CONSUMER BEHAVIOR

McGRAW-HILL SERIES IN MARKETING

Consulting Editor
Charles Schewe
University of Massachusetts

Britt/Boyd: MARKETING MANAGEMENT
Brown/Cardozo/Cunningham/Salmon/Sultan: PROBLEMS IN MARKETING
Buzzell/Nourse/Matthews/Levitt: MARKETING: A Contemporary Analysis
DeLozier: THE MARKETING COMMUNICATIONS PROCESS
Howard: CONSUMER BEHAVIOR: Application of Theory
Lee/Dobler: PURCHASING AND MATERIALS MANAGEMENT: Text and Cases
Redinbaugh: RETAILING MANAGEMENT: A Planning Approach
Reynolds/Wells: CONSUMER BEHAVIOR
Russell/Beach/Buskirk: TEXTBOOK OF SALESMANSHIP
Shapiro: SALES PROGRAM MANAGEMENT: Formulation and Implementation
Stanton: FUNDAMENTALS OF MARKETING
Wright/Warner/Winter/Zeigler: ADVERTISING

CONSUMER BEHAVIOR

Fred D. Reynolds
University of Georgia

William D. Wells
Needham, Harper & Steers Advertising, Inc.

McGRAW-HILL BOOK COMPANY
New York St. Louis San Francisco Auckland Bogotá Düsseldorf
Johannesburg London Madrid Mexico Montreal
New Delhi Panama Paris São Paulo Singapore
Sydney Tokyo Toronto

CONSUMER BEHAVIOR

1 2 3 4 5 6 7 8 9 0 K P K P 7 8 3 2 1 0 9 8 7 6

This book was set in Times Roman by Black Dot, Inc.
The editors were William J. Kane and Michael Weber;
the cover was designed by Jo Jones;
the production supervisor was Angela Kardovich.
The drawings were done by ANCO Technical Services.
Kingsport Press, Inc., was printer and binder.

Library of Congress Cataloging in Publication Data

Reynolds, Fred D
Consumer behavior.

(McGraw-Hill series in marketing)
Includes index.
1. Consumers. I. Wells, Williams D., joint author.
II. Title.
HF5415.3.R43 658.8'34 76-20580
ISBN 0-07-052031-3

Contents

Preface

Consumer Behavior is intended to meet the needs of the beginning student of consumer behavior.

Increasingly, beginning students are being exposed to a course in consumer behavior along with courses in the behavioral sciences—psychology, social psychology, and sociology—and in the applied disciplines—marketing, advertising, public relations, home economics, and journalism. While the study of consumer behavior must be congruent with this mix of courses, it should not be redundant to the mix.

The major practical use of a course in consumer behavior is to give students a better basis for understanding consumer markets, an understanding which leads toward better decisions and better solutions to problems. Consumer behavior is an applied field of study. Hence this book has a pragmatic, applications-oriented character; one designed to provide substantive insights rather than a theoretical position. We believe this approach most closely matches the needs of the beginning student of consumer behavior.

The book begins by examining the relationships among four parties vitally interested in consumer behavior: consumers, sellers, public policy makers, and "professional" students of consumer behavior (primarily educators and researchers). It then turns to an introductory foundation for the remainder of the book, providing a conceptual orientation to help put later specifics into perspective and a discussion of the major component elements that describe the boundaries of the study of consumer behavior. Building upon the introductory material, consumers are then examined in terms of their identifiable characteristics that affect their behaviors in the market place. Then the discussion shifts to an analysis of the behaviors of consumers and of the major stimuli that influence them.

Although there are alternative ways to use this book, we believe the most effective is for the text to be read outside of class; class time then can be used to allow students to further their skills though interaction with instructors and each other on material reviewed prior to class. We recommend the following procedure to students: in reviewing prior to class, first read the introductory and summary sections of each assigned chapter to get an overview of the topics included in that chapter. Next read the chapter quickly. Then read it carefully, underlining important points and making margin notes of thoughts and questions. Write some tentative answers to the review questions. But do not stop at this point. After class, review the underlined portion of the text in conjunction with class notes. Pull the two together into a detailed summary of the material covered, one that will be useful for later review and study.

A number of persons have assisted us in the development of this text. To them we express our sincere gratitude. Professors William D. Perreault, Jr. (University of North Carolina, Chapel Hill), Melvin R. Crask (University of Georgia), and Warren S. Martin (University of Texas, Dallas) used earlier versions of the manuscript in their undergraduate classes on consumer behavior. Their comments and those of their students were extremely helpful and are most appreciated. We also are indebted for insightful suggestions to these colleagues who reviewed the manuscript: Professors Kenneth L. Bernhardt (Georgia State University), Grady Bruce (University of Texas, Austin) Jeffrey A. Lowenhar (Temple University), Ivan Ross (University of Minnesota) and Charles Schewe (University of Massachusetts). Finally, we are indebted most to our coconsumers to whom this book is dedicated—our wives and children.

Fred D. Reynolds
William D. Wells

Part One

The Study of Consumer Behavior

Chapter 1

Uneasy Relationships among Four Interested Parties

One way to begin to think about consumer behavior is to start with a specific example. The great danger in starting this way is that the first example will assume undue significance, as though because it is first it is somehow most typical.

The following case is reconstructed from interviews with the participants. It describes a set of circumstances that has existed in the past, continues to exist today, and no doubt will continue to exist in the future. But it is no more typical of the behavior of buyers, or of the behavior of sellers, than any of the cases that will be presented in subsequent chapters.

This particular case is presented at the outset because it highlights many of the relationships among four parties vitally interested in consumer behavior: buyers, sellers, policymakers, and professional students of consumer behavior. Members of each of these groups would view this sequence of events from different perspectives. And, no doubt, each would have a somewhat different set of reactions.

One afternoon a young woman was ironing and watching television in her home. The telephone rang.

"Mrs. La Motta?"

"Yes."

"This is Mrs. Dunnette of the Child's World National Photo Service calling. May I ask you a few questions?"

"Yes."

"How many children do you have, Mrs. La Motta?"

"Three."

"Will you tell me their names and ages?"

"Betty—she's seventeen, and Debbie—she's fourteen, and Angelo—he's four—almost five."

"And your husband's name is—Vincent?"

"Yes."

"What does he do for a living, Mrs. La Motta?"

"He is a foreman at Jericho Steel."

"My, what a fine family! Tell me, Mrs. La Motta, do you ever take pictures of your children?"

"Yes. My uncle does, and my brother does."

"What would you say, Mrs. La Motta, if I told you that you could have a professional portrait of your children taken every year for ten years absolutely free?"

"Free?"

"Yes, absolutely free. You see, Mrs. La Motta, we have selected a few of the leading families in your neighborhood as model families who might appear in our advertising. In return for permission to use their photographs, we will furnish them with a beautiful 9 X 12 portrait every year for ten years absolutely free. Do you think you would enjoy seeing one of your children featured in our advertising in a national magazine?"

"You don't have to buy anything?"

"Absolutely not. This is our gift to you in return for permission to use pictures of your children. The pictures do not cost you anything."

"It sounds wonderful."

"You're right, Mrs. La Motta, it is wonderful, and you are very, very lucky to have such a beautiful family. Now, to explain the details, when may our representative come to call?"

"To call?"

"Yes, to explain the details of our free offer. Some evening this week?"

"I'll have to ask my husband."

"Could we say Thursday, Mrs. La Motta? Our representative, Mr. Marks, will call before he comes just to make sure the time is convenient."

"All right."

When the "representative" of Child's World National Photo Service arrived at the La Mottas' door, Vincent La Motta was pretty mad. "What's the matter with you, Lucy?" he had said. "You know they don't give you anything for free. All they want to do is sell you some pictures, and we got a million pictures already."

"Let me introduce myself, Mr. and Mrs. La Motta. My name is Peter Marks, and I am with the promotion department of the Child's World National Photo Service. Are you familiar with our company?"

"No."

"We are a subsidiary of Child Guidance, Inc., maker of educational toys and publisher of *Child Guidance* magazine. We are also affiliated with the International Publishing Company—the company that publishes many of your children's school books."

Vince said nothing. Lucy said, "I believe I have heard of the International Publishing Company."

"By the way, Mr. La Motta, what kind of work do you do?"

"I am a mechanic at Jericho Steel."

"Have you been there long?"

"Almost twenty years."

"That is a fine company. They use many of our training manuals, and with your help I hope many of your coworkers will become subscribers to our Child Guidance Photo Service. Tell me, Mr. and Mrs. La Motta, have you ever seen this advertisement?"

The salesman spread out a four-color magazine-size proof of a Child Guidance Photo Service advertisement featuring a portrait of a dark-haired, brown-eyed boy. Glancing quickly at the print at the bottom of the page, Vince noted the price: $24.95.

"I haven't seen this advertisement, and I'm not buying any pictures."

"No, Mr. La Motta. I'm not here to ask you to buy any pictures. As our interviewer explained to Mrs. La Motta, I am here to show you how you can get a beautiful portrait like this one of any member of your family every year for ten years absolutely free."

"Free?"

"You see, Mr. and Mrs. La Motta, our company has two problems. We need a continuing supply of photographs of good-looking children, like your —"

"Angelo," Lucy prompted.

"Angelo, of course. I had it right here in my notes. We need these photographs to use in our advertisements, like this one here. We also know that no matter how much advertising we do, we will never be able to reach everyone with the personal touch that is so important. You know how important the personal touch is in business, don't you, Mr. La Motta?"

For the first time Vince said, "Yes."

"We hope that if we put these fine portraits in your home—absolutely free—that you will show them to your neighbors and friends, and that some of them will become subscribers to our service. Now, does that make sense, Mr. La Motta?"

Lucy nodded. Vince said, "I don't have to buy anything?"

"The pictures are free, Mr. La Motta, absolutely free. We will supply you with one beautiful portrait of any member of your family every year for ten years at no cost to you. In return, we ask you to do only these four things. First, we ask you to allow our photographer to come into your home once a year to take pictures of the children—and of you, too, if you like. Second, when the proofs arrive, we ask you to select the one you like best to be finished as a fine 9 X 12 portrait in black and white. If you like some of the other proofs as well, we will be glad to finish them, too, at our cost, but it is not necessary that you buy any of them. You still get your free portrait. Third, after you have seen the proofs, we ask you to write a letter giving us permission to use some of the finished photographs in our advertising. You do not have to give us permission to use all of them, of course—just the ones you like. Fourth, after you have received your finished portraits, we ask you to display them in this beautiful personalized and dated album, or in your choice from our selection of fine frames."

From his briefcase, the salesman produced a photograph album bound in white "simulated leather" and etched with an ornate design in gold leaf.

"We have to pay for this album?"

"Having given you the portrait, Mr. La Motta, we cannot afford to give away the album, too, but we can let you have it for exactly what it cost us. After all, our main object is to get our work displayed, and we couldn't take the chance that some thoughtless person would get the portrait and just throw it into a drawer. Doesn't that seem reasonable, Mrs. La Motta?"

"Yes, yes."

Vince was still skeptical, but he had run his hands over the album cover, feeling the grain, squeezing the back for toughness, and testing the gold leaf with the nail of his thumb.

"How much is it?"

"Slightly more than the average family spends on a daily newspaper. Slightly more than ten cents a day."

"That is all you have to buy?"

"That is all. One album a year, as they are personalized with your name right here in gold and dated. Of course, if you should wish to purchase additional albums as gifts, we would be happy to supply you additional copies at our low, low production cost, and should you wish to have any of the portraits enlarged and tinted, we also have a beautiful selection of fine frames. Are the grandparents living, Mrs. La Motta?"

"Yes."

"Think what a fine present this would make for Christmas, a birthday, or an anniversary. This beautiful album with portraits of their grandchildren in it, and at a price that is available only to you as one of our model families."

Vince was still skeptical, but definitely interested. "How much did you say it was?"

"Just slightly more than ten cents a day. Just slightly more than the cost of a newspaper, over the year—just $39.95. Tell me, Mrs. La Motta, what do you do with the newspaper when you are finished reading it?"

"I throw it out."

"Exactly. Now, for just a little more than the cost of something that you throw away, you get a treasure you can cherish forever. Children don't stay children long, you know. Think of the years of pleasure you will have looking at them the way they are today after they have grown up. Let me show you something else."

The salesman drew a thick, leather-bound brochure from his briefcase. "This book shows our complete line of finishing and frames. Now notice, here on the first page we have a portrait finished in black and white just as your finished portraits will be, and on the facing page is the exact same portrait finished by our patented color process that makes it look like a fine oil painting. Do you know how much artists charge for oil portraits, Mr. La Motta?"

"A lot."

"A thousand dollars, and more. Now, our patented finishing process costs only $25, but I am authorized to tell you that if you agree tonight to participate as one of our model families, your first portrait will be in color—not in black and white—finished by this process absolutely free."

"The color is beautiful," said Lucy. Vince nodded.

"We have to sign up for ten years?"

"Yes, we could not make this arrangement if we could not be sure of covering our costs eventually; but on the other hand, you are guaranteed the same low price each year for ten years. You know nothing costs the same now as it did ten years ago, right?"

"Right."

"After ten years we reserve the right to increase the prices."

"The prices stay the same for ten years?"

"Exactly, Mr. La Motta. And at the rate things have been going up, that may well be the bargain of the century. Now, there is just one more thing I would like to mention. If you were to send us a dime a day, or 70 cents a week, for ten years, that would be mighty inconvenient for you, and the bookkeeping costs for us would be extremely high, so there is another plan that would benefit both of us. If you could just make it a little more—say, the price of a pack of cigarettes a day—you could take care of the whole thing in just three years, and then for the next seven years there would be nothing to pay, even though you would be getting the portraits and the albums every year right on schedule. Furthermore, if you agree to this arrangement, we will return the bookkeeping savings to you by finishing all your free portraits—not just the first one—in color."

"You mean we get nine of these color pictures free just for paying in three years?"

"Yes, indeed, and to make it easy for you, we round the monthly payment to $12.50, and that already includes the $1.50 monthly budget charge."

"How do we know that we'll get the pictures when we finish paying?"

"The International Publishing Company is one of the largest and most respected firms in its field, Mr. La Motta, and it certainly wouldn't want to cheat you. Its good name is worth far, far more than the few dollars it could make going back on its word. But just to safeguard your interests completely, we give you a signed contract."

The salesman took a document with the words "Contract and Guarantee" lettered large on the top and read it to the La Mottas slowly and carefully. It specified exactly the arrangement he had outlined. When he had finished reading the contract, Vincent L. La Motta and Lucy R. La Motta signed it, and Lucy offered the salesman a cup of coffee.

The La Mottas had just agreed to pay $399.50, plus tax, plus $52.50 budget charge, in thirty-six monthly installments, for ten photograph albums and ten color photographs. They had also created a high probability that they would be buying additional photographs, additional albums and frames—at the company's low, low production cost. They were pleased with their purchase.

As noted earlier, buyers, sellers, policymakers, and professional students of consumer behavior would view this episode from somewhat different perspectives. Before these perspectives are described, it is important to reemphasize the caution with which the episode was introduced: just because it was presented first, it is not to be construed as illustrating typical buyer or seller behavior.

The La Motta episode represents, very directly and specifically, what Kotler (1970) has called "an elementary market system" (see Figure 1-1). In its most basic form, this system consists of sellers and buyers and a set of exchanges between them. One of these exchanges is the flow of *goods and services* from seller to buyer—the photograph albums, frames, photography, and photo finishing, in this case. Another is the reverse flow from buyer to seller of *money* or a money substitute such as credit.

The episode also demonstrates another exchange that is required if the market system is to function efficiently: the flow of *communication* from seller to buyer, by which the seller attempts to convert a potential customer into an actual purchaser. In this case the communication was direct and personal, from telephone solicitor and salesman to purchaser. In other cases, it is indirect and impersonal, via advertising or "public relations."

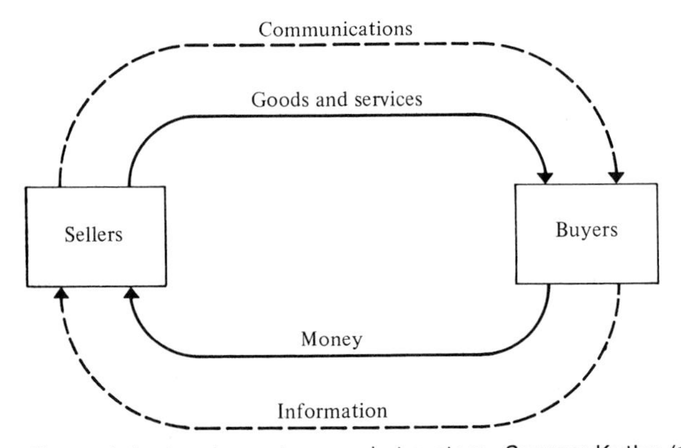

Figure 1-1 An elementary market system. *Source:* Kotler (1970: 136).

Finally, there is one other exchange that is vital to the system: the flow of *information* from the buyer to the seller. Although this flow may not be immediately and obviously evident in the episode described above, its effects are very much present. It was hardly a coincidence that the telephone solicitor called the La Motta household. Much previous experience had shown what types of families are most apt to sign a contract, and the La Mottas fit the specifications. Furthermore, the salesman's sales talk was neither created by the salesman nor extemporaneous. It had been carefully worked out in the promotion department of Child's World National Photo Service on the basis of previous experience with similar families. It had been committed, word for word, to memory by every sales representative. Thus previous buyers (and nonbuyers) in similar situations had supplied the information needed to construct and polish the presentation that led, step by step, from resistance to signature.

The buyers and sellers represented in Figure 1-1 are the principal participants in the marketing system. And both have vital interests in how well it works. Buyers are interested because the market system provides benefits—goods and services with which to live a desired style of life. Sellers are interested in it because it provides sales, profits, and return on investment. But, as the La Motta incident demonstrates, the interests of buyers and the interests of sellers are not always perfectly congruent.

At one point in history, the elementary market system depicted in Figure 1-1 might have been considered complete. Classical economists chose to think in terms of a large number of rational buyers and sellers exchanging money for undifferentiated goods or services, with exchange processes operating in such a manner as to maintain a continuous adjustment between supply and demand. The adjustment, provided by price changes, operated so as to bring the system into a state of equilibrium and enhanced the general welfare of society.

Today, however, any portrayal of the market system must also include a third group: public policy administrators who regard themselves as representing society in general and who attempt to see that both buyers and sellers are treated fairly. For our purposes, it is helpful to include a fourth group: professional students of consumer behavior. By providing valid information on the structure and function of the market system, students of consumer behavior serve the interests of the other three parties.

These expanded relationships are shown in Figure 1-2. Note that public policy administrators and students of consumer behavior are external to the market system. But they are directly related to it because they provide flows of information and influence to buyers and sellers and to each other.

Finally, it should be noted that public policy administrators and professional students of consumer behavior are themselves influenced by both buyers and sellers. The influence of buyers on public policy administrators can be seen in government's varied responses to the increasingly vocal consumer movement. The influence of sellers can be seen in the many laws and other regulations designed to promote fair competition.

Students of consumer behavior have been strongly influenced by sellers,

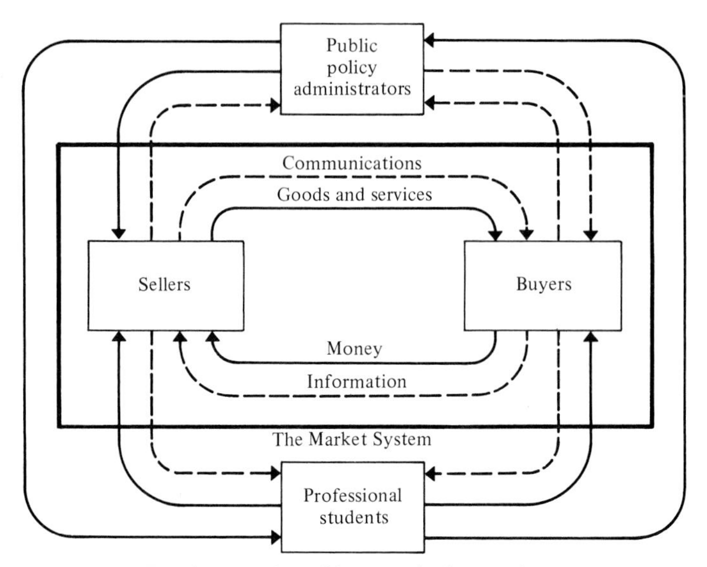

Figure 1-2 The four parties of interest in the market system.

because sellers have been a principal source of financial support for their research and a principal source of employment. To a very great extent, the research conducted on consumer behavior has been research that sellers regard as of immediate or at least potential value. Increasingly, however, consumerism groups representing the buyer's side of the marketing transaction have raised issues that students of consumer behavior have found to be of great interest. And the literature on consumer behavior, which once was almost exclusively seller-oriented, is now showing at least a partial change in direction.

Thus the four parties to the study of consumer behavior can be seen to be in constantly shifting, changing interaction. We will now examine each in turn. The first perspective is that of the seller—or, more broadly, the point of view of marketing management. Sellers represent an extremely important component of the market system because they initiate the activities and processes that create the system and help maintain it.

CONSUMER BEHAVIOR AND MARKETING MANAGEMENT

Astute businesspeople have long known that the basic purpose of a company "is to create a customer" (Drucker, 1954). For it is customers—those persons who are willing and able to pay for goods and services—who ultimately determine the success or failure of a firm.

The marketing arm of a company is charged with the task of creating customers. As the La Motta case illustrates, there have been instances in which sellers have used their knowledge of human nature to play upon and manipulate feelings and emotions. In these cases, because the marketer's skill, knowledge, and experience are so superior, the relationship between buyer and seller can be thoroughly exploitive.

But the exploitive, one-way relationship is not the only, or even the most effective, way of creating customers. It is also possible to focus on the wants of people and to develop strategies designed to satisfy these wants profitably. In the latter vein, consider the following definition.

> *Marketing Management* is the analysis, planning, implementation and control of programs designed to bring about desired exchanges with target audiences for the purpose of personal or mutual gain. It relies heavily on the adaptation and coordination of product, price, promotion, and place for achieving effective response (Kotler, 1972: 13).

This definition says that while persuasion is an integral part of marketing, the philosophy of an *exchange of values* is central. The buyer gives, but he also gets. The definition also implies that a primary concern of marketing management lies in the development of marketing programs. The development of marketing programs can be best seen in the context of two important concepts: *market segmentation* and *marketing mix*.

Market Segmentation

Shortly after the beginning of this century Charles Parlin announced, "The customer is king!" As simple as this notion is, it is difficult to implement. The needs and desires of the people who comprise markets are not readily apparent or easily uncovered. And they are heterogeneous: not all consumers want the same things at the same time to the same degree.

The heterogeneous nature of the marketplace was recognized early in the literature of marketing. Arch W. Shaw (1912) noted that "effective demand" stems not only from buying power but also from needs that result from education, habit, and environment. He observed that different people have different needs because these influences differ greatly from person to person. The market therefore splits into different "economical and social strata," which Shaw called "market contours." He suggested that each contour, or "segment," as it is now called, be viewed as a separate market problem.

This notion of market segments, as opposed to a mass, undifferentiated market, formally recognizes that there are groups of people who respond in different ways to marketing programs because of their differential needs and wants.

The existence of different segments affords marketers an opportunity to tailor their marketing programs more precisely to market needs. Before marketers can accomplish this, however, it is necessary to identify existing segments in a manner that validly reflects the underlying similarity of needs within segments and the dissimilarity of needs among segments. Just how that difficult task can be accomplished is a subject of later chapters.

Shaw also suggested that each market segment be viewed as a separate market problem. In essence, he was stating that the consumer should be given the central place in the development of marketing programs. Assigning the consumer to central placement requires that marketers first examine the results desired by a market segment and then work their way back to the specific product characteristics and marketing activities that can be employed to achieve those results.

This "backward look" is another way of saying that all marketing decisions are based on assumptions, implicit or explicit, of consumer responses to marketing efforts, on an individual basis or in combination.

The Marketing Mix

The "marketing mix" is a particular combination of variables which are (1) at least partially controllable by marketers and (2) capable of influencing consumers.

Although the elements of the marketing mix have been described differently by different authors, there seems to be an approaching consensus built around a popular mnemonic classification first suggested by McCarthy (1968)—the 4 Ps: product, price, place, and promotion. Lipson and Darling (1971) and Kotler (1972), for example, suggest four major component elements, each of which can be reduced to four major variable elements, as shown in Figure 1-3.

To return to the La Motta episode once more, the "marketing mix" exemplified by that particular instance of consumer behavior included a product line—the photographs, frames, and albums—and a group of services—photography and processing—from the "Product Component." It also included a specific basic price and a set of credit terms from the "Price Component," a particular sales territory from the "Place Component," and a particular form of presentation—personal selling—from the "Promotion Component." As will be seen in later chapters, other instances of consumer behavior include mixes that are quite different.

The marketing mix or total marketing program is based upon the marketer's beliefs about consumer behavior in each of the areas depicted. The effectiveness of marketing management depends upon the degree to which these beliefs are correct. From the marketer's point of view, then, the study of consumer behavior is an attempt to isolate, describe, and understand the interactions between consumers and elements of the marketing mix. To the degree that this enterprise is successful, it provides marketing management with the ability to make better marketing decisions.

The following example summarizes the case for consumer research from the marketer's point of view:

> Say you are a manufacturer of perfume. It's a president's business to look around. If you take your job seriously—and assume that your subordinates will do the same—there are three fundamental questions that you need to answer:
>
> **1** What will women want to smell like five years from now?
>
> **2** How much will they be willing to spend to make themselves glamorous—and who besides the perfumers will be competing for a share of that spending?
>
> **3** What sort of retail outlets will be doing the bulk of perfume sales?

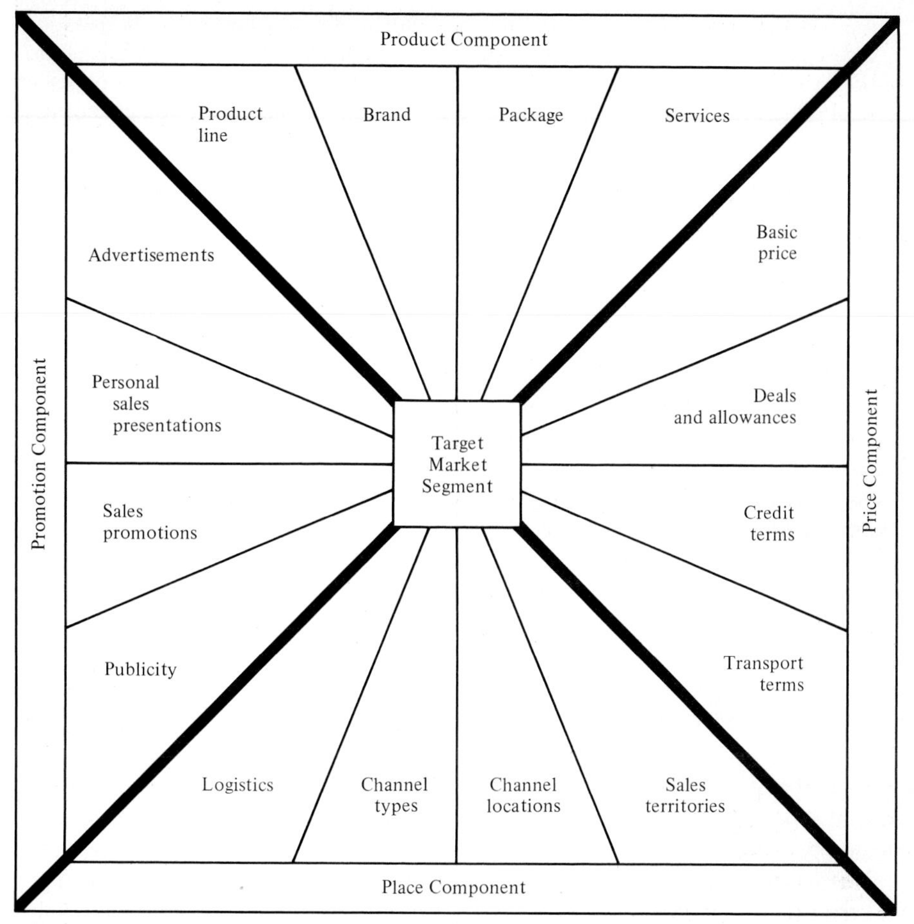

Figure 1-3 The marketing mix. *Source:* Adapted from Lipson and Darling (1971) and Kotler (1972).

Department stores? Discount houses? Drug stores? Suburban shopping centers? Downtown salons?

These are pertinent questions but broad ones. The brand managers of the different perfumes you sell will have questions of a different sort to answer. Each will want to know:

1 This square bottle my scent comes in—what does it convey to the customer? Is it exotic? Tweedy? Expensive? Sexy? Would we be better off with something slinky in swirls and gold leaf?

2 When do most of my sales take place? I advertise my stuff as a light summer scent, but most of the orders seem to come in around Christmas. Is that the time to be talking about creamy shoulders and drugged summer nights?

3 Would retailers push the brand harder if I sweetened the deal; increased the cooperative advertising allowance, or just gave the clerks more push money?

> If you have 12 brands, that means your brand managers have 36 questions among them. Add your own three, and like the Church of England with the historic 39 Articles on which it is founded, you have an equal number of points on which you must take a stand. Unlike the Church of England, however, you cannot take your 39 points as a matter of faith.
>
> So at this stage you buy yourself some market research (*Business Week*, 1964: 90).

CONSUMER BEHAVIOR AND CONSUMERS

Ideally, marketing in the aggregate is a service to society: when individual firms determine consumer wants and then develop goods and services to satisfy those wants, the welfare of consumers is enhanced.

Some would contend that American business for the most part actually operates in this manner. They cite the fact that the United States is the most prosperous country known to history. They note that in contrast to other parts of the world, and to some previous periods in history, few Americans have to worry about where their next meal is coming from or how to obtain basic shelter. And they point to the fact that most Americans are in the enviable position of worrying about what items from among an abundant selection should be on the table for the next meal and whether the house is as nice as or nicer than the neighbors'.

Others contend, however, that there is no invisible hand steering the actions of buyers and sellers so that mutual gain is always or even generally the outcome. They point out that America has pockets of poverty, even starvation, and that American businesses engage in deceptive practices and make unsafe products.

In the incident described at the beginning of this chapter, if the salesman had asked the La Mottas, "Would you like to buy ten color photographs and ten simulated leather photograph albums for $399.50 (plus tax, plus $52.50 finance charges)," they probably would not have assented. But under the impression that they were getting a bargain, flattered by being selected as a "model family" by an important company, and envisioning the pleasure of displaying these products so glowingly described, they signed without hesitation.

With some firms engaging in deceptive selling, it is not surprising that many consumers are concerned with the performance of the market system. In a nationwide survey of opinions about business practices, Barksdale and Darden (1972) found that many persons express considerable discontent with marketing activities, that many persons believe that consumers' problems are important and deserve more attention than they now receive, and that both conservatives and liberals overwhelmingly voiced support for additional government regulation as a means of solving consumer problems.

Consumers are not totally concerned with seller performance, however. Some are concerned with their own performance; they recognize that some of the imperfections in the market system result from the ineptness, carelessness, and apathy of buyers (Barksdale and Darden, 1972). These persons desire better ways of managing their consuming activities, and they seek to improve these activities by watching TV shows and reading newspaper articles and magazines intended to make them more proficient.

The outgrowth of widespread and vocal consumer dissatisfaction has taken two forms. On the one hand, businesses have responded; i.e., they have made attempts to eliminate or at least decrease causes of dissatisfaction and to establish policies and procedures for the receipt and correction of consumer complaints. On the other hand, government has become increasingly active. Such activity has come in the form of laws, regulations, and judicial decisions administered by governmental agencies.

CONSUMER BEHAVIOR AND PUBLIC POLICY ADMINISTRATION

Governmental agencies such as the Federal Trade Commission, the Consumer Product Safety Commission, and the Food and Drug Administration respond to demands that buyers be protected. They influence the market system by enforcing laws and judicial decisions and by establishing regulatory guidelines.

As shown by the solid arrow in Figure 1-2, the primary influence of public policy administrators is directed at sellers. The intent, of course, is to influence the decisions and practices of management so that the offerings of firms will not be deceptive or harmful to the welfare of consumers or to the maintenance of a competitive market system. Let us return for a moment to the La Motta incident.

Without some form of legal recourse, the La Mottas would be firmly and irrevocably bound by their "Contract and Guarantee." The FTC, however, has intervened in situations of this kind by providing consumers a recourse against deceptively presented sales presentations. Specifically, the FTC has ruled that for all door-to-door sales of $25 or more, salespersons must tell consumers orally and in writing that they have three days to obtain a full refund if they change their minds.[1]

The FTC also takes direct action through litigation. For example:

> Five dance studios in the Baltimore-Washington area have been charged with deceptive advertising and sales practices in the sale of courses of dancing instruction to the public. The complaint charges the studios with using supposed puzzles, quizzes, and other contests in which the winner is awarded a gift certificate entitling him to a specified number of Arthur Murray lessons purportedly worth from $36-$65, and with using deceptive introductory offers that purported to furnish the first lesson of a dancing course free of charge.
>
> According to the Commission, neither the contests, nor the prizes, nor the introductory offer were presented in good faith, but were used to bait prospects

[1] As of this writing, however, the Commission has not set an enforcement date. They are waiting on a federal judicial decision as to whether or not the FTC has the authority to issue legislative-type decrees (*Sales Management,* 1972).

into signing extensive dance lesson contracts sometimes for a cost in excess of $1,500.

The Commission charged that (1) the contests were not based on skill or chance but were simple enough to qualify anyone; (2) the winners of the contest received neither a gift certificate worth its stated amount nor a good faith course in dancing instruction but were subjected to a sales talk designed to induce the signing of a long-term dancing instruction contract; (3) the operators misrepresented that their club offers various types of social activities, for unless a member pays between $450 and $5,000 there are no activities in which he might participate; and (4) the studios used unfair and deceptive practices to sell initial or supplemental courses of dance instruction. Included in the practices were coercive sales effort, relay salesmanship, and intense emotional and unrelenting sales pressure during several hours to persuade people to sign a contract for a substantial number of dancing lessions at a substantial cost. (*In re Arthur Murray Studio of Washington, [D.C.], Inc., et al.,* F.T.C. Dkt. 8776, CCH 18,733, April, 1969.) Reprinted from *Journal of Marketing,* Vol. 33 (October, 1969), published by the American Marketing Association.

In addition to striking directly at deceptive practices, the FTC has experimented with another form of action—contact with the individual consumer. This form of action is shown in the following FTC *Consumer Alert* (1972: 1, 4):

FEEL RIPPED OFF? DON'T SUFFER IN SILENCE

What can a consumer do if he or she has been "ripped off" by an unscrupulous merchant?

The feeling of frustration that can result when one realizes he has been swindled does not have to be the only thing he is left with. There are a number of avenues to follow.

Compare First

Of course, the ideal solution is to shop and compare carefully in the first place. A consumer who is willing to shop for what he wants and who will take time to think realistically what quantity and quality he really should receive for his money is not an easy mark for the gyp artist. And reputable businessmen welcome the buyer who gives honest merchandising the careful consideration it deserves.

But . . .

If a consumer does find himself on the losing end of a transaction that seems unfair or downright dishonest, or even if he has seen but avoided a trap set for the less sophisticated, there are things he *can* do if he has the courage to make himself heard. Certainly it is not enough to "chalk up to experience" a purchase about which he was misled, or simply to congratulate himself on not having been duped in the way others might have been. Gypsters thrive in an environment of inaction.

Go Back to the Seller

A good starting point is to protest directly to the seller (if he can be found). Possibly the misrepresentation was done without his knowledge, in which case, he can take steps to insure against its repetition. There is even a chance he might square himself with the consumer. But if he doesn't, there are further lines of action.

Complain to Media

If advertising was involved, the consumer can complain to the radio station, television station or newspaper that carried the ad. The complaint should be backed by as many *hard* facts as the consumer can amass. Truth in advertising is too important to these media to risk gaining a reputation for carrying phony ads.

Go to Local Authorities

Another possibility is local government. This is particularly important because most of the things the consumer buys are marketed only locally, and the seller is not engaged in interstate commerce. The result is that the consumer has to depend not on the federal but on his city or state government for protection. Nearly all of the states have statutes aimed at misrepresentation of products and services. In many states these laws are enforced vigorously. (For a list of state and local consumer protection offices see the April, 1972, *Consumer Alert.*)

Go to Small Claims Court

The dissatisfied consumer also has the small claims court in his area available to him for redress against the cheat. This avenue is all too often overlooked by the aggrieved consumer, so these Courts can end up more as debt-collection agencies than potential forums for the inexpensive vindication of wronged consumers' rights.

Almost all the states have some form of small claims court, and procedures have usually been streamlined and simplified. Generally the services of a lawyer are not a prerequisite to bringing an action, although legal advice would be of assistance if it could be obtained.

Write the Federal Trade Commission

The FTC's fight against consumer deception is directed at gyp schemes that have an actual or potential impact on the public, as distinguished from actions to settle private controversies. In short, it has neither the staff nor the money to tackle cases that do not have sufficiently broad public impact. Also, the FTC concentrates its efforts on halting law violators who do at least some of their selling across state lines. Thus, while the FTC cannot undertake to settle private or purely local difficulties, it does stand ready to halt large-scale deception.

When writing a letter to the Federal Trade Commission, Washington, D.C. 20580, give as many facts as possible, including any evidence of the "rip-off", such as a copy of misleading advertising used to sell the product or the service. The consumer has the FTC's assurance that his identity will be protected.

The FTC provides the consumer with protection against many instances of deception in the marketplace. But he should remember that he can do a great deal for himself by following this advice:

1 Shop around more before buying.
2 Bring complaints first to the seller.
3 Report false advertising to the media carrying it.
4 Report deception to local organizations concerned with better business standards.

5 Consider suing the seller in small claims court.
6 Write the facts to the Federal Trade Commission.

Whether their actions are directed at sellers or buyers, public policy administrators, like marketers, must base their decisions on assumptions about consumer behavior. Indeed, the information and questions are the same; it is the perspective that may differ when dicisions are made by marketers and public policy administrators. Obviously, the validity and effectiveness of these decisions depend upon the validity of the assumptions underlying them. Former Commissioner Mary Gardiner Jones of the FTC made this point well:

> I see two broad areas which continually confront the Commission where gaps may exist in our present approaches. The first is the allocation of our resources to problem areas and the second is the development of effective remedies within problem areas.
>
> I strongly feel that our efforts in these two areas can be greatly enhanced by a systematic utilization of research on consumer behavior. The reasons for this should be obvious. Our past efforts have implicitly relied on models of the consumer, and to the extent that these models were lacking, our own efforts [were] less effective (Jones, 1971: 6).

The systematic study of consumer behavior, then, is of utmost importance to the formation and implementation of public policy.

STUDENTS OF CONSUMER BEHAVIOR

The fourth major party concerned with the market system is the professional student of consumer behavior. Like the public policy block in Figure 1-2, the student block is shown as outside the market system but also influencing it through activities aimed at sellers, buyers, and public administrators and being influenced by these groups in turn.

Several quite different academic disciplines have studied consumer behavior with relatively distinct focuses. In home economics, for example, the main concern has been to study consumer behavior as a basis for educating homemakers to become better buyers and more expert users of what is bought. In marketing, the main concern has been aiding sellers in making better decisions. And within economics, consumption has most frequently been examined with the intent of bettering the management of the total economy and with developing normative models of decision making for the firm.

In spite of these divergent points of view and distinct purposes, the study of consumer behavior is moving toward a synthesis. This trend has become so pronounced that a new interdisciplinary association, the Association for Consumer Research, has been formed, and a new interdisciplinary journal, *Journal of Consumer Research,* has been launched under the joint sponsorship of nine associations:

1 American Marketing Association
2 American Economic Association
3 American Home Economics Association
4 American Council on Consumer Interests
5 American Association for Public Opinion Research
6 American Psychological Association (Division of Consumer Pyschology)
7 Association for Consumer Research
8 American Statistical Association
9 The Institute of Management Sciences

Professional students of consumer behavior, as represented by members of these disciplines, can aid the other parties of concern with the market system by carrying out the related tasks of *(a)* adding to the existing body of knowledge in a systematic and reliable manner, and *(b)* preserving and disseminating the body of knowledge to the parties of interest.

Adding to Knowledge

Students of consumer behavior can contribute to the existing understanding of the market system in three fundamentally different ways: identifying gaps in the existing body of knowledge, developing and testing models of consumer behavior, and developing new methods for studying consumer behavior.

Identifying areas where knowledge is lacking is often accomplished by scholarly review of existing literature. For example, Ross (1972) reviewed the existing literature on consumer information handling, with particular reference to public policy decisions. He found numerous empirical studies with potential application, including information relevant to unit pricing, nutrient food labeling, open dating of foods, interest rate disclosure, corrective advertising, counter advertising, deceptive advertising, and the use of consumer-product rating publications. He also identified many areas of almost complete ignorance concerning the effects of various public policies on market interactions. This kind of review is of immediate value to decision makers who must make the best choices they can on the basis of whatever information they have at hand, and it is the essential first step toward further empirical investigation.

Another major way professional students of consumer behavior have attempted to add to basic knowledge is through the building and testing of conceptual models. Dubin has said:

> Their task is to build viable models of the empirical world that can be comprehended by the human mind. These theoretical models are intensely practical, for the predicitons derived from them are the grounds on which modern man is increasingly ordering his relationships with the environing universe (Dubin, 1969: 3).

Professional students of consumer behavior have shown great interest in model building. One author has presented an overview of no less than twenty-eight types of models of consumer behavior (Hansen, 1972). Moreover, within these various model types there are numerous specific differences. The purpose of conceptual models is to structure a group of interrelated propositions about some aspect of consumer behavior, and to use that structure to understand and predict interactions in the marketplace.

Once models have been constructed, they must be put to the test of empirical evidence. Students of consumer behavior have been quick to test their models (and the models proposed by others). Their goal is to confirm the correct features and to disprove the incorrect features of their models so as to increase the model's contribution to understand and prediciton. A very simple conceptual model will be used to help integrate the chapter that follows this one.

A third way the professional student can contribute to our understanding of consumer behavior is to develop and refine the methods used in studying consumer behavior. In model testing, for example, an ever-present question is, "Do our measures of behavior accurately reflect the behavior we are trying to measure?" The person who develops a new measure or refines an existing measure—one that is more reliable and valid than those previously existing—contributes to our understanding by contributing to our ability to do better research. Innovations of the third type, like innovations in model building, are appearing with increasing frequency in the literature. One observer (Lipstein, 1971) noted eighteen new techniques published during the 1960s.

Preserving and Disseminating Knowledge

Finally, professional students of consumer behavior are inevitably involved in preserving and disseminating knowledge of their field. Knowledge about consumer behavior or any other phenomenon is of little value unless it is shared with the parties of concern.

Initially, new knowledge is disseminated to contemporaries by the publication of scientific reports in the form of journal articles, working papers, monographs, books, or presentations at professional meetings. These publications, of course, are preserved for future students and decision makers through their systematic collection, citation, and storage in numerous public and private libraries. Later, the existing body of knowledge is transmitted via textbooks and other forms of instruction under organized systems devoted to that aim. Dissemination is carried out through the familiar medium of classroom teaching in colleges and universities and in executive development seminars, correspondence courses, and university service extension programs. In all these cases the principal purpose is to bring the knowledge generated by scholarly activities to the attention of decision makers who can use it in activities affecting the operation of the market system.

SUMMARY

To summarize our discussion thus far, return to Figure 1-2. There we outlined the major bodies concerned with the study of consumer behavior and subsequently discussed the application of the interest of these parties. Inherent in each area of discussion was the notion that better understanding of consumer behavior can improve the practices of marketers, public policy administrators, educators, and even consumers.

At this point one might well ask, "But the behavior of consumers is so vast, so complex, and so seemingly contradictory, how do we proceed?" The answer lies in systematically identifying the variables that best abstract the interactions of the marketplace and systematically unraveling their interactions. An overview of this task is the burden of the next chapter.

REVIEW QUESTIONS

1. The La Motta case is presented in this chapter because it highlights the relationships between the four parties vitally interested in consumer behavior. Identify each of these parties and the exchanges between them.
2. Discuss the differences between the "elementary market system" and the "expanded market system" developed in this chapter. Why is one system a more accurate model of our modern market environment than the other?
3. How does Kotler's definition of marketing management rely on the "exchange of values" philosophy? Is this the same as the "creating customers" approach to marketing management? Why or why not?
4. What are the two basic concepts utilized in the development of marketing programs? Why do marketers need these concepts?
5. Explain the "backward look" approach to marketing decisions. Is this idea consistent with the statement, "The customer is king"?
6. Define the "marketing mix" and identify the four component elements. What types of marketing decisions are made for each element?
7. How are the concepts of market segmentation and the marketing mix interrelated?
8. The chapter implies that the effectiveness of marketing management is directly related to the study of consumer behavior. Why are they related?
9. The study of consumer behavior is also important to the formulation and implementation of public polciy. Discuss the role of such public policy administrators in the marketing system as the FTC, the Consumer Product Safety Commission, and the FDA.
10. Identify the different academic disciplines involved in the study of consumer behavior and their respective focuses.
11. Examine the function of professional students of consumer behavior in the market system. How can this fourth party contribute to the understanding of the system?
12. What is the purpose of conceptual models in consumer behavior?

REFERENCES

Barksdale, Hiram C. and William R. Darden. "Consumer Attitudes toward Marketing and Consumerism." *Journal of Marketing,* 36 (October 1972), 28–35.

Business Week. "Why Business Is Spending Millions to Learn How Consumers Behave." *Business Week* (April 1964), 90 ff.

Drucker, Peter F. *The Practice of Management.* New York: Harper & Row, 1954.

Dubin, Robert. *Theory Building.* New York: Free Press, 1969.

Federal Trade Commission. "Feel Ripped Off? Don't Suffer in Silence." *Consumer Alert,* 2 (September–October 1972), 1, 4.

Hansen, Fleming. *Consumer Choice Behavior.* New York: Free Press, 1972.

Jones, Mary Gardiner. "The FTC's Need for Social Science Research." *Proceedings,* 2d Annual Conference, Association for Consumer Research, College Park, Maryland, 1971.

Kotler, Philip. "Corporate Models: Better Marketing Plans." *Harvard Business Review* (July–August 1970), 135—149.

———. *Marketing Management.* 2d ed. Englewood Cliffs, N.J.: Prentice-Hall, 1972.

Lipson, Harry A. and John R. Darling. *Introduction to Marketing.* New York: John Wiley, 1971.

McCarthy, E. Jerome. *Basic Marketing.* Homewood, Ill.: Richard Irwin, 1968.

Ross, Ivan. "Application of Consumer Information to Public Policy Decisions." Unpublished working paper, University of Minnesota, 1972.

Ruch, Dudley, et al. "The Mathematical Revolution and the Management of Marketing Communication." *Proceedings,* 16th Annual Conference of the Advertising Research Foundation, New York: 1971.

Sales Management. (Nov. 13, 1972), 4.

Shaw, Arch W. "Some Problems in Market Distribution." *Quarterly Journal of Economics* (August 1912), 703–765.

Chapter 2

Major Concepts in the Study of Consumer Behavior

The previous chapter began with one example of one kind of consumer behavior. Now, by way of contrast, consider a very different kind of behavior in a very different situation.

The setting is a large, well-lit, clean-looking supermarket. In its trading area, the market has the reputation of having good meat, excellent produce, and prices that are a little above average but reasonable, considering the quality.

One Thursday afternoon, a woman about thirty-five years old entered the store with two children, a boy about two and a girl about four. She lifted the boy into a shopping cart, where he sat facing her, kicking the basket frame. As she moved off toward the produce section, pushing the cart, the girl trailed along behind.

The shopper stopped first at the produce section. She glanced at the price of iceberg lettuce and selected three heads. She then placed a twenty-five-pound sack of Idaho potatoes into the rack that spanned the lower part of the cart frame. She looked at the oranges. There were four different varieties, all priced differently, packed six to a box and covered with cellophane. She reached for a box on her right, picked it up, but hesitated as she noticed a special advertised by a sign at the end of the aisle. She replaced the box, pushed the cart to the display at the end of the aisle, paused for a moment, and then selected a sack from the display. She put the sacked oranges into the shopping cart, on the bottom rack beside the potatoes.

After some more quick produce purchases (beets, squash, celery, lemons, and chives), she turned the cart up the aisle that has breakfast cereal on the left and baby food, canned vegetables, and canned fruit on the right. She passed the baby food without a glance.

The boy spied a brightly colored cereal package, pointed at it, and grunted. "Want some Fruit-Loops, Tommy?" The boy nodded, and a package of Fruit-Loops went into the cart. "What kind of cereal do you want, Jane?" The girl was inspecting the cereal packages, looking at both front and back.

"This kind,"

"We have some of that at home and nobody will eat it."

"But it has a top in it."

"We have six boxes of cereal at home, and we're not getting another box that nobody will eat. Pick some other kind."

"Tony the Tiger," said the girl, reluctantly, and a box of Sugar Frosted Flakes went into the cart.

"We need some Cheerios, and some Wheaties." Two more boxes of cereal joined the Fruit-Loops and the Sugar Frosted Flakes.

The next stop was pet food. A large bag of dog meal was placed on the bottom rack and a box of Cat Chow into the basket.

The soap and detergent section was next. A giant box of detergent, a gallon container of bleach, a container of dishwashing detergent, ten bars of Dial. The Dial was on special—ten cents off the regular price for five.

Peanut butter, a large jar, and two jars of jelly. A box of macaroni, two boxes of spaghetti, a bottle of catsup, a box of paper napkins, a four-pack of toilet tissue, two boxes of Kleenex, a two-pack (on special) of paper towels. The boy grabbed a package of Handi-Wipes from the shelf and dropped them into the basket. They were returned. Pickles, a large bag of potato chips.

The girl pointed to the Oreo cookies and said, "Mommy, get some of these." The woman dropped them into the basket without a word, then picked up a box of graham crackers and a box of vanilla wafers.

On to the meat department. Two pounds of ground chuck (also on special), two pounds of stew beef, eight pork chops, a pot roast, two chickens, two packages of hot dogs, a pound of bacon, a half-pound of sliced ham, two packages of bologna, a large box of processed cheese.

The shopping cart was getting full. The boy was getting restless, and the girl was still pouting about not getting the right cereal. In rapid order, bread (two large loaves of white), milk (two gallon cartons), two dozen eggs, a pound of margarine, ten cans of soup (also on special), a pound can of ground coffee, a jar of freeze-dried instant coffee, six large cans of frozen orange juice, two half-gallons of ice cream.

The woman looked briefly at a frozen vegetable in cheese sauce located next to the ice cream in the freezer case. She made no purchase, but while she was thus occupied, the boy reached across the aisle, grabbed a can of sardines, and dropped them into the cart. The woman did not notice what the boy did.

The family moved on the checkout line. They stood for about five minutes. During that time, the mother repeatedly told the little boy to "be still."

While standing in the checkout line, the girl asked her mother if she could have a clear plastic bag of cowboys and Indians hanging on a rack near the checkout counter. The answer was "O.K."

At the checkout counter, the checker rapidly rang up the bill while a packer loaded the groceries into bags. The shopper fished a small stack of coupons out of her purse. After the clerk subtracted these items, the total bill came to $68.72.

While the mother paid the bill, the little girl tried to open the cowboys and Indians bag. Only five of the shopping bags fit into the cart, so the packer put the remaining two into an abandoned cart nearby.

Pushing the heaviest cart ahead of her, with the little boy still in the seat, and dragging the remaining cart behind, the woman said, "Come on, Janie." and headed for the door. The door opened automatically and stood open until the woman, the two grocery carts, and the little girl (who was still trying to open the cowboys and Indians package) were outside.

Some Comments on Method

The above episode was obtained by the method of direct observation—simply watching and noting behavior as it occurs. One of the great assets of this method is that the observer may notice details of which the actor may be unaware or which the latter may consider so unimportant that they are quickly forgotten. One of the great problems associated with the method is that it leaves so many questions unanswered. In some cases, the purchaser's motives are seemingly obvious—as when the shopper exchanged the oranges on special for the oranges she had originally selected or when she bought a plastic bag of cowboys and Indians in response to a direct request from her daughter. But in other cases the reasons for her behavior are much less clear. Why did she select potatoes, oranges, beets, squash, celery, lemons, and chives, and not corn, beans, turnips, grapefruit, cherries, onions, and cabbage or cauliflower—all of which were available in the same place? Why did she deny her daughter's request for cereal and agree to her request for plastic cowboys and Indians? Why did she buy Cheerios and Wheaties even though neither child had asked for either brand? Why did she ignore "specials" on particular brands of detergent and bleach and purchase the special on Dial? Would she have bought Dial even if it had not been on sale at a reduced price? In general, of the thousands of items on display in the supermarket on this particular Thursday afternoon, why did she purchase this particular set?

One way to get at least partial answers to questions like these is to ask direct questions of the person doing the behaving. This way of obtaining explanations of consumer behavior has its own set of limitations, but since these limitations are not the same as the limitations of direct observation, direct observation and direct interviewing can usefully supplement each other.

When asked, as she was leaving the store, the following set of questions, the shopper whose purchasing behavior had been observed and recorded gave the following replies:

Question: Is Thursday the day you normally shop?

Answer: Yes. I could go Fridays just as well, but I have bowling on Friday night and, anyway, the selections are better on Thursdays and the produce is fresher.

Question: We notice that you have purchased several bags of products. Is that about what you buy each week?

Answer: Just about. I try to keep the food bill around $50 each week, but it usually comes closer to $60.

Question: Was price an important consideration in all your purchases?

Answer: Definitely! I clip coupons from the newspaper and save those that come in the mail. I used some today. I also bought a sack of oranges today instead of the regular box I usually buy because they were on special, and I didn't buy some frozen food that was too expensive.

Question: I notice that you did not take advantage of the reduced prices on detergent and bleach. Could you tell me why?

Answer: They are not my regular brands. I have tried them and they did not work as well.

Question: Did you make any purchase you did not plan to buy?

Answer: Yes, I suppose so. My daughter wanted some Oreo cookies and I got those, and that reminded me to get some crackers my son likes.

Question: Did any members of your family, other than the children who are with you, influence what you bought?

Answer: Of course. I always try to get things my husband likes when I know he is going to be eating at home. And I try to buy things I know the children will eat. I don't run a restaurant, but there is no sense buying things that no one will eat and will eventually be thrown away.

Question: Do you have other children?

Answer: Yes, two boys. I bought cereal and snacks they like.

Question: Thank you for your answers. You have been a big help.

CONSUMER BEHAVIOR: A CONCEPTUAL ORIENTATION

Hundreds of thousands of episodes of consumer behavior take place every day. Some resemble the incident in the La Mottas' living room, some resemble the sequence of events in the supermarket, and some do not resemble either one. But starting with these two incidents as a base, it is possible to abstract some of their similarities and differences and to arrive at some generalizations that will help put specific incidents and specific research findings into perspective.

Consumer Behavior Is Human Behavior

First, and perhaps the most obvious point, "consumer" behavior is a subset of human behavior in general. The fundamental processes that shape behavior in the arena of buying are those that also shape behavior regarding work-related activities, religious activities, political activities, or any other type of human behavior. Furthermore, there is no clear-cut division of human activities. Consumption of products and services and attention to advertising media can be part and parcel of many other activities, including work, play, learning about the world, interacting with other people, recovering from or avoiding illness, participating in politics, and so on.

That being the case, it is not surprising that persons who want to learn more about consumers frequently borrow concepts and methods from the behavioral sciences. Figure 2-1, for example, itemizes a number of concepts from these disciplines that have been found pertinent.

Although the study of consumer behavior is thoroughly interdisciplinary, it is important to note that not all the concepts of behavioral science are equally or directly applicable (Arndt, 1967). For example, many sociologists are interested in the study of suicide rates and many psychologists are interested in the study of "abnormal" persons. Concepts and methods developed especially for studying and understanding suicidal tendencies and other abnormal behaviors would as a rule be of little value in studying and understanding "normal" consumers. This would seem to be a rather obvious point. But, as we shall see later, some students of consumer behavior have ignored it to their peril.

The S→C→R Model

Since consumer behavior is a subset of human behavior, it is useful to develop a general orientation and then proceed to delineate those specific actions of humans that are especially relevant to humans as consumers.

When psychologists began to think about a way to describe human (and animal) behavior, they found it convenient to use a "model," usually written out as S→O→R. *Model* is a fashionable term that came in with computers. Some models are mathematical representations of sets of relationships, but many, including this one, are nonquantitative sets of symbols or words.

The S→O→R model, sometimes written R=f(S, O), is a convenient way of expressing the common-sense notion that a response (R) is a function (f) of the stimuli (S) to which the organism (O) is exposed; and, further, that the response is also a function of certain properties of the organism. Different stimuli operating on the same organism produce different responses; the same stimulus operating on different organisms produces different responses.

When stimuli are very powerful, or when the organisms being studied are much alike, it makes sense to ignore the obvious fact that organisms are different and to concentrate on working out the relationships between stimuli and responses. For instance, hunger is such a powerful stimulus that food deprivation almost always elicits food-seeking behavior. Human retinas are so

Figure 2-1 Psychological, Sociological, Anthropological, and Economic Concepts Pertinent to the Study of Consumer Behavior

Psychological:

- P_1 motivation
  - $P_{1.1}$ biogenic
  - $P_{1.2}$ sociogenic
- P_2 cognition
  - $P_{2.1}$ perception
  - $P_{2.2}$ attitudes
  - $P_{2.3}$ categorization
  - $P_{2.4}$ structuralization
  - $P_{2.5}$ decision process
- P_3 learning
  - $P_{3.1}$ instrumental
  - $P_{3.2}$ perceptual
  - $P_{3.3}$ affective
  - $P_{3.4}$ social
  - $P_{3.5}$ habit
  - $P_{3.6}$ attitudes

Sociological:

- S_1 socialization
- S_2 symbolic interaction
  - $S_{2.1}$ symbol
  - $S_{2.2}$ role
  - $S_{2.3}$ reference group
  - $S_{2.4}$ perspective
  - $S_{2.5}$ tastes and preferences
  - $S_{2.6}$ communication channels
- S_3 structure-function
  - $S_{3.1}$ social system
  - $S_{3.2}$ function
  - $S_{3.3}$ social structure
  - $S_{3.4}$ norms and values
- S_4 developmental approach
  - $S_{4.1}$ family life-cycle
  - $S_{4.2}$ careers
- S_5 social differentiation

Anthropological:

- A_1 culture
  - $A_{1.1}$ cultural patterns
  - $A_{1.2}$ cultural differences
- A_2 cultural change
  - $A_{2.1}$ processes of change
  - $A_{2.2}$ innovation
  - $A_{2.3}$ invention
  - $A_{2.4}$ diffusion
  - $SA_{2.5}$ adoption process
  - $SA_{2.6}$ change agent

Economic:

- E_1 demand (price)
  - $E_{1.1}$ utility
  - $E_{1.2}$ alternative goods
  - $E_{1.3}$ indifference
  - $E_{1.4}$ revealed preference
- E_2 consumption function (income)
  - $E_{2.1}$ permanent-income hypothesis
  - $E_{2.2}$ relative-income hypothesis
- E_3 statistical demand analysis
- E_4 consumer preference
- E_5 stocks
- E_6 flows
- E_7 dynamics
  - $E_{7.1}$ short-term
  - $E_{7.2}$ long-term
  - $E_{7.3}$ ex ante
  - $E_{7.4}$ ex post
  - $E_{7.5}$ lags
  - $E_{7.6}$ process analysis
- E_8 aggregation
- E_9 attitudes
- E_{10} expectations
- E_{11} processes
  - $E_{11.1}$ choice
  - $E_{11.2}$ use
  - $E_{11.3}$ decision making
  - $E_{11.4}$ problem solving
- E_{12} structure of consumption

Source: Burk (1967: 2).

much alike that virtually all of them show a cone-to-rod shift in dark adaptation.

Some psychologists believe that the best way to study human behavior is to concentrate on the S→R relationship, leaving out the organism, or simply treating the organism as a "black box." Other psychologists believe that understanding O is essential. They believe that the effect of a stimulus is so dependent upon the nature of the organism that in many areas of great importance, simple straightforward S→R relationships will never be found.

Students of consumer behavior also disagree on this point. Some believe that most progress will be made through careful analysis of the relationships between stimuli (display, promotion, price, etc.) and the response (purchase). Others believe that consumers are so different from each other that the effect of any stimulus will always depend upon the consumer. Instead of seeking relationships between stimuli on the one hand and responses on the other, with the consumer treated as a black box, they seek in addition to identify the characteristics of consumers that mediate these effects. That is, instead of S→R, they use S→C→R, or R=f(S, C), and a C replacing the O as a reminder that the student of consumer behavior is interested in a limited range of activities and not all behavior of all organisms. This model simply says that different stimuli operating on the same consumer will produce different results, and that different consumers will react differently to a given stimulus. Let us elaborate this point.

Thinking back to the observation and the interview with the woman in the supermarket, it seems obvious that she was, above all, an active person. She was constantly on the go, studying the signs and symbols in her environment, interacting with her children, and so on. She was not some inert object, temporarily set into motion by some push or pull stimulus.

Similarly, even though the La Mottas in the first chapter were in a certain sense manipulated, they were far from passive. They interacted with each other and with the salesman, and in doing so they emitted signals by which he moderated his behavior. Thus, consumers do not respond to stimuli such as products, advertisements, or salespersons in a simple, reflexic manner. Rather, they continually select some stimuli and ignore others, and they organize these stimuli into patterns of meaningful interrelationships.

Furthermore, consumers respond, not directly to stimuli, but to the organized interpretation of the results of a given response. Many of the La Mottas' responses, and many of the responses of the woman in the supermarket, were made with reference to the anticipated future. From something as mundane as buying Wheaties to something as important as signing a long-term contract, the behavior of the consumer was moderated and guided with a picture of the probable outcome. Consumer behavior, then, is future-oriented. Wroe Alderson (1965:144) made this point quite explicit when he wrote, "The theory of consumer buying holds that the consumer purchasing agent enters the market to replenish or extend the assortment of goods needed to support expected patterns of future behavior."

Later a great deal of emphasis will be placed upon the notion that consumers are future-oriented. To fully comprehend any aspect of human behavior, including consumer behavior, one must examine it as a process with an expected outcome, not as a function that is turned on and off by some external force.

Another and related point is that consumer behavior occurs over time. The time horizon varies, of course, for different types of activities. In the supermarket episode, the purchaser spent very little time buying some items and more time buying others. In the La Motta episode, one purchase decision took more time and probably had longer-lasting effects than the whole supermarket sequence. One must account for the fact that all behavior, even inactivity, occupies time or has a time duration.

The S→C→R model can be expanded to include the notions of time and experience, as shown in Figure 2-2.

The addition of a time line to the basic model draws attention to the dynamic aspect of consumer behavior. It illustrates three points first made by Kornhauser and Lazarfeld in 1935. First, since consumer behavior is a process through time, the consumer builds up his or her experience world as time goes on. Therefore, when analysts isolate a segment of a person's life to examine the person's interaction with some aspect of the environment, they must constantly keep in mind that the person already possesses a complex background that summarizes a vast range of previous experiences.

Second, the response a consumer makes at a given point in time can often be understood only be reference to what went before; the process must be seen in a sequence of interactions along an extended time line.

Third, each stage or set of interactions along the time line is itself a response determined jointly by the consumer as the person then is and by the existing influences or stimuli in the environment.

To illustrate, think back to the supermarket shopper for a moment and abstract certain stages of her shopping and buying experience in terms of Figure 2-2.[1] At time T_1 she was a person with a certain specific background of experience. Then she looked at the oranges in the produce section and apparently decided to purchase some; i.e., she interacted with the display (S_1) and picked up a variety packed six to a box (R_1). At that moment she became a

[1]For purposes of brevity we have ignored a number of interactions observed or reported by the shopper. Those, however, could be placed into an expanded version of Figure 2-2.

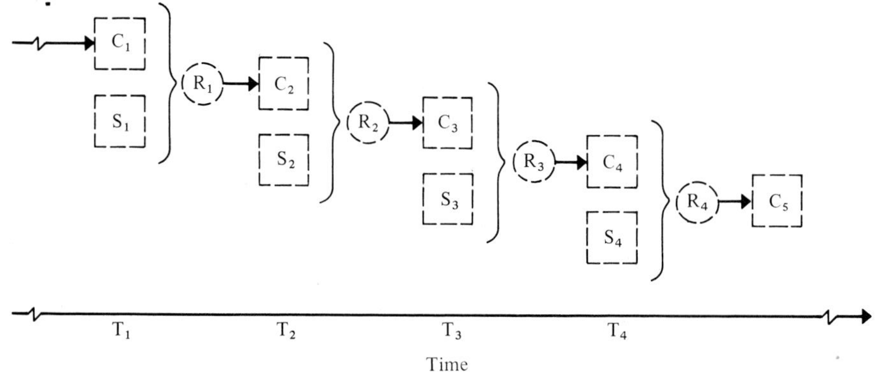

Figure 2-2 The S→C→R model over time. *Source*: Adapted from Kornhauser and Lazarfeld (1935).

different person, C_2, at least in the sense that she had apparently reached a decision to buy the pack. At time segment T_2, however, she (C_2) paid attention to a "special" advertised by a sign at the end of the aisle (S_2). Upon seeing this special, she replaced the box and selected a sack from the special display (R_2). At time T_3, she (C_3) reacted (R_3) to her son's pointing (S_3) to a cereal package by asking if he wanted Fruit-Loops. (Notice that the son's response, grunting and pointing, was also a result of his interaction with a stimulus, the brightly colored package, and that his communicating response in turn represented a source of information to his mother.) At T_4, the shopper (C_4), armed with the knowledge of her son's desire (S_4), put a package of Fruit-Loops into the cart (R_4). In short, both consumers and environments are continually changing; both can be viewed as processes over time. Furthermore, consumers individually have the capacity to interpret and represent aspects of their universe, and their organization of these representations provides the basis for their response to situations they encounter.

This brings us to a final general point: consumer behavior is, by and large, reasonable problem-solving behavior when viewed in the light of the consumer's experiences and intentions. This does not mean that the consumer invariably behaves rationally in terms of some set of objective criteria. Rather, consumers behave in terms of their perceptions of the situation. The process can be described along these lines: whenever people choose to notice some aspect of their environment, they reflect upon their experience. They recall whether or not they have ever acted toward a similar stimulus in the past; they recall their previous judgments about previous similar objects as well as their evaluation of the outcome of the actions they took; i.e., they reflect both in terms of the ends they chose and the means they chose to attain them. In relating the past to the future, they also decide whether they still desire the same ends and, if not, what different means and ends are currently possible.

This process seems generally congruent with the behavior of the woman in the supermarket, but does it fit the La Mottas' decision to pay more than $400 for a set of photographs and albums? It does because consumers often go through this process without considering all the information known or available about the situation to which they are responding. This omission may result in decisions that are seen to be foolish or "irrational" when viewed by an objective observer. Nevertheless, the pattern of interpretations that consumers build for themselves is the basis for their actions vis-à-vis an event or object of their environment, and faulty or incomplete interpretations may result in bad decisions.

THE ELEMENTS OF CONSUMER BEHAVIOR

Thus far our discussion has sketched some of the distinguishing qualities of human behavior as it relates to consumer behavior. The identification of these qualities serves two purposes. One, it provides some enlightenment not only as to what consumer behavior is but also as to what it is not; and two, it serves as a point of departure for defining consumer behavior or, more explicitly, for identifying the component elements that describe the boundaries of the study of consumer behavior.

Before rendering a definition, it might be fruitful to summarize the assumptions about consumer behavior that have been set forth in the two examples and in the discussion of the S→C→R model. These basic assumptions can then serve as the foundation for a definition.

Assumption 1. Consumers are influenced by a wide variety of stimuli or sources of information.

Assumption 2. Consumers actively and purposefully engage in many different kinds of decisions and resulting activities.

Assumption 3. Consumers engage in decisions and activities in many different settings or situations.

Assumption 4. Consumers differ greatly in many ways, and these differences mediate the effects of stimuli from various situations upon decisions and behavior.

Assumption 5. Not only do consumers differ, but these differences change over time.

Broadly speaking then, *"consumer behavior" refers to the differential behaviors of persons over time as they acquire, process, and utilize information from various sources and settings in purchasing, consuming, and communicating about brands, products, and clusters of products.*

This definition emphasizes the interactions of persons and certain aspects of their environment; it highlights the temporal dimension of behavior; and it notes the general response types resulting from people's interactions with the environment.

Each element of the definition can be explicated by organizing discussions around the components of the S→C→R model. That is, one can describe (1) consumer stimuli and situations, (2) consumer characteristics, and (3) consumer responses.

These three major divisions are introduced briefly in the remainder of this chapter.

Consumer Stimuli

As a person moves from setting to setting, the configuration of a setting at a given point in time represents the potential stimuli for a person at that point in time. Figure 2-3 represents one useful way of grouping the major consumer stimuli or sources of information. Each axis in the figure depicts a continuum of sources, one from a marketer's perspective, the other from a consumer's perspective.

From a consumer perspective, information sources can be viewed on an impersonal-to-interpersonal continuum. At the impersonal end, there are the so-called "one-way" media, such as the mass media, which direct their messages at consumers but to which consumers have little chance for

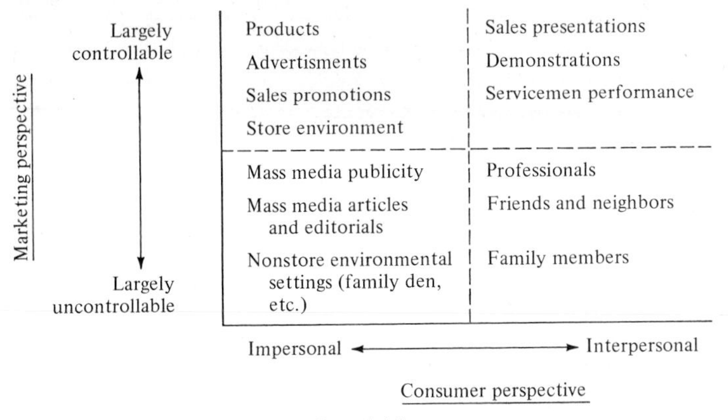

Figure 2-3 Comsumer stimuli variables.

immediate reply. At the personal end of the continuum are the "two-way" sources, where source and consumer have a chance to interact directly with each other.

From the marketers' perspective, consumer stimuli can be represented by the degree of control the marketer has over the source of information. Marketers have a relatively high degree of control over the content of advertisements, for example, but relatively little, if any, control over the thoughts imparted about a product from a friend.

It is important to classify sources in this manner in order to assess the relative effectiveness of various sources in generating a response from consumers. Since marketers must allocate communication efforts, the proportion of effort devoted to advertising as compared with direct selling will depend upon the type of response desired and the relative effectiveness of the two sources in eliciting this response. The use of the impersonal-interpersonal continuum also allows us to assess consumers' interactions with their environment. Personal selling efforts, for example, tend to be more effective than advertising in persuading consumers to buy products because of the personal two-way nature of the situation. A professional such as a lawyer, on the other hand, may be more influential than salespersons, since consumers tend to place more confidence in the advice offered by sources not highly controllable by firms.

Consumer Characteristics

Earlier we suggested that consumers differ greatly in many ways and that these differences mediate the effects of stimuli. It is possible to think of the various kinds of consumer characteristics as forming a general-specific continuum, running from demographic and socioeconomic characteristics at one end to purchasing and consumption characteristics at the other. This continuuum is illustrated in Figure 2-4.

Each box in the continuum represents a set of characteristics that have

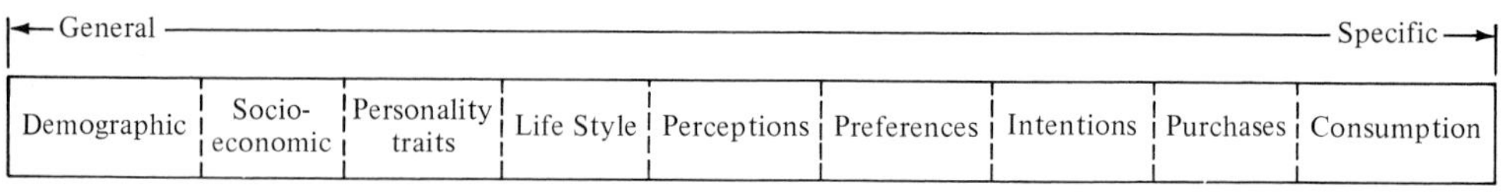

Figure 2-4 A general-specific continuum of consumer characteristics.

been used in describing consumers. The left-hand side of the continuum shows categories which contain general consumer characteristics—attributes that can be used to describe consumers without referring explicitly to a product or a stimulus. For example, a family might be described as having an income in the range of $15,000 to $24,999. Or a person might be described as a socially gregarious person who is highly interested in fashion. In so describing a consumer, however, nothing has been said about interaction with the environment, and nothing has been said about the resulting consumer responses. Figure 2-5 shows some of the most important general characteristics in which consumers differ.

In Figure 2-4 we have also referred to "specific" consumer characteristics—specific in the sense that such concepts cannot be divorced from a given product or a given source of information. For example, a person could be described as a heavy user of soft drinks (a consumption variable), or a family might be described in terms of dollars spent on groceries in a supermarket.

Figure 2-5 General Consumer Characteristics

Type of characteristic	Illustrative concepts
Demographic	Age Sex Geographical location Geographical mobility Family life cycle Racial groups Ethnic groups
Socioeconomic	Occupation Education Income Social class
Personality traits	Gregariousness Venturesomeness Self-confidence Self-esteem
Life style	Activities Interests Opinions Needs Values

Similarly, one could use any of the characteristics summarized by Figure 2-4 to describe a person or a family, or to relate these concepts to sources of information and to responses. In fact, much of the research on market segmentation employs various combinations of these characteristics as independent variables, relating consumers to responses or relating stimuli to consumers rather than relating stimuli directly to responses.

Certain consumer characteristics play a dual role in the study of consumer behavior. In general, the more specific characteristics may be considered consumer differences for descriptive and prediction purposes or they may be considered consumer response variables. For instance, families can be described in terms of their weekly grocery expenditures. But weekly grocery expenditures can also be considered a response variable—a behavior to be related to general consumer characteristics like those shown in Figure 2-5. It would also be possible to examine the relationship between two specific characteristics, such as the relationship, if any, between weekly grocery expenditures and weekly personal grooming expenditures.

Failure to recognize the dual role of specific consumer characteristics can lead to what might be termed the "descriptive-predictive" paradox. This paradox refers to the contention by some writers that general consumer characteristics are not very useful to the study of consumer behavior since they lack the predictive power of the specific variables, and to the contention by others that general variables are indeed useful even if they are "only" descriptive.

Recognition of the dual role of specific consumer characteristics leads to the conclusion that both general and specific variables are useful in studying consumer behavior, but in different contexts. Consider, for example, the categories in Figure 2-4. Among the types of data shown in the continuum, purchases are closest to consumption, purchase intentions are closest to actual purchases, brand and product preferences are next, and so on. One should therefore be able to predict purchases more accurately from intentions than from preferences; more accurately from life style variables than from personality traits; and so on. This point has been made by several authors (Ziff, 1971; Hustad and Pessemier, 1971; and Reynolds and Darden, 1972), and a substantial amount of research has shown that the closer one gets to the actual act—both temporally and psychologically—the more accurate the prediction (Bass and Talarzyk, 1972). Thus, when *prediction* is the principal objective, variables to the right of the figure are virtually certain to be superior.

Yet this greater predictive accuracy is purchased at the cost of descriptive value. To describe those who purchase Brand X as "those who intended to purchase Brand X" usually strikes marketing managers as something less than interesting, no matter how accurately intentions predict the behavior. When we move back several spaces in the figure, to life style characteristics, the data produce useful descriptions of consumers. It *does* help to have a detailed portrait of the consumer, drawn in terms of his activities, interests, opinions, needs, and values. Thus, when *description* is the goal, general consumer characteristics are superior to the more specific characteristics.

The study of consumer behavior, fortunately, does not have to be and frequently is not an "either-or" enterprise. Research can be conducted which combines both general and specific characteristics to provide data useful for both prediction and description.

Consumer Responses

We have indicated that specific consumer characteristics also represent consumer response variables. In this section we explore more explicitly the nature of these characteristics as responses. They are the results of consumers interacting with their environment.

Consumer responses can be divided into two types: observable and nonobservable. Observable responses are overt behaviors directly observable by another person. In the study of consumer behavior, these include purchasing, consuming, and communicating. Nonobservable responses are internal responses and hence cannot be directly ascertained by other persons. Since they cannot be observed directly, they must be inferred. In the supermarket incident, for example, we observed that the shopper noticed a sign promoting oranges on special, and we observed that she selected a sack from those on special. We could not, however, observe what she was thinking. On the basis of her actions, we might infer that she was price conscious. If it could be shown that this attribute was a characteristic mode of the woman's behavior in different situations it would help explain her behavior in this specific case.

Figure 2-6 depicts the major consumer response variables, along with two other relevant dimensions of consumer analysis. One, "responses toward selected aspects of one's environment," suggests the basic elements of the environment that are of importance to students of consumer behavior. These responses are shown at the bottom of the figure at various levels of aggregation. The second dimension is the unit of analysis. From a psychological viewpoint, the individual person is the basic unit of study. In research on consumer behavior, however, an aggregate of persons (ethnic groups, for example) may be the appropriate unit.

The consumer response variables shown at the left of the figure represent the basic dependent variables in the study of consumer behavior. They will now be discussed individually.

The term *information handling* refers to the ways people interact mentally with their environments. It refers to the ways a person goes about viewing things in the world, putting things into patterns of relationships, and making decisions based on these relationships. Psychologists frequently refer to these responses as "cognitive and evaluative processes." Neisser (1966), for example, has suggested that cognition includes all those processes by which a person transforms, changes, stores, recovers, and uses sensory information. Kernan (1971) describes information handling as a sequence of three processes: acquisition, processing, and utilization. "Acquisition" encompasses the sensing of stimuli and their interpretation or perception. "Processing" encompasses the

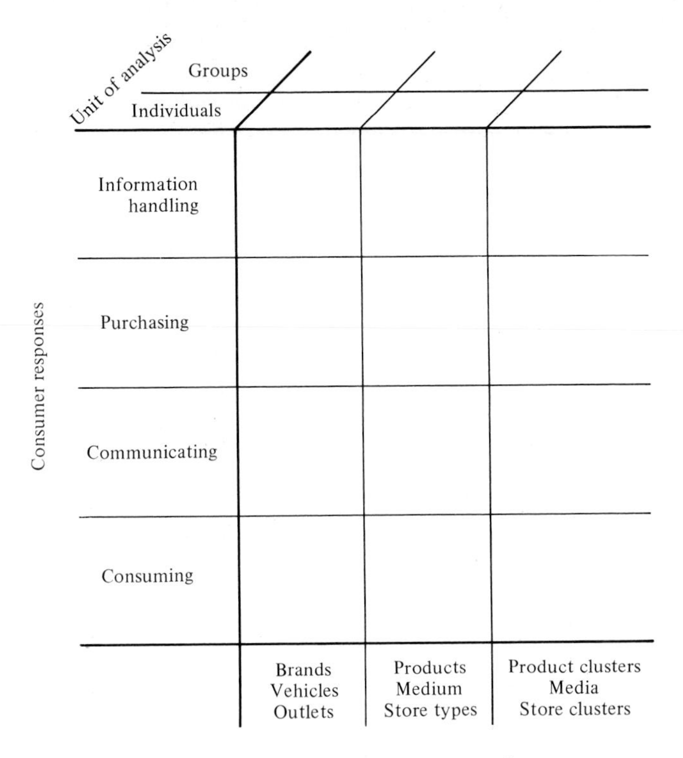

Figure 2-6 Consumer-response variables.

mental activities of a person in assessing the relative desirability of an object or idea for his own situation—a mental trial or evaluation process. "Utilization," as the name implies, refers to the use to which information is put. It is represented by decisions to respond in some manner.

Because information handling is a series of nonobservable processes, marketers typically study certain mental states postulated to be the result of information handling. Such mental states, themselves hypothetical, include such notions as attention, comprehension, attitude, image, and perceived product attribute. The understanding of these concepts is of the utmost importance to students of consumer behavior, since these concepts represent the way consumers view aspects of their world, and ultimately, the way they will react to those aspects.

Marketing has been described as "the set of human activities directed at facilitating and consummating exchanges," where exchanges or transactions occur when two or more parties each give up something of value in return for something valued (Kotler, 1972). Clearly, the marketer attempts to obtain a response from his market. The ultimate response is the exchange of money for goods or services.

The concept of *purchase,* then, is at the core of the study of consumer behavior. It includes certain decisions and activities preceding the act of purchase, such as traveling to a store, movement within a store, and the selection of a product to purchase (Webster, 1966).

The number of different purchasing behaviors of persons is almost infinite. A large number have been examined as dependent variables in the literature. It is useful to divide such behaviors into two major types: first purchase, and repeat purchase. Marketers are interested in first-purchase responses since these represent the foundation of success or failure of new-product ventures. They are interested in repeat purchasing behavior because they must be constantly alert to changes in market behavior and competitive structure in order to keep existing products profitable.

Like purchasing responses, *communication responses,* such as talking to friends about products or seeking advice from others, are observable actions of persons. Their importance to students of consumer behavior, however, lies not so much in their observable character as in their aggregate effects. The communicating activities of persons frequently are interwoven with their purchasing behaviors, and they may account for much of the transmission of information about products. Sometimes to the marketer they mean the difference between success and failure. To the consumer they frequently mean better decisions than could be made by relying on marketer-controlled information alone.

The aggregate effect of interpersonal communicating activities has been given a variety of names: *diffusion effects, social contagion, "snowballing," the interaction effect,* and *the establishment of buying patterns.* It is the process by which some persons lead others to purchase, and it is frequently posited to account for cumulative acceptance over time (Robertson, 1971; Rogers, 1962).

Marketers can no more "control" the communicating activities of consumers than they can control consumers' purchasing behaviors. But by understanding the effects of interpersonal communications, and by knowing who does the communicating to whom with what type of an effect, marketers can attempt to develop marketing programs which will facilitate favorable communications about their products. The old adage that the best advertisement is a satisfied customer attests to marketers' interest in stimulating favorable communication and to the great power that consumers can exercise by communicating their experiences to each other.

To understand the effects of interpersonal communication, it is useful to identify major interpersonal situations. Three situations have received considerable attention in the literature: interpersonal communication among friends, interpersonal communication between members of the nuclear family, and interpersonal communication between customers and salespersons. We have already encountered two of these three situations. All three will be discussed in detail in future chapters.

From the standpoint of marketing success, *consumption*—the actual experience with the product—is perhaps the most important type of response, for it is the primary basis upon which persons reassess their purchasing decisions and the information acquisition and processing strategies used to make these decisions. Reevaluation from primary experience validates or invalidates purchasing decisions and thus provides a direct influence on subsequent purchase decisions. Somewhat paradoxically, however, actual consumption has been among the least studied aspects of consumer behavior.

Some aspects of consumption have been examined. The major concepts used in consuming studies include various measures of brand and product usage rates and time spent for consumption. Because collecting observational data on product usage rates is both time-consuming and expensive, researchers have been inclined to depend upon self-reports (obtained by questionnaires through survey research) to obtain such data. Although self-reports may not be entirely accurate, they are generally considered satisfactory, at least in a relative sense. It seems reasonable to assume, for example, that if a person reports using hair spray five times a day on the average, that person consumes more hair spray than a person who reports using it only once each day.

The study of complementary (and substitute) product usage rates, relatively new in consumer research, promises to reveal sets of product consumptions with substantive marketing implications. A *complementary product* is one which tends to be used jointly with another product, whereas a *substitute product* is one which satisfies the same need as another and thus tends to be used separately (Bass et al., 1969). This type of research is, in essence, a multidimensional approach to classifying persons in terms of strength o. consumption. If, for example, hair spray and eye makeup are part of one consumption dimension and hair shampoo is part of another dimension, perhaps it would be more effective both to promote and to locate hair spray and eye makeup together rather than to promote and locate hair spray and shampoo together.

In conclusion, consuming behaviors need extensive research even though their measurement poses more problems than that of purchasing behaviors. Purchase decisions are made with consumption as the purpose, and consumption is causally related to further purchasing behavior.

ORGANIZATION OF FOLLOWING CHAPTERS

Preceding pages have introduced the major concepts which will dominate the discussion in following chapters. Subsequent chapters are organized into two Parts, (1) "Consumer Development and Market Behavior" and (2) "The Analysis of Consumer Stimuli and Responses." The reasons for this organization are explained in this section.

Earlier in this chapter we noted that there are two seemingly opposing views of the best way to approach the study of consumer behavior, the S-R and the S-C-R. Actually, there is no real need to view the study of consumer behavior from opposing positions, for the study can employ both approaches in a complementary manner, which turns out to be the essence of market segmentation. The concept of market segments formally recognizes the import of consumer differences (there are groups of *people who respond in different ways to marketing programs because of their differential needs and wants*) and consumer similarities (there are *groups of people who respond similarly . . .*). In other words, when consumers are very much alike on certain major characteristics, it makes sense to ignore the minor differences and to concentrate on working out the relationships between consumer stimuli and responses. The key, of course, lies in identifying groups of people in terms of shared major characteristics—those that accurately reflect similar needs and wants—the process called *market segmentation.*

The major theme of the chapters in Part Two is the identification of groups of consumers who share common characteristics that affect their behavior in the marketplace. In some cases generalizations about marketing efforts and consumer responses also will be discussed, but this level of analysis will be reserved primarily for the central theme of Part Three of the book.

The first five chapters in Part Two constitute an age-graded discussion of consumer behavior. Why age? Think back for a moment to the time line in Figure 2-2 and to assumption 5: consumers not only differ, but these differences change over time. These differences do not change in a helter-skelter fashion, fortunately; rather, if we start at the beginning of life, at birth and infancy, and trace the life span to its completion, we find that humans "develop"—they change in an orderly, coherent pattern. The *rate* of development from conception to death varies from person to person, of course, but all persons follow virtually the same *pattern,* and age is often a good indicator of the stage of development persons have reached. Needs of people change as they develop. Thus, age changes in the population are good indicators of demand changes for products unique to various age groups. In other words, a dynamic yet precise representation of consumer needs and goals can be sketched within the developmental framework of the various levels and phases of life. Figure 2-7 is an expanded version of the S→C→R model, expanded to show the consumer-development emphasis of Part Two.

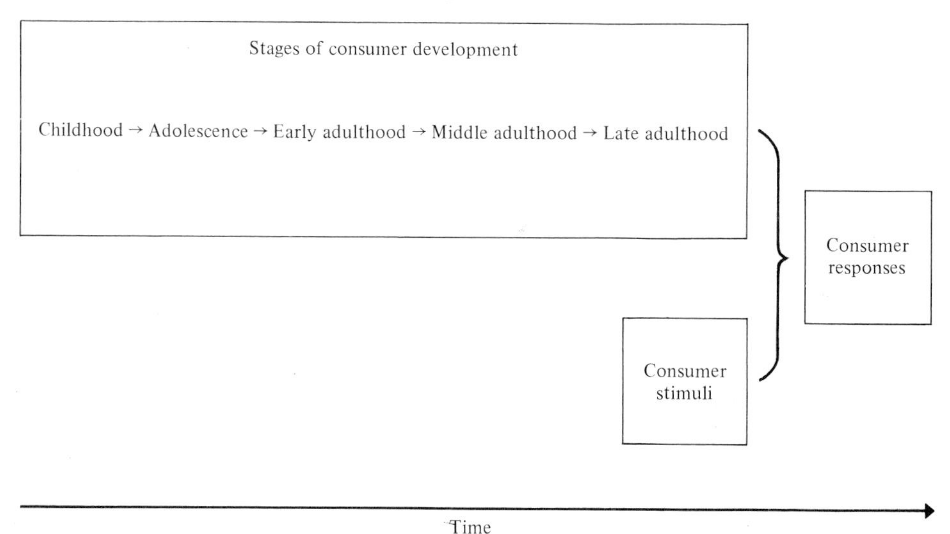

Figure 2-7 An expanded S→C→R model.

Often, of course, age must be supplemented with other consumer characteristics to define subgroups within an age group to provide greater insight into the market behavior of persons. Segmentation, viewed in this context, is hierarchical. Age, the key characteristic, resides at the top of the hierarchy because it represents development, and consumers follow fairly definite and predictable patterns of behavior as they develop. But since not all consumers follow the pattern at the same rate or express the pattern in identical behaviors, it is useful to explore subgroup identities on other characteristics, such as sex, income, and life events, to obtain a better match of needs and groups of people. Consider, for instance, the notion of the family life cycle.

In the United States today most households pass through an orderly succession of stages as defined by a combination of characteristics: age, marital status, and parenthood. These stages, shown below, are related to, but not perfectly represented by, chronological age and development level.

Age	Developmental level	Stage in the family life cycle
18-34	Early adulthood	1. The bachelor stage; young, single people
		2. Newly married couples; young, no children
		3. The full nest I; young married couples with dependent children
		a Youngest child under six
		b Youngest child over six
35-54	Middle adulthood	4. The full nest II; older married couples with dependent children
55 and older	Later adulthood	5. The empty nest; older married couples with no children living with them
		a Head in labor force
		b Head retired
		6. The solitary survivors; older single people
		a In labor force
		b Retired

Not all households pass through all these stages, of course. Some people never get married. Some married couples never have children. Some mothers and some fathers are widowed before the children leave home, and so on. But the sequence outlined above is most common.

For a great many products and services, the consumer's stage in the family life cycle has more influence on purchasing than does the consumer's chronological age. Purchases change in response to needs, and many needs change more in response to change in family status than in response to the mere passage of time. Thus, whenever a consumer characteristic exercises an influence over the consumption of goods and services, it is discussed in the chapters in Part Two within the hierarchical segmentation scheme.

The pattern of development of persons consists of not only innate physiological and psychological developments but also cultural ideas and artifacts. These cultural identities also shape behavior in the marketplace. Hence, the final chapter of Part Two is devoted to exploring these influences.

In Part Three, Chapters 9–15, the theme of the discussion shifts to major consumer stimuli and responses. By having consumers' "history" in mind—their major needs and goals over the life span—we can put the emphasis on general consumer differences into the background and focus more clearly on the analysis of consumer responses and the stimuli that influence them. In particular, as we take a more analytical approach, we can begin to examine brand choice behavior—how marketers, once they have selected a general segment of consumers with given needs and wants, study needs in a brand context and develop marketing programs aimed at getting consumers to buy and consume certain brands and to shop in certain stores or shopping centers.

Figure 2-8 depicts the emphasis of Part Three of the book. The model indicates that what consumers want from a product or service at a given point in time is a function of consumer history; that is, past experiences and position in the life span, as defined by consumer characteristics, help shape current needs and wants. What consumers are expecting, looking for, or are receptive to because of their needs, along with impersonal and interpersonal stimuli, determine product perceptions and predispositions, which, in turn, influence purchase and consumption. Each of these influences is subject to potential modifying influences, however. For instance, an advertisement may not capture consumer attention; and even if it does, consumers may distort its meaning. Thus, the intended influence is modified by selective attention and perception. Or, a consumer is predisposed to buy Brand X but an advertise-

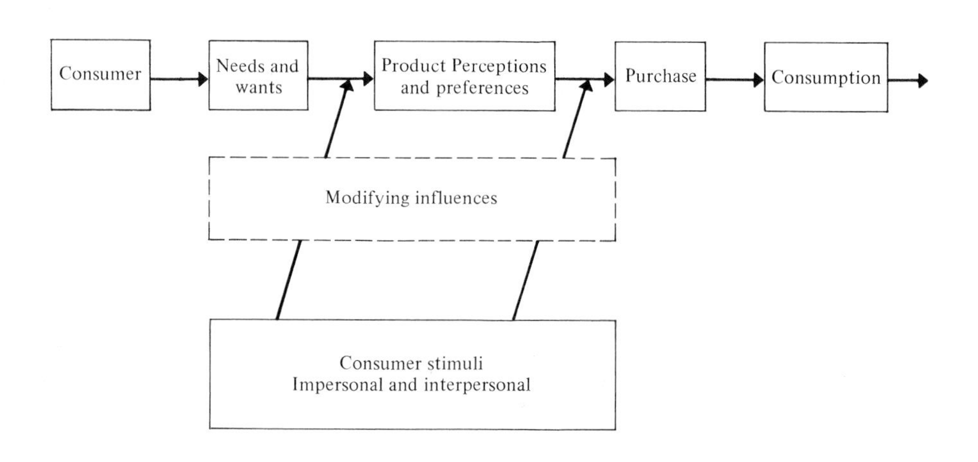

Figure 2-8 An expanded S→C→R model.

ment for Brand Y changes the consumer's mind; in this situation, the intended influence is modified by a competing stimulus.

Chapter 9 examines product perceptions and preferences. It focuses on the perception of products, product images, and attitudes toward products. It discusses the modifying influences that may prevent a direct relationship between attitudes and purchase. Chapters 10 and 11 discuss major consumer stimuli. In Chapter 10 advertising is selected to represent impersonal stimuli, and in Chapter 11 the interpersonal stimuli are friends, family members, and salespersons. Chapters 12 through 15 explore the major types of observable consumer responses—purchases of new products, repeat purchases, spatial behavior and patronage, and consumption.

SUMMARY

This chapter began with an incident of consumer behavior. The shopping incident illustrates (somewhat crudely) two ways of studying consumer behavior—direct observation and direct questioning—and it indicated some of the problems attendant to these methods. The incident also served to illustrate the complexity of consumer behavior. It showed that consumers typically can make a large number of decisions in a brief period of time, and it showed that some of these decisions are influenced by in-store factors such as price and promotions while others are influenced by stimuli not present in the buying situation, such as the anticipated needs of other family members. The incident also served as an illustration of some of the major elements of a conceptual orientation of the field of consumer behavior.

It was suggested that consumer behavior is a subset of human behavior, often appropriately studied by means of concepts and methods of the behavioral sciences. However, it was noted that not all of these methods are equally useful and that some are apt to be quite inappropriate.

In the discussion of S→C→R model of behavior, several positions were taken. We suggested that consumers do not necessarily respond directly to stimuli but may react to organized interpretations of the results expected (or predicted) from a given response. In other words, they interact with their environments in terms of past experiences and present expectations. It was also noted that consumer behavior occurs over time, that the duration of time varies for different types of activities, and that persons change over time as a result of their experiences. The position was also taken that consumer behavior is generally purposive, although not infallible in an objective sense.

Based on the discussion of the S→C→R model, the task of studying consumer behavior was outlined as identifying and measuring S→R, R→R, and S→C→R relationships. *Consumer behavior* was defined as the differential behavior of persons over time as they acquire, process, and use information from various sources and settings in purchasing, consuming, and communicating about brands, products, and clusters of products.

Consumer stimuli were shown to be the sources and settings from which persons can obtain information or be influenced. These stimuli include such major categories as products, advertisements, mass media articles, sales presentations, friends, and members of one's family. Also, a number of dimensions upon which consumers can differ were discussed, ranging from general characteristics such as demographic and socioeconomic variables to specific characteristics such as product perceptions and preferences. It was noted that special characteristics play a dual role in the study of consumer behavior in that they also represent consumer reponses. Finally, other consumer responses were reviewed briefly, all to be taken up in detail later. These responses include the results of information handling processes, observable shopping and purchasing behaviors, consuming behaviors, and communicating behaviors.

This chapter has served as an introductory foundation for the major concepts which will dominate the discussion in the remainder of the book.

REVIEW QUESTIONS

1. In the supermarket case presented at the beginning of this chapter, both direct observation and direct interviewing techniques were utilized. What are the advantages and limitations of each method?
2. Why is it possible for students of consumer behavior to borrow concepts and methods from other disciplines? Which other disciplines are pertinent?
3. Describe the differences between the S→R model, the S→C→R model, and the S→C→R model over time.
4. Define consumer behavior. What are the assumptions about consumers which are implicit in this definition?
5. Consumer stimuli variables can be viewed from a marketer's perspective and a consumer's perspective. How do the two perspectives differ? Make a list of some consumer stimuli, such as advertisements and family discussions, and then determine the relative position of each variable from both perspectives.
6. What is meant by general and specific consumer characteristics? Give examples of each. Which type of characteristic is most useful when the objective is prediction? Which is most useful for descriptive purposes?
7. Information handling is a nonobservable consumer response process. Discuss the sequence of activities involved in information handling and the method marketers use to study the consumer response variable.
8. Observable consumer response variables include purchasing, communicating, and consuming. Identify the activities involved in each response and the importance of each response to marketers.
9. What types of marketing implications can be inferred from the study of product usage rates?
10. Why are age levels used in studying the development of consumer behavior?

REFERENCES

Alderson, Wroe. *Dynamic Marketing Behavior.* Homewood, Ill.: Richard D. Irwin, 1965.
Arndt, Johan (ed.). *Insights into Consumer Behavior.* Boston: Allyn and Bacon, 1968.

Bass, Frank M., Edgar A. Pessemier, and Douglas J. Tigert. "Complementary and Substitute Patterns of Purchasing and Use." *Journal of Advertising Research*, 9 (June 1969), 19–28.

——— and Wayne Talarzyk. "An Attitudinal Model for the Study of Brand Preference. " *Journal of Marketing Research*, 9 (February 1972), 93–96.

Burk, Marguerite C. "Survey of Interpretations of Consumer Behavior by Social Scientists in the Postwar Period." *Journal of Farm Economics*, 49 (February 1967), 1–31.

Hustad, Thomas P., and Edgar A. Pessemier. "The Development and Application of Psychographic, Life Style and Associated Activity and Attitude Measures." Paper No. 287, Krannert Graduate School of Industrial Administration, Purdue University, March 1971.

Kernan, Jerome. "Human Information Handling." Unpublished working paper, University of Cincinnati, 1971.

Kornhauser, Arthur, and Paul F. Lazarsfeld. "The Analysis of Consumer Actions." *The Techniques of Market Research from the Standpoint of a Psychologist.* New York: American Management Association, 1925. Reprinted in Ralph L. Day and Thomas E. Ness (eds.), *Marketing Models: Behavioral Science Applications.* Scranton, Pa.: International Textbook, 1971.

Kotler, Philip. *Marketing Management.* 2d ed. Englewood Cliffs, N.J.: Prentice-Hall, 1972.

Neisser, U. *Cognitive Psychology.* New York: Appleton-Century, 1966.

Reynolds, Fred D., and William R. Darden. "Intermarket Patronage: A Psychographic Study of Consumer Outshoppers." *Journal of Marketing*, 36 (October 1972), 50–54.

Robertson, Thomas S. *Innovative Behavior and Communication.* New York: Holt, Rinehart and Winston, 1971.

Rogers, Everett M. *Diffusion of Innovations.* New York: Free Press, 1962.

Webster, Frederick E., Jr. "The Behavioral Sciences and the Marketing Manager." *University of Washington Business Review*, 26 (October 1966), 25–35.

Ziff, Ruth. "Psychographics for Market Segmentation." *Journal of Advertising Research*, 11 (April 1971), 3–10.

Part Two

Consumer Development and Market Behavior

Chapter 3

The Early Years

One of the most impressive aspects of this century is the *exceptional* concern with children. This is not to say that our children are loved more intensely or that their loss is mourned more deeply than in previous times, but that there is a special awareness of them as *children.*

In spite of the teachings of Jesus Christ and the subsequent growth and influence of Christianity, only occasionally in prenineteenth-century literature is a child depicted in present-day terms; rather, children are represented as smaller and weaker versions of the adults surrounding them. A reading of Chaucer or Shakespeare, for example, fails to reveal a special world of the child. Rather, the execution of the Princess in Shakespeare's *Richard the Third,* and even the labor of children in the mines and factories in the nineteenth century, were consequences of children sharing with adults the assets and dangers of their common social position of nobility or proletariat.

Yet, while there was no universal dispensation for age independent of social status in the 1800s, a change of consciousness was beginning to appear in the genius of the era. Wordsworth in poetry and Dickens in the novel both proclaimed a new and prepossessing concern for the life of the child where childhood is viewed as a unique stage during which perceptions and learning are related to age as well as to station (Gagnon, 1965).

Wordsworth stated, "The child is father to the man," thereby recognizing that many adult patterns are formed early in a person's life. This is true to a large extent—many foundations for later life are formed in childhood—and represents one reason why it is important to study children as consumers. But, more importantly, children *are* different from adults—they have their own needs and their own tastes, and their tastes change rapidly.

Another reason for studying children as consumers is their number. The sheer size of the childhood segment of the population equals demand for certain goods and services because children *are* consumers even when they are not buyers. Also, children either directly or indirectly influence the buying behavior of their parents even in areas where the child is not the consumer.

In this chapter we explore the world of child consumers, looking at their significance in terms of number and the market-related consequences of their physical and conceptual development. Before beginning this journey, a cautionary note is in order. The twentieth-century awareness of childhood as a unique stage in life correctly avoids the error of assuming that children are merely small adults. However, one of the problems of the current concern is the tendency for some authorities to view children as infinitely malleable beings subject to continual and lasting manipulation by skillful and deliberate applications of marketing efforts.

The best position is to view children somewhere between the extremes and as moving from an early tendency near the malleable end toward the adult end. From this position it is possible to divide childhood into subgroups which more closely correspond to the process of human development.

THE STAGES OF CHILDHOOD

We often hear a parent or other adult "explain" the "unacceptable" behavior of a child as, "He is just passing through a stage." There is some truth to such a remark, for psychologists have made numerous attempts in the study of the span of life to define developmental "levels" or stages in terms of behavior patterns and traits that distinguish each level from earlier and later stages. As one writer expressed it, "The basis for dividing the life span into developmental levels is demonstrated by the emergence of new qualities, as well as significant changes in trends and achievements within the basic pattern of behavior at each given stage" (Pikunas, 1969:10–11).

For the purpose of discussing children as consumers, this life period can be classified into two rough stages, early childhood and later childhood.

"Early childhood" is a period of life that extends from birth to about five years of age. The really crucial turning point is the beginning of school, which marks a major change in the mental and social development or children as they begin the stage of later childhood. Early childhood can be further divided into infancy and preschool stages. "Infancy" ranges from birth to the time when a child can walk well, roughly at age two or two and one-half.

Early childhood is a life period in which persons develop rapidly. Physically, the period is characterized by rapid growth, particularly during infancy, where babies move from almost complete helplessness to frequent movement including walking, running, and even climbing. This stage is also characterized by frequent illnesses and accidents. Psychologically, early childhood is a period in which children rapidly acquire their basic personality structures, forms of oral self-expression, and emotional and cognitive differentiation. Although the child develops rapidly during this stage, he remains largely restricted to the family environment.

"Later childhood" is a period that extends roughly from the beginning of school to the beginning of adolescence or from about age six to age twelve. This period can be further divided into the stages of "middle" and "late" childhood, or ages six to eight and nine to twelve. Physically this period is characterized by slow and steady growth, steadily increasing coordination, and good health among most children. Psychologically it is a period in which children become increasingly conscious of being evaluated—by their parents, by their peers, and by teachers at school.

Since both physical and psychological changes occur somewhat distinctly from each of these stages to the next, the stages represent important groupings of children in terms of their needs and behavior as consumers of products, listeners of media, and influences on the purchasing process of others, particularly their parents.

The following examples by age groups illustrates the interplay of the child's development and his needs. The examples were released to newspapers by the American Toy Institute in December 1974 as a "gift guide" to keep all the well-meaning Santa's helpers (grandparents) from scoring "zero" on the pleasing-gift scale.

1 Babies under 18 months. The baby needs brightly colored, lightweight toys of varied textures. They should be washable, too big for him to swallow, and free or rough edges or sharp corners.

Suggestions: Rattles, nursery mobiles, soft animals, squeak toys, crib-gym exercisers, strings of big beads, picture blocks, nested boxes of cups, push-pull toys, musical and chime toys, pounding toys, stacking toys.

2 Children 18 months to three years. These toddlers, into everything, need things to ride and climb on. They also need things that help them to imitate grown-up activity. The toddlers are great builders and sculptors. They need materials. Toy pianos and drums make great gifts, too.

Suggestions: First tricycle, little wagon, hobby horse, play furniture, balls, balloons, play appliances, and utensils, stuffed animals, dolls and doll furniture; take-apart and put-together toys with large parts. Clay, modeling dough, large crayons, blackboard and chalk, blocks.

3 Children three to six years. These like to act out grown-up roles like those of cowboys, firemen, policemen, doctors, and nurses. They also get into a young-homemaker thing and like to play house. Wheel toys go over big. For

Table 3-1 The Early Years Population

	Population (millions of persons)				
Age	1960	1970	1975	1980	1985
0–4	20.4	17.2	19.7	22.7	24.4
5–9	18.8	19.9	17.3	19.8	22.9
10–14	16.9	20.8	20.0	17.5	20.0
U.S. total	180.7	204.8	216.6	230.9	246.3

Note: Series D (moderate low series) projections for years 1975–1985. Figures include Armed Forces overseas and are as of July 1.
Source: Department of Commerce.

rainy-day activity, coloring books, paint sets, wooden puzzles. Records and easy reading books (picture stories) suit fine.

Suggestions: Dress-up outfits, puppets, storekeeping toys, cash register, toy phone and toy clock, housekeeping toys, small trucks, cars, planes, boats; items for bathing and feeding dolls; larger tricycle and other wheel toys; easy construction sets, sled; backyard gym; trains and auto racing layouts.

4 Children six to nine years. Dolls, auto-race layouts, equipment for sports and active games such as baseball, football, basketball, jump rope. Interest in group activity builds in this age period but the six to nine crowd also likes to play to-each-his-own way.

Suggestions: Board games, tabletop sports, fashion dolls, doll houses, toy typewriter or computer, printing set, marbles, tops, kites, science sets under adult supervision, handicrafts, sports equipment, swim fins and masks, larger bikes, skates, pogo stick, scooter, books.

5 Children nine to 12. In this age group serious attention is pinned on hobbies, crafts, and the building of collections—stamps, coins, rocks. There's also great interest in chemistry sets, microscopes, telescopes, computers. The desire to active physical play blooms. Team play includes hockey, basketball and you name it. Dramatic play also holds great appeal for boys and girls in this age group.

Suggestions: Model kits, makeup and good grooming kits; chemistry and other science sets; table tennis, billiard table, magic sets, advanced construction sets, marionettes, jigsaw puzzles; team-play sports equipment, card games.

SIZE AND TRENDS

Before exploring other market-related behaviors of the early years, it is useful to have some idea of the significance of these consumers to marketers. One useful measure is their number, in both absolute and relative terms.

As shown in Table 3-1, children under 15 comprise about 26 percent of the United States population, down from the figure of 30 percent in 1960 but about the same percentage that is projected to 1985. Among children under 15, those under 5 comprise about 9 percent of the population. Children in the 5–9 age group represent about 8 percent and those in the 10–14 group account for about 9 percent of the total population. While 10–14 group is expected to stay about

Percent of U.S. population				
1960	1970	1975	1980	1985
11.3%	8.4%	9.1%	9.8%	9.9%
10.4	9.7	8.0	8.6	9.3
9.4	10.2	9.2	7.6	8.1
100	100	100	100	100

the same in 1985, the other age groups are expected to grow in absolute size during this decade.

Overall, with these segments ranging in size from 17 to 20 millions of persons now and growing to range from 20 to 24 millions of children in 1985, children represent in total a substantial segment of the market in terms of their particular needs.

Since firms appealing specifically to young consumers rise and fall primarily on the basis of the rise and fall of these age groups, having an accurate projection of the future number of persons in childhood is crucial. Yet, of all age groups, children are the most difficult to predict, particularly those in early childhood. This difficulty arises because changes depend upon the birthrate, infant mortality, and the size of the childbearing population.

In the early to middle 1970s, the declining birthrate was highly publicized and we began to think in terms of, and some even advocated, a zero population growth (ZPG). This publicity upset the marketing world, particularly those appealing to children. The reaction was vividly demonstrated in 1972 when commercials began to appear stressing the benefits of "baby" powders and "baby" shampoo to women in their twenties, thirties, and beyond.

The reaction was based largely on projecting the future size of the child market solely on the assumption of one component—the declining birthrate. It is true that the fertility rate (the number of births per thousand females, aged 15–44) has dropped during this portion of the 1970s. A declining or relatively low birthrate does mean fewer children per family. It does not mean, however, fewer children, at least not in the next ten years, as the projections in Table 3-1 show.

Marketers who overreacted to falling birthrates failed to consider the effects of infant mortality and the size of the childbearing population. While fertility was declining, infant mortality was also going down. More importantly, the size of the childbearing population (females, aged 15–44) has been increasing. Indeed, 75 percent of births occur when mothers are in the age group 20–34—the age group of the population that will show the greatest increase from now to 1985. The result is a lower birthrate but *more* babies.

In general, a larger population of child consumers means a larger demand. But there is yet another and qualitative dimension to the children's market that results from a continued low birthrate, which is likely to continue for these reasons:

1 Information and devices to help contraception are more readily available and are in greater use.

2 Abortion has been made legal in many states.

3 Surveys indicate that today's young wives plan to have fewer children than their forebears. A great many say they will postpone having the first child until later in life.

4 The growing number of college graduates indicates lower fertility rates because college-educated families usually have fewer children.

5 There are more working women. In 1940 only 15 percent of America's married women were holding down jobs outside the home. The percentage had jumped to 40 percent by 1969. Predictions are that it will go higher in this decade. Working marrieds tend to have fewer children.

The qualitative dimension to the demographics is a result of the gain in young families (aged 20–36). More young families mean more first babies, and expenditures for first babies are almost always higher than for subsequent babies. Thus we can expect not only more babies during the next ten years, but, of even larger importance, more child consumers, because more money per child will be spent on them by the younger, more affluent families now being formed. More will be said of these families in a future chapter when we discuss the "era of the young affluent."

EARLY CHILDHOOD

It has been stated that in a year children in the United States consume enough peanut butter to coat the Empire State Building with a layer three feet thick and enough bubble gum to blow a bubble the size of the Rock of Gibraltar.

Children are consumers, and they use large quantities of more than peanut butter and bubble gum. In addition, they are important consumers of baby foods and bottles; cribs, clothing (including diapers), and detergents; baby-sitters and strollers; toys, wheels, and pediatric services and bandages; and milk, milk flavorings, breakfast creals, candy, and dental services. Moreover, by their very presence they have an impact on family expenditures for housing, home furnishings, automobiles, and life insurance.

Needs Change Rapidly

During early childhood many of the young consumers' needs and changes in needs can be traced directly to their physical and conceptual development during this life stage. Physically, this is a period of rapid growth. For instance, the typical American infant weighs in at 7½ pounds and is 19½ inches long but will double this weight in four to five months and triple it in a year.

Basically, physiological development (development of bones and muscles and use of locomotion) follows the "law of developmental direction," i.e., from head to foot, from trunk to extremities (Hurlock, 1968). As a result, babies do not "learn to walk"; rather, they develop to this point in a fairly structured and orderly fashion. The following age-activity pattern reflects this process:

Age	Activities
2 months	Head up, on stomach
4–6	Sit with support, head up
4	Turn over
9–10	Sit without support
10–11	Crawl
1 year	Stand
12–18 months	Walk (stiff-legged at first)
3–5 years	Hop, skip, jump, climb

Accidents are common in childhood as locomotion develops, particularly at ages two to three and five and six. Young children, boys more than girls, are also highly susceptible to several common illnesses such as respiratory, stomach, digestive, and ear ailments.

These accidents and illnesses generate a demand for "cures," and a variety of products are marketed to meet needs in a manner satisfactory to both mother and child. Thus band-aids have an "ouchless" feature or a "battle ribbon" design; there are "painless" and "tasty" medications and "baby" aspirin with "baby-proof" tops; and there are numerous brands of cough remedies, chest rubs, and room vaporizers.

For minor accidents, mercurochrome is an ideal treatment from the child's point of view—it doesn't hurt, and the red stain shows him something was done for him. (Striped toothpaste and colored band-aids convey some of the same idea to children.) Colds are the most common illness. Mothers attempt to ward them off with "magic" vitamins and treat them with "tender loving care," children's aspirin, and chest rubs, the latter being a symbol of caring.

Physiological development also affects the eating habits of young children. For infants, semi-solid foods are started during one to four months, but milk is the principal component of the diet. Physicians often recommend breast feeding because of benefits to both infant (better digestion) and mother (lower chance of breast cancer). But there are alternatives favored by many parents. One is the home-prepared formula of milk, water, and sugar. This alternative has the disadvantage of requiring preparation, sterilization, and refrigeration. Another alternative is the use of ready-to-serve formulas such as Enfamil, introduced by Mead Johnson in 1962, or Modilas, introduced by Gerber in 1968. Acceptance of ready-to-serve formulas has been rapid because of the obvious benefit of convenience. This option, however, does have a major cost disadvantage, one often increasing the cost of feeding infants by a factor of 20.

Infants can shift their food consumption from the milk-diet to "solid" foods relatively quickly with the growth of teeth. The first teeth appear in about six to eight months, and the typical child has about six teeth by the end of the first year and sixteen by the end of the second year. The first "solid" foods consumed are baby foods—a comparatively recent innovation. Baby food was first introduced by Capp's in 1921 as a high-priced line of strained fruit and vegetables and distributed in drug stores. Gerber began grocery store distribution in 1927–28 and now dominates the market because of its great distribution and variety advantages over competitors.

Babies like fruits best, then vegetables, but not strong-tasting meat. Bland food is flavorful because babies have many more taste buds than adults. Babies convert to "people" food fairly rapidly, however. This conversion takes place when mothers perceive their children growing tired of baby food and when babies who eat with their parents indicate a desire to try their food. The conversion is accelerated in families where older children are present. Also, as children get larger, they consume more, and the high cost of baby food becomes more and more apparent to parents.

Some baby food companies have introduced "junior" foods in an attempt to maintain their baby food market. These attempts, however, have never been very successful because such foods are not compatible with the reasons noted for infants' conversion to people foods.

Preschoolers, of course, cannot make an abrupt and complete change to adult foods. Since young children do not have molars or powerful jaws, they cannot grind solid food effectively. This is the reason for the popularity among this age group of hotdogs and hamburgers. Moreover, preschoolers are very sensitive to things that are too hot or cold; and they do not like sticky foods, such as mashed potatoes. Rather, they like food that is sweet, easy to chew, lukewarm, lightly seasoned, and served in small helpings with variety—a good description of presweetened breakfast cereal. Parents generally do not like these presweetened, "artificial," "yucky," expensive, cavity-inducing foods, but they buy and serve them, partly because they are convenient and partly because children will eat them.

The Influence of Younger Children

But parents also purchase cereals and other foods for preschoolers because of the interplay of three other factors: nap activity, the child's speech development, and the results of marketing efforts.

The Impact of Naps A substantial part of family activity is regulated or at least influenced by the sleep cycle of the youngest child. This is particularly true of the homemaker's daily routine. Parents can get things done while children are napping, but they cannot leave the house. On the other hand, activities such as going out in general and going to the store specifically are regulated by when younger children are awake. As a consequence, preschoolers more often than children of other age groups go to the store with the parent.

For instance, when 526 mothers of preschool children were asked, "About how often does (name of child) go with you to the grocery store—most of the time, some of the time, or not very often?" they responded as follows (ARB Surveys, 1963):

1	Most of the time	68%
2	Some of the time	15%

3 Not very often 15%
4 Never 2%

When a similar question was asked in 1966 of 1,501 mothers of children aged 4–12, respondents reported taking their preschoolers food shopping with them more frequently than children in the age groups 7–9 and 10–12 (Table 3-2).

The Power of Asking The speech development of children is another important factor bearing on the selection of products for children. In general, comprehension far exceeds expression in speed of development. Comprehension permits the child to know what he wants and expressive ability permits him to communicate it. In the illustration in Chapter Two, for example, Tommy was able to express his desire for Fruit-Loops by pointing, grunting, and nodding, while his older sister Jane was able to point and say, "This kind."

Since preschoolers often go to the store with their parent, and since they have developed to the point of comprehension with some expressive ability, their requests are frequent and in certain areas very important as to products and brands selected, as the following study indicates.

In a study conducted for the "Romper Room" television program, 526 mothers of preschool children in 21 cities scattered throughout the country were asked, "What kind of food did (name of child) ask you to get?" "What kind of food did you get?" and "Where does (name of child) get the idea of asking for certain products?" Their answers are shown in Table 3-3.
From the data in the table, children are very successful in influencing their mothers to buy cereals, cookies, party snacks, fruits, milk flavorings, and ice cream. Note, however, that requests for candy and gum are least successful. In general, there is a "child's domain" where brand choice is considered kids' business, and this domain does not extend to adult products such as milk and

Table 3-2 Frequency with which Mothers Take Children Food Shopping

	Childrens' age group (number of mothers)		
Reported frequency	**4-6 (880)**	**7-9 (827)**	**10-12 (711)**
Normally take children	70.1%	63.0%	61.5%
Number of times out of every ten food shopping trips that children are taken along:			
10 times	27.6	20.6	17.6
8-9 times	13.8	10.5	9.1
5-7 times	13.3	12.5	12.6
2-4 times	10.9	13.4	13.4
1 time	2.4	3.3	4.6
Don't know	2.1	2.7	4.2
Don't normally take	29.9	27.0	38.5

Source: Bruskin (1966).

Table 3-3 Child and Television Power

Product category	Asked for	Bought	Source of idea	
Cereals (in general, and specific brands)	61%	59%	Television	94%
Candy; gum; buble gum	35	19	Friends	11
Cookies, cakes, cupcakes, doughnuts	30	27	At home (parents, siblings, etc.)	10
Party snacks, popcorn, potato chips, pretzels, etc.	18	16	Newspapers, magazines	8
Fruits, canned and fresh	14	13	Box seen at home	7
Milk flavorings	7	7	Radio	3
Ice cream; popsicles	6	5	Other	5

Source: ARB Surveys (1963).

meat. A more comprehensive list of child-adult products and degree of influence is shown in Table 3-4.

The Residual Effects of Advertising The third factor influencing parental purchasing for children is the efforts of marketers, particularly advertising. When parents were asked where their children got their ideas of asking for certain products, the impact of TV showed up quite clearly: 94 percent of the parents in the survey said the idea for the product requested came from television (Table 3-3).

Before the advent of radio, products could not be advertised to preschool children. And food advertisers, for example, formerly addressed themselves to parents, counting on the parents to buy the food and develop the child's interest in that food. Advertisers now directly address children. Television makes such advertising easy, and television has a measurable effect even before children begin their formal schooling.

Starting at about age two—long before they can read—children begin to pay some attention to TV commercials, and by the time they are ready to enter first grade, children have already acquired a large fund of information about products they find interesting.

This information has at least two effects. The effect most direct and obvious is that it encourages children to ask their parents to buy special products, especially food and toy items. Children quickly learn that these requests, like other requests, are not all granted, and that even when requests are granted, the product does not always live up to the advertising. By age six or seven almost all children have become selective about when they ask for what, and most can describe when something they managed to get did not live up to expectations.

The more subtle effect of exposure to television advertising is that it associates the brand name with a variety of appealing characters and pleasant experiences. While remaining skeptical of any specific claims made for what is seen advertised, the child can still prefer certain brands because of their favorable associations. If all brands are about equal as far as the parent is concerned, and if the child takes to one more readily than to another, that brand has an advantage even in the absence of strong direct child pressure.

The cartoon characters that advertisers have associated with products (especially read-to-eat breakfast cereal) are much more meaningful and much more memorable to preschool children than are the brand names, which after all are only words (at this stage of concept development, anything abstract is hard for children, even names). Instead of referring to "Kellogg's Sugar Frosted Flakes," young children speak of "Tony Tiger Cereal."

Quaker has taken advantage of this characteristic of preschoolers by naming cereals for the characters that advertise them—Cap'n Krunch, Quisp and Quake. In addition to being featured in the advertising, these characters figure prominently on the cereal boxes themsleves. The association between

Table 3-4 Influence of Children

	Percent of women stating, "Children influence my choice of brand"			
Product	Almost all the time	Fairly often	Some-times	Never
Bologna	8%	9%	20%	63%
Cake mixes	4	9	31	56
Candy	15	23	35	27
Canned puddings	7	9	19	65
Canned spaghetti	9	9	21	61
Cheese	8	16	28	48
Children's clothes	20	23	26	31
Children's shoes	23	21	22	34
Cold cereal	26	25	24	25
Cookies	17	26	31	26
Fast food restaurant	14	19	31	36
Hot cereal	10	16	26	48
Hot dogs	9	14	27	49
Ice cream	15	19	30	36
Jam or jelly	10	15	26	49
Lunch meat	9	15	26	50
Milk	12	9	15	64
Milk shake in a can	3	3	9	85
Packaged dry spaghetti, macaroni, noodles	4	5	13	78
Peanut butter	12	15	27	46
Potato chips	12	16	28	44
Powdered orange drink such as Tang	9	10	21	60
Pretzels	5	9	23	63
Snack cakes (Tasty Kake, etc.)	9	10	26	55
Soft drinks	12	19	32	37
Soup	11	22	29	38
Toys	25	25	25	25
White bread	9	9	19	63

Source: Needham, Harper & Steers, 1975.

product and character thus remains firm, and the preschooler can identify the product easily in the store.

Another example of personification is the use by Pillsbury of Funnyfaces—Jolly Olly Orange, Goofy Grape, and assorted friends—to portray flavors. This product's major competitor, Kool-Aid, uses the more abstract flavor names; and as a consequence, preschool children often ask for "the red kind" or "the green kind." At this stage of concept development, colors are more immediate than flavors.

In both these cases, the concreteness of a personified brand name and the favorable association with an appealing character give the brand an advantage that adds to whatever advantage it may gain from physical characteristics.

In summary, children view commercials uncritically at first and tend to confuse them with program episodes. Skepticism increases with age and with the corresponding counterpressure from adults and from their own experiences with advertised products, particularly toys. Yet children still react favorably toward commercials because they like the entertainment, want to try new things, "half" believe them, and like the information provided in commercials.

For these and other reasons, another residual effect of advertising upon children has emerged: strong criticism, as the following excerpts from Charren (1972:104-108) illustrate:

> Elimination of advertising on children's programs would affect only a small percentage of companies in the United States. Almost all advertising on children's TV falls into one of three categories: 1) toys, 2) edibles, 3) vitamins. TV advertisements for children's vitamins place the manufacturer's profit motive ahead of the real health needs of children. The ads suggest that children are competent to make judgments about their need for medicine. Most pediatricians feel that children who eat an adequate diet do not require vitamin supplements after one year of age. TV ads for vitamins ignore or obscure the very real health hazard to children who ingest too many candy-like pills. Ingestion of a single bottle of children's vitamins with iron added can seriously endanger a child's health. The amount of iron contained in one bottle of vitamin pills can put a four-year-old child into a coma. Yet, these vitamins are sold to children every day on television. . . . [Another] . . . category of advertising directed to children is food, which includes cereal, candy, and snack foods. Even a casual examination of ads for edibles is enough to establish that the aim of these ads is not to lead the child along the pathways to proper nutrition, but rather to cater to his fondness for sugar, to his need to be as big or as strong as his peers, or to his passion for premiums. Parents, who are concerned about what their children eat, try to limit sugar intake and encourage their children to eat fruit or raw vegetables between meals. If advertisers had their way, children's cereal would be sugared, their milk would be syrupped, and their snacks would be candy. . . .
>
> It should also be pointed out that many ads feature standards of performance and enjoyment which are quite unattainable by children. Children can make cookies, but they can not decorate them like a master chef; they can play with target games, but not hit the bull's eye every time; they can manipulate some mechanical toys, but often not as easily as the ads promise. While an adult automatically discounts some of the promise in a commercial, a child does not—and will often blame himself if he cannot measure up to the standards he saw

in the commercial. Advertising of toys on television should be confined to adult programs, with the sales message directed to adults.

Advertisements directed at children via TV are unfair because they put additional stress on the parent-child relationship. Dr. John Condry, Professor of Human Development and Psychology, Cornell University, points to the serious consequences of manipulating children to reach parents: "I believe advertisements directed toward children may seriously interfere with family life by creating conflicts between parents and children, by teaching children to be materialistic, and by disrupting attempts to teach the child responsibility." (Testimony to the Federal Trade Commission, November 10, 1971)

Parents resent advertisers who make it more difficult for them to raise responsible children. A study, *Mothers' Attitudes Toward Children's Television Programs and Commercials,* by Daniel Yankelovich, Inc., (March, 1970), found that "there is a great deal of hostility and resentment toward most commercials on children's programs. Mothers' complaints center around misrepresentation of the product, manipualtion of the child, stresses and strains imposed on low income mothers by the demands created by the commercials and a general unhealthy environment." (p.4) Among the specific findings were the following: The most serious criticisms are directed at those commercials which manipulate or 'use' the child to get the mother to buy a broad variety of products from soap powder to vitamins." (pp. 6, 7). Misrepresentation is another important complaint. Mothers feel that the children are fooled into wanting something due to actual misrepresentation. Examples were given of toys and games which seem large or exciting on television—but then turn out to be very inferior once they are actually bought. This type of misrepresentation leads to frustration, disappointment, tears, etc., *Often the anger is expressed against the mother, not the sponsor."* (pp. 7, 8, emphasis added). In all income strata, the constant duel of children asking for things and mothers having to say yes or no creates, mothers feel, an unheatlhy environment and relationship." (p. 8).

It is unfair to consider children as miniature consumers. At the first National Symposium on Children and Television, held in Boston in 1970, Fred Rogers, of "Misterogers' Neighborhood," said: "Commercialism bombards us all and all too frequently with messages which say you have to have something besides yourself to get along. You have to have a pill for a headache or a smoke to feel cool or a drink to cope, or, worst of all, a toy to play. Your resources are not enough, so be sure to buy ours. Our children are being raised on messages like this; and what is more, they think we adults condone them."

In the past few years, the amount of TV advertising directed to children has increased. Earlier, ads to children were for child-oriented products—such as toys and cereals. Today, vitamin pills, frozen dinners, bread, gasoline, shoes, and snack foods are all being advertised directly to children, with the clear implication that they should pressure their parents into buying the adult-oriented products. In the next decade we may see advertising directed to children used to promote an even wider and less-child-oriented range of products as a growing number of advertisers realize that you can sell anything to a child through television.

However, the possibility also exists that we may see advertising eliminated from children's television if enough people demonstrate their concern. Consumer groups have alerted the Federal regulatory agencies to the special needs of children, and parents and teachers are becoming more aware of the importance of television in the lives of children. Public pressure is needed to take children's television out of the marketplace, and the public has started to act.

In general, critics charge that commercials to children are deceptive, create materialistic desires, cause have-nots to feel inferior, create distrust and cynicism, and promise instant solutions. For these and perhaps other reasons, many critics would like to see advertising to children banned. Many parents agree: in 1975, 64 percent of adult Americans (men and women) agreed to the statement, "Advertising directed to children should be taken off television."[1]

Advertisers are not unaware of parents' feelings. Consider the toy industry, which has been revolutionized by television. Before TV, most toys were distributed through high-mark-up outlets like department stores and there was little consumer advertising. With TV, toys are distributed more by discount and other self-service outlets, frequently as loss leaders. But with TV came complaints about false advertising, high prices, and poor construction. In the early 1960s, such complaints brought "guidelines" from the National Association of Broadcasters:

1 Do not make misleading statements such as "only $29.95" to youngsters.
2 Do not imply child will be a social outcast if he doesn't have the toy.
3 Do not dramatize a toy in a way that could not be duplicated in the home.

Nevertheless, parents still complain about toys that are falsely advertised, that will not work as shown, that are not constructive, and that are dangerous. This may well be the reason for the partial effectiveness critics have had in influencing public policy (partial, since a total ban on children's commercials has not been mandated).

The Federal Communications Commission conducted a four-year study of advertising practices and issued guidelines in 1974 which called for more educational content in children's TV programming, along with a reduction in children's commercials by 20 percent during 1975.

LATER CHILDHOOD

Later childhood begins with entry into school. This is an important point in the life of children because school widens their world, accompanies and encourages vast cognitive development, and introduces children to peer competition.

Physically, it is a period of slower and more uniform growth with fewer accidents. Conceptually, however, it is a period of rapid development; both the children's active and passive vocabularies increase; sex roles which the children began to acquire in early childhood become ingrained by peer-reinforced school activities, books and TV, toys, clothes, and parental behavior; status and status symbols (particularly such visible and sizable symbols as household possessions) become important; social acceptability becomes important as in-groups and out-groups form (boys' gangs and girls' clubs); and influence on product consumption increases and shifts in a number of ways.

Children in later childhood remain important market segments because,

[1]Data from Needham, Harper & Steers, 1975.

like those in early childhood, they consume specific products, including food, toys, clothes, lessons, and medical and dental care. But, more importantly, they become relatively more influential in determining product consumption in the family than they were in earlier years. In this section, then, we will explore the influence of children and note how it has changed from the stage of early childhood.

Influence on Product Consumption

Children influence the consumption of products in several quite different ways, some obvious and some subtle. To assess the influence of children on purchases, it is necessary to understand and account for the various forms the influence takes (Wells, 1965).

Personal Purchases When children get to be about five or six years old, they begin to get small amounts of money to spend on their own. At first this money usually comes in the form of allowances or presents at special occasions; but as children approach the teens, more and more of it comes from odd jobs like lawn mowing, baby-sitting, paper delivering, and/or rewards for doing something well.

The source of money, the amount of money, and how it is spent are often highly interrelated. What a child does with his money depends in part on how much he has, and how much he has is often controlled by his parents. In addition, parents may affect what children buy as a result of what they buy for the children. But children's accounts of how they spend "their" money suggest that much of it goes for things their parents consider either unnecessary or even slightly evil. Much is spent on candy, gum, soft drinks, and other sweets; and a lot is spent on comic books and inexpensive toys. Almost none is spent on things that parents consider virtuous, like orange juice, cereal, milk, or shoes.

Why, then, do parents put their children "on the dole"?

According to the parents, the basic need kids have for money is for the purchase of hard-to-define, subjectively determined "extras." Parents accept the doctrine that they should (and must) provide shelter, food, and clothing for children, but the categorizing of other products into "necessities provided for by parents" and "extras provided for by children" is not always a clean-cut matter.

Although white-collar families may have more disposable income (on the average) than blue-collar families, willingness to spend money on children is more readily apparent among blue-collar mothers.

Specific "extras" differ from family to family, but generally an extra is a small product wanted solely for personal enjoyment rather than for need.

In addition to needing money for extras, parents feel that children need to handle money in order to learn its value. A difference seems to appear between the atitudes of blue- and white-collar parents toward this learning experience. Among white-collar families, parents seem to let the children learn about the value of money on their own rather than by being taught. If the child does not value money very highly, he is not always given more to replace what he spent, but rather is lectured on the need for "stretching the dollar." Parents exercise a minimum of control over what children buy.

Among the blue-collar families, there is more evidence that parents expect children to get the most for the money they spend. Blue-collar families tend to be more restrictive toward what their children can buy—especially younger children. In addition, the role of savings is stressed.

Both white- and blue-collar women, however, express the idea that if the children pay for the item themselves, they tend to take better care of it.

Direct Requests in the Store When children are taken along on trips to the store, they have an opportunity to influence both the purchase of products and the choice of brands. During later childhood, however, children have less influence in the grocery store because they are taken along less often than during early childhood. But a higher percentage of their requests are granted. A similar age pattern is found within later childhood: younger children ask for more things, but they don't get everything they ask for because parents act as dampening intermediaries; older children are more selective and more circumspect based on their past successes and failures, but they are still effective as they become more persuasive and are viewed more as "full members" of the family with equal rights—especially when the product is one they are going to consume themselves.

To illustrate the in-store influence, one study questioned 1,500 parents with children 4-12 from across the nation about allowing their children to select items when shopping. Over 55 percent of the parents reported that they normally allow their children to select items for purchase. Moreover, beyond the obvious preferences for cereals, cookies, and candies, children are allowed to select a wide range of products (Bruskin, 1966):

Ready-to-eat cereal
Packaged cookies
Candy
Soft drinks, Kool-Aid
Potato chips
Gum
Fruits
Fruit juices or drinks
Peanut butter
Ice cream
Soups
Chocolate drink additives
Bubble bath
Jams, jellies, and preserves
Toothpaste
Desserts
Pretzels
Dessert mixes
Spaghetti and macaroni products
Cakes
Fresh vegetables
Hot cereal
Milk, cheese, and butter
Soap, detergent
Toys
Meat
Lunch meat
Canned fruits
Tuna fish
Frozen dinners
Bread
Peanuts
Frozen vegetables
Canned vegetables
Corn chips
Seasoning and spreads

It should be noted that the selection and purchase of food products in the store are not only an influence on consumption but also a part of consumer training—children learn about buying largely through observing others and then making small purchases themselves (McNeal, 1964). Making purchases in turn reinforces the use in schools of consumer-related materials in teaching reading and arithmetic.

Direct Requests at Home "Mommy buy me . . . !" has become the rallying cry of the young consumers in the home as well as in the store. As Wells (1965) has reported, children in the 5–7 age group have little difficulty remembering and describing episodes in which they asked their parents for products they saw advertised on TV, especially toys and cereals. Older children, 10–12, tend to describe fewer requests—they are more skeptical of TV advertising than younger children and have found that things advertised on television do not always turn out to be as good as they appear. Children in late childhood have also learned to be more selective in their requests—after five or six years of being told "no," they no longer ask for everything they see on TV, just as they do not ask for everything they see in the store.

Parents report a similar pattern of requests and effectiveness of request by age. As the data in Table 3-5 show, Ward and Wackman (1972) found that children frequently attempt to influence purhcases of food products, and that these attempts decrease with age. Also, purchase influence attempts were found to generally decrease with age for the other product categories. Exceptions were clothing and record albums, where older children made more requests. The authors also found that across most of the products, the older the child, the more likely parents are to yield to the influence attempts of their children.

Some mothers and fathers, of course, yield more often than others to their childrens' requests. One study, for example, found that parents who were less concerned with their children were more frequent buyers of their children's favorite brand of cereal (Berey and Pollay, 1968). Other differences will be discussed in the chapter on interpersonal communications.

But, in general, the single, direct, overt "Mommy, Daddy, buy me . . ." response to TV advertising seems to reach a peak in the elementary school years. After that period, response begins to take another, harder-to-trace form—passive dictation.

Passive Dictation Although children in late childhood report fewer direct requests for products than younger children do, their influence on parents' purchases is still very much alive. In addition to getting a higher proportion of their requests granted, older children influence the purchase of products and the choice of brands in a way similar to the way a baby influences the choice of baby food. Even when children do not ask for certain brands and products in so many words, their parents observe what they consume willingly and what they resist, and govern their purchases accordingly. At times, this passive dictation

Table 3-5 Frequency of Children's Attempts to Influence Purchases and Percentage of Mothers "Usually" Yielding

	Frequency of requests[a]				Percentage of yielding			
Product	5-7 years	8-10 years	11-12 years	Total[b]	5-7 years	8-10 years	11-12 years	Total[b]
Relevant foods								
Breakfast cereal	1.26	1.59	1.59	1.59	88	91	83	87
Snack foods	1.71	2.00	1.71	1.80	52	62	77	63
Candy	1.60	2.09	2.17	1.93	40	28	57	42
Soft drinks	2.00	2.03	2.00	2.01	38	47	54	46
Jell-o	2.54	2.94	2.97	2.80	40	41	26	36
Overall mean	1.82	2.13	2.16	2.03				
Overall percentage					51.6	53.8	59.4	54.8
Less relevant foods								
Bread	3.12	2.91	3.43	3.16	14	28	17	19
Coffee	3.93	3.91	3.97	3.94	2	0	0	1
Pet food	3.29	3.59	3.24	3.36	7	3	11	7
Overall mean	3.45	3.47	3.49	3.49				
Overall percentage					7.6	10.3	9.3	9.0
Durables, for child's use								
Game, toy	1.24	1.63	2.17	1.65	57	59	46	54
Clothing	2.76	2.47	2.29	2.52	21	34	57	37
Bicycle	2.48	2.59	2.77	2.61	7	9	9	8
Hot wheels	2.43	2.41	3.20	2.67	29	19	17	22
Record album	3.36	2.63	2.23	2.78	12	16	46	24
Camera	3.91	3.75	3.71	3.80	2	3	0	2
Overall mean	2.70	2.58	2.73	2.67				
Overall percentage					25.6	28.0	35.0	29.4
Notions, toiletries								
Toothpaste	2.29	2.31	2.60	2.39	36	44	40	39
Bath soap	3.10	2.97	3.46	3.17	9	9	9	9
Shampoo	3.48	3.31	3.03	3.28	17	6	23	16
Aspirin	3.64	3.78	3.97	3.79	5	6	0	4
Overall mean	3.13	3.09	3.26	3.16				
Overall percentage					16.8	16.3	18.0	17.0
Other products								
Automobile	3.55	3.66	3.51	3.57	2	0	0	12
Gasoline brand	3.64	3.63	3.83	3.70	2	0	3	2
Laundry soap	3.69	3.75	3.71	3.72	2	0	3	2
Household cleaner	3.71	3.84	3.74	3.76	2	3	0	2
Overall mean	3.65	3.72	3.70	3.69				
Overall percentage					2.0	.75	1.50	1.75

[a]On a scale from 1 = Often to 4 = Never.
[b]5-7 years, n = 43; 8-10 years, n = 32; 11-12 years; n = 34; n = 109.
Source: Ward and Wackman (1972). Reprinted from the *Journal of Marketing Research*, published by the American Marketing Association.

governs product choice and brand choice for the whole family—if other family members, including Mom and Dad, have no objections, the child is likely to carry the day.

Some Implications The ways children influence product purchasing and consumption have several implications for marketers. They suggest, first of all, that it is easy to underestimate the influence of children if all types of influence are not taken into account. Yet many studies have been and still are conducted which ask about only one or two types of influence.

Another implication is that the difference between the child's and the parents' evaluation of a product can be an important dimension in planning advertising strategy. What the advertiser should say, and how, when, and where he should say it, will obviously depend a great deal on the type or types of influence present—in other words, whether he is addressing children only (for personal-purchase products or products parents do not value highly) or both children and parents. The following discussion of toys illustrates some problems and prospects for advertising that can be gained from understanding the web of influence on toy buying.

Toys[2]

Women tend to put toys into two categories: creative and noncreative. The creative category includes "educational" toys, as well as such things as blocks, watercolors, and clay. Any toy that helps a child develop mentally and/or physically beyond his present level of achievement would be considered a creative toy. Toys that are only for a child's amusement and are not considered necessary for his development would fall into the category of noncreative. In general, mothers perceive that there is a basic division between toys that look pretty but do nothing, and toys which encourage the child to create or to make things.

The mother of the family appears to do most of the toy buying, and she tries to buy those toys she feels will benefit her children most, i.e., creative toys.

There appear to be several reasons why most mothers prefer creative toys. As previously mentioned, they feel these toys contribute to their children's development. Some women also state that their children seem to be more interested in the creative toys and use them long after their other toys have been put away and forgotten. This popularity of creative toys suggests a need for more inexpensive toys in this category.

Children have the greatest influence on which toys their parents purchase just prior to holidays, birthdays, and other special occasions. On these occasions children usually receive as presents the toys that they have requested or that their parents know they want. These toys are often the noncreative kind; parents feel justified in purchasing them because it is for a special occasion.

Television advertising of toys seems to exert a strong influence on children. Parents believe that many television commercials take advantage of the fact that a toy can be a status symbol among children and that many toys

[2]The material in this section is a summary of results of proprietary studies.

may appear even more fun and interesting than they actually are. Parents have negative reactions to some toy commercials, knowing that their children are not discriminating enough to know whether what they are asking for is worthwhile.

Parents turn down many of their children's requests for toys. They probably know that in many cases the child does not really know what he is asking for; he just wants it at the moment. Once the novelty of a new toy wears off, he may never play with it again. Some parents, however, admit they occasionally "break down" and buy their children some toy for no special reason. For instance, in a 1975 survey of 1,797 homemakers, 75 percent said children influence their choice of toy brands at least sometimes; only 25 percent said "never" in response to the influence question.[3] Usually these toys are inexpensive. (Many parents may be reluctant to make such an admission, however, for fear that they would be judged "too permissive.")

There may be several reasons for these purhcases. If the child has been pestering his parent to buy him a toy, it may be easier to buy the toy and shut him up than to have to say "No" again. Then there is the problem every parent faces of maintaining a happy medium between being too strict with the child on the one hand and being too permissive on the other. So perhaps the occasional purchase of an inexpensive toy solves this dilemma. The parent keeps the child happy but does not feel guilty about spoiling him. Nor does the parent worry about being a spendthrift.

In summary it may be said that mothers appear to be the primary buyers of toys. They seem to prefer creative toys to the noncreative ones because they feel those toys will contribute to their children's development.

Noncreative toys are purchased less frequently, and then usually for special occasions, birthdays, Christmas, etc., It is on these occasions that children have the greatest influence on the purchase decision.

Many of the requests that children make for toys are turned down by parents. Once in a while parents give in to such requests, most often with the purchase of an inexpensive toy.

How does all this affect the toy advertiser? Advertisers of toys are able to create a demand in children for the intricate, expensive toys that leave very little to a child's imagination. Parents resent this kind of advertising because they do not approve wholeheartedly of this type of toy. Thus, the child is angry because he cannot have the toy and the parent is angry that the child is deluged with advertising for this kind of toy. One solution would be to produce and advertise toys that meet the parents' conception of a "creative" toy and yet to promote them to kids with the same degree of enthusiasm as is shown for the "noncreative" toys. Educational and creative toys do not have to be dull in concept or promotion.

Children and Television

This is an age of television. Children of all ages report watching TV and watching it frequently. During later childhood, for example, about 75 percent of

[3]Data from Needham, Harper & Steers, Ic., 1975.

the children report viewing television every day, as the following data from a typical survey show (*Bruskin Metromedia,* 1965):

	Age			
Viewing frequency	**4-5**	**6-8**	**9-12**	**Total**
Every day	84%	71%	73%	75%
Almost every day	15	27	26	24
Once a week	1	2	1	1

Change in Viewing Habits Although most children view television frequently, there is a change in viewing habits from one developmental level to another. In a comparison of early versus later childhood, the amount of time spent viewing television decreases slightly. Nielsen data for the 1970–71 season, for instance, indicate that children in the age group 2–5 averages 22.6 hours of viewing TV each week, while those in later childhood (6–11) averages 21.7 hours per week in front of an activated set.

Viewing time decreases primarily because children in later childhood engage in more peer group activities such as active play with other children. Lower-socioeconomic-level children, however, spend more time with TV than upper-socioeconomic-status children, who partly switch to reading in addition to active play.

More important, though, is the shift in viewing times as children move from early into later childhood. As the following Nielsen data for the 1967–68 season indicate, when children enter school, there is a substantial shift from daytime to prime time viewing:

	Age	
Time period	**2-5**	**6-11**
Monday–Sunday 7:30 P.M.–11:00 P.M.	25%	39%
Monday–Friday 7:00 A.M.–5:00 P.M.	34	14
Saturday–Sunday 7:00 A.M.–5:00 P.M.	16	18
All other	25	29

In early childhood the primary viewing time is weekday daytime; during later childhood, it is prime time. Note, however, that even during early childhood, one-fourth of viewing is during prime time.

The shift in viewing time, along with the sizable proportion of children viewing during prime time, has several implications. The most obvious is that indication for advertisers of when to broadcast commercials for products that children buy or influence others in purchasing. Also, since adults spend more time watching television during the evening hours than during any other day part, children often are viewing in the company of one or more of their parents. This fact becomes important from the standpoint of consumer learning, as children's reactions to commercials and programs are moderated by the views of their parents. This benefit, of course, could be weakened as more and more families become multiset owners and children view "children's" programs and parents view "adult" programs.

The joint adult-child viewing during prime time traditionally had an implication for network programming. Basically, programs telecast between 7:30 and 9:00 in the evening frequently were "all-family" programs. Because of the FCC's prime time access rule, however, the number of network all-family programs (excluding Westerns and adult-oriented situation comedies) dropped from 30 in 1967 to 14 by 1972. Thus, an unforeseen consequence of public policy was to reduce the amount of programming that was attractive to children and had the added benefit of causing them to view in the company of their parents (Banks, 1973).

Shifts in Program Preferences At about age ten, children's television program preferences begin to undergo a substantial change. Younger children (boys and girls) are most attracted by slapstick comedies, stories featuring young children and animals, and cartoons. By the middle of the teens, boys' preferences shift away from these simpler offerings to sports, action and adventure, and more sophisticated comedy; and girls' preferences shift toward situation comedies, drama and romance, such as stories of young doctors and evening soap operas. Below are some examples of the favorite programs of boys aged 6 through 11 and boys aged 12–17.

Programs Most Often Rated "One of My Favorites" by Boys

Boys 6–11	Boys 12–17
"Flintstones"	"The FBI"
"Alvin"	"Bonanza"
"Lassie"	"The Virginian"
"Bugs Bunny"	"NFL Football"
"Wonderful World of Disney"	"NCAA Football"
"Top Cat"	"Baseball Game of the Week"
"Red Skelton"	"Mod Squad"
"Three Stooges"	"Felony Squad"

At about this same time, many children also begin to shift away from nearly exclusive interest in television to at least some interest in books, newspapers, and magazines. After the early teens, print media in general become active competitors with television as sources of information and entertainment, as well as carriers of messages about products and brands (Schramm, Lyle, and Parker, 1961).

In view of the shift in program preferences, it would be reasonable to expect a similar change in reactions to TV commercials; for example, we would expect older children to scorn cartoon commercials as they do cartoon shows. Such a change does not seem to occur, however. Children who spurn cartoon programs as too juvenile to be worthy of their attention still react positively to cartoon commercials. For advertisers, the absence of a major age change means less guidance, because it reduces the value of program preferences as patterns for commercials; but it also means more freedom, for, in eliminating program preferences as patterns, it eliminates restrictions which if present could not safely be ignored (Wells, 1965).

In general, commercials remain effective even though children become more skeptical as they grow older and cognitively develop: children report it and mothers report it.

Children and Print Media

Because of our national preoccupation with children and television, we sometimes forget that children are exposed to another medium—print.

Few preschoolers, of course, can read; but they like to look at pictures and to have stories read to them. Their favorite stories are the classic fairy tales, things that "could happen" rather than fact, and, in comics, things that are funny more than things that are actionable.

During later childhood, interests shift from fairy tales to adventure, and sex differences become more pronounced somewhat along the same lines as those discussed for television program preferences.

One illuminating study by Gaier and Collier (1960) compared story preferences of American and Finnish grade school children. The children were asked by their teachers to complete a questionnaire which included questions about their favorite story and certain features of the story.

The children, regardless of sex or culture, clearly preferred fiction over fairy tales, information, biographical, animal, or religious stories. They also expressed a preference for story content about travel and about exciting, dangerous pursuit and escape.

Beyond these general similarities in story taste, however, the authors found some important sex differences but not cultural differences. The girls, unlike the boys, chose fairy tales next in order after fiction. And in both story categories, the girls chose several highly characteristic features rarely observed in the favorite stories of the boys:

1 The leading characters tended to be of the same age as the children or only slightly older.

2 These characters were often multiple, orphaned, of interchangeable appearance, and male.

3 The most obvious story themes were of mystery; of positive and cooperative social relationships with siblings, schoolmates, or friends of either sex; and of small, helpless children or animals who triumphed over stronger, older, usually male characters.

The boys, unlike the girls, chose information stories next in order of frequency after fiction. In their selections there were characteristic features which seldom occurred in the girls' favorite stories:

1 The leading characters were older than the children and usually were adult.

2 These characters tended to be solitary rather than multiple and were almost always male.

3 The themes of favorite stories tended to be of high physical adequacy or of intellectual adequacy reinforced by information (often gained through travel) about other places, people, and times.

To summarize some of these differences, the lists below are some examples of the favorite story features of boy's and girls:

Girls	Boys
Home, family, and school	Hunting, fighting, murder, war, and cruelty
Friendship, helpfulness, and kindness	Information and travel
Mystery	Overcoming odds through intelligence, alertness, and ingenious behavior
Sadness, death, poverty, and orphanhood	Strength, bravery, and spiritedness
Love, happiness, marriage, and clothes	

Newspaper reading also begins in later childhood. Children start with comics, then go on to headlines and some stories of immediate interest such as sports for boys and the columns for girls (Schramm, et al., 1961).

Children in later childhood are also avid readers of comic books. And while not as effective as television in reaching children, advertising in comics can be a useful supplement. Gold Key Comics, for example, distributes about 18 different titles each month and estimates an average monthly circulation of 5 million children and a monthly readership of 30 million (including many parents of the children).

The appeal of the comics is chiefly emotional and is achieved by their being "skewed toward reality," with real people in unreal situations, or vice versa. Moreover, most are adventure stories in which the characters are engaged in dangerous adventures or noble deeds. Like television, there is a great deal of criticism of children's reading of the comics, but no one has demonstrated conclusively that they are detrimental (Hurlock, 1968).

SUMMARY

In this chapter, the importance and the development of children as consumers from early to late childhood is documented. Although children are not often buyers, they are consumers and they exert considerable influence on family purchase and consumption patterns.

Childhood is a series of life periods, each characterized by its own set of needs and preferences which change as children proceed from infancy through late childhood. Many of these changes have important marketing implications in terms of package design; placement, timing, and character of advertisements; as well as product offerings. As children become older, they tend to ask for things less, to be more skeptical and discriminating concerning advertisements, and consequently to gain more influence with parents. Parents grant requests more often as children grow and also give older children allowances and the opportunity to buy items themselves.

As childhood progresses, then, children gain consumer experience. They are exposed to grocery stores and TV advertisements at early ages, are often allowed to influence purchase decisions as soon as they are capable of expressing their wishes, and are allowed to make small purchases on their own as they proceed through middle and late childhood. By the time they have reached twelve years of age, most children have developed some skepticism toward advertisements and some skill in making purchases and spending money—experience which will be needed and used in later years.

In addition to the developmental stages of childhood, we also discuss such factors as the declining birthrate and the highly critical attitudes of many parents toward TV advertisements directed toward children. It is crucial for marketers to be aware of such factors and to understand their inherent threats and opportunities.

In the next chapter the life journey of consumers is continued as we explore the world of adolescents.

REVIEW QUESTIONS

1 Why are children important to the study of consumer behavior?
2 Identify the different childhood life periods and the characteristics and needs of each period. Try to relate these changing characteristics to their marketing implications.
3 Some marketers have viewed the declining birthrate as a serious threat. Why is it not always a serious threat?
4 Are young children often successful in influencing their parents to buy specific products and brands? Is this influence equally strong for all types of products? Why or why not?
5 Although advertising to children on TV seems to offer significant advantages to marketers, many parents feel that such advertising should be eliminated or curtailed. Discuss both viewpoints.
6 Studies have shown that older children tend to ask for things less, but have their requests granted more frequently by parents, than younger children. What are the marketing implications of this development?
7 Describe the differences between blue- and white-collar families in their attitudes toward the spending of money on and by the children.
8 Discuss the changing patterns of children's TV viewing habits and preferences in relation to age and sex. What are some marketing implications inherent in these changes?
9 Differences in sex-related preferences increase as children grow older. How does this phenomenon affect the reading habits of children?

EXERCISE

Children frequently influence their parents' brand choices of products. By reordering the products in Table 3-4 by magnitude of influence, describe which products are in the adult domain. Discuss the reasons why you think children are effective (or not effective) in influencing brand choice for these products.

REFERENCES

ARB Surveys. "The Pre-School Child's Role in Buying Decisions." Study conducted for Romper Room, Inc., 1963.

Banks, Seymour. Statement to the Federal Communications Commission. Washington, D. C., Jan. 8, 1973.

Berey, Lewis A. and Richard W. Pollay. "The Influencing Role of the Child in Family Decision Making." *Journal of Marketing Research,* 5 (February 1968), 70–72.

Bruskin, R. H., Associates. *Bruskin Metromedia,* 1965.

———. "Child Power." New York: ABC Television Research Department, 1966.

Charren, Peggy. "The Child Market." BAEYC *Reports,* 8 (April 1972), 103–109.

Gagnon, John H. "Sexuality and Sexual Learning in the Child." *Psychiatry,* 28 (1965), 212–228.

Gaier, Eugene L. and Mary Jeffery Collier. "The Latency-Stage Story Preferences of American and Finnish Children." *Child Development,* 31 (1960), 431–451.

Goldberg, Marvin E. and Gerald J. Goin. "Children's Reactions to Television Advertising: An Experimental Approach," *Journal of Consumer Research,* 1 (September 1974), 69–75.

Hurlock, Elizabeth B. *Developmental Psychology.* 3d ed. New York: McGraw-Hill, 1968.

McNeal, James U. *Children as Consumers.* Austin, Tex.: University of Texas Bureau of Business Research, 1964.

Pikunas, Justin. *Human Development: A Science of Growth.* New York: McGraw-Hill, 1969.

Rubin, Ronald S. "The Effects of Cognitive Development on Children's Responses to Television Advertising." *Journal of Business Research,* 2 (October 1974), 409–420.

Schramm, Wilbur, Jack Lyle, and Edwin B. Parker. *Television in the Lives of Our Children.* Stanford, Calif.: Stanford University Press, 1961.

Ward, Scott. "Consumer Socialization." *Journal of Consumer Research,* 1 (September 1974), 1–14.

——— and Daniel B. Wackman. "Children's Purchase Influence Attempts and Parental Yielding." *Journal of Marketing Research,* 9 (August 1972), 316–319.

Wells, William D. "Communicating with Children." *Journal of Advertising Research,* 5 (June 1965), 2–14.

Chapter 4

Young Consumers

The Mule started out as a Madison Avenue special—a dance craze created, packaged, and promoted like a new product. A leading vodka distillery, bent on putting some kick into its sales, hired New York dance master Killer Joe Piro ("King of the Discotheque") to fashion the Mule's steps and Skitch Henderson to compose music for it. The dance, teamed up with a new vodka drink also called "the Mule," was launched in the spring of 1966 by a $2 million publicity campaign employing television, magazines, newspapers, and billboards. And, just in case anyone had missed the word, the dance turned up on the Ed Sullivan and Johnny Carson shows.

The Mule, of course, never got off its hind legs. It died of neglect; the teenagers would not buy it—and without their endorsement, no adult would, either.

ADOLESCENCE

This period episode represents the flop of an "outside" fad—outside because those who fashioned and promoted it did not understand the world of America's young consumers. In this chapter we will seek such an understanding as we turn our attention from children to teenagers, from childhood to adolescence—a time when young people are expected to prepare for adulthood by replacing childish behavior patterns with those of an adult type.

Traditionally, adolescence has been regarded as a period in life which begins when a person becomes sexually mature and ends when young person reaches legal maturity. For this reason the "youth" market is sometimes referred to as though youth formed a single, homogeneous group of consumers. More recently, it has become common to divide adolescence into two periods—early and late adolescence—which conform more closely to changes occurring between puberty and legal maturity.

Early adolescence covers the life period from puberty to about age fifteen, and late adolescence ranges from age sixteen through age eighteen, nineteen, or twenty. These age boundaries are somewhat arbitrary and are used mainly for the sake of convenience, since development during the period is continuous, especially during late adolescence—the longer age span of the division. Yet there are some significant changes which occur during adolescence that warrant using these age boundaries. Puberty, for example, is used as the beginning point because it represents major changes in status and activities for both boys and girls, changes that shape many of their needs and behaviors as consumers.

Age sixteen is an important cutting point. At that age, in many states, young consumers are first able to get the "working papers" that permit them to earn substantial sums through part-time employment. Even more ominous, sixteen is the minimum age in most states for obtaining a driver's license. Thus at a single age two factors combine which can produce both added and discretionary spending power and the mobility to exercise that power in new ways.

In addition to early and late adolescence, we will often find it useful to explore the consumer behaviors within these groups on the basis of sex, since in many cases the resources, interests, and activities of girls differ from the resources, interests, and activities of boys.

THE IMPORTANCE OF YOUNG CONSUMERS

There are several factors that, when taken together, substantiate the significance of the nation's adolescents as consumers. These include their number, their purchasing power, their influence on family spending patterns, and their formation of attitudes and interests that affect their purchase patterns in later life.

Size and Trends

One useful measure of the importance of any segment of the market is the number of persons comprising it. Currently, adolescents number some 21 million persons, roughly equivalent to the current number of preschoolers but substantially less than the number in later childhood. Historically, however, this age group has been as volatile as other age groups of the population. In 1950, for example, the number of teenagers declined by 1 million persons from the number in 1945 as a result of the low birth level of the depression-ridden

1930s. Conversely, as a result of the baby boom of the early postwar years, the mid-1950s and the 1960s and early 1970s became the years of an adolescent boom—see Figure 4-1. The "teen tide" has, however, crested, and we can expect the size of the teenage population to level off and decline by about 3 million persons by 1985. These projections can be noted graphically in Figure 4-1 by comparing the beginning of the decline of the 6–12 age group (1970) with the lagged decline in the 13–17 age group beginning in 1975.

Two conclusions emerge from the trend of change in the size of the adolescent market. First, since the total population of the United States will be increasing during this decade, the young consumer market will become relatively less important in terms of number. Thus, the industries which have catered to adolescents will be confronted with different market parameters in the coming decade than they were during the prosperous past fifteen years. Second, companies appealing to the teens will need a deeper understanding of adolescents as consumers if they are to compete successfully in a smaller market.

Spending Power

Another dimension of the young consumer market is spending power. For the first time in their lives, adolescents have significant amounts of money to spend, and much of it is discretionary, particularly as they move from early to late adolescence.

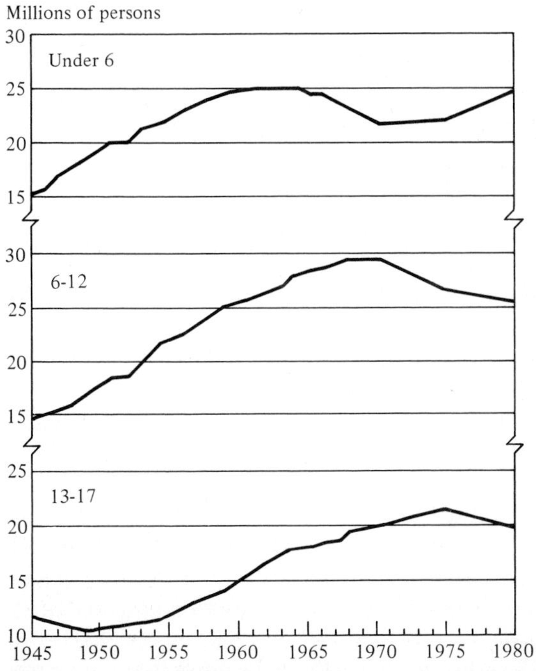

Figure 4-1 Children by age groups. *Sources:* U. S. Department of Commerce; The Conference Board Record (1970).

For instance, a study by the Youth Research Institute for the Los Angeles Chamber of Commerce (1967) showed the following differences in average weekly income between younger and older teenage boys in 1966:

	Ages 13–15	Ages 16–19
Allowance	$2.45	$ 7.10
Earnings	2.60	9.95
	$5.05	$17.05

In these data, the cutting age of sixteen becomes apparent as boys in late adolescence not only have a weekly income over three times that of their younger counterparts but also earn an increasingly larger proportion of their income. Moreover, weekly expenditures by young teenage boys differ both absolutely and relatively from expenditures by boys over sixteen, as the following figures, also collected by the Youth Research Institute (1967), show:

Boys 13–15			Boys 16–19		
Candy, ice cream, soda	$1.35	30.3%	Movies, dating, entertainment	$ 4.35	28.8%
Movies and entertainment	1.15	25.8	Gasoline and auto	3.00	19.9
Hobbies	0.60	13.5	Clothing	2.80	18.5
Clothing	0.55	12.4	Candy, ice cream, soda	1.50	9.9
Comic books, magazines	0.40	9.0	Hobbies	0.95	6.3
Records	0.40	9.0	Records	0.80	5.3
			Magazines, paperbacks	0.65	4.3
			Personal grooming	0.60	4.0
Total	$4.45	100%		$15.10	100%

These expenditure differences are a result of a combination of the resources and the stage in life. Not only is the young teenage boy relatively immobile because he cannot drive a car, and relatively poor because he is generally limited to sporadic, low-paying jobs, he is also as yet painfully unsure of his ability to maintain his cool in the face of the opposite sex. These factors work together to ensure that he will spend much of his time and much of his limited money alone, with members of his own family, or with other teenage boys. As a consequence, many of his activities and interests are hangovers from late childhood, including collections, models of various kinds, school activities, and competitive sports.

The older teenage boy usually has money, and usually he has wheels. He uses his money to buy clothes, grooming aids, records, and food for himself, to support his car if he has one of his own, and to pay for dates. He maintains much of his interest in competitive sports, especially if he is skilled enough to gain status in this way, but baseball, football, and basketball now begin to suffer severe competition from girls.

Adolescent girls also have considerable spending power. In general, girls tend to have slightly higher incomes than boys and to earn a slightly large proportion of it, regardless of age group. The Youth Research Institute study (1967) revealed the following average weekly income differences between early and late adolescent girls in 1966:

	Age 13–15	Age 16–19
Allowance	$2.25	$ 7.55
Earnings	2.90	10.35
Total	$5.15	$17.90

The following figures, from the same study, show how expenditures by young teenage girls differ from those by girls over sixteen (Youth Research Institute, 1967):

Girls 13–15			Girls 16–19		
Candy, ice cream, soda	$0.85	18.9%	Clothing	$ 3.50	23.4%
Clothing	0.85	18.9	Cosmetics and fragrances	2.20	14.7
Cosmetics and fragrances	0.70	15.6	Movies and entertainment	1.95	13.0
Records	0.65	14.4	Beauty parlor and hair	1.80	12.0
Movies and entertainment	0.60	13.3	products		
Magazines	0.45	10.0	Gasoline and automobile	1.55	10.4
Jewelry, trinkets and	0.40	8.9	Jewelry, trinkets and	1.20	8.0
notions			notions	0.95	6.4
			Records	0.95	6.4
			Magazines and paperbacks	0.70	4.7
			Candy, ice cream, soda	0.70	4.7
			Cigarettes	0.40	2.7
Total	$4.50	100%		$14.95	100%

Note that girls, when compared with boys, have more similar expenditure patterns, particularly for clothing and other personal-appearance items. The early emergence of interests in appearance among girls is due largely to the sex-appropriate peer values placed on being "glamorous and fascinating," the earlier interest girls show in boys, and the changing recreational patterns of girls, where a larger percentage of girls than of boys enjoy sports as spectators.

Adolescent interests will be discussed in more detail later in the chapter. For the moment, it is sufficient to conclude that adolescents have spending power and that they exercise it in rather predictable ways because of their stage in life.

Influence on Others

While many marketers view young consumers primarily as teens with "money to burn," it is also important to recognize that adolescents are still influential in family spending patterns, at least when the family has money to spend.

The role of teens as influences represents a historical shift in the basic role of children in the family from "producers" to "consumers." Historically, in our agrarian era, children were "producer durables" for the family—the income they produced clearly outweighed the cost of raising them. Now they are "consumer durables"—costs clearly outweigh the income they provide to the family.[1] Thus, by their presence, adolescents influence family expenditures. As Cateora (1963:16) observed:

> The teenager requires major portions of the typical family's income for food, clothing, medical care (especially dental) and, depending upon the extent of indulgence by the family, second telephones, television sets, automobiles and a host of other purchases. Basically the family with one, two or more teen-agers to feed, clothe, educate, and entertain must switch spending away from what the adult members may want to the needs and demands of the younger members of the family.

In addition to influencing expenditures for "basics" of life, adolescents to a larger extent than children are recipients of relatively expensive presents, such as radios, TV sets, shavers, hair care products, watches, and pocket calculators.

Moreover, they are granted their requests for a number of products. Teenage influence is strongest on products that are used exclusively by the teens and not apt to be a gift: shoes, fountain pens, and records. Influence is least on items shared with others and gift items: watches and vacations.

Influencing Future Purchases

The dimensions of adolescence discussed thus far—number, income and expenditures, and influencing family purchases—were each concerned with the significance of young consumers during their transition through the development stages of adolescence. These, of course, are important—of utmost importance to marketers directing their efforts to these market segments. But there is an additional dimension of importance, one that affects future behavior. This dimension is the stabilizing of personality development during adolescence.

The personality pattern that is established during childhood and changes somewhat during early adolescence begins in late adolescence to take the form that it will maintain, with few modifications, during the remaining years of life. And even the subsequent modifications are more quantitative than qualitative, such as the strengthening of desirable traits and the weakening of undesirable traits. In general, the attitudes and behavior patterns established during late adolescence can be carried over into adulthood and become a way of life (Hurlock, 1968).

In consumer research it has been shown that brand preferences established during adolescence tend to be followed through by subsequent purchases in later life. The relationship is not perfect, but it is present.

[1]Gary S. Becker, "Markets of the Sixties," quoted in Cateora (1963).

Orth (1963), for example, reported that young people who indicated a brand preference for cameras, fountain pens, or typewriters during an interview conducted in 1954 were followed up in 1963 to find out whether their expressed brand preferences had been translated into purchasing behavior. The question in the second interview was, "What was the brand of the last fountain pen, camera, and typewriter you bought, if any?" The figures in Table 4-1 show that between one-third and two-thirds of the brand preferences expressed in 1954 had been translated into behavior by 1963.

Note that there are substantial differences among these three products, and that preferences expressed in the late teens seem to have a much higher probability of being acted upon than preferences expressed during the early teens.

ACTIVITIES AND INTERESTS OF ADOLESCENTS

New and preposessing interests develop during the period of adolescence. These result not only from the physical changes occurring during the period but also from the numerous social changes, particularly the shifting of reference groups from family to peers and the deeper identification of friends as small, select groups rather than the "crowd" or class.

The specific activities and interest of adolescents depend on a number of factors, including sex, intelligence, resources and opportunities, prestige value among peers, and personal abilities. There are, however, certain interests and activities that are fairly universal in the American culture, although these may be expressed in somewhat different ways in different sections of the country or in different social classes within the different areas (Hurlock, 1968). In this section we examine some of these major activities and interests of adolescence.

Games and Sports

Interest in games and sports which require high energy expenditure reaches its peak during early adolescence. Table 4-2 illustrates some of the favorite outdoor sports of young male and female teens. While the sample, drawn from Catholic schools, may not be representative, the pronounced sex-different

Table 4-1 The Durability of Brand Preference*

	Young people who were	
Product	8–14 years of age in 1954	15–19 years of age in 1954
Camera	40%	68%
Fountain pen	32	54
Typewriter	29	41
Average brand-preference longevity	34	52

*Percentages of young people who named as the "last" brand purchased in 1963 the brand they had said they preferred in 1954.
Source: Orth (1963:76).

Table 4-2 Sex Differences in Outdoor Sports

	Favorite sport		
Sport	12-14-year-old boys (*n*=794)	12-14-year-old girls (*n*=791)	Total
Swimming	8.4%	43.6%	26.0%
Baseball	33.1	13.8	23.5
Football	35.9	2.6	19.3
Basketball	7.4	3.9	5.7
Softball	0.5	5.7	3.1
Tennis	1.0	5.1	3.0
Horseback riding	0.1	4.6	2.3
Badminton	0.4	3.3	1.8
Ice skating	0.4	3.3	1.8

Source: Seventh Triennial Youth Market Survey (1966:20).

interests tend to hold across most adolescents. In general, there is a shift away from games that require high energy expenditure toward recreations of the amusement type where the player is a passive spectator. This is particularly true for girls, who, earlier than boys, begin to enjoy sports as spectators. Boys, however, retain their interest in active, competitive sports longer than girls, primarily because of the peer rewards given boys for athletic ability. But even boys gradually lose their interest in participating in strenuous physical activities unless they have the ability to play and excel on a school team.

Not only is there a general shift away from strenuous games and sports to "inactive" games such as playing cards and loafing around, but there is also a general reduction in the range of interest in different forms of recreation. Because of schoolwork and studies, school activities, part-time jobs, and other time-demanding activities, many adolescents simply have less time for games and sports. As a result, young consumers select those few activities that give them greatest pleasure, either because they can excel or, more frequently, because the activities offer greater opportunities for social contacts, especially with members of the opposite sex.

Automobiles

The automobile is a basic trait in the material culture of young consumers. We have already shown its importance in the average weekly expenditure figures earlier in the chapter. But the relatively large proportion of income spent on cars does not reveal the underlying reasons for the significance of the automobile to teens. Cars are more than a means for transportation; they represent the opportunity for socialization and dating in contemporary society. Thus, an automobile is much more than a convenience; it is a sign of adulthood to the adolescent—perhaps even something which takes the place of the adolescent "rite of passage," a ceremony ushering in adulthood in most nonliterate cultures.

Indeed, it is taken for granted that all teenagers will learn to drive and that, if they do not have a car of their own, they will certainly have access to one. Many car dealers even take it for granted that when a boy reaches the age of sixteen he will be in the market for a used car. Moreover, the automobile represents the interconnecting tie between many of the activities of adolescents and thus becomes an absorbing interest, particularly among boys. As Bernard (1961) has observed:

> Automobiles have become a factor of great importance in adolescent culture. For example, in many cities it is an accepted pattern that in order to date a girl, a boy must be able to provide a car for transportation; she may not go in a cab or allow herself and her date to be driven by parents. To many boys the car itself becomes a dominant motivating force. Having acquired a car for transportation, socialization, and dating, a boy becomes so involved in its care and upkeep he has little time or interest left for other activities. . . . "For many, the clubhouse on wheels is a medium for holding a party. . . ."

Food

The eating patterns of teenagers are quite distinct from those of childhood. As children leave childhood and pass into the teen years, their craving for sweets diminishes somewhat, especially in the case of cereal. Conversely, interest in salty things increases, as does interest in sharply flavored things.

In part the diminished use of sweets is an attempt to combat skin problems; and, especially for girls, diminished sweet intake may be the result of attempts at weight control, since obesity is a common adolescent physical development problem. Notice, for example, the less importance of candy, ice cream, and soda expenditures for girls and for boys in the data presented earlier.

Generally, teens have somewhat erratic eating habits and will eat large quantities of "almost anything." Cereal does not fit the "anything" category, however. During adolescence, both boys and girls eat less cereal than they did during childhood. Some say, "Cereal is for little kids." Others find it tasteless, and some do not want to take the time to have a formal breakfast. Some (again, especially girls) think it is too high in calories and the milk contains too much fat. Indeed, milk consumption among girls declines rapidly after age fifteen, but the high rate of male consumption is sustained up to age twenty.

Reading

Throughout adolescence there is less reading for fun because of the reading required by school and because of other time pressures. Also, adolescents would rather spend their leisure time with their close friends or talking with them on the phone, rather than alone reading.

When adolescents do read, they specialize in the type of subject matter that appeals to them; and they read magazine stories more often than books, or they read paperback editions of the popular novels of the day. Particularly during early adolescence, boys' preferences center around science and invention, while the girls' favorite topic is romantic stories.

Since teens do read magazines, a host of "teen" magazines have been marketed to appeal to adolescent tastes and to "help" them with their "problems." In general, the content of these magazines reveals the major positive values—fun and popularity—and negative concerns—overweight or underweight and acne—of their readers. How to be popular in order to have fun is the major focus of the content. The execution of content, however, varies with the social class background of the intended audience. Many teen-type magainzes, for example, differ from their slick counterparts—*Seventeen* and *Mademoiselle*—in a way analogous to the way true-story magazines for adult women differ from the service-type women's magazines. The class background of these differing publics is revealed in the relative sophistication of the contents as well as in the nature of the advertising. The values, however, are the same at both class levels—beauty, fun, and popularity (Bernard, 1961).

The ability to reach the teen market through magazines is illustrated in the figures in Table 4-3. While the data are of circulation and not total readership, they do illustrate the differential popularity of certain magazines among adolescents. *Seventeen* has by far the largest circulation among the girls' magazines and *Boys' Life* the largest circulation among the boys'. However, the Scholastic Group circulation compared with total circulation of other teen periodicals indicates the relative reading-for-fun versus reading-for-school time available to adolescents. Other magazines with large adolescent circula-

Table 4-3 Teenage Magazine Circulation

Magazine	Sex of audience	Year	Average audience circulation (000)
American Girl	F	1974	700
Co-ed	F	1974	878
The New Ingenue	F	1975	700
Seventeen	F	1975	1,450
Young Miss	F	1972	350
Boys' Life	M	1975	2,000
Scouting	M	1975	1,200
Teen	M–F	1975	750
Right On	M–F	1974	150
Teen Star Gossip	M–F	1974	150
Tiger Beat	M–F	1974	205
Scholastic magazines*	M–F	1974	4,172
Scholastic Newstime	M–F	1971	1,100
Xerox education publications, comprised of:			
1. Current Events	M–F	1974	795
2. Current Science	M–F	1974	855
3. You and Your World	M–F	1974	399

*Six magazines distributed to high school students.

Source: "Consumer Magazine and Farm Publications Rates and Data." *Standard Rate & Data Service,* 57 (Jan. 27, 1975), 355–374, 377–381.

tion include *The Reader's Digest* for both boys and girls and *McCall's, Family Circle, Woman's Day,* and *Ladies' Home Journal* for females.

Magazines, however, do not claim all the adolescents' reading time. Interest in newspapers increases rapidly during the teen years. In fact, a large majority claim high readership: 72 percent during early adolescence and 81 percent during late adolescence (Bogart, 1971). Moreover, newspapers, relative to magazines and electronic media, are regarded by teens as most informative and most dependable.

Adolescents, of course, do not read everything in the newspaper—no one does, for that matter. What specific parts of the paper are read, however, show a fast shift toward adult interest patterns. For instance, the findings of a national study on readership of both editorial matter and advertising of over 1,600 young people, aged 14–25, look remarkably similar to the usual adult model. These findings are presented in Table 4-4. Notice that traditional sex differences in readership also are revealed in the study. Males read the sports pages and females the fashion pages. Males, more than females, read political columns and business news, while females dominate the readership of advice and etiquette columns, teen columns, weddings and engagements announcements, and society social events. As the data show, the advertisements, too, draw differently from boys and girls.

Radio and TV

Both younger and older adolescents enjoy "listening" to the radio. We have put *listening* in quotations because much of the time spent with the radio is not active listening time. Rather, the radio often is on when the adolescent is dressing, reading, and studying—many teenagers claim that listening to the radio while studying helps them to concentrate better. Actually, radio acts as a form of companionship in the absence of human companionship (Hurlock, 1968).

According to one survey (Popazian, 1967), 75 percent of America's adolescents listen to the radio on a daily basis and average almost three hours' listening per day, mainly during the evening when they are studying. Females tend to listen more than males do, and older adolescents are heavier listeners than younger teens. The pattern for all, however, is to tune into the favorite station and stay tuned; favorite stations are those presenting the favorite programming—pop or rock music.

While listening to the radio increases throughout adolescence, television viewing drops somewhat in popularity as the following Nielsen data for the six-week period ending December 3, 1967, show:

	Time viewed per week	
Age group	Male	Female
6–11 (not divided by sex)	22 hr 1 min	
12–17	19 hr 40 min	18 hr 39 min
Adults under 35	19 hr 9 min	29 hr 4 min

Table 4-4 Sex Differences in Newspaper Readership

Advertising	Percent reading several times weekly	
	Male	Female
Movie and theater announcements	49	59
Women's clothing and accessories	5	77
Employment	31	34
Men's clothing and accessories	39	26
All car references (net)[1]	42	22
New cars	35	15
Used cars	33	15
Records	29	30
Supermarkets and other food ads	16	40
Household items, furnishings	14	35
Total classified (net)	24	19
Furniture	12	30
Recording and hi-fi equipment	26	13
Television and radio sets	18	16
Real estate	14	16
Personal notices	10	18
Travel agencies and airlines	11	12
Banks, finance companies	12	6
Do not read any ads	7	2
Base: Total respondents = 100%[2]	100	100
Average number of kinds of ads read	3.5	4.5

Editorial features	Percent reading several times weekly	
	Male	Female
News	81	81
Comics	65	68
Program listings: TV, radio	61	66
Sports page	77	36
Horoscope	33	66
Editorial page	50	47
Movie reviews	40	54
Reviews: TV, radio	38	51
Fashion	11	69
Advice and etiquette columnists	19	54
Political columnists	43	32
Teenage column and news	26	42
Weddings and engagements	13	45
Food	14	39
Puzzles and games	23	29
Society social events	12	38
Music, music reviews	21	27
Business, finance, stock exchange listings	31	15
Gossip columnists	10	32
Recording reviews	17	20
Theater, ballet reviews	16	21
Obituaries	11	20
Art, painting, sculpture reviews	9	17
Book reviews	10	16
Sewing	1	21
Hobbies, miscellaneous	10	9
Gardening	3	9
Bridge	4	3
None of these	7	2
Base: Total respondents = 100%	100	100
Average number of features read	7.6	10.3

[1] Includes classified car ads.
[2] Adds to more than 100% due to multiple mentions.
Source: Bogart (1971:38).

Note that the viewing time is reduced only about three hours from the childhood years to the adolescent years, and that viewing is heavier, by about one hour per week, among males. The big change in the data is that, among "adults under 35," male viewing continues to drop slightly while female viewing increases dramatically—almost ten and one-half hours.

Generally, television has less appeal for adolescents than has radio, partly because it is impossible to study or work or engage in social activities with peers while watching television, and partly because adolescents become more critical of programming content as they grow older. In addition, programming that appeals to teenagers is not generally available when they are free to watch.

These data, of course, are averages. How great a drop in time spent on television viewing there will be as time passes varies greatly among adolescents. Intelligence is one discriminating factor. Bright teens tend to be more critical of programming and more interested in reading and studying than those who are less bright. Popularity and emotional adjustment are other discriminating factors. Popular, well-adjusted teens prefer recreations with their friends to staying at home to watch television, while those with poor adjustments during adolescence use TV as an escape.

Thus, while television is *the* medium for reaching children with advertisements, the teens are more elusive to this approach. One innovative approach to overcome this problem was the launching of programs like "Midnight Special." Such programs offer music, pop and rock stars, and familiar in-concert format, all at a time (1-2:30 A.M.) when teens tend to be home and have access to the family TV set. According to Grey Advertising, this formula was on target, producing twice the average viewing time among late adolescents ("Grey Matter," 1974).

Recordings

Buying, swapping, and listening to recordings—records and cassettes—have been and still are highly popular activities of adolescents. These activities are popular because they are highly compatible with a number of other teenage interests and activities. With recordings, more than with radio and TV, adolescents can control what they listen to, and this is highly consistent with their desire for independence from parental control. Listening to recordings is also a popular activity and interest because current "hits" offer conversation opportunities, and conversation is one of the favorite social activities of teenagers. Similarly, recordings can be used at parties and dances, which also rate high among the social interests of adolescents.

A 1967 survey for *Seventeen* magazine of the ownership and use of phonographs and records offers a conservative perspective of the magnitude of the recording interests of teenagers today. The survey showed that 7 out of 10 teens personally owned phonographs, and that these were mainly received as gifts from specific requests for them. Moreover, virtually all the respondents (92 percent) reported that they lived in a household with one or more phonographs available to them to use. As to records, 9 out of 10 respondents reported owning a record collection averaging 45.3 albums and 42.8 singles and chalking up an average listening time of 9 hours per week. The *Seventeen* respondents reported the following record purchase patterns:

	Albums		Singles
Purchased in last six months	78%		62%
Average number of purchases	3.2		4.9
Median price paid	$ 3.57		$0.84
Expenditure per buyer	$11.42		$4.12
Total		$15.54	

All totaled, the annual volume for records was estimaed as $286,352,000—and the current volume is bound to be substantially higher in today's inflated recording prices.

Personal Appearance

One of the strongest and most persuasive interests of adolescents is their interest in themselves. This interest is expressed in their worries about and behavior in buying and using personal care items and clothing. This interest is a result of several factors of development: teens have an awakening and growing interest in members of the opposite sex as they move through puberty into adolescence; they also develop a strong desire for social acceptance among their peers; and they recognize that social acceptance is highly influenced by their appearance as well as by other symbols of status such as material possessions, money, and independence.

Interest in personal appearance includes but is not limited to clothing and accessories. Hair, body shape and size, facial features, skin, and nails are each points of extreme importance to teens; indeed, any feature not up to the standards set by peers and the mass media is of great concern. For instance, a 1968 study for *Seventeen* magazine quizzed 1,439 girls 13–19 years old about their skin problems, and 93 percent reported having some problem. The problems included pimples and blackheads, flaking, and chapping, as well as a host of others. Table 4-5 shows the percentage of girls who reported having various types of skin problems.

Because of these skin and other related problems, cosmetic manufacturers have become the most avid advertisers to teens, trying to make the adolescent needs more prepotent and trying to show them how the advertisers' brands will "solve" the adolescents' problems. Indeed, there are now as many different cosmetics and lotions for teenagers as for older women, and many of the products, such as astringents and facial masks, traditionally designed for mature women are now being promoted to adolescents.

Moreover, the magazines published for the adolescent market—*Seventeen, Glamour, Charm, Teen, Mademoiselle, Eye,* and *Cheetah*—provide a great deal of encouragement to cosmetic and other manufacturers of teen-type products to continue their advertising, particularly in their respective publications. For

Table 4-5 Skin Problems of Teenage Girls

Type of problem	Ever have	Recency among those having	
		Past week	Past month
Pimples/blemishes	75%	60%	32%
Blackheads	54	59	30
Oiliness	48	64	27
Dryness	31	55	35
Large pores	26	61	29
Flaking	25	55	38
Chapping	25	55	36
Acne	15	44	32
Allergies	7	31	42

instance, a full-page ad for *Seventeen* appeared in the April 15, 1974, issue of *Advertising Age* proclaiming:

> SUPERSPENDER!
>
> There are a lot of girls in this country who walk around disguised as typical teenagers.
>
> In reality, they're all Superspenders.
>
> There are some 14 million of them. And they spend over 20 billion dollars every year.
>
> Not just on cosmetics and clothing, but on everything from food to sporting goods to trips to Europe to automobiles.
>
> And, as you've already guessed, the magazine Superspender reads is Seventeen.
>
> So now that we've exposed her, you should have no trouble contacting her.

And, after tying a number of spending-power traits to a picture of a teenage girl holding a copy of *Seventeen,* the ad concludes:

> SUPERSPENDER
> BUYS WHAT
> SHE READS IN
> SEVENTEEN!

The combination of product availability and advertising designed to appeal to adolescents has been effective. The data in Table 4-6, for example, show how teenage girls changed their grooming habits from 1948 to 1964. During this time period, a big switch occurred from the use of traditional "girl-like" cosmetics to those associated with adult women.

Clothing, like cosmetics, becomes highly important to adolescents as they seek to present themselves in the best light possible (according to the contemporary definition of "best light").

Both boys and girls discover quickly that clothing can be used to hide or cover up undesirable features, to signify status, to proclaim group membership,

Table 4-6 How Teenage Girls Changed Grooming Habits

Product	Extent of use	
	1948	1964
Mascara	20%	90%
Liquid foundation	10	60
Lipstick	90	100
Eyebrow pencil	10	50
Medicated creams	10	40
Perfume (daily usage)	10	30
Nail enamel	30	90
Sun-tan aids	40	70

Source: *Printer's Ink* (Nov. 20, 1964).

and to signify sophistication—all crucial variables in the process of making friends and keeping them. Thus, one of the primary requirements of clothing for adolescents is that their clothes meet the approval of the peer group. Being fashionable, moreover, is so important to a teenager that "becomingness" from the parents' viewpoint must often be sacrificed where possible. Furthermore, as teen fashion leaders adopt new styles and these are quickly imitated by the majority of teens, frequent replacements of garments must take place for an adolescent to stay in style (Ryan, 1966). Thus, the desire to appear "glamorous and fascinating" to their peers, particularly on the part of teenage girls, becomes a common source of friction between parents and teens.

And whenever there is a conflict between parents and adolescents about products used, there are problems for marketers: "To whom do we appeal, teens, parents, or both?" and "What appeals do we use?" In the following two subsections, we elaborate on the meaning to marketers and advertisers of the effects of parent-teen interaction on clothing and cosmetics.[2]

Clothing How do parents react to their children's choice of clothing? The situation here is very complex, and the answer depends largely on the age of the children involved. In general, parents tend to give younger children a freer rein in picking their clothes because they know that young children are unconsciously influenced by their parents and that they have not yet developed "far-out" fad tastes in clothing. The young child will probably pick an item of clothing from within a range of selections acceptable to the parent.

Teenagers, on the other hand, come into conflict more often with their parents because their choice of clothing falls within a range that, for economic and aesthetic reasons, is not nearly as acceptable to the parent. The parents in this situation are forced to exert more pressure in order to prevail over their child. Teenagers, then, come into conflict more often with their parents over clothing selection than do younger children. This leads to situations in which

[2]The material in these sections is a summary of results of proprietary studies.

both parent and child are forced to compromise and each side wins a few battles and loses a few battles.

There are obvious reasons for the conflict between teenagers and parents over clothing selection. The parents are interested in economy and conservative good taste; the teen is interested in modish style and fitting in with friends. Perhaps the parents also feel threatened because the child is increasingly challenging their authority and is seeking the advice of peers rather than parents in the choice of clothes. This infringes on an area where the discretion of the parents has always been rather telling, and it reminds the parents that their child is growing up. The teenager's increased monetary independence, resulting from part-time jobs and increased allowance, also allows the teen more freedom and removes from the parents even this area of control.

Clothing advertising campaigns can benefit from this knowledge in several ways. For children's wear, anything that appeals to a woman's sensibilities (i.e., quality, long-lasting clothing at a moderate price) and yet still appeals to a child's desires to have something stylish and "in" would have strong appeal to the purchasing mother.

Teen advertising that parents are likely to see should not be "flashy" and should not make children appear more adult than they really are. Parents continually argue against this very thing, and advertising showing grown-up-looking teens only adds fuel to the fire. Since parents have the final say in most cases, it makes more sense to appeal to their sensibilities in all advertising, except for inexpensive fad items. For items of this type, teens may be appealed to more in their own terms. Many have their own money, and for items of this type they spend freely, with relatively little parental control.

Cosmetic and Toilet Articles Teens have more success influencing their parents to buy face and hair care products than makeup. Here, the comparison with the purchase of clothing is clear. Eye makeup, as well as flashy or fad clothing, has connotations of the daughter's growing up—a process many parents wish they could retard. But interest in hair and complexion care products indicates an interest in healthy good grooming and cleanliness—traits all parents encourage, just as they encourage an interest in good taste and value in clothing.

Teens all have different methods of convincing their parents of what they need. Some will suggest a brand they like, and if the parent thinks other members of the family will also use it, the parent will buy it or pay for part of it, with the teen paying part. But in order to have exclusive use of a product, teens often have to part with their own money.

Teens seem particularly well-qualified to choose shampoo and complexion care products. Much of their time is spent in search of products to make them look better. They experiment freely, often with their parents' approval. Teenaged girls study labels, read magazines, listen to TV ads, and talk to girl friends—all in search of the magic potion that will make them beautiful. Self-conscious teens feel that it is crucial to be as attractive as possible at all times. Stringy hair or a stubborn pimple can be "devastating." When a teen's whole self-image is at stake, it is no wonder she wants to believe what cosmetic advertising tells her. She relies on promotional promises enough to try the product at least once and then judge it.

The teens' influence in this area, for the most part, is welcomed by their parents. Parents seem to feel that it is desirable for their daughters to take an interest in personal care and are willing to purchase almost anything their girls request. One problem remains: how to reconcile cosmetic advertising to the teens, who are interested in appearing more glamorous and grown-up, with advertising to the parents, who buy the products and want their daughters to remain clean and shining little girls. The answer seems to lie in the image a product projects and in its packaging. Perhaps if, as some companies are doing, makeups are given a pure, natural image and are shown on lovely young girls, the parents will read "nice, innocent." But the girls will study the back of the box, where the product claims are listed, and will read, "This will *work;* this will make me beautiful."

INFLUENCE OF PEERS

Underlying the discussion of teens' activities and interests has been the common thread of peer influence. This thread is directly related to the coping of adolescents with their physical and psychological changes—changes that can be extremely difficult because the teenagers are facing them for the first time without the benefit of experience. Outside of a few close friends, there are few who seem to really understand the conflicts, anxieties, and frustrations of this developmental period. Children do not understand what their older brothers and sisters are facing and really do not care; parents are sympathetic, but it has been some time since their teen years, and memories and impressions tend to fade. To the teen, the only other people who really can feel and understand what is happening are teen friends.

Therefore, it is not surprising that teenagers find great closeness and friendship in their peers. As a group, adolescents can relate to each other's problems because their problems are quite similar. Unity is found through similar problems, frustrations, and anxieties. So when we look at adolescents and recognize their strong peer group relationships and need for approval from each other, we should not be surprised. It is only within this peer group that complete understanding can be found, and if not understanding, then a willingness to listen to each other's problems and a feeling for the emotional trauma stirring within. Maybe adolescents are not qualified to solve each other's problems or do not have the insight to always help each other, but they do have one thing—trust. One teenager can confide and trust in another teenager, and, therefore, they can talk to each other and express pent-up emotions and feelings that may otherwise never be aired. Although problems may not be solved, the act of expression and discussion with another interested person who strongly relates to those problems is highly beneficial.

It naturally follows that teenagers will do their utmost to maintain good relationships with other teenagers. Since there is really nowhere else to turn, the teenager is very reluctant to risk losing a peer group relationship. Hence, within this age group there tends to be considerable conformity in behavior, thinking, actions, customs, and mores. Teenagers are very sensitive about understanding and practicing those norms that help them maintain group membership. Wide deviations from norms are usually met with disapproval and the threat of severance from the particular subgroup in which one finds membership. Norms are reflected in almost everything that is done or worn. Teenagers have a cult that dictates a complete life style that each one strives to reach. Being part of the in-group depends upon understanding and performance of the life style. Playing the "role" is both recognized and approved. Not to play the role can lead to expulsion, with few options for companionship. Teenagers rejected by the cult find other fringe groups to belong to, but even those on the fringe recognize their status and are not entirely happy.

Moreover, since young consumers do not feel that "outsiders" understand them, they generally are not responsive to words. They have learned to mistrust them. Words are the vehicles for polite social hypocrisies, broken promises, evasion tactics, insincere expressions of affection, and meaningless convention. Thus, teens express themselves in other, nonverbal ways. When asked how to tell a "friend" from an "enemy," teens may talk about "feeling the vibes" (vibrations). When pressed, however, they will mention specifics like dress, gait, demeanor, and grooming. These are the visual symbols by which individuals express, often exactly and subtly, mood, status, and values. The garb worn by young people is not just the bizarre affectation which some oldsters think it is. It is the announcement of affiliation in a particular group. The shape of a shoe, the styling of hair, the material or fit of a coat, the degree of cleanliness (or uncleanliness) and the adoption of particular garment styles convey life styles.

Much of the teenage verbal communication is really not a prime form of communication at all. "Ring my chimes," "doing your own thing," and "letting it all hang out" are ambiguous expressions with many meanings depending on the intonation pattern and associated gestures. These few expressions can cover most situations, so that the teen does not have to open himself up and say what he or she really thinks—thus escaping getting hurt.

For marketers, the uncommunicative nature of teen life makes their life style, thoughts, and feelings that much more difficult to identify. Advertisers must learn the other conventions, such as dress and behavior, which cue the teens, and must signal to them that the advertiser has something to offer the group. A wrong signal can also drive teens away, never more to return.

SUMMARY

Adolescence is a transitional period between childhood and adulthood which is characterized by major shifts in such important areas as activities, interests, and reference groups. We examine how these changes affect purchasing, consumption, and media patterns in order to illustrate the problems and opportunities facing marketers who cater to the teen market.

Actually, the youth market is composed of two age groups, each with its own characteristics. As young consumers proceed from early adolescence through late adolescence, their behavior patterns normally shift toward progressively adult forms. In fact, many of the patterns established during late adolescence are carried over into later life.

It is important to realize, however, that many factors which affect the behavior of teens stem directly from the teens' unique, transitional life period. The dramatic physical and emotional changes which distinguish this period result in an intense need for peer acceptance and companionship, assurances of personal attractiveness, and increasing independence from parental control—all with concurrent needs and desires in terms of products, fashions, and life styles. Such unique preferences often cause conflicts with parents, who still hold the final authority and the purse strings in respect to large or important purchasing decisions. In order to successfully market to teens, then, the desires and needs of parents must also be satisfied or at least appeased.

REVIEW QUESTIONS

1 When studying the consumer behavior of teens, it is advisable to separate adolescence into early and late life periods. Discuss the differences between the two periods in terms of interests, employment, and life styles. Why is sixteen years the turning point in our culture?
2 Sex-related differences in behavior patterns are important during the adolescent years. Describe the types of behavior which show significant differences between boys and girls. What are the marketing implications?
3 Is the teenage population expected to grow or decline during the next decade? How will marketers catering to the teen market adjust to this population trend?
4 Teens have a great deal of influence in deciding family purchases for certain products. Identify the types of products where teen influence is important.
5 In what ways does the fact that attitudes and behavior patterns established during late adolescence often carry over into adulthood relate to marketing?
6 Automobiles represent more than a means of transportation to teens, and they figure heavily in teen expenditures. Why are they so important?
7 Describe the differences between children and teens in respect to eating patterns and interest in games and sports.
8 Perhaps one of the most significant shifts in behavior during adolescence, from a marketing viewpoint, occurs in media habits and exposure. Discuss these changes in terms of reading, radio, and TV.
9 Discuss the purchasing, consumption, and media patterns affected by the increasing importance of personal appearance among teens.
10 Changing reference groups from parents to peers results in conflicts within families where teens are present. Why is this factor important in studying consumer behavior, and how can marketers overcome this problem?

EXERCISE

Compare on a point-by-point basis the weekly expenditures of late adolescents presented in the first part of the chapter with advertisement readership in Table 4-4. Is the relationship high, low, or nonexistent? How do you account for any differences in the rank orderings of expenditures and readership? In general, does style of life lead to readership of ads, or does advertising capture attention and lead to readership? Explain.

REFERENCES

Bernard, Jessie. "Teen-Age Culture: An Overview." *Annals of the American Academy of Political and Social Sliences,* 338 (1961), 1–12.

Bogart, Leo. "Youth Market Isn't All That Different." *Advertising Age* (Apr. 12, 1971), 37–39.

Cateora, P. P. *An Analysis of the Teen-Age Market.* Studies in Marketing No. 7. Austin, Tex.: Bureau of Business Research, University of Texas, 1963.

Gilkison, Paul. "Teen-agers' Perceptions of Buying Frames of Reference: A Decade in Retrospect." *Journal of Retailing,* 49 (Summer 1973), 25–37.

Grey Advertising, Inc. "Grey Matter." March 1974.

Hurlock, Elizabeth B. *Developmental Psychology.* 3d ed. New York: McGraw-Hill, 1968.

Linden, Fabian. "Under 18—The Younger Population." *The Conference Board Record* (February 1970), 22–4.

Moore, Roy L. and Lowndes F. Stephens. "Some Communication and Demographic Determinants of Adolescent Consumer Learning." *Journal of Consumer Research,* 2 (September 1975), 80–92.

Orth, P. "Teenager: What Kind of Consumer?" *Printer's Ink* (September 1963), 7.

Papazian, Edward. "Teenagers and Broadcast Media." *Media/Scope* (December 1967). *Printer's Ink,* Nov. 20, 1964.

Ryan, M. S. *Clothing: A Study in Human Behavior.* New York: Holt, Rinehart and Winston, 1966.

Schiele, George W. "How to Reach the Young Consumer." *Harvard Business Review* (March–April 1974), 72–84.

Schwartz, Gary and Don Merten. "The Language of Adolescence: An Anthropological Approach to the Youth Culture." *The American Journal of Sociology,* 72 (March 1967), 453–468.

Seventh Triennial Youth Market Survey. Seventeen, 1966.

Stuteville, John R. "Sexually Polarized Products and Advertising Strategy." *Journal of Retailing,* 47 (Summer 1971), 3–13.

Weale, W. Bruce and John R. Kerr. "Brand Choices of Teen-Age 'In-Group' Versus 'Out-Group.'" *Journal of Retailing,* 45 (Winter 1969–1970), 30–35.

Youth Research Institute. *The Dynamics of the Youth Explosion.* Los Angeles Chamber of Commerce, 1967.

Chapter 5

Young Adults

The sixties were the decade of the teenager! And because teenagers were so extraordinarily visible, politically and socially, during the period, marketers, politicians, and other concerned citizens showed an inordinate interest in the life styles, opinions, and consumption habits of these young consumers (Bogart, 1971).

In contrast, this is the era of the young adult! The youngsters of the sixties now are maturing into early adulthood. By 1980, more than 2 out of every 5 of the nation's adult population—or some 66 million persons—will be over 18 but under 35. Indeed, the size of this age group will increase twice as fast as the total adult population, and its growth will continue for the next ten years. The rising importance of the young adult—the young affluents—will have significant consequences for a wide range of consumer industries, marketing practices, and public policy. Author and demographer Ben Wattenberg (1975: 51) encapsulates the new era well and succinctly: "Simply put, the situation is this: Never before and probably never again will one age group and one social group wield such disproportionate and newly-found economic potency in the marketplace."

But early adulthood, roughly the 18–35 age group, like all developmental levels of adulthood, is quite heterogeneous in terms of important market needs.

It will be useful, then, to define more explicitly the major dimensions of early adulthood before proceeding to develop an understanding of the major issues and their consequent market-related behaviors of this growing segment of the population.

EARLY ADULTHOOD

As adolescents mature and become adults, both in the legal and the developmental sense, there are a number of continuities of the behaviors and interests acquired during adolescence and even during childhood. But there are also major discontinuities—major shifts resulting from almost inescapable adult role patterns. As Neugarten (1969:124) has explained:

> Every society is age-graded, and every society has a system of social expectations regarding age-appropriate behavior. The individual passes through a socially-regulated cycle from birth to death as inexorably as he passes through the biological cycle; and there exists a socially-prescribed timetable for the ordering of major life events: a time when he is expected to marry, a time to raise children, a time to retire. Although the norms vary somewhat from one socioeconomic, ethnic, or religious group to another, for any social group it can easily be demonstrated that norms and actual occurrences are closely related.

What are the societal expectations of early adulthood? What new roles is the young adult expected to play that differentiate this period of the life span from those preceding and succeeding? As Neugarten (1969) has noted, the major issues of early adulthood are related to intimacy, to parenthood, and to meeting the expectations of the world of work, with the attendant demands for restructuring the roles, values, and sense of self.

The issue of intimacy generally relates to the period from graduation from high school to the birth of the first child. This life period differs in length for different people more than previously discussed periods because it is more issue-related than strictly age-related. For example, the period usually is longer for men than for women. Also, the period differs in the sense that the boundaries apply to the majority of consumers but not all—some never marry; and some married remain childless. Nevertheless, for most United States consumers, the period contains several major episodes which strongly condition peoples' behaviors as consumers. These episodes include serious dating and preparation for marriage, marriage, an occupational choice, and, for some, more education, mostly without marriage but sometimes with it.

For most, but again not for all, consumers, these episodes occur during the age period 18–25. For this reason, this age group provides most of the demographic data as to the size and trends of adults in the intimacy-related issues of life. Moreover, two of the episodes denote two fairly distinct and time-ordered groups, the premarrieds and the marrieds without children. Within these two groups, there is considerable variation of the timing of occupational choice—some gain employment before marriage, some after;

some go on to college before making an occupational choice, others do not. For these reasons, educational and occupational effects on behavior will be discussed where appropriate within the two broader segments, premarrieds and young marrieds.

The other major issue of early adulthood identified by Neugarten is related to parenthood. The birth of a child, particularly the first child, sets off a chain of events which affect consumer behavior as strongly as the dating and mating games.

In singling out young parents as the third major group of early adulthood, we have departed almost entirely from an age-graded definition of consumer groups to a family life-cycle gradation. Most people face the issue of parenthood in the 25–34 age bracket, since these are the prime years of family building. But the role changes brought about by the event of one or more children is more significant than the age of the people in explaining their market needs and behavior. Age grading was satisfactory through high school because school experiences are relatively standard at different ages in the United States and because roles and expectations of appropriate behavior are age-graded more than event-graded.

In adulthood, however, many of the activities of individuals, and especially their consumption of products and media, are more related to their position in the family life cycle than to their chronological age, because role changes are inevitable with the events faced regardless of the age of the person facing them. These ideas are expressed graphically in Figure 5-1.

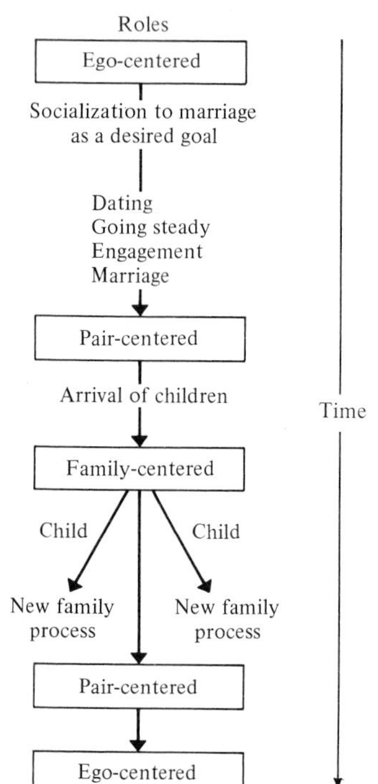

Figure 5-1 Role changes and the family process. *Source:* Clavan (1969). Copyright 1969 by National Council on Family Relations. Reprinted by permission.

Thus, in the following sections on the premarrieds, the marrieds, and young parents, we subtly move from an age-graded to an event-related or family life-cycle definition of consumer groups.

Before dealing with these major issues of early adulthood, we examine the various dimensions of early adulthood that, when taken together, substantiate the significance of these persons as consumers; much in the vein of previous chapters, we provide an overview of the importance of this segment of the population in terms of numbers and spending power.

THE IMPORTANCE OF YOUNG ADULTS AS CONSUMERS

We alluded to the size dimension of the young adult population in the introduction. Table 5-1 shows the raw magnitude of the number of persons in early adulthood. Certainly, the arithmetic is impressive! Currently, young adults number some 57 million persons, roughly equivalent to two and one-half times the number of adolescents.

Moreover, as the trend data indicate, young adults will acount for an increasingly larger share of the United States population through 1980, and then slacken in relative growth around 1985. Currently, persons in early adulthood represent about 27 percent of the population; in 1980 they will acount for almost 29 percent, and in 1985 about 28 percent. As shown in Table 5-1, the slackening growth at the end of the next ten years is accounted for by the under-25 age group; the 25–34 age group, which has more economic clout in the market, will continue its impressive growth, moving from 12 percent of the population at the beginning of this decade to 16.5 percent by 1985.

One inescapable conclusion of these aggregate data is that there currently is and will continue to be (for a time) a huge bulk of young adults in the population promising potentially prosperous years for those industries catering to the needs of these segments of the market.

But what are they doing? We have noted that behavior is not entirely homogeneous for the two young adult age groups, and this is particularly so for the 18–25 group: it includes young persons just out of high school, some of

Table 5-1 The Young Adult Population: 1970-1985

Year	Total population (in millions)	Age group: 18-24 (number and % of total)		Age group: 25-34 (number and % of total)	
1970	204.8	24.6	12.0%	25.3	12.4%
1975	216.6	27.7	12.5	31.2	14.4
1980	230.9	29.4	12.7	36.9	16.0
1985	246.3	27.4	11.1	40.7	16.5

Note: Series D (moderate low series) projection. Data include Armed Forces overseas and are as of July 1.

Source: Department of Commerce, *Current Population Reports,* Series P-25, No. 470 (November 1971).

those in college, some who have completed college and have formed families of their own, some who are in the labor force, and some who are in the Armed Forces.

Table 5-2 gives a brief profile of the individuals in the 18–24 age group. Note that while the male-female percentages are roughly comparable for those in school and those unmarried, a larger percentage of young males than of young females are working, or at least are in the labor force.

But underlying these aggregate percentages are some revealing sex differences. By age 20, one-half of the females are married; for males, the median age of marriage is 23. For both males and females, however, the median age at first marriage is increasing and reversing a trend toward earlier marriages that lasted from 1920 to 1955 (see Table 5-3). Delaying a marriage, even by a few months, adds up to a longer period of the premarried stage of life and the corresponding discretionary income that goes with being single—a factor discussed later.

Also, the big change in school status occurs around the ages 18 and 19. After these ages, the proportion of males in school is much higher than of females. But for both sexes, the proportion in school drops rapidly below the average figures shown in Table 5-2; at age 24, for example, only about 13 percent of the males are still in school and 4 percent of the females.

The working percentages also disguise some sex differences by individual ages. By age 20, about two-thirds of the males are working; by age 22, the proportion rises to three-fourths. For females, about 40 to 45 percent work during the ages 19–23; the percentage drops at 24, however, because of the presence of children.

Spending Power

The reshuffling of the age mix of the population is but one indicator of the importance of young adults; another critical factor is the distribution of income, a good indicator of the spending power of any segment of the population.

Demographic developments, except for young children, over relatively short time periods are readily predictable—we know, for example, that all persons who will be of adult age by 1980 or 1985 are already with us. Projecting the income mix of the population is far more difficult. Much of our ability to predict it depends on the nation's overall economic position and growth and, by

Table 5-2 1970 Profile of Young Adults, Ages 18-24

Category	Male	Female
Unmarried	28.6%	22.6%
In school	56.6	52.0
Working	76.6	41.4
Armed Forces	2.9	0.06

Source: Department of Commerce, *1970 Census of Population,* Part 1, United States Summary, June 1973.

Table 5-3 Median Age at First Marriage: 1920–1970

Year	Male	Female
1920	24.6	21.2
1930	24.3	21.3
1940	24.3	21.5
1950	22.8	20.3
1955	22.6	20.2
1960	22.8	20.3
1970	23.2	20.8

Source: Department of Commerce, *Statistical Abstract of the United States*, 1971.

implication, the gain in average household earnings. During the past two and a half decades the United States economy has expanded at a real average rate of about 4 percent. But there is an increasing doubt that the United States can sustain this pace for the next twenty-five years: the energy crisis, the deep recession of the mid-seventies, double-digit inflation, and the expectation of a less rapidly expanding labor force after 1980 all point to a lower rate of economic growth (Linden, 1974). The income projections presented in Table 5-4 are based on a slower rate of growth—3 percent annually. These projections may be on the cautious side, but it is not likely that the traditional 4 percent will be maintained.

When young adults are viewed in terms of households, the under-25 group is seen to be markedly different from the 25–34 age group. Households whose heads are under 25 account for 8 percent of the household population but only 5.5 percent of the nation's household income. These percentages are projected to decline to 7 percent and 5 percent, respectively, by 1985. In contrast, the 25–34 household group contains one-fifth of the nation's households and a corresponding amount of income. Moreover, by 1985, this rapidly growing segment will account for about one-fourth of the households and one-fourth of the income. Thus, while those in the earlier stage of the life cycle are relatively poor, those in the 25–34 group generally parallel the national average in income.

Incomes within each group are expected to increase considerably, adding to the groups already substantial buying power. In 1972, only 7 percent of those under 25 earned over $15,000; by 1985 approximately 14 percent will earn in excess of $15,000. An even more dramatic improvement is shown in Table 5-4 for the 25–34 households: within this group, the proportions earning above $15,000 are expected to shift from 24 percent in 1972 to over 36 percent in 1985—a substantial jump and one that underlies much of the optimism concerning the growth potential this segment provides to the marketplace.

We should note that the income data are for households, not individuals. Such data are more accurate in reflecting the spending power of the 25–34 age group of young adults than that of the under-25 adults simply because about half of the young adults under 25 do not constitute households—they are single and living at home or are at school. Thus, they are in a more discretionary spending position than those under 25 who must maintain a household and the

Table 5-4 Young Adult Households by Age of Head and Income Class (All Figures in 1972 Dollars)

	All households	Age of household head: Under 25	25-34
1972			
Households			
Millions	68.3	5.5	13.6
Distribution	100.0%	8.0	20.0
Spending power			
Total	100.0%	5.5	20.5
Discretionary	100.0%	1.5	14.5
Household income distribution	100.0%	100.0%	100.0%
Under $3,000	14.0	15.5	6.0
$3,000-5,000	11.0	16.5	7.5
$5,000-7,000	10.5	17.5	10.0
$7,000-10,000	16.0	24.0	20.0
$10,000-15,000	23.0	19.5	32.5
$15,000-25,000	19.5	6.5	20.5
$25,000 and over	6.0	0.5	3.5
1980			
Households			
Millions	77.3	6.0	18.3
Distribution	100.0%	8.0	23.5
Spending power			
Total	100.0%	5.5	25.0
Discretionary	100.0%	1.5	19.5
Household income distribution	100.0%	100.0%	100.0%
Under $3,000	12.0	13.0	5.0
$3,000-5,000	10.5	14.5	6.5
$5,000-7,000	10.0	17.0	8.5
$7,000-10,000	14.5	23.0	17.0
$10,000-15,000	23.0	22.5	32.5
$15,000-25,000	22.0	9.0	25.0
$25,000 and over	8.0	1.0	5.5
1985			
Households			
Millions	84.2	6.0	20.5
Distribution	100.0%	7.0	24.5
Spending power			
Total	100.0%	5.0	26.0
Discretionary	100.0%	1.5	20.5
Household income distribution	100.0%	100.0%	100.0%
Under $3,000	11.0	12.0	5.0
$3,000-5,000	10.0	13.5	5.5
$5,000-7,000	9.0	14.5	8.0
$7,000-10,000	14.0	23.0	15.5
$10,000-15,000	22.0	23.5	29.5
$15,000-25,000	25.0	12.5	30.5
$25,000 and over	9.0	1.0	6.0

Source: Linden (1974).

many captive expenditures that go along with an apartment or house. Also, they maintain a stronger influence on the expenditure of parents than do the elder members of the young adult population, as we shall note when discussing the intimacy period of young adulthood.

In general, then, the era of the young adult is more than an era of numbers; it is also an era of the young affluent to an extent not witnessed before in the history of the nation. An enormous market, obviously, for necessities like food, clothing, transportation, and shelter—not to mention numerous durables relating to family formation.

General Mood

In highlighting the number and income of young adults relative to the general population, we identified two of most important determinants of consumer demand. In addition, there is an important qualitative dimension—the general mood of young adults, especially when compared with other stages in the life cycle of adulthood.

The general mood of the population is becoming recognized by consumer researchers as an indicator of willingness to spend. When their mood is low, consumers are more reluctant to spend and more inclined to save, and vice versa. The general mood of the population is also an indicator of the style of life consumers can be expected to live.

Within any general-population level of mood, young adults to a greater degree than any other adult group say their lives are going well (they are happy) and that they are optimistic about the future. This ebullience is somewhat more pronounced for those under 25 but remains high through the 25–34 age period.

Here are some of the specific findings on young adults' outlooks and self-appraisals found in both the 1971 and 1975 nationwide Life Style Surveys[1] studies available for publication:

1 Young adults are *optimistic and happy.* They agree more than other groups in the population with such statements as: "I am much happier now than I ever was before," and "My greatest achievements are still ahead of me." And they agree less with "I dread the future."

2 They have *modern ideas.* They answer affirmatively to "I like to think I am a bit of a swinger," and negatively to "There is too much emphasis on sex today."

3 They consider themselves *cosmopolitan,* strongly agreeing with "I would like to take a trip around the world," "I'd like to spend a year in London or Paris," and "I like to visit places that are totally different from my home."

And here are some supporting findings from the extensive studies of America's youth conducted by Daniel Yankelovich (1974:83–84) and his associates:

[1]Needham, Harper & Steers, (1975).

1 *Personal life.* A large majority of both college (78 percent) and noncollege (75 percent) youth say their lives are going well.

2 *Self-evaluation.* Roughly three-fourths of all young people say they enjoy their lives and are satisfied with themselves.

3 *Outlook for the future.* Approximately two-thirds of all young people say they have a clear idea of what they want to do in the future. Eighty-one percent of the college students feel they have good opportunities for the future, compared with 75 percent of noncollege youth.

THE PREMARRIEDS

Inevitably, young adults in the premarried stage of life must face two major choices: deciding whether, when, and whom to marry and selecting an occupation.

Occupational choice is somewhat different for the college-educated minority of young adults. They have more alternatives; they choose when they are older and more mature; and they display more sophistication in an "exploitive" sense: they ask, "What will I do with my life?" instead of "What will life do for me?" For college youth, then, occupational choice (except during periods of high unemployment in the economy) is largely a function of interest; in contrast, noncollege occupations are almost fortuitous, brought about by circumstances in lieu of interests, as reflected in the behavior of many young adults who go through a period during which they try out one job after another.

For both college and noncollege youth, however, occupational choice becomes increasingly difficult for each successive generation. Much of this difficulty can be traced to these factors (Hurlock, 1975):

1 The ever-increasing number of different kinds of work from which to choose.

2 Rapid changes in work skills due to increased use of automation.

3 Long and costly preparation, which makes job shifts impossible.

4 Unfavorable stereotypes of some occupations.

5 A desire for a job that will give the individual a sense of identity, rather than one that makes him feel like a cog in a large machine.

6 The individual's ignorance of his own capacities due to lack of job experience or vocational guidance.

7 Unrealistic vocational aims carried over from adolescence.

8 Unrealistic vocational values, especially concerning prestige and autonomy.

The choice problem varies greatly by sex, especially among noncollege youth. For females, it is only something to do until they get married. And while attitudes toward women in the labor force are shifting, the future social status of a noncollege female still depends on her husband's occupation, not hers. In contrast, for men, occupation determines status in the community.

Whatever the choice, occupation often is related to consumption patterns, particularly of socially visible products, as we shall explore in Chapter Eight under the discussion of social class.

In Figure 5-1, we showed that role changes are almost inevitable during early adulthood. Indeed, in our society there is a strong socialization to marriage as a desired goal. Thus, for both college and post-high school young adults, marriage choice leads to a focus on dating activities that consume much leisure time and much psychic energy, whether or not the final choice is to marry or not to marry. The marriage choice also leads to a focus on physical appearance as well as to a number of other premarital interests and activities.

Activities and Interests

Typically, individuals carry over into early adulthood many of the interests and activities acquired during adolescence or even during childhood. Interests change, however, as they become less appropriate to the adult role.

Money Interest in money among premarried adults is similar to that of adolescents. Money is more for immediate use than for planning or saving for the future. One notable exception is the engaged girl who buys a lot of items for the "hope chest." Mainly, though, the premarrieds are interested in money because they want to have and to do what their reference group has and does. Again, as in adolescence, the reference group is usually peers—but sometimes parents, as revealed in the following self-description by one of the author's former graduate students:

> For about one year after graduation from undergraduate work, I had the blessed classification of being single, and, therefore, foot-loose and fancy-free. I had a decent job, money burned a hole in my pocket, charge accounts were available, so I indulged myself at every opportunity. As a single man, I lived at home and paid no rent, had very few regular bills (clothes cleaning and gas only), so my money was mine to spend. (According to some writers on life cycle and consumer behavior, I was not really a separate consumption unit, since I was living at home. However, for many products I was a distinct unit, and for my purposes here, I will count myself as a spending/consuming unit.)
>
> Although my parents had started off in the upper-lower, or lower-middle social class, as far as income, living accommodations, and material possessions were concerned, by the time I entered junior high school, they had advanced on all class scales to the middle-middle or even the upper-middle class. Both of their parents had been in this social class, so from the standpoint of cultural and social measurements, they had finally equated themselves to their proper social class.
>
> Since I was very accustomed to living like a person in the upper-middle class, I saw no reason to change things, although my salary certainly was nowhere near a level that would maintain living like this, as I was soon to find out. (This is probably the main reason that some writers do not consider the single person living at home a separate consumer unit.)
>
> During my short spree, I managed to buy much in the way of new clothes, a new car, squander most of the money and save a little (very little). The clothes and car were both purchased from local retail outlets which I had frequented when my

> father was paying the bill. As I later learned, these were some of the most expensive places in town for the quality received, but even if I had known this at the time, it would have made little difference.
>
> My actions bore out the fact that I felt I had to keep up with my parents and with all of the other young people my age (place in the life cycle). Everything had to be just as good (or at least very nearly as good) as what my father bought, or already owned, while on the other hand, it had to be the latest style, fashion, or be as sporty as what others my age had.
>
> My sphere of reference at this stage in my life cycle was very limited, since I had generally been raised in one particular group (social class) and had attended a college made up of people from basically the same overall social background. Economics played no role in my behavior except as the uppermost limit, which I did not reach since my income could easily satisfy my every whim.

Recreations and Amusements Many of the recreations and amusements of premarrieds are centered around the "dating game." Male interests become more girl-oriented and female interests become more boy-oriented but to a lesser degree.

Young unmarried adults often go to the *movies* on dates, as they did in adolescence. And while groups of girls go together, unmarried males are not too interested in movies except as a date site. *Dancing* is also important for its role in dates, and also of much more intrinsic interest to females than to males. *Music* maintains a high level of interest among premarried adults. Not only is it necessary for dancing, but young adults listen to recordings frequently as a way of relieving feelings of boredom or loneliness. The preference is mostly for popular music, as in adolescence.

There is less participation in *sports* by males because school facilities are not available, school routine does not demand it, and it no longer is the single most important road to status. The sports interests that remain generally are of either a passive nature (attending a football game) or an individual nature, such as tennis or golf among the white-collar unmarrieds and hunting and bowling among the blue-collar unmarrieds.

In general, leisure activities become more individualized during early adulthood. When youth moves from an age-graded, school-regulated society to a status-graded society, ready-made activities and ready-made groups suddenly evaporate. In turn, the young adults must provide for their own recreation, including paying for it, and must find compatible friends to replace those conveniently at hand during high school.

Physical Appearance Interest in physical appearance remains strong during young adulthood, as it was in adolescence. The continuing high level of interest is a result of similar but subtly different influences, however. For the adolescent, with rapidly changing physique, the interest is related to the desire for popularity and peer group acceptance. For the premarried, with physique pretty much established, the interest primarily is related to the "dating game"—to the desire for acceptance by the opposite sex—as expressed in the use of items of personal adornment and cosmetic applications to enhance good features and camouflage the less attractive ones.

For this reason there has been a more or less continuous line of critical commentary (directed mainly at the female) running from the Old Testament through the medieval moralists to Shakespeare ("The harlot's cheek beautified with plastering art") to modern times. The epitome of this line of criticism is found in the following quotation from a law passed by the British Parliament in 1770:

> All women, of whatever age, rank, profession or degree, whether virgins, maids or widows, that shall impose upon, seduce or betray into matrimony any of His Majesty's subjects, by scents, paints, cosmetics, washes, artificial teeth, false hair, iron stave hoops, high-heeled shoes, bolstered hips, or padded bosoms shall incur the penalty of the law enforced against witchcraft and like misdemeanors and, upon conviction, that marriage stand null and void.[2]

But, as Murray Wax (1957: 593) has emphasized:

> The function of grooming in our society is understandable from the perspective of sociability, not of sexuality. A woman grooms herself to appear as a desirable sexual object, not necessarily as an attainable one. In grooming herself, she is preparing to play the part of the beauty, not the part of the erotically passionate woman. In this sense, cosmetics and grooming serve to transmute the attraction between the sexes from a raw physical relationship into a civilized game.
>
> Some may carp at the game, feeling that activity should be functional and that beauty should therefore denote the superior female, the ideal sex partner and mother. Here the question becomes evaluative: Should cosmetics and grooming be judged as a form of play, engaging and entertaining its participants, or should they serve a nobler purpose?

But whether the importance-of-appearance role of clothing and grooming for the dating game is viewed as good, bad, or indifferent from a moral standpoint, it always has and probably always will be an important artifact of human nature.

In addition to the role of clothing in the dating game, there is an increased use of items of personal appearance among young adults as an indication of status, a symbolic expression of occupational group identity. This role is especially prominent among those who are vocationally and socially mobile, such as many college students, the topic of the next section.

COLLEGE STUDENTS

As noted in the chapter introduction, one episode that strongly conditions people's behavior as consumers is the choice to continue formal education

[2]Quoted in *The Marketing News,* 1 (Jan. 1, 1968), p. 1.

beyond high school. A choice for post-high school training affects behavior both in the present and in the future, not only of those attaining the education but also of those not attaining it.

There are several compelling reasons for examining the college market as present-day consumers. One is the large number of young adults attending college—a result of a larger proportion of young adults who enter college today than in previous generations and a larger number of young adults in the population. Data in Table 5-5 show that enrollment in institutions of higher education jumped from 1.5 million in 1940 to 8.6 million in 1973. In 1940, only 16 percent of those persons who graduated from high school entered college; today the figure is over 43 percent. In essence, there are a lot of college students, absolutely and relatively, as compared with past decades.

A second reason for considering the "now" behavior of college students is their spending power and expenditures. Exclusive of educational costs and room and board, the college market represented persons with an aggregate income of over 9 billion dollars in 1969, or, on the average, $1,300 per student in disposable income. While this figure may seem low when compared to per capita disposable income of the population in 1969 ($3,130), it should be noted that college students have fewer taxes and minimum food and medical expenses. Thus "disposable" is truly disposable for this group.

How is this 9 billion dollars spent? Data in Table 5-6 show that it goes mainly for entertainment, clothes and toiletries, and automobile gas and accessories—just the sort of things found important to the dating game. And these data do not include the items purchased to take along to college, such things as towels and bedspreads, luggage, irons, pens and typewriters, calculators, cameras, and tennis racquets.

Another important dimension of the college market is that increased education is a passkey to higher-paying, higher-status occupations. Thus, over the remainder of the life span, the college-trained youth can expect to earn considerably more and spend considerably more than from the noncollege-trained youth and to spend it differently. This obvious relationship takes on new meaning, however, in the context of today's larger college enrollment.

College youth also affect the life styles of noncollege youth and even of older adults, as they represent the experimenters with new ideas that later

Table 5-5 College Enrollment, 1940–1973 (In Millions)

Year	Number
1940	1.5
1950	2.3
1960	3.6
1970	7.4
1972	8.3
1973	8.6

Source: Wattenberg (1974:58).

Table 5-6 How Disposable Income Is Spent (Average per Student)

Category	Males	Females
Auto	$ 272	$ 192
Clothing	220	300
Entertainment	400	350
Toiletries	80	120
Travel	50	75
Other	268	253
Totals	1290	1290

Source: Taylor (1969:5).

diffuse to other youth and to many older persons. Much has been written about the "new morality" (or old immorality, if you prefer) of college youth during the period 1967–1974. To gain a perspective, consider the following major changes between the late 1960s and early 1970s documented by Yankelovich (1974: 3–5):

Late 1960s	Early 1970s
The campus rebellion is in full flower.	The campus rebellion is moribund.
New life styles and radical politics appear together: granny glasses, crunchy granola, commune-living, pot smoking, and long hair seem inseparable from radical politics, sit-ins, student strikes, protest marches, draft card burnings.	An almost total divorce takes place between radical politics and new life styles.
A central theme on campus: the search for self-fulfillment in place of a conventional career.	A central theme on campus: how to find self-fulfillment within a conventional career.
Growing criticism of America as a "sick society."	Lessening criticism of America as a "sick society."
The Women's Movement has virtually no impact on youth values and attitudes.	Wide and deep penetration of Women's Liberation precepts is under way.
Violence on campus is condoned and romanticized, there are many acts of violence.	Violence-free campuses; the use of violence, even to achieve worthwhile objectives, is rejected.
The value of education is severely questioned.	The value of education is strongly endorsed.
A widening "generation gap" appears in values, morals, and outlook, dividing young people (especially college youth) from their parents.	The younger generation and older mainstream America move closer together in values, morals, and outlook.
A sharp split in social and moral values is found within the youth generation, between college students and the noncollege majority. The gap within the generation proves to be larger and more severe than the gap between the generations.	The gap within the generation narrows. Noncollege youth has virtually caught up with college students in adopting the new social and moral norms.
A new code of sexual morality, centering on greater acceptance of casual premarital sex, abortions, homosexuality, and extra-	The new sexual morality spreads both to mainstream college youth and also to mainstream working-class youth.

Late 1960s	Early 1970s
marital relations, is confined to a minority of college students.	
The challenge to the traditional work ethic is confined to the campus.	The work ethic appears strengthened on campus but is growing weaker among noncollege youth.
Harsh criticisms of major institutions, such as political parties, big business, the military, etc., are almost wholly confined to college students.	Criticisms of some major institutions are tempered on campus but are taken up by the working-class youth.
The universities and the military are major targets of criticism.	Criticism of the universities and the military decreases sharply.
The campus is the main locus of youthful discontent; noncollege youth is quiescent.	Campuses are quiescent, but many signs of latent discontent and dissatisfaction appear among working-class youth.
Much youthful energy and idealism is devoted to concern with minorities.	Concern for minorities lessens.
The political center of gravity of college youth: left/liberal.	No clear-cut political center of gravity: pressures in both directions, left and right.
The New Left is a force on campus: there are growing numbers of radical students.	The New Left is a negligible factor on campus: the number of radical students declines sharply.
Concepts of law and order are anathema to college students.	College students show greater acceptance of law and order requirements.
The student mood is angry, embittered, and bewildered by public hostility.	There are few signs of anger or bitterness and little overt concern with public attitudes toward students.

Based, in part, on Yankelovich surveys among cross sections of the general population.

In assessing these changes, Yankelovich (1974:7) concludes: "If there are any patterns which underlie the dense variety of findings described in the main body of this report, they are the story of the transmission of the New Values from the campus to the mainstream of American youth, the efforts of both college and noncollege youth to find a satisfactory means of blending the new values with older, more traditional beliefs, and the search for new modes of adaption to the highly institutionalized structure of American society."

To the conclusion that college youth are in many ways life style pacesetters, a foonote should be added. The life styles of youth, whether hip or straight, do not mean a rejection of spending; new life styles may imply a new materialism (buying sailboats rather than motorboats, vans rather than convertibles), but not the absence of material possessions.

YOUNG MARRIEDS

It is no secret, of course, that when a young man and a young woman decide to get married, they trigger a vast amount of economic activity that continues throughout their remaining lives. Consider, for instance, a brief time span before and after marriage:

> In short, only one simple thought: the formation of a "family," starting at the moment of betrothal, triggers an astonishing spurt of economic activity. It is difficult to measure the entire breadth and scope of that activity, but to give just a flavor of how it is at its beginning, consider projections from a 1972 study by Trendex dealing with the brief six-month period surrounding a marriage (three months before and three months after). Persons involved in that frenetic family-forming situation comprise only 2.5 percent of all households. Yet they represent sales amounting to 58 percent of the total for sterling flatware, 25 percent of total bedroom furniture sales, 41 percent of stereo and hi-fi equipment, 11 percent of hard surface floor coverings, 27 percent of sewing machines, 12 percent of refrigerators, 16 percent of vacuum cleaners, 13 percent of electric blankets (pre-energy crisis data), 9 percent of clothes dryers, and so on—and of course, 100 percent of wedding gowns, . . . These numbers reflect the fact that of all the life-stages people go through, the most economically intense time surrounds the actual time of marriage. But that, of course, is still only the intense beginning. The spending goes on and on through the early years of marriage (Wattenberg, 1974:52).

Marriage is not only an economically intense time, it is an emotionally intense aspect of the period of intimacy; it is a transition period which involves many adjustments to new roles.

The Transition

Figure 5-1 positions marriage prior to the pair-centered role of adulthood. And so it is. The first months or the first year of marriage is a crucial time because in a very real sense it represents a move into a new culture—a transition into new roles. Only occasionally has courtship or going steady (the dating game) prepared the couple for this shift of roles, in terms of either the role tasks or the complexities of role relationships (Perlman, 1968).

From the standpoint of consumer behavior, the transition is more of a problem for the female than for the male, especially for middle-class women. The male generally continues his occupational role as worker or as student preparing to work, while the woman, even if she continues at her occupation, must also undertake the tasks of housekeeper, cook, and domestic manager; overnight she becomes a "homemaker"—a role of obvious importance in purhcasing behavior. Assuming this role is a problem because United States children and adolescents receive little preparation for domestic skills; they simply are on relatively unfamiliar terrain. Lopata (1966:7-8) explains:

> The housewife is not "adequately" trained for the role. . . . Although each young girl usually lives in a home run by her mother up till the time of marriage, the American system of education and occupation removes her from its walls for most of her conscious hours starting at the age of five, and even impinges upon her time within it. Training in "home economics" and the voluntary learning of homemaking skills are not highly evaluated by the society and especially by teen-aged school-work-boy-leisure-oriented girls. Attention tends to be directed "outside" the home, and the focal point of interest in the role cluster of each teen-ager tends to be not a role, but the individual.

> The process of becoming a housewife includes the phase of the learning the various skills used in maintaining the home and relating to those who are involved in its maintenance. The process of shifting identifications and space placements is also important to the young woman. The stress upon the location of the self "inside" the home as opposed to "outside" life roles, or persons, so important to housewives in the next stage of the cycle, begins with a gradual shift of the image of the self from a rather functionally diffused "outside" existence to a role-focused and geographically placed identity within a home.
>
> The newly married bride, still engaged in occupational or school roles typical of the American pattern, sees herself as located outside of the home. Living in her own place is important, but it is seen mostly as part of being a wife, and then in terms of primary relations with the husband, rather than as a potential center of multiple relations. She talks of her life in terms of personality changes and feelings to a degree not used again till very old age.
>
> The role of housewife begins to enter her life pattern with a grow-awareness [sic] of the complexity of duties involved in the role of wife, duties beyond those of primary attitudes, and, with shifting significance, the role of customer. The meaning of money does change, reflecting and perhaps even leading the changes in the role cluster. The role of worker becomes used more instrumentally than before, as a source of obtaining means for housekeeping activities. The role of consumer begins to involve purchasing for a unit, budgeting, and accounting to the self for expenditures. The role of customer no longer serves only the ends of personal pleasure and adornment. Although "fixing up the apartment" is accomplished with external eyes, the process of bringing the self and purchases "inside" the house begins to acquire a symbolic tone.
>
> The shifting of roles into new clusters often results in the placement of the role of wife in the center, and in the pushing of the roles of daughter, worker, and colleague into the background. The role of housewife or "homemaker" and of consumer are gradually pulled into the foreground.

During the beginning of this transition, the past has an important influence. While, as Lopata notes, homemaking skills are not valued highly in our society, homemaking does not suddenly begin at the time a woman marries. Rather, homemaking has its antecedents in early life, when the homemaker is still a child. Our culture encourages little girls to play "house," to pretend they are keeping house in the way their mothers do. Through play-acting of this sort, children learn to experiment with various kinds of homemaking roles. They are "preparing" themselves for the real-life adult role to come.

The influence of this earlier period of play-acting at homemaking, reinforced by the poor formal training in adolescence, is especially marked among women in the early years of marriage. As they go through the process of "shifting identifications" described above, their interests shift. But during the early part of the transition, the childhood fantasies about what it means to "keep house" linger on or gain new impetus, influencing the homemaker's attitudes and behavior toward what she wants to achieve in the new role. The ideal tends to be to establish a home which fulfills girlhood fantasies.

For example, a *Better Homes and Gardens* research report ("Today's

Changing Consumer") illustrates this type of influence in the case where recently married women manifest a strong attachment to their mothers. The report indicated that homemaking, for these women, is a way of being like mother and remaining close to her. These women are especially attracted to furnishings which seem feminine, beautiful, delicate, and light in appearance and meaning. They enjoy taking people on "tours" about their homes and "showing off" their furnishings. They are fond of ornamental styles, with many fancy flourishes and curving lines, and they strive to surround themselves with objects of this sort.

Women of this sort are most readily motivated by appeals to their sense of vanity and their wish to adorn their homes in a way that would make them feel like "queens." Colors and fashions that women know about are items which especially interest them, and they are eager to learn more about them. Families—husband and children—are less central to their concerns. They want their husband to take little active part in selecting furnishings, but they need their husband to serve as an admiring audience (they are inclined to feel relatively lonely and isolated from neighbors and female friends). They tend to have few or no children, have problems disciplining the children they do have, and regard the changing needs of their family as having relatively little influence on their decisions to buy furnishings. All in all, children seem to spoil some of the fun these homemakers derive from their home furnishings and home life.

To a large extent, contemporary society seems to be redefining the role of the housefrau. While most young women want to and do play the role of wife and mother when they reach adulthood, they do not necessarily want to do so in a traditional sense of being subordinate to their husbands. Indeed, many are opting for more egalitarian sex roles or those that stress similar behavior patterns for men and women (see Figure 5-2). The reason for wanting to avoid playing the traditional female role has been explained by Arnott and Bengtson (1970:495):

> The role of "homemaker" is undervalued in the United States where occupation is the key to the assignment of role status, and achievement and monetary value tend to provide the criteria for social ranking. In contemporary America, women tend to absorb the same values as the men with whom they are educated, and to use these men as reference persons in comparing role rewards. Educated women in the "homemaker only" role may feel a sense of "relative deprivation" in the distribution of social status. A "homemaker-plus" role (such as the addition of employment to home duties) may promise greater social recognition.

And, somewhat ironically, their ability to opt for nontraditional feminine roles has been fostered by technology and marketing. The convenience of prepared foods and household labor-saving devices reduces the time *and* the skills it once took to run a household. Perhaps the feeling of "relative depriviation" is an illusion fostered not only by socialization and status

Figure 5-2 Concepts of Adult Sex Roles

Traditional Concepts

Traditional concepts of sex roles empahsize a prescribed pattern of behavior regardless of individual interests or abilities. They emphasize masculine supremacy and intolerance toward any trait that hints of femininity or any work that is considered woman's work.

Men

Outside the home the man holds positions of authority and prestige in the social and business worlds; in the home he is the wage earner, decision maker, adviser and disciplinarian of the children, and model of masculinity for his sons.

Women

Both in the home and outside, the role of the woman is other-oriented in that she gains fulfillment by serving others. She is not expected to work outside the home except in cases of financial necessity, and then she does only work that serves others, such as nursing, teaching, or secretarial work.

Egalitarian Concepts

Egalitarian concepts of sex roles emphasize individuality and the egalitarian status of men and women. Rules should lead to personal fulfillment and not be considered appropriate for only one sex.

Men

In the home and outside, the man works with the woman in a companionship relationship. He does not feel "henpecked" if he treats his wife as an equal, nor does he feel ashamed if she has a more prestigious or remunerative job than he does.

Women

Both in the home and outside, the woman is able to actualize her own potentials. She does not feel guilty about using her abilities and training to give her satisfaction, even if this requires employing someone else to take care of the home and children.

Source: Hurlock (1975:223).

recognition but also by a lot of time with which to become bored, restless, and self-searching.

It is true that many women today give (or at least would like to give) the nontraditional role a try. In the 1975 Needham, Harper & Steers Life Style Survey women were asked:

> In today's society there are many different life styles, and some are acceptable today that weren't in the past. Regardless of what you may have done or plan to do with your life, and thinking just of what would give you personally the most satisfying and interesting life, which one of these different ways of life do you think would be best as a way of life?
>
> **1** A traditional marriage with the husband assuming the responsibility for providing for the family and the wife running the house and taking care of the children.
>
> **2** A marriage where husband and wife share responsibilities more—both work, both share homemaking and child responsibilities.
>
> **3** Some other arrangement, such as staying single, living with a group of other persons, etc.

A majority (54 percent) of women opted for the egalitarian role, number 2; 45 percent for the traditional; and only 17 out of 1,797 (1 percent) preferred some other arrangement. Many of these egalitarians flock out of their homes to take courses, to give courses, to work for money, or to work as volunteers—all seeking to experience themselves as competent over and beyond marriage (Table 5-7). And, as Perlman (1968) has observed and the data in Table 5-7 confirm, some succeed and take pleasure in their sense of self-discovery and competence; others succeed but at the cost of chronic tension in themselves or stress created in other family members; and still others find the outside orientation was not what it promised to be and return to marriage and motherhood as their chief source of self-expression and gratification.

Working Wives

Whether from a traditional or a nontraditional orientation, the working-wife phenomenon also is very real; and when wives are working, it subsantially affects both the ability of the family to purchase and consume as well as the distribution of family expenditures. Not all working wives are young marrieds. But a larger proportion of young married women are working than any other proportion. For this reason, we discuss the consumption implications of working wives in this section.

Reasons for Working While in general a working wife's income is not as great as her husband's, it is often large enough to move the family up in income class; for example, if total family income is in the $7,000–$10,000 category when the husband is the sole earner, it often jumps to the $10,000–$15,000 class when income is earned by both husband and wife.

This increment to the family income is one of the reasons wives work, and it is especially important as an influence on consumer behavior because it often is discretionary income. In many families the husband's income provides the necessities while the wife's income provides the extras.

But many wives get more out of their jobs than just a paycheck to add to their husband's. For women who do not have the traditional feminine orienta-

Table 5-7 Some Traditional-Egalitarian Differences

	% Agreeing	
Statement or activity	Traditional	Egalitarian
	%	%
Attended school at least once during the past year	22	32
Attended a lecture at least once last year	35	42
Gave a speech at least once last year	23	30
Brought work home at least once during the past year	22	41
Employed (at least part time) outside the home	26	56
If I had my life to live over, I would sure do things differently	47	54
I wish I could leave my present life and do something entirely different	22	30
I often wish for the good old days	55	50

Data source: Needham, Harper & Steers, (1975).

tion toward homemaking and children, a job outside the home is both an escape from boredom and drudgery and a positive source of self-actualization. These women do not want to spend all their time "staring at four walls." They enjoy other things and place a higher priority on them than did their mothers and grandmothers.

The discretionary income that a second paycheck provides and the chance to escape into the wider world provided by a job outside the home supplement each other as reasons for working. Together they are a more powerful force than either one working alone.

Effect on Consumer Behavior Because income from the second paycheck is more discretionary than income from the first, two-earner families are able to afford more luxuries. Compared with families in which the husband is the only earner, families with both husband and wife working spend proportionately more on food away from home, on convenience foods such as frozen fruits and vegetables, on small appliances, on entertainment, and on vacation travel.

They also spend more on some products that are luxuries in one sense and necessities in another. They spend more on transportation, partly because the working wife must get to and from work. They spend more on women's medical and group life insurance, on laundry and dry cleaning, and, of course, on baby-sitting and housecleaning services (National Industrial Conference Board, 1967; and Bureau of Advertising, 1972).

A job outside the home affects the wife's pattern of exposure to advertising media. If it is a full-time job, her exposure to daytime weekday television is drastically curtailed. Even when the job is not full-time, the working wife is apt to spend little time with daytime television because her household duties must be compressed into the fewer at-home hours that are available.

Compared with full-time homemakers, working wives read more and somewhat different types of magazines. They spend less time with magazines devoted to cooking, sewing, and other homemaking activities and more time with magazines that deal with fashion, home decoration, and news of what is going on in the wider outside world. In part this difference in reading preferences must reflect the varied sources of stimulation a working wife receives. It probably also reflects the basic difference in orientation that faces some women toward home and children and some women toward the world outside.

Interests and Activities

As pointed out in the premarried section, interests of the young married change from those appropriate to adolescence to those more congruent with adult roles. And they become more individualized, that is, less pervasive. Still, young marrieds maintain a high level of interest and a high degree of involvement in many things when compared with later stages in the life span. In this section we highlight the interests and activities of young marrieds, using age-graded data from nationwide life style surveys of American consumers.

Physical Appearance The young married's interest in physical appearance remains strong as a carry-over from premarried days. Basically, the reasons are the same—sociability and status.

Data in Tables 5-8 and 5-9 show the relatively high degree of interest among young marrieds in personal adornment and self. Young women and men under twenty-five years of age tell us that dressing well is important, that they want to look a little different from others, and that they like to feel attractive to members of the opposite sex. Young marrieds, of course, do not yet have the income to dress in more stylish clothing or to wear expensive cologne to the degree that older consumers do.

The tables also show that young marrieds remain highly interested in being social. They often visit friends in the evening, like parties, dislike quiet evenings at home when a party is available, and do not consider themselves homebodies when compared with consumers in later age groups.

Being social, of course, is an interest in and of itself. But its importance to understanding consumer behavior lies more in its impact on interest in physical appearance and related purchasing of items of personal adornment than as a sociological topic.

Money and Material Possessions To be active socially and to keep up to date fashionwise takes money. Young marrieds not only express high interest in money, they have a lot of it. Not as much as they will have later in life, of course; but with more husbands and wives working and before child-related expenditures become necessary, they do not mind spending what they earn, and they are really better off financially than they will be in the near future.

Tables 5-8 and 5-9 show that this group of consumers are financially optimistic. Their view toward future income is more positive than that of any other age group in the adult population, and their view toward personal equity suggests that they spend accordingly.

They want many material things, and the things they want, and buy, carry considerable symbolic value—living, dining, and bedroom furniture; TV sets and appliances; rugs, carpeting, and draperies. It is not just wanting these things that is important economically; rather, young couples must have them to start their new household. Further, marriage precipitates a philosophy of impulsiveness, self-expression, and self-gratification in the home. It is a time for saying, "Let's enjoy our furnishings now, while we can, before we start a family." This philosophy is suggested by the data in Tables 5-8 and 5-9, where young housewives and husbands do not say (when compared with other groups) that they choose comfort over style in furnishing their homes.

In addition to home-related durables, young marrieds are especially likely to buy a car if one of them does not have a car already, and a second car if they do not already own two at the time of marriage. This statement, of course, does not mean they buy a second car immediately after marriage, or ever, for that matter. Rather, car ownership is disproportionately higher for married couples with no children when compared with ownership of all families or of single

Table 5-8 Female Interests and Opinions (Percent Agreeing by Age Group)

Statement	Sample total	Age group: Under 25	25–34	34–44	44–54	55 and older
Optimism and happiness						
My greatest achievements are still ahead of me	64%	92%	84%	73%	52%	28%
I dread the future	23	20	18	17	24	30
I am much happier now than I ever was before	79	85	82	80	74	74
Modern – traditional ideas						
I have somewhat old-fashioned tastes and habits	86	78	84	87	88	89
There is too much emphasis on sex today	87	70	74	90	89	93
I like to think I am a bit of a swinger	26	43	34	26	19	15
A woman's place is in the home	46	39	39	44	49	60
The working world is no place for a woman	17	15	11	14	19	28
Young people have too many privileges	76	57	74	77	76	83
The U.S. would be better off if there were no hippies	55	32	37	46	54	82
My days seem to follow a definite routine – eating meals at the same time each day, etc.	67	59	62	61	67	75
Travel						
I would like to take a trip about the world	67	78	83	73	65	51
I would like to spend a year in London or Paris	34	38	40	34	34	25
I would feel lost if I were alone in a foreign country	68	66	66	64	68	76
I like to visit places that are totally different from my home	85	85	83	86	82	88
Mobile						
We will probably move at least once in the next five years	38	71	53	27	28	23
Our family has moved more often than most of our neighbors have	24	36	32	26	18	17
Anxious						
I have trouble getting to sleep	33	29	24	26	33	49
I wish I knew how to relax	52	51	49	49	51	59
Personal adornment and self						
Dressing well is an important part of my life	81	84	80	78	79	83
I like to feel attractive to members of the opposite sex	85	93	91	77	82	72
I want to look a little different from others	69	71	78	70	63	72
I often wear expensive cologne	28	19	24	28	27	33

Table 5-8 Female Interests and Opinions (Percent Agreeing by Age Group) (Continued)

Statement	Sample total	Age group: Under 25	25–34	34–44	44–54	55 and older
I have more stylish clothes than most of my friends	30%	31%	34%	27%	29%	27%
View toward income, personal equity, and spending						
I will probably have more money to spend next year than I have now	45	71	70	58	53	30
Five years from now our family income will probably be a lot higher than it is now	65	87	85	75	61	26
Our family income is high enough to satisfy nearly all our important desires	74	59	66	78	78	80
No matter how fast our income goes up we never seem to get ahead	53	62	65	61	47	32
Investing in the stock market is too risky for most families	86	79	83	82	85	87
Our family is too heavily in debt today	27	36	33	37	23	11
I like to pay cash for everything I buy	77	83	79	74	71	77
I pretty much spend for today and let tomorrow bring what it will	22	33	21	22	25	18
Staying at home						
I would rather spend a quiet evening at home than go out to a party	65	50	66	64	68	78
I am a homebody	69	59	65	64	72	79
I stay home most evenings	83	81	95	80	83	83
Husband and children						
A wife's first obligation is to her husband, not her children	69	53	65	74	74	76
When children are ill in bed, parents should drop everything else to see to their comfort	74	61	71	73	80	83
Children are the most important thing in a marriage	52	42	44	49	56	64
When making important family decisions, consideration of the children should come first	54	69	58	44	48	56
A wife should have a great deal of information about her husband's work	82	83	84	75	88	85
View toward durable goods						
Our home is furnished for comfort, not for style	90	83	88	88	94	94
If I must choose, I buy stylish rather than practical furniture	17	19	31	13	15	15
When buying appliances, I am more concerned with dependability than price	90	85	89	89	89	94
A subcompact car can meet my transportation needs	66	85	74	60	61	57

Table 5-8 Female Interests and Opinions (Percent Agreeing by Age Group) (Continued)

Statement	Sample total	Under 25	25–34	34–44	44–54	55 and older
		Age group				
Housekeeping and cooking						
When I see a full ashtray or wastebasket, I want it emptied immediately	71%	77%	70%	72%	64%	64%
I am uncomfortable when the house is not completely clean	67	76	67	70	61	68
The kind of dirt you can't see is worse than the kind you can see	77	77	72	73	79	85
I am a good cook	91	93	92	88	90	91
I like to cook	87	91	88	84	85	87
I like to bake	40	43	43	42	39	38
Meal preparation should take as little time as possible	42	42	41	40	41	44
Grocery shopping						
Shopping is no fun anymore	54	49	43	58	55	51
Before going shopping, I sit down and prepare a complete shopping list	72	68	73	71	69	74
I try to stick to well-known brands	74	58	67	71	82	86
I find myself checking prices even on small items	90	89	93	92	89	86
I like to save and redeem savings stamps	75	72	70	70	75	83
I pay a lot more attention to food prices now than I ever did before	90	92	91	88	88	87
I am an impulse buyer	38	39	40	37	42	27
I shop a lot for specials	84	85	86	83	84	81
Health and nutrition						
I am very concerned about nutrition	87	87	89	87	82	89
I am concerned about how much salt I eat	56	52	55	56	50	66
I am careful what I eat in order to keep my weight under control	57	63	57	58	62	68
I try to avoid foods that are high in cholesterol	62	37	53	60	65	79
I try to avoid foods that have additives in them	56	45	52	57	53	62
I get more headaches than most people	28	30	31	28	27	22
I eat more than I should	70	68	70	75	73	69

Data source: Needham, Harper & Steers, (1975).

persons with no children. Data in Table 5-10 show the degree of car ownership for these groups and how the growth in ownership has increased during the two time periods. Also, young marrieds are more likely than other age groups to buy a subcompact car.

In general, the formation of a family requires couples to acquire a lot of durables—things to sleep on, to eat with, and to get about in. It is not surprising, then, that studies of family expenditures by stage in the family life cycle

Table 5-9 Male Interests and Opinions (Percent Agreeing by Age Group)

Statement	Sample total	Age group: Under 25	25–34	34–44	44–54	55 and older
Optimism and happiness						
My greatest achievements are still ahead of me	64%	98%	93%	76%	55%	25%
I dread the future	20	21	19	19	23	23
I am much happier now than I ever was before	78	87	92	97	76	74
Modern – traditional ideas						
I have somewhat old-fashioned tastes and habits	85	73	78	84	92	89
There is too much emphasis on sex today	66	56	65	74	81	93
I like to think I am a bit of a swinger	31	51	43	29	26	15
A woman's place is in the home	54	45	52	53	52	62
The working world is no place for a woman	27	24	20	25	26	37
Young people have too many privileges	75	60	63	77	74	88
The U.S. would be better off if there were no hippies	59	33	38	57	67	81
My days seem to follow a definite routine – eating meals at the same time each day, etc.	63	50	53	59	67	76
All men should be clean shaven every day	67	47	55	66	75	85
Travel						
I would like to take a trip around the world	67	74	73	77	68	53
I would like to spend a year in London or Paris	34	38	39	40	32	23
I would feel lost if I were alone in a foreign country	52	59	46	47	44	67
I like to visit places that are totally different from my home	72	80	73	75	73	67
Mobile						
We will probably move at least once in the next five years	37	75	52	28	23	20
Our family has moved more often than most of our neighbors have	22	27	30	23	18	17
Anxious						
I have trouble getting to sleep	24	20	20	23	25	30
I wish I knew how to relax	47	40	48	51	44	50
Personal adornment and self						
Dressing well is an important part of my life	72	70	73	72	72	67
I like to feel attractive to members of the opposite sex	81	87	87	87	66	74
I want to look a little different from others	55	74	62	55	49	42

Table 5-9 Male Interests and Opinions (Percent Agreeing by Age Group) (Continued)

Statement	Sample total	Age group: Under 25	25-34	34-44	44-54	55 and older
I often wear expensive cologne	14%	16%	14%	12%	15%	13%
I have more stylish clothes than most of my friends	25	24	26	28	24	22
View toward income, personal equity, and spending						
I will probably have more money to spend next year than I have now	56	74	65	64	58	29
Five years from now our family income will probably be a lot higher than it is now	68	87	85	79	69	28
Our family income is high enough to satisfy nearly all our important desires	75	63	72	78	78	79
No matter how fast our income goes up we never seem to get ahead	58	60	68	56	52	39
Investing in the stock market is too risky for most families	83	86	82	81	87	86
Our family is too heavily in debt today	28	41	42	28	25	11
I like to pay cash for everything I buy	75	79	74	70	69	81
I pretty much spend for today and let tomorrow bring what it will	26	31	29	23	23	26
Staying at home						
I would rather spend a quiet evening at home than go out to a party	73	65	67	73	75	79
I am a homebody	72	55	67	73	79	82
I stay home most evenings	80	70	77	79	78	89
Husband and children						
A wife's first obligation is to her husband, not her children	57	43	52	54	64	66
When children are ill in bed, parents should drop everything else to see to their comfort	70	66	68	66	73	78
Children are the most important thing in a marriage	53	37	44	50	57	78
When making important family decisions, consideration of the children should come first	53	63	54	48	49	53
A wife should have a great deal of information about her husband's work	77	74	75	73	80	82
Our family is a close-knit group	87	86	94	89	83	88
View toward durable goods						
Our home is furnished for comfort, not for style	93	89	92	94	95	94
If I must choose, I buy stylish rather than practical furniture	15	18	20	14	15	9
When buying appliances, I am more concerned with dependability than price	93	91	93	90	94	95

Table 5-9 Male Interests and Opinions (Percent Agreeing by Age Group) (Continued)

Statement	Sample total	Age group: Under 25	25–34	34–44	44–54	55 and older
When buying appliances, the brand name is more important than the reputation of the store	56%	56%	53%	49%	55%	64%
A subcompact car can meet my transportation needs	59	71	57	56	58	57
Housekeeping and cooking						
When I see a full ashtray or wastebasket, I want it emptied immediately	56	56	46	54	60	63
I am uncomfortable when the house is not completely clean	51	57	48	53	49	52
The kind of dirt you can't see is worse than the kind you can see	77	68	74	73	79	86
I am a good cook	51	63	57	50	48	41
I like to cook	50	60	58	48	48	41
I like to bake	30	34	35	27	26	30
Meal preparation should take as little time as possible	42	42	41	38	40	46
Grocery shopping						
Shopping is no fun anymore	59	54	55	55	63	64
Before going shopping, I sit down and prepare a complete shopping list	44	35	42	38	38	56
I try to stick to well-known brands	79	71	79	76	71	86
I find myself checking prices even on small items	79	78	74	75	78	84
I like to save and redeem savings stamps	43	43	31	35	42	58
I pay a lot more attention to food prices now than I ever did before	81	81	79	81	81	84
I am an impulse buyer	38	46	47	40	33	30
I shop a lot for specials	60	61	59	63	56	61
Health and nutrition						
I am very concerned about nutrition	61	66	65	60	57	63
I am concerned about how much salt I eat	40	28	32	32	46	54
I am careful what I eat in order to keep my weight under control	51	38	43	44	55	64
I try to avoid foods that are high in cholesterol	49	31	42	41	60	63
I try to avoid foods that have additives in them	44	36	35	39	49	56
I get more headaches than most people	17	18	17	19	21	12
I eat more than I should	66	57	67	68	70	64

Data source: Needham, Harper and Steers, (1975).

Table 5-10 Car Ownership by Young Families – Percent Owning

Type of family	Own a car		Own two or more	
	1966	1970	1966	1970
Under age 45				
Single, no children	53	69	5	8
Married, no children	91	96	17	34
All families	79	82	25	28

Source: *Survey of Consumer Finances* (1967, 1970).

inevitably show that young marrieds without children have the highest purchase rate of durables and the highest average expenditures for durables. Nor should it be a big surprise to find that installment debt of these young couples is disproportionately higher than for singles and all families combined—see Table 5-11—and that they are substantially above average in agreeing with, "Our family is too heavily in debt today."

Where do young marrieds put all these durables they have gone into debt for? Many, of course, buy single-family houses, condominiums, and mobile homes. But, as Table 5-12 shows, the majority still rent—usually, an apartment. That substantially more marrieds than singles own a home is a reflection of increased incomes, veterans' benefits, and the like. That a majority still rent, of course, is a reflection of the diversity of income groups within the young marrieds and the fact that not all can fork over the down payment *and* acquire the durables which must come first.

But whether one rents, owns, or has some other arrangement, marriage facilitates an interest in keeping house and grocery shopping for the housewife. Table 5-8 shows that young married females view themselves as meticulous housekeepers and as enjoying grocery shopping, cooking, and baking. They are not overly cautious or lacking confidence in shopping. It is here we see the truth of Lopata's statement, "The role of housewife or 'homemaker' and of consumer are gradually pulled into the foreground."

Recreations and Amusements We have already noted that leisure pursuits become less pervasive and more individualized during early adulthood. Data in Tables 5-13 (for females) and 5-14 (for males) show how true this is. If we

Table 5-11 Installment Debt of Young People (Percent in Debt)

Type of family	Any debt		$2,000 or more	
	1966	1970	1966	1970
Under age 45				
Single, no children	45%	41%	10%	11%
Married, no children	67	63	21	17
All families	49	NA	10	NA

Source: *Survey of Consumer Finances* (1967, 1970).

Table 5-12 Housing of Young People

Type of family	Own 1966	Own 1970	Rent 1966	Rent 1970	Other[a] 1966	Other[a] 1970
Under 45						
Single, no children	9%	14%	59%	78%	32%	8%
Married, no children	35	31	57	59	8	10
All families	62	62	30	31	8	7

[a] Includes trailer owners, families that rent part of another family's dwelling, and families that neither own nor rent.

Source: *Survey of Consumer Finances* (1967, 1970).

define *pervasive* as 80 percent of the population participating in a pursuit at least once during the year, we get the following count: for females under 25, 6 of the 22 leisure pursuits are pervasive; for males, the figure is also 6 and the number becomes still smaller over the life span. Also, it is evident in the tables that the more inactive pastimes are favored by more young adults than the

Table 5-13 Female Leisure Activities (Percent Engaged in by Age Group)

Activity	Sample total	Age group: Under 25	25-34	35-44	45-54	55 and older
Active recreations						
Went for a walk	91%	96%	94%	92%	88%	86%
Went swimming	62	84	80	73	55	31
Went boating	37	44	41	39	37	26
Went bowling	35	54	45	40	30	12
Went camping	30	42	38	36	26	15
Jogged	24	41	30	24	22	13
Played tennis	14	24	23	20	99	2
Went hunting	7	20	8	7	6	3
Went skiing	6	14	8	7	4	0
Went backpacking	3	10	4	3	2	.1
Inactive recreations/hobbies						
Took color photographs	89	97	95	91	87	78
Played a game (monopoly, bingo, etc.)	85	95	95	94	81	77
Played cards	83	93	91	87	80	71
Went on a vacation	77	71	75	79	81	77
Went to the movies	74	95	88	82	71	43
Attended an X-rated movie	20	42	28	20	15	7
Attended a sporting event	53	56	60	63	53	36
Visited an art gallery or museum	49	35	48	57	52	46
Worked on a collection (stamps, coins, etc.)	31	22	27	30	34	36
Went to a classical concert	22	13	14	21	28	30
Went to a pop or rock concert	13	24	18	11	11	5
Went to an auto race	8	16	12	7	6	4

Data source: Needham, Harper & Steers, (1975).

Table 5-14 Male Leisure Activities (Percent Engaged in by Age Group)

Activity	Sample total	Age group: Under 25	25–34	35–44	45–54	55 and older
Active recreations						
Went for a walk	82%	81%	83%	83%	80%	71%
Went swimming	61	82	76	75	67	32
Went boating	44	54	46	51	43	34
Went bowling	36	65	47	42	30	14
Went camping	34	48	41	44	32	18
Jogged	27	43	37	31	19	14
Played tennis	14	26	25	17	7	3
Went hunting	33	53	38	33	30	21
Went skiing	7	14	14	5	4	2
Went backpacking	6	9	10	8	4	2
Inactive recreations/hobbies						
Took color photographs	82	95	91	82	78	70
Played a game (monopoly, bingo, etc.)	79	99	92	86	70	60
Played cards	81	96	91	83	72	69
Went on a vacation	76	66	80	79	81	72
Went to the movies	72	94	89	79	69	42
Attended an X-rated movie	24	44	40	23	21	6
Attended a sporting event	61	64	67	72	64	42
Visited an art gallery or museum	36	24	40	43	37	32
Went to a classical concert	15	9	12	19	16	19
Went to a pop or rock concert	11	26	17	9	6	5
Went to an auto race	11	23	16	10	8	3

Data source: Needham, Harper & Steers, (1975).

active recreations are. More play a game, attend movies, and take photographs than swim, bowl, jog, or camp. And when it comes to organized sports, substantially more participate as spectators than as active participants.

Even so, young marrieds are highly active as compared with later stages in the life span: With few exceptions, both males and females engage more in active and inactive leisure pursuits and social activities; and they participate less in church and community activities and home and garden activities.

But, while they are more active now than they will be in the future, it should be remembered that they are less active than in the past—reflecting the transition into adulthood. Consider reading, for instance. Young adults read less than adolescents because they no longer have school assignments and they are busy at work. And while they spend more time on magazines and newspapers, they read books less. Males like newspapers better than magazines, and women, in keeping with their new role, prefer magazines to papers. There are, of course, class differences in readership. For example, upper-class adults read more serious books—more nonfiction; lower-class adults read more fiction. Class differences will be discussed in more detail in the chapter on subculture.

YOUNG PARENTS

Having struggled through adolescence and "mooned" through the pair-centered issue intimacy, young adults come—soon, in our modern world—to parenthood, the next major issue in the life span.

Parenthood

The arrival of children fosters many changes in the behavior of persons, as well as in their needs and their behavior as consumers. Before documenting these changes, the role of parenthood is discussed: the nature of the role change, its meaning, and its importance.

Role Change Parenthood affects both husbands and wives. As indicated in Figure 5-1, there must be a shift from pair-centered to family-centered roles.

For the wife, there is an increased importance in the role of homemaker. This increase begins with pregnancy. Outside roles, especially employment roles, fade out for most women. For both men and women, employment rates are lowest among the very young and the old. But whereas for men employment rates follow a regular curve, peaking in the 35–44 age bracket, for women the curve takes a dip in the age range 25–34.

The reason for the dip in female employment is, of course, the presence of young children who need care. This effect is shown most clearly when the population is divided into married and unmarried, and when divided to show the presence of children, as in Figure 5-3.

In 1969, the employment rate of all married women (with husband present) was 39.6 percent. Among married women with no children—a group that includes older women as well as young women who have not had a child—the rate was 41 percent. Among married women with all children over six, the rate was 48.6 percent. And among married women with at least one child six years of age or younger, the rate was 28.5 percent. This rate is low compared with the

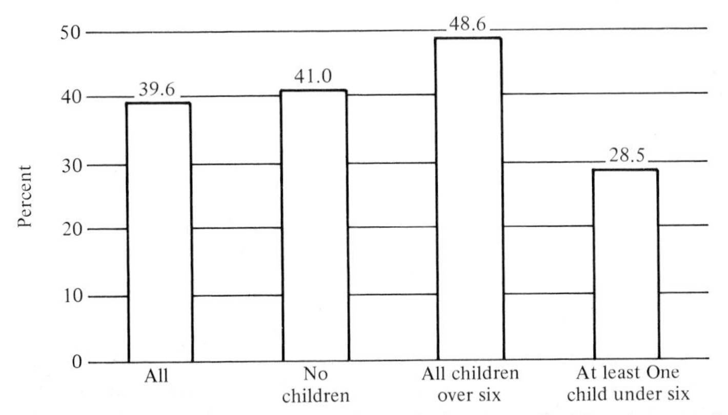

Figure 5-3 Employment rates of married women (husband present) in 1969. *Source:* The Conference Board Record (1970).

other rates, but it is still far from zero. Even among women with young children, the employment rate is above 1 out of 4.

Even so, for most women, pregnancy and the birth of the first child constitute a dramatic event, changing the whole life pattern of the wife. New roles are added, old ones dropped. Lopata (1966:9) explains:

> Because of the utter dependence of newborn infants upon practically 24-hour care by an adult, the number of activities such care necessitates, and the society's preference for its being undertaken by the biological mother, the young housewife suddenly finds herself confined to her house, carrying on a variety of housekeeping tasks; often inexpertly and alone.
>
> Not only does the infant require many housewifely actions, and its birth expand the social circle to include new people, but new sets of duties arise in new role relations with people already present in other circles. The husband now becomes also the father of the child and must relate to the mother on that level. The shift of attention often pushes the role of wife to the background, temporarily if not permanently. One of the characteristics of the role of housewife is the fact that competence acquired in the previous stage of the role may not actually help the new mother. A housekeeping schedule, for example, may be dysfunctional to, or made ineffective by, the demands of a newborn baby in a society which stresses its needs above those of adults.

Figure 5-4 Factors Influencing Adjustment to Parenthood

Attitudes toward Pregnancy
The woman's attitude toward parenthood is colored by her physical and emotional condition during pregnancy. In most cases if her attitude has been unfavorable it improves after the baby's birth.

Attitudes toward Parenthood
Adults adjust better to parenthood if they want children because the feel they are essential to a happy marriage rather than because of family or social pressures.

Age of Parents
Young parents tend to take their parental responsibilities lightly and not allow them to interfere too much with their other interests and pleasures. Older parents tend to be more anxious and concerned. Thus younger parents often make better adjustments.

Sex of Children
Adults' attitudes toward parenthood are more favorable if they have a child or children of the sex they prefer.

Number of Children
When adults have the number of children they consider ideal, their adjustment to parenthood will be better than if they have more or fewer children than they want.

Parental Expectations
If parents have a "dream child" concept, their adjustment to parenthood will be affected by how well the child measures up to this ideal.

Feelings of Parental Adequacy
Conflicts about child training methods lead to confusion and to feelings of anxiety about doing the job well. This has an unfavorable effect on the adult's adjustment to parenthood.

Attitudes toward Changed Roles
Parenthood means that both the man and the woman must learn to play family-centered rather than pair-centered roles. How the individual reacts to this role change will have a profound influence on his adjustment to parenthood.

The Child's Temperament
A child who is easy to manage and who is responsive and affectionate makes parents feel rewarded for their time and effort.

Source: Hurlock (1975:243).

Role Meaning Parenthood is at once the most harassing and the most rewarding period of life. The arrival of the first child often is viewed as a crisis. Old patterns of behavior no longer are appropriate, and both parents may feel inadequate for the parenthood role, partly because they have highly romanticized concepts of parenthood, and partly because of the personal, social, and economic privations brought about by parenthood (Hurlock, 1975). Most parents, however, adjust to their new roles even though it can be an harassing period. Figure 5-4 gives the most important factors influencing adjustment to parenthood.

However harassing, parenthood is viewed as rewarding. Figure 5-5, for instance, shows that parental satisfaction is highest among childbearing families and aging families. The lack of satisfaction between these periods is due to the increasing demands and conflicts occurring as children grow older. But at the beginning satisfaction is high. As Brayshaw (1962) suggests, "This surely is the most richly significant and rewarding time of life. Never again will we mean so much to another person as we do to our young children. Our smile or frown means everything to them. Without us they could scarcely survive." Parental satisfaction is high at the end also; here parents experience a recurrence when their grandchildren come along.

Importance of Parenthood Parenthood not only is a major issue of life, it is a role of extreme importance, as expressed by Perlman (1968:116):

> Parenthood may just happen or it may be calendar-planned; it may be dreaded or dreamed of; it may, in its long and varied course, be mostly pain or mostly pleasure. But under all and any circumstances its long-term commitment, its firm

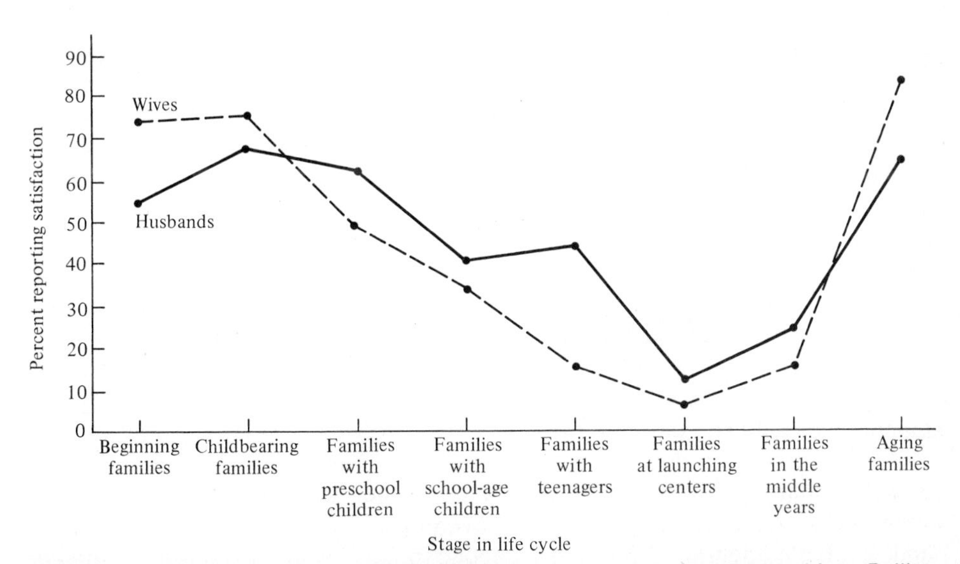

Figure 5-5 Parental satisfaction at different life-cycle stages. *Source:* Adapted from Rollins Feldman (1970). Copyright 1970 by National Council on Family Relations. Reprinted by permission.

> duties and demands, its emotionally-charged expectations and involvements, its viscerally experienced hurts and gratifications drive deeper into the core of the personality, probably, than any other life role.
>
> Parenthood requires a basic, consistent, continuous willingness and capacity to give or lend oneself to the nurture and protection of another. But it requires more than this. Because that "other" is a growing, changing, developing being in a sequence of evolving life stages under changing circumstances, the parent-person is thrust and pulled, willy-nilly, into moving, changing, and developing himself.

The effects of giving oneself to children in a consumer context has been documented, partially, in the childhood and adolescence chapters. In essence, we noted the large magnitude of direct purchases of a wide variety of goods and services having to do with young children. The advent of children affects more than buying diapers, toys, and games, however. With parenthood come substantial changes in many other consumer needs, such as the need for larger dwellings and installment credit. These and other needs and changes during this period are discussed in the following section.

Activities and Interests

We have seen that in the beginning parenthood is a rewarding period in life. It is also the beginning of the decline in satisfaction and *general mood.* The harrassment begins to take its tole during this period of early adulthood. As the data in Table 5-8 show, housewives in the 25–34 age group are less happy and optimistic than those under 25. Husbands, too, are less optimistic, but children do not affect their happiness in a negative sense—at least, not at first (Table 5-9).

The advent of children also brings about the beginning of a more conservative or *traditional outlook* on life. Young mothers and fathers are much less likely to consider themselves swingers and are much more likely to endorse discipline and old-fashioned tastes than they did as young housewives and husbands without children—a manifestation of the commitment to more dependent others required by parenthood.

The commitment to the role of parent produces other significant changes in outlook. For one, *companionship* with the spouse drops. It is now the child or children rather than the husband who goes shopping with the homemaker and the mother, while still not so much as the average, begins to emphasize the importance of children in the home more than the newly married wife. For another, interest in the *outside world* increases. Young homemakers are more likely to want to take a trip around the world even while realizing they are homebound with the kids.

Also, there is a decline in *social* interests. Tables 5-8 and 5-9 show, for example, that the 25- to 34-year-olds increase their agreement with statements such as, "I would rather spend a quiet evening at home than go out to a party," and "I am a homebody." There is a decline in *fashion and personal adornment* interest among females which coincides with being less social. This pattern is revealed in the drop in agreement with statements such as, "Dressing well is an important part of my life," and "I like to feel attractive to members of the opposite sex." The corresponding drop in fashion consciousness and social activity, while triggered by children and their demands, reinforces our earlier discussion of the relationship between social life and personal adornment.

Not all changes with parenthood are "negative," however. While obviously tired, young mothers are *less anxious*—they tell us they have less trouble getting to sleep and have virtually no trouble relaxing. Moreover, young parents are more concerned about *health and nutrition* and they obviously buy more chest rubs and cough medicine and vitamins than the average family. They do not take health for self and husband for granted, however; they are very concerned about salt and cholesterol and food with additives.

Now let us consider changes related to financial position, housing and keeping house, and recreation and media habits of young parents.

Financial Position Tables 5-8 and 5-9 show that young parents are still above average in financial optimism, but not as high as the young married group. The data also show that people in this life period become concerned about their financial position. More than any other age group, young parents are more likely to agree with "No matter how fast our income goes up we never seem to get ahead"; and males say, "Our family is too heavily in debt today."

This dissatisfaction with personal equity is justified. Not only are young marrieds among the heaviest users of credit cards and charge cards, their installment debt is at a peak. Table 5-15 shows installment debt outstanding by life-cycle stage; it reveals that the peak stages of families having any debt and

Table 5-15 Installment Debt Outstanding by Life-Cycle Stage (Percentage Distribution of Families)

	Early 1970	
Life-cycle stage	Have debt	$2000 or more
Younger than age 45		
Unmarried, no children	41%	11%
Married, no children	63	17
Married, youngest child under age 6	71	21
Married, youngest child age 6 or older	71	22
Age 45 or older		
Married, has children	57	16
Married, no children, head in labor force	43	10
Married, no children, head retired	15	3
Unmarried, no children, head in labor force	29	2
Unmarried, no children, head retired	14	*
Any age		
Unmarried, has children	53	9

*Less than 0.5 percent.

Note: The term "no children" means no children younger than age 18 living at home. Unemployed people and housewives age 55 and older are considered retired; unemployed people and housewives younger than age 55 are considered to be in the labor force.

Source: *Survey of Consumer Finances* (1970).

having debt of $2,000 or more are found in the married families with children where the household head is under age 45. The reasons, of course, are the changes in housing, durable needs, and child products and the fact that the wife is not working—all brought about by the presence of children.

Housing and Homemaking The advent of children is an occasion for a big shift from renting to owning housing. Table 5-16 reveals an almost perfect reversal in owning and renting between young marrieds and young parents; i.e., 59 percent of young marrieds rent and 31 percent own, while 34 percent of young parents rent and 58 percent own. The table also shows ownership increases as families move into the next life-cycle stage. The basic reasons for owning, of course, are the need for more room, the need for location nearer schools (for older children), and, for more affluent families, an added and needed tax break.

Although ownership percentages continue to rise until late in the life cycle, traditionally house *purchasing* is at a peak among young parents, closely followed by young marrieds. Table 5-17 shows the percent of nonfarm families purchasing in the early adulthood stages during 1966, 1968, and 1969. These data show that the peak purchasing rate may be shifting in favor of young marrieds, but that the peak rate remains closely in favor of the young parents. One possible reason for the shift, if it continues, is the rising affluence of young marrieds armed with foreknowledge of needs to come and the availability of condominiums—in other words, anticipatory purchases.

Within the home there are additional changes brought about by the advent of children. It is a time for "baby-proofing" both the house and the furnishings. Parents focus on things that wear, that will not be easily damanged or soiled, or that are inexpensive so that it will not matter too much if they are broken. The object is not just to spare the house. The object is also to spare growing youngsters too much restriction and to spare parents the need to punish (*Better Homes and Gardens*, 1967). Along with this baby-proofing theme, the life style data in Table 5-8 show that young mothers begin to take a different view of household goods in general. When compared with young marrieds, they begin to agree more with the need for comfortable furnishings and dependable appliances.

Table 5-16 Housing Status during Early Adulthood — 1970 (Percentage of Nonfarm Families)

	Housing status		
Early adulthood stages	Own	Rent	Other[a]
Single, no children	14%	78%	8%
Married, no children	31	59	10
Married, youngest child under age 6	58	34	8
Married, youngest child age 6 or older	79	17	4

[a]Includes trailer owners and families who neither own nor rent.
Source: *Survey of Consumer Finances* (1970).

Table 5-17 Percent of House Purchases in 1966 and 1969 among the Stages of Early Adulthood

Life-cycle stage	New or used houses		
	1966	1968	1969
Single, no children	2%	4%	2%
Married, no children	9	12	11
Married, youngest child under age 6	10	11	10
Married, youngest child age 6 or older	8	9	8
All nonfarm families	6	6	5

Source: *Survey of Consumer Finances* (1967, 1970).

Housekeeping, cooking, and shopping interests and activities also show a substantial change during parenthood. Interest in housework and grocery shopping drops during this period. Young mothers agree less than any other age group with "Shopping is no fun anymore."

There is a drop in housekeeping standards, probably as a result of constantly trying to clean up after children. Instead of expressing the meticulous-housekeeper pattern of responses found for young marrieds, we find in Tables 5-8 that young mothers are now below average in agreement with housekeeping statements such as, "The kind of dirt you can't see is worse than the kind you can see."

All is not "lost," however. Females in the 25–34 age group tell us they are somewhat more skilled in shopping—they increasingly prepare a shopping list before going shopping, shop for specials, and check prices more carefully. They remain self-indulgent or impulsive, however.

Recreations and Media Habits Tables 5-13 and 5-14 show that both females and males remain relatively active during the years 25–34 and are pursuing about the same leisure-time activities and pastimes, although not quite to the same degree.

More importantly, the changes which occur, either up or down, are almost entirely explained by the presence of children and the confinement to the home or to the ownership of a house. For example, there is a sharp increase among males and females in home repairs and yard work and in participation in community and school activity, and a general decline in recreations outside the home. Also, for males, there is a sharp increase in job-related reading or studying—with the wife not working and occupied with children, there apparently comes a pressing need to get ahead faster in one's occupation.

Media habits also change. Generally there is a substantial jump in newspaper readership of the young mother over that of the young wife. Newspaper readership, of course, goes along with preparing a shopping list and being at home more. When children are less than age five, baby magazines are important also. And when these are not purchased or subscribed to, they are read in the doctor's office—and that office is visited frequently.

Television viewing also is high for females. Nielsen data in 1968, for example, revealed that adult females under 35 viewed TV, on the average, over 29 hours per week, compared with 27 hours for those between 35 and 49 years of age. Males, on the average, watched about 10 hours less each week. The viewing times also differed. While a larger percentage of males and females viewed during prime time, females (17 to 9 percent) were the daily, afternoon viewers.

Table 5-18 shows that favorite TV shows vary between sexes as well as between age groups. For males, preferences during parenthood center around football as opposed to male preference for comedy and detective shows during the young married stage. For females, interest declines somewhat, but the favorite shows remain family drama and comedy such as "The Waltons" and "Happy Days."

Not only are young mothers heavy viewers; they are also interested in commercials. Because they have so many needs for new products, they like

Table 5-18 Consumers' Favorite TV Programs

		Age group				
Sex/program	Sample total	Under 25	25-34	35-44	45-54	55 and older
Females						
"The Waltons"	36%	43%	35%	34%	30%	42%
"M*A*S*H"	31	42	30	28	33	25
"All in the Family"	29	31	24	25	31	36
"Little House on the Prairie"	28	26	27	25	26	37
"Wonderful World of Disney"	22	13	22	23	24	24
"Emergency"	22	26	27	23	20	15
"Streets of San Francisco"	21	21	23	23	22	18
"Mary Tyler Moore"	21	26	22	18	21	21
"Kojak"	19	22	20	20	20	16
"CBS Evening News"	19	12	15	15	22	29
"Roda"	19	36	23	15	14	13
"Happy Days"	18	36	24	19	13	7
Males						
"Weekend Pro Football"	34	27	40	39	35	27
"Monday Night Pro Football"	31	27	36	35	30	24
"All in the Family"	29	28	26	26	32	31
"M*A*S*H"	29	42	32	27	31	20
"Sanford and Son"	24	27	21	22	28	23
"Kojak"	23	22	28	20	26	20
"Streets of San Francisco"	19	29	19	16	22	16
"The Waltons"	19	11	16	15	19	30
"CBS Evening News"	19	11	13	16	19	28
"Emergency"	18	20	20	17	17	16
"Wonderful World of Disney"	18	12	18	17	19	20
"Hawaii Five-O"	17	17	15	15	16	21

Source: Needham, Harper & Steers, (1975).

advertised products—TV advertisements provide a quick way to obtain information about brands which fit their new needs as mothers. Advertisers, of course, are aware of their needs and are quick to promote their brands to the young parents as well as to all others.

SUMMARY

Young adults comprise a large and growing population segment which is distinguished by high discretionary income levels and highly active purchasing rates relative to other consumer groups. Within the ranks of the young adult groups are the premarrieds and young marrieds (ages eighteen to twenty-four), and the young parents (ages twenty-five to thirty-four)—three rather diverse groups, in terms of roles, issues, and needs. It is important to note that, throughout adulthood, chronological age is less important in determining consumer behavior than position in the family life cycle, although most consumers go through each stage during the same relative age bracket.

Premarrieds, who are primarily concerned with choosing an occupation and a mate, are closest in activities and interests to adolescents. Many are in college, still somewhat tied to parental purse strings. For both males and females, the median age at first marriage is increasing, thereby lengthening the premarried stage. Incomes for this stage are expected to rise, over the next decade, as they are expected to do for all stages of young adulthood, which will mean significantly increased disposable income for those young adults not burdened with the expenses of marriage and parenthood.

Interest in money among premarrieds centers around immediate use rather than long-term planning, similarly to adolescent patterns. Recreation for premarrieds revolves around dating, with a corresponding high interest in personal appearance, grooming, and clothing. These interests are translated into high expenditure patterns for appropriate products, especially among college students.

Expenditure patterns change as consumers progress from premarried to young married stages. Intense needs for durables are matched with relatively strong levels of purchasing power and result in high expenditure patterns for all types of household goods. Young marrieds progress toward adult activities and interests as they begin establishing their own homes and settling into careers. The transition from premarried to married is often fraught with emotional tension and problems, especially for women, who suffer from a lack of confidence concerning the housewifely role and duties. Many newly married women continue to work, thus providing a second paycheck and remaining in touch with the world outside the family home.

Young families in which both husband and wife work have more discretionary income than families in which only one partner works. Consequently, two-earner families spend more on such items as convenience goods, small appliances, and vacation travel, reflecting higher disposable income and greater need for time- and labor-saving devices. Although she is in a stronger position to spend, the working wife has less time to shop and is less exposed to weekday advertising, which is generally geared toward housewives, than is the stay-at-home wife. Young marrieds tend to be financially optimistic, tend to borrow relatively heavily on an installment basis in order to buy the goods they want and need, and are important markets for subcompact cars, silverware, furniture, and other household durables. As consumers progress through the young adult stage, participation in active sports begins to decline, as it will continue to do throughout adulthood.

Once consumers reach the parenthood stage, leisure activity begins to center more and more around the home, and there is a general decline in recreations outside the home. Young mothers are heavy viewers of TV programs and advertisements, especially during weekdays. The level of employment for married women with at least one child under six at home is lower than for any other group of married women, indicating that the homemaker role is dominant for many women during this stage of the family life cycle.

Young parents tend to experience a decline in general mood, seem less optimistic, and adopt a more conservative, or traditional, outlook on life. For women, interest in fashion and personal adornment, as well as in social activities, tends to decline, while interest in the outside world, health, and nutrition tends to increase. Financial position for young parents is somewhat less favorable than for young marrieds, as a result of fewer working wives and increased expenses due to child care. However, young parents represent strong markets for family-owned housing and are interested in comfortable furnishings and dependable appliances.

While young adults are, in general, socially and recreationally active, increasing demands on their time and resources have a curtailing effect as they progress through the family life cycle. This trend toward a narrowing of outside activities and interests will become more pronounced in later stages.

REVIEW QUESTIONS

1 Identify the major issues and roles that characterize the young adult life period and their corresponding effects on consumer behavior.
2 Although the young adult period is generally attributed to the eighteen-to-thirty-four age bracket, family life-cycle stages rather than chronological ages are often more directly related to consumer behavior. Why is this true? What are the pertinent stages?
3 How do young adults compare with other population groups in terms of their general mood and outlook on life? Do consumers' moods affect their behavior? In what ways?
4 Young adults in the premarried stage face two major choices. Identify the two choices and discuss how this unsettled state affects consumer behavior.
5 Why are college students examined as a separate group within the premarried group?
6 Besides increasing discretionary income, the presence of a working wife has many

effects on the consumer behavior of her family. Identify these effects and discuss the resultant opportunities and problems they bring to marketers.

7 Would you agree that, as a group, the young marrieds seem to be on a perpetual shopping spree? What factors precipitate and support this behavior?

8 The arrival of children results in significant changes in the consumer behavior of young families. Discuss the differences between young families without children and those with children in terms of fashion and social consciousness, choice of dwelling, financial position, and other pertinent areas.

EXERCISE

As pointed out in the chapter, a majority of American women now prefer an egalitarian life style. Working individually or as a small group with other students, prepare a portrait of the egalitarian female. That is, if a woman adopts this posture, how is this likely to differentiate her from traditional females in terms of (1) views toward home, work, and family relationships; (2) satisfaction with life; (3) leadership; (4) social activities; (5) self and adornment interests; (6) attitude toward travel; (7) views of income and financial position of the household; (8) attitudes toward business and advertising and national events; (9) views toward transportation vehicles, housekeeping, grocery shopping, and traditions such as eating breakfast; (10) leisure activities engaged in; (11) idea of enjoyable entertainment; (12) influence of children on brand choice, exposure to the magazine, television, and radio media, and products personally used?

REFERENCES

Arnott, C. and F. L. Bengtson. " 'Only a Homemaker': Distributive Justice and Role Choice among Married Women." *Sociology and Social Research,* 54 (1970), 495–507.

Better Homes and Gardens. Today's Changing Consumer, A Condensation of Research Presented at the 2nd All-Industry Home Furnishings Conference.

Bogart, Leo. "Youth Market Isn't All That Different." *Advertising Age* (Apr. 12, 1971), 37–39.

Brayshaw, A. Joseph. "Middle-Aged Marriage: Idealism, Realism and the Search for Meaning." *Marriage and Family Living,* 24 (November 1962), 358–364.

Bureau of Advertising. *The Working Women.* New York: Bureau of Advertising, April 1972.

Clavan, S. "The Family Process: A Sociological Model," *Family Coordinator,* 18 (1969), 312–317.

Hawes, Douglass K., W. Wayne Talarzk, and Roger D. Blackwell. "Consumer Satisfaction from Leisure Time Pursuits." In Mary Jane Schlinger (ed.), *Advances in Consumer Research.* Vol. 2. Chicago: Association for Consumer Research, 1974, 817–836.

Hurlock, Elizabeth B. *Developmental Psychology.* 4th ed. New York: McGraw-Hill, 1975.

Linden, Fabian. "Reshuffling the Age-Income Mix." *The Conference Board RECORD* (March 1974).

———. "Young Adults." *The Conference Board RECORD* (April 1971), 53–56.

Lopata, Helena Znaniecki. "The Life Cycle of the Social Role of Housewife." *Sociology and Social Research,* 51 (1966) 5–22.

National Industrial Conference Board. *Market Profiles of Consumer Products.* New York: National Industrial Conference Board, 1967.

Neugarten, B. L. "Continuities and Discontinuities of Psychological Issues into Adult Life." *Human Development,* 12 (1969), 121–130.

Perlman, Helen Harris, *Persona, Social Role and Personality.* Chicago: The University of Chicago Press, 1968.

Reynolds, Fred D., Melvin R. Crask, and William D. Wells. "The Modern Feminine Life Style." *Journal of Marketing* forthcoming, 1977.

Rollins, B. C. and H. Feldman. "Marital Satisfaction over the Family Life Cycle." *Journal of Marriage and Family,* 32 (1970), 20–28.

Survey Research Center. *1966 Survey of Consumer Finances.* Ann Arbor, Mich.: University of Michigan, Survey Research Center, 1967.

———. *1970 Survey of Consumer Finances.* Ann Arbor, Mich.: University of Michigan, Survey Research Center, 1970.

Taylor, Richard. "The College Market Today." A study for Transcontinental Enterprises, Inc., July 1969.

The Conference Board. *A Guide to Consumer Markets, 1970.* New York: The Conference Board, 1970.

VanDusen, R. A. and E. B. Sheldon. "The Changing Status of American Women: A Life Cycle Perspective." *American Psychologist,* (February 1976), 106–116.

Wax, Murray, "Themes in Cosmetics and Grooming." *American Journal of Sociology* 62 (1957), 588–593.

Wattenberg, Ben J. "The Forming-Families: The Spark in the Tinder, 1975–1985." 1974 Combined Proceedings of the American Marketing Association. Chicago: American Marketing Association, 1975.

Wells, William D. and George Gubar. "Life Cycle Concept in Marketing Research," *Journal of Marketing Research,* 3 (November 1966), 355–63.

Yankelovich, Daniel. *The New Morality, A Profile of American Youth in the '70's.* New York: McGraw-Hill, 1974.

Chapter 6

The Middle Years

"Life begins at forty" is a popular phrase, at least among those persons about to reach the fortieth anniversary of their birth. The phrase and its popularity can be traced back forty-five years: "In 1932, Walter B. Pitkin wrote *Life Begins at Forty* and it became an overnight inspirational bestseller precisely because people thought life ended at 40 and there was nothing left to do but wait around for retirement and death" (*Time,* 1966).

People in their middle years, of course, know that life does not end at forty. Yet many behavioral scientists and many marketers have acted as if the life span suddenly stopped at age thirty-five, went into a period of suspended animation, and began again in old age just in time to decline rapidly to death. In other words, the middle-aged seem to be the forgotten generation, both in terms of scientific investigation and in marketing practice. The reasons for this "forgetfulness" are understandable: to the behavioral scientist, preoccupied with studying children, adolescents, young adults, and old people, the middle-aged seem to offer few problems worthy of serious attention; and to marketers and consumer researchers, also preoccupied with the other life stages, the no-longer-younger seem dowdy and uninspiring when compared with the glamor of the young.

Fortunately, the situation is being corrected—now that a number of researchers are surveying the adult life cycle with vigor. We say "fortunately" because many issues must be faced in the middle years, and many of these issues have an impact on our needs and behaviors as consumers.

In this chapter we explore the middle years, following much the pattern of previous chapters. We begin with a discussion of the major dimensions of the middle years of the life span, turn to a documentation of their importance, and then proceed to discuss the major divisions of this part of the life span.

THE MIDDLE YEARS

The middle years of the life span can be divded into two primary stages, middle and later adulthood. These stages roughly correspond to the age groups 35–44 and 45–54, but, as in the divisions of early adulthood, the ages are only approximate and are useful mainly in documenting certain trends and issues related to middle and later adulthood.

Middle adulthood might aptly be termed the "full house" stage of life. It is the time when family size is at a peak, and generally it consists of older couples with dependent children, especially children in school. Because of family composition, parental roles take on new dimensions and new meanings. For example, persons in middle adulthood become more aware that they are the socializers rather than the socialized and turn their attentions to relations with their children and adolescents, thereby helping them become responsible and socially integrated adults.

It is also the period of life when the individual attains the peak in performing many of life's roles, especially vocationally and when one comes to terms with one's degree of success, becoming one's own man or woman. Consequently, it is a time of heightened introspection, of being "on or off time" with the social calendar. Coupled with this new introspection and socializing of children and adolescents is a developing of new adjustments with one's spouse.

Middle adulthood gradually shades into later adulthood as families "empty the nest." "Later adulthood" refers to the time between when children leave home and the household head retires from the work force. It is a time of settling down, of mellowing, of coming to grips with physical and psychological changes that first began during middle adulthood, of coping with children leaving home, and of preparing for retirement and old age.

IMPORTANCE AS CONSUMERS

Table 6-1 shows the proportion and trends of persons in their middle years. Currently, 21 percent of the population falls into the middle years category compared with 27 percent in early adulthood, but neither is it a figure to ignore, as we shall see when discussing income and expenditures.

The percentage of the population in the 35–44 and 45–54 age groups will begin to decline as we move into the 1980s, principally because of the shrinking

Table 6-1 The Middle Years Population: 1970–1985
(In Millions)

		Age group			
Year	Total population	35–44 (number and %)		45–54 (number and %)	
1970	204.8	23.1	11.3%	23.3	11.4%
1975	216.6	22.8	10.5	23.6	10.9
1980	230.9	25.5	11.0	22.5	9.7
1985	246.3	31.3	12.7	22.1	9.0

Note: Series D (Moderate low series) projections. Data include Armed Forces overseas and are as of July 1.
Source: Department of Commerce, *Current Population Reports,* Series P-25, No. 470 (November 1971).

size of the 45–54 age group—the depression babies of the 1930s. There will be a moderate increase in the importance of the 35–44ers as we enter the 1980s, and this group will continue its growth as the young adults of this decade grow into middle adulthood.

A similar perspective on size can be seen in Table 6-2, which shows the number of households in the United States for these two age groups. But the table also reveals the incomes of households in the middle years.

As the data show, the households headed by someone in middle adulthood represent about 17 percent of the households but account for over 21 percent of total household income. In other words, persons in middle adulthood are above average financially—and they will remain better off in the 1980s. As we enter the 1980s, middle-adult households will account for almost 20 percent of American homes but 25 percent of household spending power. This is slightly below the total figures for young adults, but significantly more middle-aged adults will be earning more than $15,000.

The real affluence, however, is in the later adulthood households. Households in the 45–54 category account for less than a fifth of the total number but a commanding 25 percent of the income and an even more impressive 33 percent of the discretionary income. This segment, of course, will decline in relative importance during the 1980s. It will remain, however, a significant luxury market—the percentage of households earning over $25,000 is highest in this age group and will remain so.

The uses to which income is put show some major changes as people move into middle and later adulthood. It is not only that they are better off financially, but they have less demand placed on their income by durable goods purchases. The demands on income shift according to the child-age composition of the family.

In the previous chapter we showed that the peak purchasing rate of certain durables occurred during early adulthood, noting that the major culprits requiring these expenditures were marriage and children. As these children grow older, many new and different demands are placed on the family. When the

Table 6-2 Middle-Years Households by Age of Head and Income Class
(All Figures in 1972 Dollars)

	All household	Age of household head: Under 25	25–34	35–44	45–54
1972					
Households					
Millions	68.3	5.5	13.6	11.7	12.8
Distribution	100.0%	8.0	20.0	17.0	19.0
Spending power					
Total	100.0%	5.5	20.5	21.5	24.5
Discretionary	100.0%	1.5	14.5	25.0	33.0
Household income distribution	100.0%	100.0%	100.0%	100.0%	100.0%
Under $3,000	14.0	15.5	6.0	5.0	6.5
$3,000–5,000	11.0	16.5	7.5	6.0	6.5
$5,000–7,000	10.5	17.5	10.0	8.0	7.5
$7,000–10,000	16.0	24.0	20.0	15.5	14.0
$10,000–15,000	23.0	19.5	32.5	28.0	25.0
$15,000–25,000	19.5	6.5	20.5	29.0	29.0
$25,000 and over	6.0	0.5	3.5	8.5	11.5
1980					
Household					
Millions	77.3	6.0	18.3	13.1	11.8
Distribution	100.0%	8.0	23.5	17.0	15.5
Spending power					
Total	100.0%	5.5	25.0	21.5	20.0
Discretionary	100.0%	1.5	19.5	26.5	27.5
Household income distribution	100.0%	100.0%	100.0%	100.0%	100.0%
Under $3,000	12.0	13.0	5.0	4.0	5.5
$3,000–5,000	10.5	14.5	6.5	5.5	6.0
$5,000–7,000	10.0	17.0	8.5	7.0	6.5
$7,000–10,000.	14.5	23.0	17.0	13.0	12.0
$10,000–15,000.	23.0	22.5	32.5	25.5	22.5
$15,000–25,000	22.0	9.0	25.0	32.0	32.0
$25,000 and over	8.0	1.0	5.5	13.0	15.5
1985					
Households					
Millions	84.2	6.0	20.5	16.3	11.7
Distribution	100.0%	7.0	24.5	19.5	14.0
Spending power					
Total	100.0%	5.0	26.0	24.5	18.0
Discretionary	100.0%	1.5	20.5	29.5	25.0
Household income distribution	100.0%	100.0%	100.0%	100.0%	100.0%
Under $3,000	11.0	12.0	5.0	4.0	5.5
$3,000–5,000	10.0	13.5	5.5	5.0	5.5
$5,000–7,000	9.0	14.5	8.0	6.0	6.0
$7,000–10,000	14.0	23.0	15.5	11.5	10.5
$10,000–15,000	22.0	23.5	29.5	24.0	21.0
$15,000–25,000	25.0	12.5	30.5	35.5	33.5
$25,000 and over	9.0	1.0	6.0	14.0	18.0

Source: Linden (1974).

family consists of "some children under six and some over six" (a transition from early to middle adulthood, in many cases), a host of items get their highest average expenditure. The list includes a long list of foods: cornflakes, sugar, flour, lard, dried vegetables, evaporated and condensed milk, raisins, margarine, cold wheat cereal; macaroni, spaghetti, and noodles; syrup, molasses, and honey; eggs, canned chicken soup, fresh whole milk, potatoes, peanut butter, white bread, frankfurters, ice cream; jellies, jams and preserves, candy, pancake and waffle mix; and potato chips. Also in this group of items, and for the same reasons, are bleaches and disinfectants, packaged detergents, soap, electric irons, dolls and accessories, toys and play equipment, wagons, sleds, and skates.

As children grow older, the list of items purchased shifts again. These items receive peak expenditure in the "all children six to eleven" category: bicycles, games, puzzles, and mechanical toys; comic books, hardback books, pianos and organs, and music lessons. Also included are some nonessential appliances: electric floor waxers, air conditioners, hand and power tools, and insect sprays and powders.

When all the children in the home are twelve or over, these products get peak expenditures: auto operating expenses, auto liability insurance, auto repairs and parts, hand luggage, lodging out of the home town; boats, motors, and trailers; dental services, electric shavers and repairs, haircuts, home permanent kits, school and technical books, and magazines (National Industrial Conference Board, 1965).

Finally, as the nest is emptied, there are increased expenditures for vacations, home improvements, and luxuries in general (Wells and Gubar, 1966).

In summary, the middle years of life are filled with changes in consumption needs and with the economic ability to fill these needs. Families in middle and later adulthood are important segments for a host of products, but for a time they will be relatively less important than in prior years. Students of consumer behavior should not ignore these groups, however; the middle years should be understood both for their existing level of important and for the simple reason that the huge bulge of young adults of this decade will become a big group of persons in the middle years in the not too distant future.

In seeking this understanding we turn now to middle adulthood, examining the major changes occurring during this life period.

MIDDLE ADULTHOOD

According to Hurlock (1975), middle adulthood should be a time of "payoff" and of newfound freedom, not only from the cares and responsibilities of the home, but also from economic problems and worries. Is it? To answer this question we will explore the changing female role of homemaker and the male role of worker. Then we will see how these changes influence the activities and interests of middle adulthood.

The Female Role: Homemaker

Marriage starts the woman in her career as homemaker, and parenthood redefines the role. The next major change in the role starts when the youngest child enters school and ends when the children start leaving home and taking up residence elsewhere.

Young mothers, those with preschoolers, often anticipate this next stage with hopes for "relaxation" and "time for oneself," but these anticipations reflect their reaction to the new intensity of being a young parent, of shifting from "outside" to "inside" roles (Lopata, 1966).

In reality, the "full house" stage of homemaking does not turn out as anticipated. Figure 5-5, for instance, shows an almost linear decline in parental satisfaction of women during the full-house stage, dropping from the 50 percent satisfaction level in the previous stage to a low of less than 10 percent at the end of the full-family period.

It is true, of course, that as children grow older and increase in ability to care for self and belongings, there is some relief of household chores. But this does not necessarily mean more spare time for relaxing. The presence of school-aged children frequently results in the expansion of the homemaker's circle and of duties toward the expanded circle. Playmates, teachers, tutors, or organization leaders may ask for special attention or impose special demands upon the child, requiring more, not less, work of its mother.

Other life change-related roles may impinge on her time for home as well. For instance, mothers of teenaged daughters often spend more time in worrying, in arguing about proper taste in clothing and cosmetics than they did in supervising their daughters during preadolescent days. This intensity is well expressed by Perlman (1968):

> If ever there is a time when the ordered, patterned personality is subject to the impact and upheaval of a barrage of stimuli and to the necessity for fast-stepping adaptations and accomodations and revisions and reconsolidations, it is during adolescence—during the adolescence of one's children, that is. Everyone knows of the problems and perils of the adolescent period for a child. Scant attention has been given to its significance for parents. Yet it is almost inevitably a long-time crucial period for them when changes in the child's body, status, attitudes, feelings, and behaviors strike off clamorous resonances and haunting echoes in the parental personality and sense of self. Probably not since the child's conception and infancy has the parent as person been so assailed and rocked by changing relationships and tasks.

Another time demand can come from the husband's career advancement. For example, the career cycle of the husband is likely to have resulted in a consistent improvement of the family's economic position due to occupational role performance and upward mobility. If this improved position is used to add to the home more objects for the sake of beauty or class status, then more work is the consequeuence to the wife. In contrast, the consequence may mean less work if the money is converted into services and labor-saving devices (Lopata, 1966).

Finally, the changes in the housewife role during the full-nest stage depend on the woman's view toward "inside-outside" role clusters. During this stage, the rest of the family are now all "outside" the home a great deal of time, both physically and in mental orientation. The wife, then, can opt to be the only "inside" person and can continue focusing on the roles of wife, mother, housewife—on "cooking for the family," "sewing for the family," and "waiting for the family to come home." But, as already documented, women can opt for an "outside" role—and many wives return to work after their children are in school and/or increase their participation in community affairs.

What do housewives say about this life period in terms of their role of homemaker? Several items in the life style data (Table 6-3) suggest they are less than happy with many housewifely duties. More than any other age group, they agree that shopping is no fun anymore, and they are below average on many shopping activities. They view themselves as about average in keeping the house neat and clean but no longer enjoy cooking as much as do younger age groups and fewer believe they are good cooks.

Also, the demands brought by the family all being "outside" the house apparently precipitate more outside activities for the homemaker. As Table 6-3 shows, women in the 35–44 age group agree less than any other group with "I stay home most evenings." In general, these women are highly active, when compared with other age periods, in community organizations and activities. They tell us they are substantially higher now than during early adulthood in participating in PTA and service organizations, and in raising money for charities. Not surprisingly, they agree less than other age groups that a subcompact car can meet their transportation needs.

Upper-class women, of course, opt more for a nonhousekeeping orientation that lower-class women, partly because of financial ability and societal expectations and rewards at various class levels and partly because of higher education and a consequent recognition of the importance to society of the "outside" roles.

The Male Role: Worker

Persons in the middle years of life are continually ranked by their friends, associates, employer, and neighbors. The status to which they are assigned largely depends upon their occupational position, which leads also to their economic standing. In other words, the work role provides the security of a position in the social system; it names one's function in the network of functions that constitute society.

Indeed, in superficial social relationships what people work at is the first, quick way they are identified; hence, the frequently asked question of new acquaintances: "What do you do?"

The role of work also has several implications for the family during the middle years. For instance, work and earning power are vital in validating the

Table 6-3 Female Interests and Opinions
(Percent Agreeing by Age Group)

Statement	Sample total	Age group: Under 25	25–34	34–44	44–54	55 and older
Optimism and happiness						
My greatest achievements are still ahead of me	64%	92%	84%	73%	52%	28%I
I dread the future	23	20	18	17	24	30
I am much happier now than I ever was before	79	85	82	80	74	74
Modern — traditional ideas						
I have somewhat old-fashioned tastes and habits	86	78	84	87	88	89
There is too much emphasis on sex today	87	70	74	90	89	93
I like to think I am a bit of a swinger	26	43	34	26	19	15
A woman's place is in the home	46	39	39	44	49	60
The working world is no place for a woman	17	15	11	14	19	28
Young people have too many privileges	76	57	74	77	76	83
The U.S. would be better off if there were no hippies	55	32	37	46	54	82
My days seem to follow a definite routine – eating meals at the same time each day, etc.	67	59	62	61	67	75
Travel						
I would like to take a trip around the world	67	78	83	73	65	51
I would like to spend a year in London or Paris	34	38	40	34	34	25
I would feel lost if I were alone in a foreign country	68	66	66	64	68	76
I like to visit places that are totally different from my home	85	85	83	86	82	88
Mobile						
We will probably move at least once in the next five years	38	71	53	27	28	23
Our family has moved more often than most of our neighbors have	24	36	32	26	18	17
Anxious						
I have trouble getting to sleep	33	29	24	26	33	49
I wish I knew how to relax	52	51	49	49	51	59
Personal adornment and self						
Dressing well is an important part of my life	81	84	80	78	79	83
I like to feel attractive to members of the opposite sex	85	93	91	77	82	72
I want to look a little different from others	69	71	78	70	63	72
I often wear expensive cologne	28	19	24	28	27	33
I have more stylish clothes than most of my friends	30	31	34	27	29	27

Table 6-3 Female Interests and Opinions (continued)

Statement	Sample total	Age group: Under 25	25–34	34–44	44–54	55 and older
View toward income, personal equity, and spending						
I will probably have more money to spend next year than I have now	45%	71%	70%	58%	53%	30%
Five years from now our family income will probably be a lot higher than it is now	65	87	85	75	61	26
Our family income is high enough to satisfy nearly all our important desires	74	59	66	78	78	80
No matter how fast our income goes up we never seem to get ahead	53	62	65	61	47	32
Investing in the stock market is too risky for most families	86	79	83	82	85	87
Our family is too heavily in debt today	27	36	33	37	23	11
I like to pay cash for everything I buy	77	83	79	74	71	77
I pretty much spend for today and let tomorrow bring what it will	22	33	21	22	25	18
Staying at home						
I would rather spend a quiet evening at home than go out to a party	65	50	66	64	68	78
I am a homebody	69	59	65	64	72	79
I stay home most evenings	83	81	95	80	83	83
Husband and children						
A wife's first obligation is to her husband, not her children	69	53	65	74	74	76
When children are ill in bed, parents should drop everything else to see to their comfort	74	61	71	73	80	83
Children are the most important thing in a marriage	52	42	44	49	56	64
When making important family decisions, consideration of the children should come first	54	69	58	44	48	56
A wife should have a great deal of information about her husband's work	82	83	84	75	88	85
View toward durable goods						
Our home is furnished for comfort, not for style	90	83	88	88	94	94
If I must choose, I buy stylish rather than practical furniture	17	19	31	13	15	15
When buying appliances, I am more concerned with dependability than price	90	85	89	89	89	94
A subcompact car can meet my transportation needs	66	85	74	60	61	57
Housekeeping and cooking						
When I see a full ashtray or wastebasket, I want it emptied immediately	71	77	70	72	64	64

Table 6-3 **Female Interests and Opinions (continued)**

Statement	Sample total	Under 25	25–34	34–44	44–54	55 and older
		Age group				
I am uncomfortable when the house is not completely clean	67%	76%	67%	70%	61%	68%
The kind of dirt you can't see is worse than the kind you can see	77	77	72	73	79	85
I am a good cook	91	93	92	88	90	91
I like to cook	87	91	88	84	85	87
I like to bake	40	43	43	42	39	38
Meal preparation should take as little time as possible	42	42	41	40	41	44
Grocery shopping						
Shopping is no fun anymore	54	49	43	58	55	51
Before going shopping, I sit down and prepare a complete shopping list	72	68	73	71	69	74
I try to stick to well-known brands	74	58	67	71	82	86
I find myself checking prices even on small items	90	89	93	92	89	86
I like to save and redeem savings stamps	75	72	70	70	75	83
I pay a lot more attention to food prices now than I ever did before	90	92	91	88	88	87
I am an impulse buyer	38	39	40	37	42	27
I shop a lot for specials	84	85	86	83	84	81
Health and nutrition						
I am very concerned about nutrition	87	87	89	87	82	89
I am concerned about how much salt I eat	56	52	55	56	50	66
I am careful what I eat in order to keep my weight under control	57	63	57	58	62	68
I try to avoid foods that are high in cholesterol	62	37	53	60	65	79
I try to avoid foods that have additives in them	56	45	52	57	53	62
I get more headaches than most people	28	30	31	28	27	22
I eat more than I should	70	68	70	75	73	69

Data source: Needham, Harper & Steers, (1975).

roles of husband and father in the family. The husband is "supposed" to work and be a "good provider." Also, his work links the family to the larger world outside the home, thereby affecting children's ideas about their work experiences and their attitudes toward work itself. The husband's job provides an established defense system—it gives him the "right" not to be bothered by many problems or relationships he considers peripheral to his central function (Perlman, 1968). Thus, while both men and women must make role changes as their children grow up and leave home, these changes are much easier for the husband than for the wife. Not surprisingly, then, men in this age group (but not women) tell us they are much happier now than ever before (Table 6-4). Because of the ascribed position of earner, the role of father is less time- and energy-consuming than the mother's, and the husband can place greater

Table 6-4 Male Interests and Opinions
(Percent Agreeing by Age Group)

Statement	Sample total	Age group: Under 25	25–34	34–44	44–54	55 and older
Optimism and happiness						
My greatest achievements are still ahead of me	64%	98%	93%	76%	55%	25%
I dread the future	20	21	19	19	23	23
I am much happier now than I ever was before	78	87	92	97	76	74
Modern — traditional ideas						
I have somewhat old-fashioned tastes and habits	85	73	78	84	92	89
There is too much emphasis on sex today	66	56	65	74	81	93
I like to think I am a bit of a swinger	31	51	43	29	26	15
A woman's place is in the home	54	45	52	53	52	62
The working world is no place for a woman	27	24	20	25	26	37
Young people have too many privileges	75	60	63	77	74	88
The U.S. would be better off if there were no hippies	59	33	38	57	67	81
My days seem to follow a definite routine — eating meals at the same time each day, etc.	63	50	53	59	67	76
All men should be clean shaven every day	67	47	55	66	75	85
Travel						
I would like to take a trip around the world	67	74	73	77	68	53
I would like to spend a year in London or Paris	34	38	39	40	32	23
I would feel lost if I were alone in a foreign country	52	59	46	47	44	67
I like to visit places that are totally differend from my home	72	80	73	75	73	67
Mobile						
We will probably move at least once in the next five years	37	75	52	28	23	20
Our family has moved more often than most of our neighbors have	22	27	30	23	18	17
Anxious						
I have trouble getting to sleep	24	20	20	23	25	30
I wish I knew how to relax	47	40	48	51	44	50
Personal adornment and self						
Dressing well is an important part of my life	72	70	73	72	72	67
I like to feel attractive to members of the opposite sex	81	87	87	87	66	74
I want to look a little different from others	55	74	62	55	49	42

Table 6-4 Male Interests and Opinions (continued)

Statement	Sample total	Age group: Under 25	25–34	34–44	44–54	55 and older
I often wear expensive cologne	14%	16%	14%	12%	15%	13%
I have more stylish clothes than most of my friends	25	24	26	28	24	22
View toward income, personal equity, and spending						
I will probably have more money to spend next year than I have now	56	74	65	64	58	29
Five years from now our family income will probably be a lot higher than it is now	68	87	85	79	69	28
Our family income is high enough to satisfy nearly all our important desires	75	63	72	78	78	79
No matter how fast our income goes up we never seem to get ahead	58	60	68	56	52	39
Investing in the stock market is too risky for most families	83	86	82	81	87	86
Our family is too heavily in debt today	28	41	42	28	25	11
I like to pay cash for everything I buy	75	79	74	70	69	81
I pretty much spend for today and let tomorrow bring what it will	26	31	29	23	23	26
Staying at home						
I would rather spend a quiet evening at home than go out to a party	73	65	67	73	75	79
I am a homebody	72	55	67	73	79	82
I stay home most evenings	80	70	77	79	78	89
Husband and children						
A wife's first obligation is to her husband, not her children	57	43	52	54	64	66
When children are ill in bed, parents should drop everything else to see to their comfort	70	66	68	66	73	78
Children are the most important thing in a marriage	53	37	44	50	57	78
When making important family decisions, consideration of the children should come first	53	63	54	48	49	53
A wife should have a great deal of information about her husband's work	77	74	75	73	80	82
Our family is a close-knit group	87	86	94	89	83	88
View toward durable goods						
Our home is furnished for comfort, not for style	93	89	92	94	95	94
If I must choose, I buy stylish rather than practical furniture	15	18	20	14	15	9
When buying appliances, I am more concerned with dependability than price	93	91	93	90	94	95

Table 6-4 Male Interests and Opinions (continued)

Statement	Sample total	Age group: Under 25	25-34	34-44	44-54	55 and older
When buying appliances, the brand name is more important than the reputation of the store	56%	56%	53%	49%	55%	64%
A subcompact car can meet my transportation needs	59	71	57	56	58	57
Housekeeping and cooking						
When I see a full ashtray or wastebasket, I want it emptied immediately	56	56	46	54	60	63
I am uncomfortable when the house is not completely clean	51	57	48	53	49	52
The kind of dirt you can't see is worse than the kind you can see	77	68	74	73	79	86
I am a good cook	51	63	57	50	48	41
I like to cook	50	60	58	48	48	41
I like to bake	30	34	35	27	26	30
Meal preparation should take as little time as possible	42	42	41	38	40	46
Grocery shopping						
Shopping is no fun anymore	59	54	55	55	63	64
Before going shopping, I sit down and prepare a complete shopping list	44	35	42	38	38	56
I try to stick to well-known brands	79	71	79	76	71	86
I find myself checking prices even on small items	79	78	74	75	78	84
I like to save and redeem savings stamps	43	43	31	35	42	58
I pay a lot more attention to food prices now than I ever did before	81	81	79	81	81	84
I am an impulse buyer	38	46	47	40	33	30
I shop a lot for specials	60	61	59	63	56	61
Health and nutrition						
I am very concerned about nutrition	61	66	65	60	57	63
I am concerned about how much salt I eat	40	28	32	32	46	54
I am careful what I eat in order to keep my weight under control	51	38	43	44	55	64
I try to avoid foods that are high in cholesterol	49	31	42	41	60	63
I try to avoid foods that have additives in them	44	36	35	39	49	56
I get more headaches than most people	17	18	17	19	21	12
I eat more than I should	66	57	67	68	70	64

Data source: Needham, Harper & Steers, (1975).

emphasis on work to compensate for changes in family life to a larger extent than the wife. The working wife, however, does not generally attain such a defense system—she, if anything, adds to her homemaker-role pressures.

Generally, vocational success reaches its peak during the middle years, as reflected in the fact that earnings normally peak during middle age. Middle age is a time not only of financial and social success but also of vocational reevaluation. It is a time when men evaluate their accomplishments in the light of earlier aspirations and expectations (Archer, 1968).

Erikson (1967) states that middle age is a crisis age, in which either "generativity" or "stagnation" will dominate. That is, a person will become more and more successful or will stand still on past accomplishments. Whether one will "generate" or "stagnate" depends in part on the goals previously set in life and the degree of success in achieving them—in general, the "achievement motive" of the person.

The Achievement Motive Psychologists have long been interested in the way people set goals for themselves. One approach they use to study goal setting is through the analysis of imagination. In a typical study of this kind, subjects are shown a series of pictures and asked to tell a story about each one. What led up to the events shown in the picture? What is going on? What are the characters feeling and thinking? What is going to happen in the future?

Analysis of these stories that the subject makes up in response shows that some people tend to think rather consistently in terms of goal setting and goal attainment. The stories they tell are full of chances taken, achievements attained by the actor's efforts, obstacles successfully overcome, and accomplishments accompanied by applause and elation. The stories told by other subjects lack these themes or show them much less often. Some people "think achievement" much more than others do.

The tendency to "think achievement," measured by the story-telling test, influences behavior outside the laboratory. Students with high achievement motivation get better grades than students of equal intelligence who are low in achievement motivation. People with high achievement motivation move up in the executive ranks faster than executives whose achievement motivation is lower. When given the opportunity, high-achievement businessmen and businesswomen undertake projects with high risk and the prospect of high payoff, while business people with low achievement motivation undertake projects that provide more security.

How do people with strong achievement motivation get that way? Present evidence suggests that childhood training plays an important role—both the childhood training that is attributable to the society in which the child is raised and the childhood training that is attributable to the child's immediate family. Children raised in societies that emphasize achievement in folk tales, myths, and schoolbook stories have stronger achievement needs than children raised in other societies. And children raised in families that identify and reinforce achievement-related behavior have stronger achievement needs than children raised in families that reinforce other motives.

Achievement motivation influences more than grades and vocational attainment. It also influences consumer behavior—partly, of course, through the income it is instrumental in producing. In addition, achievement motivation influences decisions about investment and saving, biasing decisions away from low-risk, low-return savings accounts and life insurance policies and toward riskier investments, like common stock, that promise more return if they are successful.

Achievement motivation influences many other expenditures, although the influence is often subtle and often combined with the influence of other forces. Because a college education provides the training required for the most challenging occupations, many persons have sacrificed present income to get through college themselves, and have given up luxuries to provide a college education for their children. Because job changes often mean locality changes, achievement motivation contributes to decisions that result in use of long-distance moving companies and the services of real estate agents.

Activities and Interests

As Tables 6-3 and 6-4 reveal, persons in middle adulthood express some notions about their life styles that are highly consistent but also some that are contradictory. There is a consistent pattern of decline in *general mood.* Housewives in the 35–44 age group report they are less happy and optimistic than in previous life periods, and males report they are less optimistic. There is a particularly sharp drop in the percentage of those who agree with the statement, "My greatest achievements are still ahead of me." This is understandable in light of a characteristic of the middle years that people become more emotionally aware that death will come and that time is running out.

Some psychologists have termed the age period 35–44 as the "mid-life explosion." They see this stage of life as an unstable, explosive time resembling a second adolescence where all values are open to question (*Time,* 1975). It is certainly a time of introspection, of reflecting on the past and the future. It is not surprising, then, to find some seemingly contradictory views on *modern/traditional ideas.* On the one hand, the middle-adulthood women tell us they have some old-fashioned ideas, that there is too much emphasis on sex, and that they are not swingers. On the other hand, they do not report their days as routine and settled. Thus, at the same time that people are questioning, they are also beginning a transition into later adulthood, which is a time of truly settling down.

This seemingly contradictory pattern is also found in Tables 6-3 and 6-4 in the views expressed on *travel* and *mobility.* Here we find that women in middle adulthood are less mobile, are less cosmopolitan in viewing mobility, but are beginning to anticipate emptying the nest and vacationing; thus, while they are less likely to want to spend a year in London or Paris or to want to take a trip around the world, they are more likely to want to visit places totally different from home and they would probably settle, at this point, for a vacation without the children. Men, however, have wider travel horizons.

There is a continuing drop in interest in physical appearance as women move through middle adulthood. Although middle adulthood is a time for introspection, it is also a time when appearance has been accepted, when women indicate to a lesser degree an interest in dressing well and in stylish clothes. Men, not completely willing to accept decline of physical appearance maintain their interest in personal adornment and self. This, of course, is attributable to their successful position in life, and things like dressing in stylish clothes are symbolic of their position.

Views toward *finances* during middle adulthood continue the pattern established during earlier time periods. There is a general drop in financial optimism, largely because of a recognition that income is better than in the past and because it is likely to peak in the intermediate future. There is a heavy use of credit, especially via credit and charge cards, but less bank borrowing. This pattern, of course, is consistent with the peak expenditure items discussed earlier and the ability of this group to use credit more from a convenience than an installment standpoint.

As Table 6-3 shows, people in middle adulthood, when compared with earlier periods, express more interest in comfort in purchasing home *durables.* There is no longer a pressing need to acquire basic durables, and there is a new maturity in expressing one's self in the home. Thus, as durables are replaced, the emphasis shifts more to comfort and less to frills or fashions. Men and women tell us they furnish "for comfort, not for style." They are not yet ready to sacrifice price for dependability, however, when buying appliances.

Leisure pursuits also change during middle adulthood. Americans have more leisure time now than ever before and have more time than most other cultures because of shorter workweek, longer vacations, and numerous holidays, not to mention more mechanization of the home.

In spite of these increases, leisure time is cut by family responsibilities, community activities, wives working, and moonlighting. For families in the full-house stage, especially those with young children, recreation tends to be home-centered, such as playing with the kids, picnics, driving around for pleasure, and yard work. These activities, of course, continue to decrease with increasing age.

As children grow older, leisure pursuits often reflect more individualization for the parents. This is especially true for females. Their time for recreation (and type of pursuit) depends on the age of the children and the amount of labor-saving devices in the home. The young mother, for example, has little time except early afternoon when the children nap, and even then she is limited to what she can do alone, such as reading, listening to the radio, or watching TV. In contrast, when children are adolescents, mothers (if not working) have more time on their own for their own activities. They also attend more sporting events and concerts as spectators as children grow into the adolescent years than do husbands—see Tables 6-5 and 6-6.

Tables 6-5 and 6-6 show few pervasive activities for adults in the 35–44 age category. Only walking is found in the active recreations. Some leisure pursuits, however, continue to be engaged in by 80 percent or more of the population. For females, these are taking photographs, attending movies,

Table 6-5 Female Leisure Activities
(Percent Engaged in, by Age Group)

Activity	Sample total	Age group: Under 25	25-34	35-44	45-54	55 and older
Active recreations						
Went for a walk	91%	96%	94%	92%	88%	86%
Went swimming	62	84	80	73	55	31
Went boating	37	44	41	39	37	26
Went bowling	35	54	45	40	30	12
Went camping	30	42	38	36	26	15
Jogged	24	41	30	24	22	13
Played tennis	14	24	23	20	9	2
Went hunting	7	20	8	7	6	3
Went skiing	6	14	8	7	4	0
Went backpacking	3	10	4	3	2	1
Inactive recreations/hobbies						
Took color photographs	89	97	95	91	87	78
Played a game (monopoly, bingo, etc.)	85	95	95	94	81	77
Played cards	83	93	91	87	80	71
Went on a vacation	77	71	75	79	81	77
Went to the movies	74	95	88	82	71	43
Attended an X-rated movie	20	42	28	20	15	7
Attended a sporting event	53	56	60	63	53	36
Visited an art gallery or museum	49	35	48	57	52	46
Worked on a collection (stamps, coins, etc.)	31	22	27	30	34	36
Went to a classical concert	22	13	14	21	28	30
Went to a pop or rock concert	13	24	18	11	11	5
Went to an auto race	8	16	12	7	6	4

Data source: Needham, Harper & Steers, (1975).

playing games, and playing cards. For males, the pervasive pursuits are more limited to those that can be done with the wife and/or chiildren. Also, the data show that few activities increase in percent of the population engaging in them during middle adulthood. Those that show an increase, such as vacationing and attending sporting events, are related to economic position and the age of children in the home.

Media habits also change during middle adulthood. In the previous chapter we noted a general decline of about two hours in TV viewing as women move into the middle adult years. For males, there is an increase of about an hour per week. The number of hours viewed remains higher for females, however. Nielsen data for the six weeks ending December 3, 1967, for example, indicated that middle-aged males watch TV 20 hours and 30 minutes each week; the corresponding figure for middle-aged females was 27 hours and 13 minutes.

What do they watch? Table 6-7 shows the rankings for the Fall 1973 nighttime shows for females by age group and for working women. Women in

Table 6-6 Male Leisure Activities
(Percent Engaged in, by Age Group)

Activity	Sample total	Age group: Under 25	25–34	35–44	45–54	55 and older
Active recreations						
Went for a walk	82%	81%	83%	83%	80%	71%
Went swimming	61	82	76	75	67	32
Went boating	44	54	46	51	43	34
Went bowling	36	65	47	42	30	14
Went camping	34	48	41	44	32	18
Jogged	27	43	37	31	19	14
Played tennis	14	26	25	17	7	3
Went hunting	33	53	38	33	30	21
Went skiing	7	14	14	5	4	2
Went backpacking	6	9	10	8	4	2
Inactive recreations/hobbies						
Took color photographs	82	95	91	82	78	70
Played a game (monopoly, bingo, etc.)	79	99	92	86	70	60
Played cards	81	96	91	83	72	69
Went on a vacation	76	66	80	79	81	72
Went to the movies	72	94	89	79	69	42
Attended an X-rated movie	24	44	40	23	21	6
Attended a sporting event	61	64	67	72	64	42
Visited an art gallery or museum	36	24	40	43	37	32
Went to a classical concert	15	9	12	19	16	19
Went to a pop or rock concert	11	26	17	9	6	5
Went to an auto race	11	23	16	10	8	3

Data source: Needham, Harper & Steers, (1975).

their middle adult years preferred "All in the Family," followed by "Friday Night Movies" (CBS), "The Waltons," and "Sanford and Son"—a heavy dosage of comedy and family drama. Notice the shift in preference from the under-35 group, who are relatively heavier movie viewers.

Male TV preferences are illustrated in Table 6-8, which shows the program rankings by occupation of household head—mostly males. Many of the same shows emerge as popular with males as with females. The major exception, of course, is "NFL Football," which ranked second for professional/white-collar household heads.

In general, although not completely revealed in Tables 6-7 and 6-8, males prefer sports, news, and adventure programs and females prefer romance and family comedy.

LATER ADULTHOOD

Later adulthood, the period of life from the time the children have left home until retirement of the breadwinner(s), mostly covers the age span 45–65, but the 45–54 age group is used for benchmark data in the discussion because the frequency of emptying the nest increases dramatically during these years and there are some marked changes in persons which occur during the late forties and early fifties, particularly physical changes. These changes affect behavior and opinions of persons in later adulthood.

Physical Changes

Physical changes during later adulthood, of course, do not start during this period; they just become more apparent. Basically, the changes are an acceleration of the aging process that has been going on since birth.

Although gradual rather than sudden, physical changes do become pronounced during the latter part of the middle years and affect many behaviors of consumers. The most obvious—and to most people, the most troublesome—changes are shown in Figure 6-1—the "telltale signs of aging."

Weight gain, especially at the waistline, frequently contributes to a diet consciousness during later adulthood. More than members of any earlier age group, persons in the 45–54 category say they are careful what they eat in order to keep their weight under control. They also agree that they eat more than they should. And, although they are concerned about the consequences of cholesterol, diet consciousness does not generally run to nutritional concern.

Table 6-7 Female Ratings for Network Nighttime Series

	Rank and rating — female group							
	Under 35		35-49		50 +		Working women# all ages	
Program	Rank	Rating	Rank	Rating	Rank	Rating	Rank	Rating
"All in the Family" (CBS)	7	25.7	1	34.9	1	36.4	1	30.0
"Sanford and Son" (NBC)	—	23.5	4	32.0	2	35.2	2	28.6
"Friday Movie" (CBS)	1	33.1	2	34.6	—	—	3	27.9
"Wonderful World of Disney" (NBC)	4	27.8	7	27.4	—	—	4	25.4
"The Waltons" (CBS)	2	30.4	3	33.0	5	26.9	5	25.3
"Maude" (CBS)	—	23.8	8	26.8	6	26.5	6	24.7
"M*A*S*H" (CBS)	—	21.9	5	29.1	4	27.8	7	23.8
"Hawaii Five-O" (CBS)	—	20.8	6	27.7	7	25.0	7	23.8
"Sunday Movie" (ABC)	—	23.8	—	—	—	—	9	23.1
"Monday Movie" (NBC)	9	24.9	—	—	—	—	10	22.7
"Tuesday Movie of the Week" (ABC)	3	28.4	—	—	—	—	—	—
"Sunday Mystery Movie" (ABC)	5	27.0	—	—	—	—	—	—
"Thursday Movie" (CBS)	6	26.9	—	—	—	—	—	—
"NFL Football" (ABC)	8	25.5	—	—	—	—	—	—
"Marcus Welby" (ABC)	10	24.3	—	—	—	—	—	—
"Sonny and Cher" (CBS)	—	22.8	9	26.3	—	—	—	—
"Mary Tyler Moore" (CBS)	—	20.8	10	26.2	8	24.5	—	—
"Gunsmoke" (CBS)	—	—	—	—	3	28.0	—	—
"Adam 12" (NBC)	—	—	—	—	9	23.5	—	—
"Bob Newhart" (CBS)	—	—	—	—	10	23.3	—	—

#Employed outside home at least 30 hours weekly.
Source: A. C. Nielsen Co. (1974: 45).

Table 6-8 Household Heads' Ratings for Network Nighttime Series, by Occupation

	Rank and rating, by household heads grouped by occupation					
	Professional/ white collar		Blue collar/ skilled		Not in labor force	
Program	Rank	Rating	Rank	Rating	Rank	Rating
"All in the Family" (CBS)	1	31.4	2	33.1	1	34.3
"NFL Football" (ABC)	2	28.4	—	—	—	—
"Friday Movies" (CBS)	3	27.5	1	33.7	—	—
"Sanford and Son" (NBC)	4	27.0	3	31.8	2	33.7
"The Waltons" (CBS)	4	27.0	5	30.6	3	28.0
"M*A*S*H" (CBS)	6	26.4	7	26.6	6	24.6
"Sunday Mystery Movie" (NBC)	7	25.1	6	27.9	—	—
"Maude" (CBS)	8	25.0	—	—	4	26.9
"Mary Tyler Moore" (CBS)	9	23.7	—	—	6	24.6
"Wonderful World of Disney" (NBC)	10	23.4	4	31.6	—	—
"Kung Fu" (ABC)	—	—	9	25.8	—	—
"Thursday Movie" (CBS)	—	—	8	25.9	—	—
"Monday Movie" (NBC)	—	—	9	25.8	—	—
"Gunsmoke" (CBS)	—	—	—	—	5	26.5
"Hawaii Five-O" (CBS)	—	—	—	—	8	24.0
"Bob Newhart" (CBS)	—	—	—	—	9	23.8
"Adam-12" (NBC)	—	—	—	—	10	23.0

Source: A. C. Nielsen Co. (1974: 45).

In addition to weight gain, a number of other changes in appearance tend to produce a person unlike the youth model of American society—less hair in some parts, more in others, baggy eyes, and rounded shoulders typically are not characteristics seen in models for clothing and cosmetic advertisements.

How do later adults react to their appearance? Of all age groups, members of the 45–54 group are least happy with their appearance—38 percent generally or strongly disagree with the statement, "I like what I see when I look in the mirror," compared with the population average of 26 percent and the following percentages for other age groups: under 25, 18 percent; 25–34, 12 percent; 35–44, 24 percent; and 55 and over, 32 percent.[1] Such dissatisfaction should not be surprising, however. As Hurlock (1975) has suggested, "Having known, since early adolescence, the important role appearance plays in social judgements, social acceptance, and leadership, the middle-aged person rebels against threats to the status he fears he may lose as his appearance deteriorates."

Persons (especially females) in their later years still have hopes, aspirations, and personal care activity—they generally increase their interest in fashion over members of the 35–44 age group (Table 6-3)—but age is creeping up.

[1]Unpublished data from Leo Burnett, 1971.

In addition to the external changes in appearance depicted in Figure 6-1, internal changes also take place during later adulthood; chief among these are sexual change—the much dreaded menopause in women; and in men, the male climacteric. Because much mystery surrounds the sexual changes for most women and men, there tends to be an accompanying psychological or emotional change producing headaches, fatigue, choking, sleep difficulty, restlessness, and irritability. Small wonder members of the 45–54 age group say they have trouble getting to sleep and that they wish they knew how to relax (Table 6-3).

Small wonder, too, are the further changes in *general mood.* Persons in this age group are less happy and optimistic than those in any earlier age group. They are more *settled,* agreeing more that their days seem to follow a definite routine and less that they have moved more frequently than their neighbors. Also, they consistently express more traditional or *conservative* attitudes (Tables 6-3 and 6-4).

Change in Family Pattern

One of the most dramatic changes in the middle years is the withdrawal of children from the home, leaving husband and wife as the family unit. The consequence of this change is depicted in Figure 5-1 as a role shift from family-centered to pair-centered.

This transition time is tougher for wives than for husbands. Children or no

Figure 6-1 Telltale Signs of Aging

Weight Gain
During middle age, fat accumulates mainly around the abdomen and on the hips.

Loss and Graying of Hair
The middle-aged man's hairline begins to recede, the hair becomes thinner, and baldness on the top of the head is very common. Hair in the nose, ears, and eyelashes becomes stiffer, while facial hair grows more slowly and is less luxuriant. Women's hair becomes thinner, and there is an increase of hair on the upper lip and chin. Both men and women have a predominance of gray hair by fifty, and some have white hair before middle age ends.

Skin Changes
The skin on the face, neck, arms, and hands becomes coarser and wrinkled. Bags appear under the eyes and dark circles become more permanent and pronounced. Bluish-red discolorations often appear around the ankles and on the mid-calf.

Body Sag
The shoulders become rounded and there is a general sagging of the body which makes the abdomen appear prominent and causes the person to look shorter.

Muscle Changes
Most middle-aged people's muscles become soft and flabby in the areas of the chin, upper arms, and abdomen.

Joint Problems
Some middle-aged people develop problems in their joints and limbs that cause them to walk with difficulty and to handle things with an awkwardness rarely found in younger adults.

Changes in Teeth
The teeth beocme yellowed and must often be replaced with partial or complete dentures.

Changes in Eyes
The eyes look less bright than they did when the individual was younger, and there is a tendency for mucous to accumulate in the corners of the eyes.

Source: Hurlock (1975:266).

children, the husband continues in his primary life role, that of worker and doer outside the home. But his wife is freed—or stripped, depending on her view—of her most essential and long-absorbing role. For the wife, especially if she feels stripped, there is a loss of the sense of function and usefulness. She has mixed emotions—release and emptiness, freedom and ambiguity, achievement-pleasure and nostalgia-regret—and these are carried into behaviors that may or may not lead to new ways of self-fulfillment. For example, housing arrangements may change—the uprooting from long-familiar quarters to settle into new and smaller ones, or some radical, even frantic "redecorating" as if to symbolize that a new and different life has begun (Perlman, 1968).

The marriage relationship also is affected by the childless state—the empty nest. Husband and wife may draw more closely together, find one another again, and celebrate their "second honeymoon"; or they may find that, now the children are gone, there is "nothing to talk about," a situation that leads in many cases to infidelity, separations, and divorces. For those who find one another again, life styles change and couples enjoy entertaining, visiting, and vacationing together; they enjoy many of their new activities and interests.

Changes in Activities and Interests

While there are changes in interests and activities during later adulthood, they are not as marked as were the changes of earlier years. The changes that take place now are the result of changes in health, in duties and responsibilities, and in roles in life.

In men, interests narrow somewhat because of concentration on vocational advancement. This is especially true for more successful men. In women there is a more pronounced change because of role change. Women have fewer responsibilities with children, but men are still quite occupied with a career, so women must find more things they can do outside the home.

For both sexes, interests shift from energy-consuming and social to more sedentary and solitary ones as age increases; for example, sports, dancing, and active recreations decrease, while reading, art, and attending lectures increase. During later adulthood there is also a lessening of sex differences in interests and activities; especially large are the changes in males, from active and mechanical to artistic and cultural.

The most common activities and interests of later adulthood are discussed below.

Appearance and Clothes As noted, people react negatively to the telltale signs of aging. Thus, interest in appearance, which declined during the years of parenthood, again becomes salient with advancing age. Both men and women attempt to conceal the signs of aging through dieting, exercising, and the use of cosmetics and clothing. Men attempt to reverse their age advance or hide their appearance because a youth image is a business asset; women, while not as fashion conscious as during the early phases of adulthood, still want to be attractive. Working women are especially conscious of appearance for the same reason males are; but housewives also are appearance and clothes conscious because of critical appraisal by their children and because of the social image relative to their new roles in community activities. And women do not want to look older than their husbands.

The refound interest in clothing during later adulthood is reflected in Table 6-3 in the increase in the percentage of women agreeing with these statements: "I have more stylish clothes than most of my friends" and "I like to feel attractive to members of the opposite sex."

Money As shown by the data in Tables 6-3 and 6-4, persons in later adulthood recognize that they are nearing their peak in earning income. But generally they are less concerned about money than in prior years. While they are near the peak of earning power, they also know that demands on their incomes are fewer, and they express different views about personal equity and spending: they are not too heavily in debt and do not feel that they never seem to get ahead.

Concern for money, of course, varies by occupational level and sex. While men in professional fields are relatively secure, working-class men often are greatly concerned with money, especially during dislocations of the economy, because their employment is less stable and they cannot "retread" as easily if job technology changes. The female is more interested in money than the male during later adulthood because she wants the status symbols money can buy and she feels threatened by possible loss of support by her husband in case of his death or illness. Indeed, one reason many middle-aged women return to the labor force is the goal of ensuring their security both at the time and for old age.

Status Symbols When entering later adulthood, many people are able to afford material possessions reflecting status because they have more money and because the drains on it are less. Status symbols are especially important to those who are anxious to move up the status ladder and to those who wish to express their actual rank. Almost all visible items represent status symbols, but the home is the major one because it costs so much more than cars and clothes and because it can be used to display other symbols of status such as art objects and antiques.

The importance of the home is reflected in the overall pattern of responses to questions relating to it in Tables 6-3 and 6-4. Women and men in later adulthood tell us, for instance, that they are homebodies and that they would rather stay at home than go out to a party.

Community Affairs Later adulthood is a time for community service. Men generally are well established in their occupation and for women home responsibilities are lower. Community responsibility and activity emerge throughout the years of adulthood, but generally these reach the peak in this stage of life, particularly for such activities as collecting money for the Red Cross, United Fund, or other charities. Generally, persons in later adulthood engage more in community affairs because they are given positions of leadership in recognition of their life accomplishments.

Leisure Pursuits During later adulthood there is a major increase in leisure time, especially when compared with early adulthood, and especially for females. The young adult cannot afford the labor-saving devices, whereas persons in later adulthood can afford them, and they increase leisure time. Also, the demands of parenthood are diminished, and this, too, increases the time available for leisure pursuits.

From the standpoint of consumer behavior, the major question is, "What changes in leisure pursuits accompany the increased time for leisure activities?" In general, four important changes in leisure interests occur during later adulthood: strenuous activities continue to decline; activities are more individualized; pursuits tend to become adult- as opposed to family-oriented; and there is a continual narrowing down of interests (Hurlock, 1975).

As Tables 6-5 and 6-6 show, participation in the more active recreations declines markedly during later adulthood. With few exceptions, males and females in the 45–54 age group are well below the population average for participation in the more strenuous events. The decline in level of participation, of course, is consistent with the aging process, as are those few active pursuits engaged in most often, such as swimming and walking, which aid physical appearance and health.

Persons in later adulthood prefer less formal and smaller-group activities where sociability is stressed and where there are few rules and obligations to the large, organized-group activities. When persons in later adulthood engage in group activity, it is usually in connection with community organizations such as civic, social, and church organizations. In general, though, there is a shift to more individualized pursuits of an adult nature and to a smaller number of leisure pursuits. Tables 6-5 and 6-6 show these interrelated shifts. Notice, for example, the decline in attending sporting events and the increase in working on a collection such as stamps and coins.

There also is a shift in television viewing and program preferences during later adulthood. For both males and females, the amount of time spent viewing television increases by about six hours per week beginning around age fifty. Programming preferences become more selective, however; there is a move toward variety and panel shows and away from adventure and soap opera.

Travel and "trips" also are more common in later adulthood than in middle adulthood. With fewer family responsibilities and more income, people in later adulthood are able to take more trips to visit friends, to sightsee, or to go on extended travel. This latter interest is revealed in the increased percentage of persons reporting taking a vacation in Tables 6-5 and 6-6.

SUMMARY

The middle years are marked by role changes which significantly affect outlook on life and consumer behavior. We have divided the middle-years period into two categories which reflect these role changes: middle adulthood and later adulthood.

Middle adulthood is characterized by the "full nest" family life-cycle stage, during which children increasingly are becoming oriented toward activities outside the home rather than inside, husbands are becoming increasingly oriented toward their work, and wives are pulled in two directions, both toward family-related activities and away from them. Middle-aged women become involved in PTA and youth organizations, but many also become involved with social or community groups and in jobs of their own. For women, roles reflect family changes which are not always seen as favorable, resulting in a decline in general outlook, optimism, and satisfaction, while men are reaching their peak in career and community roles.

Later adulthood, characterized by the "emptying nest" and "empty nest" life-cycle stages, is accompanied by increasing amounts of leisure time and discretionary income but declining physical condition. Although older adults now have the means to engage in a variety of leisurely pursuits, the type of activities may be curtailed by physical limitations. Discretionary income is often expended on goods which indicate the increasing prestige of the family resulting from the husband's advancement in his career, thus creating a luxury market reflected in sales of durables and travel. This life period is often marred by emotional problems as children leave home, husband-wife relationships change, and the telltale signs of aging become more apparent.

As consumers progress through the middle years, their leisure activities change in directions that continue through later life periods: strenuous activities continue to decline, activities are more individualized, pursuits tend to become adult as opposed to family-oriented, and there is a continual narrowing of interest. Older people watch more TV and are more interested in travel but change residences less than their younger counterparts. Generally, they are becoming more settled in their ways and will continue to do so as age progresses.

REVIEW QUESTIONS

1 Both age groups included in the middle years will be declining as a percentage of the total population through the 1970s. Why, then, is it important to continue to study and understand these groups?
2 Purchasing and consumption patterns during the middle years change as the children in the family grow older. What types of products reach their highest average expenditure when children's ages are: some under six and some over six, six to eleven, and twelve or over?
3 Males and females differ markedly in the degree of role changes faced during the

middle years. Discuss these changes for each sex and determine why they are so much more pervasive for women. How do these role changes affect consumer behavior?

4 How is "achievement motivation" related to consumer behavior? Give some specific examples of purchasing and consumption patterns that are related to degree of achievement motivation.

5 Generally, activities and interests in the middle years follow trends established in earlier years. One exception seems to be interest in physical appearance. How does this interest change during each age period in the middle years? Are the changes the same for men and women? Why or why not?

6 Middle adulthood usually spans a full-nest family situation while later adulthood involves in emptying-the-nest situation. How do these changes in family structure affect the activities and consumer behavior of parents? What effect do these changes have on discretionary income?

7 In addition to changes in the family situation, physical and emotional changes have important effects on consumer behavior in later adulthood. Identify specific changes that accompany increasing age and their corresponding effects on behavior and mood.

8 Later adulthood is often referred to as the "luxury market." Why? What types of products are especially important for this group?

9 Are older adults more likely to be thinking about, or actually taking, vacations and travel trips than younger adults? Why or why not?

10 Do you agree that the middle years are a period of "payoff" for consumers? Why?

11 Identify the four important changes that occur in leisure interests during later adulthood. What are the factors contributing to these changes?

EXERCISE

Later adulthood represents the affluent years of the life span. Persons comprising it generally represent a significant proportion of the luxury market. Yet it is declining as a percent of the United States population. When will this trend change? Show by "aging" the current young adult population, and take into account the net change occurring through immigration, emigration, and death.

REFERENCES

Archer, D. "The Male Change of Life." *Yale Alumni Magazine* (March 1968), 33–35.

Erikson, E. H. "Identity and the Life Cycle: Selected Papers." *Psychological Issues Monograph.* Vol. 1. New York: International Universities Press, 1967.

Franzblau, R. N. *The Middle Generation.* New York: Holt, 1971.

Hawes, Douglas K., W. Wayne Talarzyk, and Roger D. Blackwell. "Consumer Satisfaction from Leisure Time Pursuits." In Mary Jane Schlinger (ed.), *Advances in Consumer Research.* Vol. 1. Chicago: Association of Consumer Research, 1974, 817–836.

Hurlock, Elizabeth B. *Developmental Psychology.* 4th ed. New York: McGraw-Hill, 1975.

Linden, Fabian. "Reshuffling the Age-Income Mix." *The Conference Board RECORD* (March 1974).

Lopata, Helena Znaniecki. "The Life Cycle of the Social Role of Housewife." *Sociology and Social Research,* 51 (1966), 5–22.

McClelland, D. C. *The Achieving Society.* Princeton, N.J.: Van Nostrand, 1961.

National Industrial Conference Board. *Expenditure Patterns of the American Family.* New York: *Life,* 1965.

Neugarten, B. L. "Continuities and Discontinuities of Psychological Issues into Adult Life." *Human Development,* 12 (1969), 121–130.

Nielsen, A. C., Co. Reported in *Advertising Age* (Feb. 4, 1974), 45.

Perlman, Helen Harris. *Persona, Social Role and Personality.* Chicago: The University of Chicago Press, 1968.

Pressey, S. L., and R. G. Kuhlen. *Psychological Development through the Life Span.* New York: Harper & Row, 1957.

Time article. "The Command Generation." *Time* (July 19, 1966), 50–54.

———. "New Light on Adult Life Cycles." *Time* (Apr. 18, 1975), 69.

Wells, William D., and George Gubar. "Life Cycle Concept in Marketing Research." *Journal of Marketing Research,* 3 (November 1966), 355–363.

Chapter 7

Older Consumers

Throughout history older persons have occupied a precarious position in society. Some primitive people, while respecting the elderly, left them to die when they could no longer care for themselves. This idea of abandoning the elderly is not unique to primitive societies. A 1966 Rand Corporation study concluded that if the United States survived a nuclear war it would be "better off without old and feeble" citizens, and suggested that no provisions be made to care for the surviving elderly. And in the 1968 novel *They,* Marya Mannes postulated a world in which everyone over fifty was herded into public institutions and eventually liquidated (*Time,* 1975).

Americans, fortunately for the aged, have not followed such "advice" and have tried to live up to the Fifth Commandment of honoring their parents. American marketers, however, have been extensively criticized for, if not abandoning, at least forgetting the needs of older consumers. It is true the marketing community has lionized youth in lieu of the old for years. As expressed in the header to a *Forbes* (1969) article: "Youth will be served, and youth is being served. But the elderly, who have twice as much money to spend as the teenagers, are getting scant attention from the marketing men." It also is true that few, if any, cosmetics are positioned for the elderly and that dress designers and manufacturers do not market clothes especially for older women.

This lack of attention may or may not be sound business. Heinz Foods, for example, tried to market "senior foods." These were a failure because older consumers preferred to buy baby food, saying it was for their grandchildren (*Forbes*, 1969). Even so, many of the elderly have eating problems and need special food regardless of what it is called.

Today, a new interest is emerging in older consumers, in understanding and meeting their needs and problems. The new interest is encouraging, and any resulting action is not only humane but pragmatic as well.

OLDER CONSUMERS

Age sixty to death is the traditional definition of old age in the American culture. However, there is an increasing trend toward using sixty-five—the age of compulsory retirement in many businesses—to mark the dividing line between middle and old age. Retirement, especially in the study of consumer behavior, is an important event which sets off a new chain of consumer activities. Even so, age sixty-five is not a universal age for retirement; many institutions, such as educational and religious ones, allow persons to work until sixty-seven or seventy, while others, including the military services, allow much earlier retirement. Thus many persons have retired when they were in the age group fifty-five to sixty-four, and many are still in the labor force at seventy.

In the following sections we will use age fifty-five and older to provide data about older consumers. But it should be remembered that chronological age is a poor criterion to use in marking off the beginning of old age because there are wide individual differences in the relation between age and the aging process.

The period of old age, like every other period in the life span, is characterized by certain changes and new issues which affect the behavior of persons as consumers. The most obvious characteristic is that it is a period of decline, physically and mentally. Aging also requires role changes, as suggested in Figure 5-1. Some of the issues are those related to "renunciation"—adapting to losses of work, friends, spouse, a sense of competency, and authority; others relate to "reconciliation"—with members of one's family, one's achievements, and one's failures; and some relate to the need to maintain a sense of integrity in terms of what one has been rather than of what one is, or to the concern with "legacy"—how to leave traces of oneself (Neugarten, 1969). Many of these issues of aging and old age will be discussed after the documentation of the importance of older consumers as consumers.

THEIR IMPORTANCE

The size of the population of older consumers and its trends are shown in Table 7-1. Currently, slightly over 19 percent of the population is age 55 or older, a group slightly smaller than the middle-years population and substantially smaller than the young adult population. Into the 1980s older consumers will

Table 7-1 The Older Consumer Population: 1970–1985
(Millions of Persons)

Year	Total population	Age group: 55–64 (number and %)		65 and older (number and %)	
1970	204.8	18.6	9.0%	20.2	9.9%
1975	216.6	19.8	9.1	21.9	10.1
1980	230.9	21.2	9.1	23.7	10.3
1985	246.3	21.4	8.7	25.5	10.4

Note: Series D (moderate low series) projections. Data include Armed Forces overseas and are as of July 1.
Source: Department of Commerce (1971).

hold their own, percentagewise, and increase slightly in aggregate number. The major change, as shown in the table, will be among the persons 65 and older—a growth in the next 10 years of almost 4 million persons.

Table 7-2 shows the number of households and their incomes for these older-consumer age groups. As the data reveal, the 55–64 age group will become somewhat less important in the 10 years ahead. Although the number of households, like the number of persons in this age group, will increase slightly, the growth will be below average. Furthermore, when compared with the preceding age group, there is a significant change in household income. While 27 percent (in 1972) have incomes above $15,000, this fares poorly against the 40 percent who have earnings of over $15,000 in the 45–54 age group. Moreover, close to 1 out of every 4 households has earnings of less than $5,000, compared with 1 of 8 for the 45–54 age group households. By 1985 the income situation will improve somewhat for this age, but the group will remain less well off than the 45–54 age group. The income change from later adulthood to early old age is explained largely by the large number of working wives who have withdrawn from the labor force, as well as by retired male heads of households.

In contrast to the soon-to-be-retired group, the already retired—the 65-and-over—are expected to increase in number at a slightly faster than average rate in the years ahead. Being already retired, by and large, the group's incomes drop sharply. In 1980 and in 1985, the over-65 will account for 20 percent of the households but only 11 percent of household income.

While older consumers are not as well heeled as in previous years, they should not be ignored—their obligations are less than those of the younger adults. In many cases the house is paid for and there is an adequate inventory of furniture, appliances, and other durables, leaving the household income for basic necessities and luxury goods and services.

What specifically is the distinguishing expenditure pattern of older consumers? One set of items where purchasing is heavily skewed to older consumers is clearly a function of age-related physical difficulties: laxatives, denture products, pain-relieving rubs, indigestion remedies, medical applianc-

Table 7-2 Older Consumer Households, by Age of Head and Income Class
(All Figures in 1972 Dollars)

	All households	Age of household head: Under 25	25–34	35–44	45–54	55–64	65 and over
			1972				
Households							
Millions	68.3	5.5	13.6	11.7	12.8	11.2	13.5
Distribution	100.0%	8.0%	20.0%	17.0%	19.0%	16.5%	19.5%
Spending power							
Total	100.0%	5.5	20.5	21.5	24.5	17.0	11.0
Discretionary	100.0%	1.5	14.5	25.0	33.0	19.5	6.5
Household income distribution	100.0%	100.0%	100.0%	100.0%	100.0%	100.0%	100.0%
Under $3,000	14.0	15.5	6.0	5.0	6.5	13.5	35.5
$ 3,000– 5,000	11.0	16.5	7.5	6.0	6.5	10.0	23.0
$ 5,000– 7,000	10.5	17.5	10.0	8.0	7.5	10.5	13.5
$ 7,000–10,000	16.0	24.0	20.0	15.5	14.0	16.0	12.0
$10,000–15,000	23.0	19.5	32.5	28.0	25.0	23.0	8.5
$15,000–25,000	19.5	6.5	20.5	29.0	29.0	19.0	5.5
$25,000 and over	6.0	0.5	3.5	8.5	11.5	8.0	2.0
			1980				
Households							
Millions	77.3	6.0	18.3	13.1	11.8	12.4	15.6
Distribution	100.0%	8.0%	23.5%	17.0%	15.5%	16.0%	20.0%
Spending power							
Total	100.0%	5.5	25.0	21.5	20.0	17.0	11.0
Discretionary	100.0%	1.5	19.5	26.5	27.5	18.5	6.5
Household income distribution	100.0%	100.0%	100.0%	100.0%	100.0%	100.0%	100.0%
Under $3,000	12.0	13.0	5.0	4.0	5.5	12.0	31.0
$ 3,000– 5,000	10.5	14.5	6.5	5.5	6.0	9.0	23.0
$ 5,000– 7,000	10.0	17.0	8.5	7.0	6.5	10.0	14.5
$ 7,000–10,000	14.5	23.0	17.0	13.0	12.0	14.0	12.0
$10,000–15,000	23.0	22.5	32.5	25.5	22.5	23.0	10.0
$15,000–25,000	22.0	9.0	25.0	32.0	32.0	22.5	6.5
$25,000 and over	8.0	1.0	5.5	13.0	15.5	9.5	3.0
			1985				
Households							
Millions	84.2	6.0	20.5	16.3	11.7	12.7	17.1
Distribution	100.0%	7.0%	24.5%	19.5%	14.0%	15.0%	20.0%
Spending power							
Total	100.0%	5.0	26.0	24.5	18.0	15.5	11.0
Discretionary	100.0%	1.5	20.5	29.5	25.0	17.0	6.5
Household income distribution	100.0%	100.0%	100.0%	100.0%	100.0%	100.0%	100.0%
Under $3,000	11.0	12.0	5.0	4.0	5.5	11.0	28.5
$ 3,000– 5,000	10.0	13.5	5.5	5.0	5.5	8.5	23.0
$ 5,000– 7,000	9.0	14.5	8.0	6.0	6.0	9.0	14.0
$ 7,000–10,000	14.0	23.0	15.5	11.5	10.5	14.0	13.5
$10,000–15,000	22.0	23.5	29.5	24.0	21.0	22.0	11.0
$15,000–25,000	25.0	12.5	30.5	35.5	33.5	24.5	7.0
$25,000 and over	9.0	1.0	6.0	14.0	18.0	11.0	3.0

Source: Linden (1974).

es, drugs, and "other medical care" such as nursing homes and outpatient hospital service; also, color rinses, artificial sweeteners, dietetic canned foods, and prunes. Generally, these items are heavily purchased by all older-consumer groups.

Another set of items show a steady increase in expenditure with age but peak during the 55–64 age period. This set consists primarily of luxuries or near luxuries: fur coats and stoles; men's jewelry and watches; blended whiskey, bourbon, Scotch and rye; manicures, massages, and slenderizing treatments; gifts and contributions; laundry and cleaning sent out; and repairs by contractors (Wells and Gubar, 1966, and Reinecke, 1964).

And, while vacationing is not as high as for the 45–54 age group, older consumers are above average in foreign travel, higher in frequency of air travel, and way ahead of the under-35 group in possession of passports, air travel and auto rental credit cards, and traveler's checks (Grey Advertising, Inc., 1973).

In summary, the older consumer market consists essentially of two different segments, the soon-to-be-retired and the already retired. The younger group is, of course, more appealing from an income viewpoint but less so in terms of proportion of population. The older group, however, has more pressing needs and will maintain its earned buying power and transfer payments in the decade to come. In the following sections we examine the major changes occurring during old age, physical and mental changes, loss of work role (retirement), and shifting interests and activities.

PHYSICAL CHANGES

Old age is the closing period in the life span and it generally is marked by decline or physical deterioration. Yet there are wide individual differences in the *rate* of aging, so one should not expect to characterize all sixty-seven-year-olds as at the same state of deterioration. The rate of aging varies according to hereditary factors, body build, and life experiences, including diet, amount of work, and diseases. The rate is controlled by endocrine glands, especially pituitary, adrenal cortex, thyroid, and gonads. Sooner or later, however, major physical changes occur in old age.

Appearance

Figure 7-1 gives the changes in appearance that normally occur during old age. The face presents the first and most obvious signs of aging, especially the lower part—smaller jaw, sagging chin, and jowly cheeks. Also, the eyes are baggy, dull, and lusterless, and the nose appears longer by comparison.

The hands, like the face, are another telltale sign of old age. Scrawny hands with prominent veins are difficult to hide with cosmetics and may even be more telling of a person's age than the face.

How do people react to these changes in appearance? Obviously not with joy. Persons over fifty-five, to a less degree than any other age group, tell us

Figure 7-1 Common Appearance Changes during Old Age

Head Region

The nose elongates

The mouth changes shape as a result of tooth loss or the necessity of wearing dentures

The eyes seem dull and lusterless and often have a watery look

A double or triple chin develops

The cheeks become pendulous, wrinkled, and baggy

The skin becomes wrinkled and dry, and dark spots, moles, or warts may appear

The hair on the head becomes thin and turns gray or white and tough, bristly hair appears in the nose, ears, and eyebrows

Trunk Region

The shoulders stoop and thus seem smaller

The abdomen bulges and droops

The hips seem flabbier and broader than they did earlier

The waistline broadens, giving the trunk a sacklike appearance

The woman's breasts become flabby and droop

Limbs

The upper arm becomes flabby and heavy, while the lower arm seems to shrink in diameter

The legs become flabby and the veins prominent, especially around the ankles

The hands become scrawny, and the veins on the back of the hand are prominent

The feet become larger as a result of sagging muscles, and corns, bunions, and callouses often appear

The nails of the hands and feet become thick, tough, and brittle

Source: Hurlock (1975:317).

they like what they see when they look in the mirror (Table 7-3). Also, a fairly large number (32 percent) generally or strongly disagree with the statement, "I like what I see when I look in the mirror." Also, older consumers seem to have lost some of their hopes and aspirations for retaining their appearance—they no longer wish they were "more glamorous," but they do continue brushing their hair and emphasizing its natural color (Table 7-3).

Many of the physical changes listed in Figure 7-1, of course, are difficult to camouflage, and this leads to a change in fashion interest, discussed later.

Physiological and Sensory Functions

In addition to visible outward changes and certain internal changes in the skeleton from bone hardening, there are a number of changes in the functioning of the organs during old age. Some of these, such as reduced metabolic rate and

Table 7-3 Older Consumers: Reactions to Appearance

	Percent agreeing	
Statement	Total population	55 years and older
I like what I see when I look in the mirror	16%	9%
I wish I were more glamorous than I am	39	35
I brush my hair at least twice a day	23	21
I like the natural color of my hair	48	64
Eye makeup is more important than lipstick	29	10

Data source: Leo Burnett (1971).

muscular vigor, affect the ability of older consumers to tolerate temperature extremes, which in turn leads them to more stable environments such as staying indoors or moving, if they can afford it, to a better climate. Others, such as elevated blood pressure, lead them to the doctor's office more often than in the past.

Still others affect consumer behavior. During old age, the need for sleep decreases and many old people suffer from insomnia—notice the highest percentage of agreement with "I often have trouble getting to sleep" is in the 55-and-over age group (Tables 7-4 and 7-5)—making the older consumer a prime prospect for sleep aids of the variety advertised on the Lawrence Welk show.

Digestive problems also are common during old age, mainly because of dental difficulties but also because of changes in sensory functioning, especially taste—see Figure 7-2—food becomes tasteless. Digestive problems also occur because the stomach glands no longer produce the fluids to lubricate and to dissolve food elements to the degree necessary for proper digestion.

With these and other deteriorating health changes in old age, older consumers become increasingly conscious of health and nutrition, as is reflected in the pattern of responses to a number of items in Tables 7-4 and 7-5. They shun serving high-cholesterol foods and limit their salt intake; and they generally recognize the need for nutritional foods to help fight off illnesses. Unfortunately, though, as aging progresses and mental changes occur, older consumers lose this consciousness and malnutrition becomes common, especially among those old persons living alone. This problem is almost predictable from the above-average agreement among the over-55 group that meal preparation should take as little time as possible.

Among the changes in sensory functioning, the organs most affected by aging are the eyes and ears, but all sense organs function less effectively—see Figure 7-2. Sensory changes all work to cut the older person off from his or her environment and from other people, the latter being reflected in the responses to such items in Tables 7-4 and 7-5 as those asking about being a homebody and spending quiet evenings at home.

MENTAL CHANGES

Traditionally it has been assumed that mental deterioration inevitably accompanies physical decline. Physical deterioration does contribute to mental decline in learning ability, in reasoning, in creativity, in recall, and in memory. But it is important to recognize that the mental decline associated with old age may not be as great as is popularly believed (Hurlock, 1975). Moreover, we do not have to emphasize Verdi's *Falstaff*, composed at age eighty, or other major accomplishments of selected elderly persons to document the point.

Rather, some mental abilities decrease more rapidly than others. Those abilities most likely to decline first involve the execution of tasks requiring

Table 7-4 Female Interests and Opinions
(Percent Agreeing, by Age Group)

Statement	Sample total	Age group: Under 25	25-34	35-44	45-54	55 and older
Optimism and happiness						
My greatest achievements are still ahead of me	64%	92%	84%	73%	52%	28%
I dread the future	23	20	18	17	24	30
I am much happier now than I ever was before	79	85	82	80	74	74
Modern-traditional ideas						
I have somewhat old-fashioned tastes and habits	86	78	84	87	88	89
There is too much emphasis on sex today	87	70	74	90	89	93
I like to think I am a bit of a swinger	26	43	34	26	19	15
A woman's place is in the home	46	39	39	44	49	60
The working world is no place for a woman	17	15	11	14	19	28
Young people have too many privileges	76	57	74	77	76	83
The U.S. would be better off if there were no hippies	55	32	37	46	54	82
My days seem to follow a definite routine—eating meals at the same time each day, etc.	67	59	62	61	67	75
Travel						
I would like to take a trip around the world	67	78	83	73	65	51
I would like to spend a year in London or Paris	34	38	40	34	34	25
I would feel lost if I were alone in a foreign country	68	66	66	64	68	76
I like to visit places that are totally different from my home	85	85	83	86	82	88
Mobile						
We will probably move at least once in the next five years	38	71	53	27	28	23
Our family has moved more often than most of our neighbors have	24	36	32	26	18	17
Anxious						
I have trouble getting to sleep	33	29	24	26	33	49
I wish I knew how to relax	52	51	49	49	51	59
Personal adornment and self						
Dressing well is an important part of my life	81	84	80	78	79	83

Table 7-4 Female Interests and Opinions (continued)

Statement	Sample total	Age group: Under 25	25–34	35–44	45–54	55 and older
I like to feel attractive to members of the opposite sex	85%	93%	91%	77%	82%	72%
I want to look a little different from others	69	71	78	70	63	72
I often wear expensive cologne	28	19	24	28	27	33
I have more stylish clothes than most of my friends	30	31	34	27	29	27
View toward income, personal equity, and spending						
I will probably have more money to spend next year than I have now	45	71	70	58	53	30
Five years from now our family income will probably be a lot higher than it is now	65	87	85	75	61	26
Our family income is high enough to satisfy nearly all our important desires	74	59	66	78	78	80
No matter how fast our income goes up we never seem to get ahead	53	62	65	61	47	32
Investing in the stock market is too risky for most families	86	79	83	82	85	87
Our family is too heavily in debt today	27	36	33	37	23	11
I like to pay cash for everything I buy	77	83	79	74	71	77
I pretty much spend for today and let tomorrow bring what it will	22	33	21	22	25	18
Staying at home						
I would rather spend a quiet evening at home than go out to a party	65	50	66	64	68	78
I am a homebody	69	59	65	64	72	79
I stay home most evenings	83	81	95	80	83	83
Husband and children						
A wife's first obligation is to her husband, nor her children	69	53	65	74	74	76
When children are ill in bed, parents should drop everything else to see to their comfort	74	61	71	73	80	83
Children are the most important thing in a marriage	52	42	44	49	56	64
When making important family decisions, consideration of the children should come first	54	69	58	44	48	56
A wife should have a great deal of information about her husband's work	82	83	84	75	88	85
View toward durable goods						
Our home is furnished for comfort, not for style	90	83	88	88	94	94

Table 7-4 Female Interests and Opinions (continued)

Statement	Sample total	Age group: Under 25	25-34	35-44	45-54	55 and older
If I must choose, I buy stylish rather than practical furniture	17%	19%	31%	13%	15%	15%
When buying appliances I am more concerned with dependability than price	90	85	89	89	89	94
A subcompact car can meet my transportation needs	66	85	74	60	61	57
Housekeeping and cooking						
When I see a full ashtray or wastebasket, I want it emptied immediately	71	77	70	72	64	64
I am uncomfortable when the house is not completely clean	67	76	67	70	61	68
The kind of dirt you can't see is worse than the kind you can see	77	77	72	73	79	85
I am a good cook	91	93	92	88	90	91
I like to cook	87	91	88	84	85	87
I like to bake	40	43	43	42	39	38
Meal preparation should take as little time as possible	42	42	41	40	41	44
Grocery shopping						
Shopping is no fun anymore	54	49	43	58	55	51
Before going shopping, I sit down and prepare a complete shopping list	72	68	73	71	69	74
I try to stick to well-known brands	74	58	67	71	82	86
I find myself checking prices even on small items	90	89	93	92	89	86
I like to save and redeem savings stamps	75	72	70	70	75	83
I pay a lot more attention to food prices now than I ever did before	90	92	91	88	88	87
I am an impulse buyer	38	39	40	37	42	27
I shop a lot for specials	84	85	86	83	84	81
Health and nutrition						
I am very concerned about nutrition	87	87	89	87	82	89
I am concerned about how much salt I eat	56	52	55	56	50	66
I am careful what I eat in order to keep my weight under control	57	63	57	58	62	68
I try to avoid foods that are high in cholesterol	62	37	53	60	65	79
I try to avoid foods that have additives in them	56	45	52	57	53	62
I get more headaches than most people	28	30	31	28	27	22
I eat more than I should	70	68	70	75	73	69

Data source: Needham, Harper & Steers, (1975).

Table 7-5 Male Interests and Opinions
(Percent Agreeing, by Age Group)

Statement	Sample total	Age group: Under 25	25-34	35-44	45-54	55 and older
Optimism and happiness						
My greatest achievements are still ahead of me	64%	98%	93%	76%	55%	25%
I dread the future	20	21	15	19	23	23
I am much happier now than I ever was before	78	87	92	97	76	74
Modern-traditional ideas						
I have somewhat old-fashioned tastes and habits	85	73	78	84	92	89
There is too much emphasis on sex today	66	56	65	74	81	93
I like to think I am a bit of a swinger	31	51	43	29	26	15
A woman's place is in the home	54	45	52	53	52	62
The working world is no place for a woman	27	24	20	25	26	37
Young people have too many privileges	75	60	63	77	74	88
The U.S. would be better off if there were no hippies	59	33	38	57	67	81
My days seem to follow a definite routine—eating meals at the same time each day, etc.	63	50	53	59	67	76
All men should be clean shaven every day	67	47	55	66	75	85
Travel						
I would like to take a trip around the world	67	74	73	77	68	53
I would like to spend a year in London or Paris	34	38	39	40	32	23
I would feel lost if I were alone in a foreign country	52	59	46	47	44	67
I like to visit places that are totally different from my home	72	80	73	75	73	67
Mobile						
We will probably move at least once in the next five years	37	75	52	28	23	20
Our family has moved more often than most of our neighbors have	22	27	30	23	18	17
Anxious						
I have trouble getting to sleep	24	20	20	23	25	30
I wish I knew how to relax	47	40	48	51	44	50
Personal adornment and self						
Dressing well is an important part of my life	72	70	73	72	72	67

Table 7-5 Male Interests and Opinions (continued)

Statement	Sample total	Age group: Under 25	25-34	35-44	45-54	55 and older
I like to feel attractive to members of the opposite sex	81%	87%	87%	87%	66%	74%
I want to look a little different from others	55	74	62	55	49	42
I often wear expensive cologne	14	16	14	12	15	13
I have more stylish clothes than most of my friends	25	24	26	28	24	22
View toward income, personal equity, and spending						
I will probably have more money to spend next year than I have now	56	74	65	64	58	29
Five years from now our family income will probably be a lot higher than it is now	68	87	85	79	69	28
Our family income is high enough to satisfy nearly all our important desires	75	63	72	78	78	79
No matter how fast our income goes up we never seem to get ahead	58	60	68	56	52	39
Investing in the stock market is too risky for most families	83	86	82	81	87	86
Our family is too heavily in debt today	28	41	42	28	25	11
I like to pay cash for everything I buy	75	79	74	70	69	81
I pretty much spend for today and let tomorrow bring what it will	26	31	29	23	23	26
Staying at home						
I would rather spend a quiet evening at home than go out to a party	73	65	67	73	75	79
I am a homebody	72	55	67	73	79	82
I stay home most evenings	80	70	77	79	78	89
Husband and children						
A wife's first obligation is to her husband, not her children	57	43	52	54	64	66
When children are ill in bed, parents should drop everything else to see to their comfort	70	66	68	66	73	78
Children are the most important thing in a marriage	53	37	44	50	57	78
When making important familiy decisions, consideration of the children should come first	53	63	54	48	49	53
A wife should have a great deal of information about her husband's work	77	74	75	73	80	82
Our family is a close knit group	87	86	94	89	83	88
View toward durable goods						
Our home is furnished for comfort, not for style	93	89	92	94	95	94

Table 7-5 Male Interests and Opinions (continued)

Statement	Sample total	Age group				
		Under 25	25-34	35-44	45-54	55 and older
If I must choose, I buy stylish rather than practical furniture	15%	18%	20%	14%	15%	9%
When buying appliances I am more concerned with dependability than price	93	91	93	90	94	95
When buying appliances, the brand name is more important than the reputation of the store	56	56	53	49	55	64
A subcompact car can meet my transportation needs	59	71	57	56	58	57
Housekeeping and cooking						
When I see a full ashtray or wastebasket, I want it emptied immediately	56	56	46	54	60	63
I am uncomfortable when the house is not completely clean	51	57	48	53	49	52
The kind of dirt you can't see is worse than the kind you can see	77	68	74	73	79	86
I am a good cook	51	63	57	50	48	41
I like to cook	50	60	58	48	48	41
I like to bake	30	34	35	27	26	30
Meal preparation should take as little time as possible	42	42	41	38	40	46
Grocery shopping						
Shopping is no fun anymore	59	54	55	55	63	64
Before going shopping, I sit down and prepare a complete shopping list	44	35	42	38	38	56
I try to stick to well-known brands	79	71	79	76	71	86
I find myself checking prices even on small items	79	78	74	75	78	84
I like to save and redeem savings stamps	43	43	31	35	42	58
I pay a lot more attention to food prices now than I ever did before	81	81	79	81	81	84
I am an impulse buyer	38	46	47	40	33	30
I shop a lot for specials	60	61	59	63	56	61
Health and nutrition						
I am very concerned about nutrition	61	66	65	60	57	63
I am concerned about how much salt I eat	40	28	32	32	46	54
I am careful what I eat in order to keep my weight under control	51	38	43	44	55	64
I try to avoid foods that are high in cholesterol	49	31	42	41	60	63
I try to avoid foods that have additives in them	44	36	35	39	49	56
I get more headaches than most people	17	18	17	19	21	12
I eat more than I should	66	57	67	68	70	64

Data source: Needham, Harper & Steers, (1975).

Figure 7-2 Changes in Sensory Functioning in Old Age

Vision
There is a consistent decline in the ability to see at low levels of illumination and a decline in color sensitivity. Most old people suffer from presbyopia—farsightedness—which is due to the diminishing elasticity of the lenses.

Hearing
Old people lose the ability to hear extremely high tones as a result of atrophy of the nerve and end organs in the basal turn of the cochlea, although most can hear tones below high C as well as younger people. Men tend to experience greater hearing loss in old age than women.

Taste
Marked changes in taste in old age are due to atrophy of the taste buds in the tongue and the inner surface of the cheeks. This atrophy becomes progressively more widespread with advancing age.

Smell
The sense of smell becomes less acute with age, partly as a result of the atrophy of cells in the nose and partly because of the increased hairiness of the nostrils.

Touch
As the skin becomes drier and harder, the sense of touch becomes less and less acute.

Sensitivity to Pain
The decline in the sensitivity to pain occurs at different rates in different parts of the body. There is a greater decline, for example, in the forehead and arms than in the legs.

Source: Hurlock (1975:319).

quick, accurate decisions in complex situations. Elderly persons cannot be expected to engage effectively in on-the-spot "horse trading" for an automobile or to make complex financial decisions quickly, for instance. This generalization is shown graphically in Figure 7-3; digit symbol substitution, tapping, and

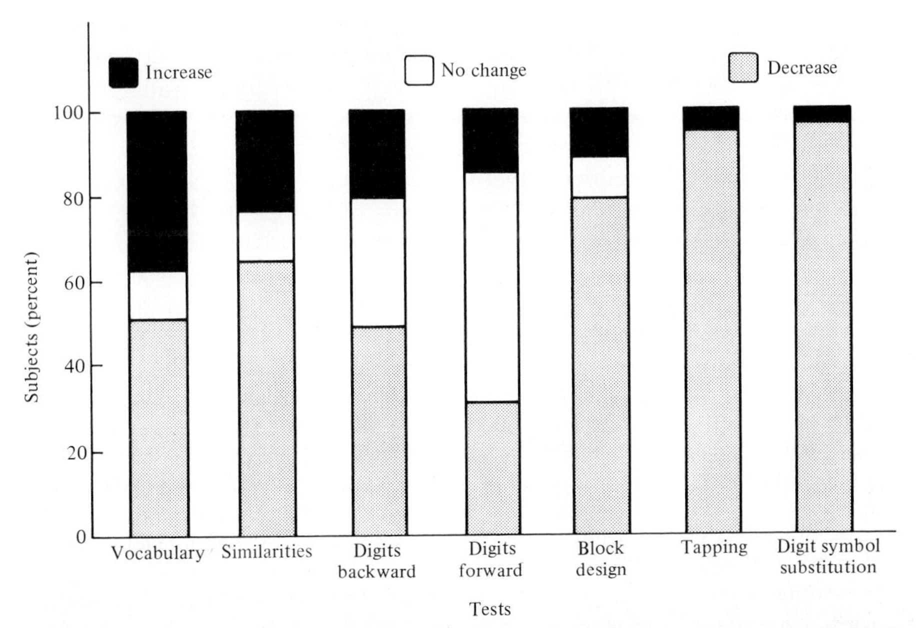

Figure 7-3 Changes in test scores for different mental abilities among the elderly. *Source:* Blum, Fosshage and Jarvik (1972: 181). Copyright 1972 by the American Psychological Association. Reprinted by permission.

block design tests revealed the most dramatic and consistent pattern of decline during a twenty-five-year study of elderly persons. Those abilities least affected by aging include recognition and vocabulary—indeed, many of the elderly scored higher over time on the vocabulary and similarities tests in the study summarized in Figure 7-3.

Some of the most marked mental changes during old age, however, are not purely a function of ability, but rather of general mood. Mental rigidity, for example, becomes more pronounced with aging not only (or chiefly) because of learning problems but also because of a decline in optimism and a belief that old values and ways of doing things are better than the new. In Tables 7-4 and 7-5 members of the 55-and-older group express the lowest level of happiness and optimism; and, while not a majority, they also tend to dread the future. They are the most vocal in their affirmation of traditional ideas: "I have somewhat old-fashioned tastes and habits"; "A woman's place is in the home"; "Young people have too many privileges"; "There is too much emphasis on sex"; and "The working world is no place for a woman."

RETIREMENT

Certain role changes are inevitable during the life span. For families with children, as noted in the last chapter, the mother much more than the father is affected by the empty nest. In old age, by contrast, the role shock typically belongs to the husband when he retires.

Most people assume that to be old is to be "over the hill" or "finished," and about one-half of the labor force today is employed by organizations that have institutionalized this assumption by mandating retirement at age sixty-five, if not earlier (*Time,* 1975). Compulsory retirement can be traumatic. Not only are incomes reduced substantially, but the male work role is largely eliminated. Even family relations can be affected.

For most older consumers, there is a marked difference between the expectations before retirement and the realities of retirement. Perlman (1968: 68–69) explains:

> It is the nature of man that he is more aware of his pain than of his pleasure. We tend more to count our misfortunes than our blessings, or if we count the latter it is to reinforce ourselves against a misfortune that has already occurred or is looking over our shoulder. Thus the manifest and ordinary everyday rewards of our work are scarcely noted. We take them for granted—they are "coming to us." We know them only, suddenly and acutely, when they are snatched away. The rewards of work that anchor a man in the social system, that secure him in the eyes of his neighbors and wife and children, that furnish his economic independence and the choices that go with it—these are most acutely appreciated and longed for when they are lost, when work is lost and missing. The unemployed man knows what he is missing, if only in a vague, inarticulate way. The employed man rarely knows what he has, rarely asks himself, "How come I feel settled, doing all right, looking forward to my kids' doing even better?"

As mentioned, the loss of work tends to affect the male more than the female. The male lacks the feeling of "rightfully belonging" to the home that is generally held by the female, and consequently he has a more difficult time adjusting to an "inside" orientation. Retirement automatically tends to place the focus of life inside the home. The woman, who has always had the role of housewife, with its location "inside," as one of her principal roles, finds herself inside the home more comfortably than the man, for whom this focus is foreign (Lopata, 1966).

Often accompanying the male role change is a change in husband-wife interactions. Because retired men feel lost inside the home, they tend to become bored and unhappy and may become critical of their wives' behaviors as consumers or in general. The extent to which this friction does not occur depends on a number of factors, but the chief one is the number of interests and activities shared by husbands and wives.

INTERESTS AND ACTIVITIES

In general, interests and activities continue to narrow during old age; new ones are seldom acquired. This narrowing is reflected in a number of statements in Tables 7-4 and 7-5, including the extremely high level of agreement in later years relative to earlier years to "I am a homebody," and "My days seem to follow a definite routine—eating meals at the same time each day, etc.," as well as the decreased interest shown in travel.

New interests can be acquired (or old interests revived), however, if the elderly are provided or made aware of the appropriate opportunity. For instance, Greyhound has been able to interest oldsters in travel with television commercials showing older people (as well as young) traveling by bus and saying, "Leave the driving to us." Older people now account for over half of Greyhound's business (*Forbes*, 1969). And, in the mid-1970s, a number of "granny bike clubs" began to emerge throughout the country with the availability of three-wheel bikes giving the obvious benefit of balance.

The interests and activities of the elderly, although much narrower than in earlier years, vary along a number of dimensions. Persons in poor health have fewer and less varied interests than those with better health; elderly persons of higher socioeconomic status have more varied interests than those of a lower position; and women have more than men, just as they do throughout adulthood (Hurlock, 1975). Even so, there are some major changes in interests which are fairly typical of older consumers. These are discussed in the following sections.

Self and Appearance

Older people become increasingly self-centered and preoccupied with the bodily processes as they grow older. They tell us they "hate to lose at anything." They talk endlessly about their past, have little regard for others' wishes and interests, want to be the center of attention, and expect to be waited on or catered to. This heightened interest in self frequently contributes to the unfavorable attitudes toward the old held by many people today (Hurlock, 1975).

At the same time that self-interest increases, interest in physical appearance declines, including an interest in grooming, as reflected in the over-55 age group's lower response levels to "I wish I were more glamorous than I am" and "Eye makeup is more important than lipstick" (Table 7-3). Elderly persons who are socially active, however, are more interested in their appearance than those who are isolated. And with the growing interest in social groups for the elderly, there may be an opportunity for marketers to make a socially beneficial and business-pragmatic contribution by developing and promoting grooming products for the elderly.

Interest in clothing also is believed to decline in old age. In Tables 7-4 and 7-5 older consumers tell us they do not have more stylish clothes than their friends. But they do not reject the concept of dressing well. One of the reasons for lack of fashionable clothes among elderly women is that clothes are made for youngsters and do not fit well, and those that do fit the elderly are often drab. Perhaps Seventh Avenue is correct; as one garment marketer said, "Older women will want to see ten dresses and they'll buy one; with the juniors, we can show three and two will be in the running" (*Forbes,* 1969). Another reason, of course, is that many older people do not have the income to keep wardrobes up to date.

Money

As noted earlier, there is a sharp drop in income at retirement. This focuses the elderly's attention on money, but, unlike the young adult's, the older consumer's interest in money is oriented more toward preserving independence than acquiring possessions.

Income is low for the elderly, but on a per capita basis it is not as low as it looks. Persons over 65 have larger tax exemptions, social security is tax-free income, pension benefits up to $1,200 are not taxed, there is a special tax break on the sale of the house, and indebtedness is less—there is less need to "save for old age."

Older consumers generally express a realistic view of their financial situation and shift their expenditures accordingly. In Tables 7-4 and 7-5 they tell us their income is less but that it is high enough to satisfy their most important desires; moreover, they express the belief they are not too heavily in debt and are not likely to be. The availability of time plus the need to conserve money tend to make older consumers careful shoppers, especially in the context of preparing for shopping. More than any other age group, the older consumers agree that before going shopping, they prepare a complete shopping list. However, because of their relatively limited mobility, we would expect less physical store-to-store comparison among older consumers than their emphasis on price would suggest. Also, since many do not have cars, shopping is often local and on foot, especially in the urban areas. Going to the store can be a major problem for maintaining proper nutrition, however. For the very old, inclement weather may force the shoppers to stay home and make do with the food they have or go on an enforced fast.

Leisure Pursuits

Older consumers, of course, have more time for leisure pursuits than consumers at any other stage of the life span. Yet changes in the activities are inevitable with advancing age. Poor health, lower economic status, and living at home, alone, all contribute to a narrowing of the leisure pursuits in which the older consumer can participate. Figure 7-4 lists the factors contributing to changes in leisure pursuits during old age.

Tables 7-6 and 7-7 reveal the low participation rates in leisure pursuits by older consumers when compared with earlier age groups. Generally the shift is a continuation of the overall pattern toward inactivity as age progresses, and the pursuits that remain popular are largely sedentary or home- and hobby-oriented, such as reading, writing letters, collecting things, playing shuffleboard, listening to music, and engaging in handicrafts.

While many of these changes are inevitable, most are made of necessity rather than by choice; the elderly tend to remain interested in the leisure pursuits they enjoyed during early adulthood even though they can no longer participate in them (Hurlock, 1975).

One of the most common forms of "spending" leisure time among the elderly is viewing television—they are heavy viewers, especially of daytime

Figure 7-4 Factors Contributing to Changes in Leisure Pursuits

Health
As health gradually fails and as physical disabilities such as poor eyesight set in, the individual acquires an interest in recreational activities that require a minimum of strength and energy and can be enjoyed in the home.

Economic Status
Reduced income after retirement may force the individual to cut down on or eliminate recreational activities, such as moviegoing, that cost money. This is especially true of older people in the lower socioeconomic groups.

Education
The more formal education a person has, the more intellectual recreational activities, such as reading, he cultivates. Because these require little energy, they can be enjoyed in old age. Those with limited education must often depend mainly on television for recreation.

Sex
Women tend to cultivate a wide range of recreational interests throughout life, many of which are sedentary in nature and thus can be carried into old age. Men, by contrast, tend to limit their recreational interest to sports, which they must give up when their health fails. Thus they have a paucity of recreational interests in old age and may depend mainly on television.

Living Conditions
Elderly persons who live in a home for the aged have recreations provided for them that are suited to their physical and mental abilities. Those who live in their own homes or with a married child have fewer opportunities for recreation, especially if their economic status is poor or if failing health or transportation problems prevent them from participating in community-sponsored recreational activities.

Source: Hurlock (1975:325).

Table 7-6 Female Leisure Activities
(Percent Engaged in, by Age Group)

Activity	Sample total	Age group: Under 25	25–34	35–44	45–55	55 and older
Active recreations						
Went for a walk	91%	96%	94%	92%	88%	86%
Went swimming	62	84	80	73	55	31
Went boating	37	44	41	39	37	26
Went bowling	35	54	45	40	30	12
Went camping	30	42	38	36	26	15
Jogged	24	41	30	24	22	13
Played tennis	14	24	23	20	99	2
Went hunting	7	20	8	7	6	3
Went skiing	6	14	8	7	4	0
Went backpacking	3	10	4	3	2	1
Inactive recreations/hobbies						
Took color photographs	89	97	95	91	87	78
Played a game (monopoly, bingo, etc.)	85	95	95	94	81	77
Played cards	83	93	91	87	80	71
Went on a vacation	77	71	75	79	81	77
Went to the movies	74	95	88	82	71	43
Attended an X-rated movie	20	42	28	20	15	7
Attended a sporting event	53	56	60	63	53	36
Visited an art gallery or museum	49	35	48	57	52	46
Worked on a collection (stamps, coins, etc.)	31	22	27	30	34	36
Went to a classical concert	22	13	14	21	28	30
Went to a pop or rock concert	13	24	18	11	11	5
Went to an auto race	8	16	12	7	6	4

Data source: Needham, Harper & Steers, (1975).

programs. Weekly viewing time generally runs about 33 hours for the over-65 as compared with 25 hours for persons 50–64 and 20½ hours for adults under 50; approximately two-thirds of this is daytime viewing. Program preferences are similar for males and females and lean toward variety and music, followed by panel shows and news. In 1968, for example, the most popular programs were dominated by variety and music: "Mayberry RFD," "Here's Lucy," "Family Affair," and "Lawrence Welk."

Older consumers also have favorite performers. As shown in Table 7-8, the favorite entertainers among the older age groups tend to be vintage names and mostly from motion pictures. Among the younger viewers, in contrast, the favorites are relatively new names in show business who primarily have come into prominence via the medium of television.

While TV viewing increases with age, social activity declines. A major factor accounting for this decline is that social contacts contract during old age.

Table 7-7 Male Leisure Activities
(Percent Engaged in, by Age Group)

Activity	Sample total	Age group: Under 25	25-34	35-44	45-55	55 and older
Active recreations						
Went for a walk	82%	81%	83%	83%	80%	71%
Went swimming	61	82	76	75	67	32
Went boating	44	54	46	51	43	34
Went bowling	36	65	47	42	30	14
Went camping	34	48	41	44	32	18
Jogged	27	43	37	31	19	14
Played tennis	14	26	25	17	7	3
Went hunting	33	53	38	33	30	21
Went skiing	7	14	14	5	4	2
Went backpacking	6	9	10	8	4	2
Inactive recreations/hobbies						
Took color photographs	82	95	91	82	78	70
Played a game (monopoly, bingo, etc.)	79	99	92	86	70	60
Played cards	81	96	91	83	72	69
Went on a vacation	76	66	80	79	81	72
Went to the movies	72	94	89	79	69	42
Attended an X-rated movie	24	44	40	23	21	6
Attended a sporting event	61	64	67	72	64	42
Visited an art gallery or museum	36	24	40	43	37	32
Went to a classical concert	15	9	12	19	16	19
Went to a pop or rock concert	11	26	17	9	6	5
Went to an auto race	11	23	16	10	8	3

Data source: Needham, Harper & Steers, (1975).

Work associates are lost with retirement; friendship and family contacts decrease when friends and relatives die and when grown children live in distant communities. The result is withdrawal or "social disengagement." Social withdrawal can be either voluntary or involuntary. It is voluntary when people withdraw from group events because these no longer meet their needs, especially the more preposing self-interest. It is involuntary when older consumers want and need social contacts but are deprived of the opportunities to have them. Indeed, one of the major values of retirement communities such as Sun City in Arizona is that they supply social contacts with similar interests, problems, experiences, and abilities.

Housing

Table 7-9 reveals the housing status of older consumers relative to younger consumers. In the upper part of the table, the data show a steadily increasing percentage of families owning their homes until age 65 or older—then there is increased rental and less ownership. These data suggest there is much mobility

Table 7-8 Favorite Television Performers, by Age Group

Age group	Performer	Rank
6–11	Elizabeth Montgomery	1
	Sally Fields	2
	The Monkees	3
	Jim Nabors	4
	Rowan and Martin	5
	Barbara Eden	5
12–17	Bill Cosby	1
	Sidney Poitier	2
	Rowan and Martin	3
	Pat Paulsen	4
	Smothers Brothers	5
18–34	John Wayne	1
	Bob Hope	2
	Sidney Poitier	3
	Bill Cosby	3
	Paul Newman	5
	Herb Alpert	5
35–49	Bob Hope	1
	John Wayne	1
	Gary Cooper	3
	Spencer Tracy	3
	Clark Gable	5
50 and older	Spencer Tracy	1
	Bob Hope	2
	Walter Cronkite	3
	Clark Gable	4
	Lawrence Welk	5
	Brian Keith	5
	Chet Huntley	5
	Lorne Greene	5

Source: Variety (1968:30).

in old age, and there is: changed economic conditions upon retirement, too much space, failing health, loneliness, and a change in marital status all contribute to mobility among older consumers. Probably the greatest of these mobility contributors is widowhood. By far the lowest ownership and highest rental percentages during later years of life are found in the two unmarried stages of the life cycle in Table 7-9. There is also a big increase in "other" living arrangements during widowhood. "Mobile" homes are popular because they are inexpensive, easy to maintain, and modern.

Mobility, while precipitated by one or more of the factors mentioned above, is not necessarily unwanted by older consumers. In a 1971 survey, for instance, the smallest percentage of disagreement with "I would rather live in an apartment than a house" is found in the 55-or-older age group. Actually, the housing needs and wants of older consumers vary greatly, and not all of them

Table 7-9 Housing Status of the Elderly: 1970
(Percentage Distribution of Nonfarm Families)

Age or life-cycle stage	Housing Status		
	Own	Rent	Other[a]
Age of family head:			
18–24	12%	77%	11%
25–34	48	45	7
35–44	72	24	4
45–54	74	22	4
55–64	77	18	5
65 or older	71	22	7
Age 45 or older:			
Married, has children	79	16	5
Married, no children, head in labor force	81	15	4
Married, no children, head retired	82	14	4
Unmarried, no children, head in labor force	58	35	7
Unmarried, no children, head retired	62	28	10

[a]Includes trailer owners, and families who neither own nor rent.
Source: Survey Research Center (1970).

will find the same living arrangements suitable. Whatever the dwelling style, however, almost all older consumers have certain physical and psychological needs that must be met within their dwelling quarters. These are given in Figure 7-5.

Figure 7-5 Living Arrangement Needs of Older Consumers

Physical Needs

The house temperature should be comparatively even from floor to ceiling because poor circulation makes the elderly person especially sensitive to chilling.

The elderly person needs large windows to ensure plenty of light because of the gradual impairment of his vision.

Provisions should be made for the safety of the elderly person. He should have to climb few steps, and floors should be unwaxed.

There should be adequate space for indoor and outdoor recreation, a condition best met in multiple housing developments or homes for the aged.

Noise should be controlled, especially during the night. This can be done by locating the elderly person's sleeping quarters in a quiet part of the house.

The elderly person should have labor-saving devices, especially for cooking and cleaning.

The living quarters should be on one floor to avoid possible falls on steps.

Psychological Needs

The elderly person should have at least one small room of his own so that he can have an opportunity for privacy. The living arrangements should include space for sedentary recreations, such as reading and television watching.

There should be provisions for storage of cherished possessions.

The elderly person should live close to stores and community organizations so that he can be independent in his activities, and he should also be near relatives and friends so that frequent contacts are possible.

Source: Hurlock (1975:353).

How these needs and wants are met is more than a public policy question. It is a challenge to marketers. As the *Forbes* article (1969) concluded: "It's hard to believe that the smart, almost infinitely diverse U.S. marketing system will fail to come up with some better approaches to the burgeoning over-65 market than nursing homes and rocking chairs."

SUMMARY

Similar to the other life periods, advancing age involves pervasive changes which result in behavior shifts. Although older consumers generally experience declines in physical and mental condition, income levels, and opportunities for recreational activities, they represent an important market segment whose needs and wants marketers can profitably satisfy. In order to do so, marketers must understand the changes which occur during old age and the new requirements that correspond to these changes.

Older consumers have been divided into two segments, the 55–65-year group, and the over-65-year group. The beginning of retirement, with its resultant drop in income, social opportunities, and general mood, is often a more accurate indicator of the change between the two groups than is chronological age. Once retirement occurs, men face significant role changes while their activities become focused toward the home.

Physical decline results in a narrowing of leisure pursuits to sedentary activities, a drop in interest in fashion and personal grooming, and an increase in interest in nutrition and body functions. Physical, and even financial, decline does not mean older consumers are of less importance to marketers, but that these consumers have needs for products and activities which are different from those of their younger counterparts. Older consumers represent a strong market for medical care, products which relieve their discomforts, labor-saving devices, hobbies that can be performed at home, and specially designed dwellings. Mobility is high for this segment, as is television viewing. Available leisure time is higher for this group than for any other, and opportunities for social contact and shopping which accommodate physical limitations are needed.

This chapter concludes our examination of consumers in terms of their life periods. Throughout our discussion, we have stressed the constant changes which face consumers as they progress through life and which face marketers if they are to successfully meet the needs and wants of their prospective customers. The following chapters will build on the foundation of consumer development presented in the first seven chapters.

REVIEW QUESTIONS

1 Identify the two different segments within the older consumer market. Which group is growing faster? How do the two groups compare in terms of income?
2 The physical changes which take place during old age create needs (markets) for

many types of products. Discuss some of the important physical changes and give examples of products these changes necessitate.

3 General mood sustains marked changes during old age. What are these changes, and how do they affect consumer behavior?
4 Retirement results in significant role changes for most men which may cause a feeling of loss and unhappiness. Do women generally experience the same problems? Why or why not?
5 Identify and discuss the major factors contributing to changes in activities of older consumers. How do these changes affect shopping habits?
6 How do housing needs change as consumers grow older? Indicate some ways marketers can meet these changing requirements.
7 Do retirement communities offer any advantages for older consumers? Any disadvantages? What are they?
8 An important characteristic of aging is a gradual narrowing of leisure pursuits. Discuss the types of leisure pursuits generally engaged in by older consumers. Identify some marketing opportunities and problems presented by the narrowing activities of this market segment.

EXERCISE

Using Figure 7-5, prepare a checklist fo the living needs of older consumers. Visit several retirement or elderly housing developments in or near your community and record how well these needs are being met. Discuss your findings with local developers and service agency personnel. What are the factors (economic, legal, and so forth) contributing to the degree to which needs are being met? Is your selection of areas to visit representative of your community? your state? Explain.

REFERENCES

Bernhardt, Kenneth D. and Thomas Kinnear. "Profiling the Senior Citizen Market." In Beverlee B. Anderson (ed.), *Advances in Consumer Research.* Vol. 3. Proceedings of the Association for Consumer Research, 1976.

Blum, J. E., J. L. Fosshage, and L. F. Jarvik. "Intellectual Changes and Sex Differences in Octogenarians: A Twenty-five Year Longitudinal Study of Aging." *Developmental Psychology,* 7 (1972), 178–187.

Boone, Louis E. and J. A. Bonno. "Food Buying Habits of the Urban Poor." *Journal of Retailing,* 47 (Fall 1971), 79–84.

Carp, Frances M. "The Impact of Environment on Old People." *Gerontologist,* 7 (June 1967), 106–108 ff.

Decker, Patricia M. "Color Choices of Older Women: Preferences or Necessities?" *Journal of Retailing,* 39 (Winter 1963–1964), 16–25.

Department of Commerce, *Current Population Reports,* Series P-25, No. 470 (November 1971).

Forbes article. "The Forgotten Generation." *Forbes* (Jan. 15, 1969), 22–29.

Grey Advertising, Inc., "Grey Matter," New York: May 1973.

Hawes, Douglas K., N. Wayne Talarzyk, and Roger D. Blackwell. "Consumer Satisfaction from Leisure Time Pursuits." In Mary Jane Schlinger (ed.), *Advances in*

Consumer Research. Vol. 2. Chicago: Association for Consumer Research, 1974, 817–836.

Hurlock, Elizabeth B. *Developmental Psychology.* 4th ed. New York: McGraw-Hill, 1975.

Linden, Fabian. "Reshuffling the Age-Income Mix." *The Conference Board RECORD* (March 1974).

Lopata, Helena Znaniecki. "The Life Cycle of the Social Role of Housewife." *Sociology and Social Research,* 51 (1966), 5–22.

Martin, Claude R., Jr. "A Transgenerational Comparison—The Elderly Fashion Consumer." In Beverlee B. Anderson (ed.), *Advances in Consumer Research.* Vol. 3. Proceedings of the Association for Consumer Research, 1976.

Neugarten, B. L. "Continuities and Discontinuities of Psychological Issues into Adult Life." *Human Development,* 12 (1969), 121–130.

Perlman, Helen Harris. *Persona, Social Role and Personality.* Chicago: The University of Chicago Press, 1968.

Reinecke, John A. "The 'Older' Market—Fact or Fiction?" *Journal of Marketing,* 28 (January 1964), 60–64.

Samli, A. Coskun. "The Elusive Senior Citizen Market." *University of Washington Business Review,* 25 (September 1966), 29–343.

Schiffman, Leon G. "Sources of Information for the Elderly." *Journal of Advertising Research,* 11 (October 1971), 33–37.

Sherman, E. M. and M. R. Brittan. "Contemporary Food Gatherers—A Study of Food Shopping Habits of an Elderly Urban Population." *Gerontologist,* 13 (Autumn 1973), 358–364.

Survey Research Center. *1970 Survey of Consumer Finances.* Ann Arbor, Mich.: University of Michigan, Survey Research Center, 1970.

Time article. "New Outlook for the Aged." *Time* (June 2, 1975), 44–51.

Variety. Report of TvQ performer study by Home Testing Institute. *Variety* (Sept. 11, 1968), 30.

Wells, William D. and George Gubar. "Life Cycle Concept in Marketing Research." *Journal of Marketing Research,* 3 (November 1966), 355–363.

Chapter 8

The Impact of Subculture and Geography

Human needs and consumer behaviors are molded in decisive ways as people are born, grow, mature, and decline. Human development, however, does not take place in a vacuum. As Kluckhohn (1949:18) notes: "Even those of us who pride ourselves on our individualism follow most of the time a pattern not of our own making. We brush our teeth on arising. We put on pants—not a loincloth or a grass skirt. We eat three meals a day—not four or five or two. We sleep in a bed—not a hammock or on a sheep pelt."

Kluckhohn, of course, is emphasizing the role of the culture within which we live. In essence, much behavior is learned and performed within the bounds or norms for behavior that are established and transmitted from generation to generation and form one society or group to another.

We all are aware of the notion of culture as it exists from country to country and of its implications to marketers in international markets. In this chapter, however, our outlook is not so global. Rather, we are more concerned with understanding the influence of the subgroups or subcultures that inevitably exist within a so-called "national" culture. Specifically, we focus on two groups that are particularly valuable to the study of consumer behavior in the American culture: *ethnic group* and *social class.* Then we turn to the impact of geography, especially in relation to seasons, on consumers' behavior.

ETHNIC GROUPS

Every society breaks into subgroups within which there is close personal contact. Inevitably, members of these subgroups develop a shared set of customs and values and a shared way of looking at themselves and at outsiders.

In the United States today subgroups often are composed of people of the same racial and ethnic origin, so that, in any town of any size, there are subsocieties that are consciously Jewish, or Polish, or black, or White Anglo-Saxon Protestant, or Italian. Members of one of these groups are apt to regard themselves as similar to other members of the group and to feel more comfortable with them. They are apt to share social and leisure-time activities with other members of the group, to have similar tastes in food, clothing, home decoration, and home furnishings. They may want to live in the same neighborhood as other members of the group.

When ethnic groups cluster within neighborhoods, they are especially important to small retailers. Italian bakeries, Jewish delicatessens, restaurants that serve soul food, and grocery stores that feature snow peas and water chestnuts draw their patrons largely, though of course not exclusively, from groups of people to whom these foods are native. If the ethnic character of the neighborhood changes, a retailer may be forced to change with it, to move, or to go out of business.

Occasionally a distinctly ethnic product is adopted by other segments of the population. Chinese, Italian, and Mexican foods are now served, or at least imitated, in a great many non-Chinese, non-Italian, and non-Mexican restaurants. The Japanese style of furniture is more popular on the West Coast than is the style called Early American. And jazz, an art form that originated in the black community of New Orleans, has dominated many apsects of popular entertainment nationally.

Thus the ethnic origins of Americans influence consumption of products and services in two somewhat different ways. Styles, tastes, and values that are established within ethnic communities influence purchases that support ethnic retailers and symbolize ethnic identities. As these are diffused into the wider American society, they add color, richness, and variety to consumption patterns that would otherwise be much more uniform.

An illustration of the first type of influence is found in the study of Alexander (1959) of the acceptance of six prepackaged food products by members of four ethnic groups in New York City. He found the following pattern:

Product	Degree of acceptance by			
	Italian homemakers	Jewish homemakers	Puerto Rican homemakers	Black homemakers
Frozen dinners	Low	Very low	High	Moderate
Frozen red meat	Low	Low	Moderately high	Low
Frozen fruit pie	Very low	Very low	High	Low
Instant coffee	Very low	High	Moderately high	Very low
Cake mixes	Low	Very low	High	Low
Dehydrated soups	Moderate	Low	High	Very low

Source: Alexander (1959).

Like most consumer behavior, the pattern in this case turned out to be the outcome of a mixture of forces. A "deep-seated ethnic preference" for fresh meat and vegetables hampered acceptance of frozen dinners and frozen meat among Italian homemakers. Jewish homemakers and black homemakers indicated similar biases against these products; but for the Jewish homemakers the bias against nonfresh products was reinforced by the influence of dietary laws, and for many of the black homemakers the bias was reinforced by lack of freezer space.

Italian homemakers and Jewish homemakers often serve sweet goods, but the pastry they serve is usually baked at home or purchased at neighborhood ethnic bakeries, so they had little interest in frozen fruit pies. For black homemakers, lack of freezer space was the major negative factor.

Italian homemakers serve a lot of coffee, but the coffee they serve has a stronger, sharper flavor than instant coffee made for the general market. On the other hand, the very low consumption of this product by blacks was attributed to the black homemakers' belief that this product was too expensive.

The low acceptance of cake mix by Italian and Jewish homemakers was, like their low acceptance of frozen fruit pies, mainly the result of a preference for baked products associated with their own ethnic backgrounds. The low acceptance by blacks, however, was again a matter of cost.

The Puerto Rican homemakers were the only respondents in this study to show much interest in dehydrated soups. Their favorable reaction to this product was based on the fact that also made them favorably disposed toward the other convenience products on this list: a great many of them were working full time outside the home.

Thus each of these foods was accepted and each of these foods was rejected by at least one of the ethnic groups, and the pattern of reasons for acceptance or rejection was the result of how well the product fit into the life circumstances of each group and into their needs and values.

Since people of the same racial or ethnic origin are so readily identifiable by that characteristic, it is possible to think of these subgroups as extending beyond individual communities to the national community. In doing so, the concept of subculture is broadened and becomes, perhaps, more generally useful in identifying large segments of the market. But at the same time the concept loses some of its original meaning. It no longer refers to specific groups of persons interacting with each other; nor does it necessarily imply the diffusion of richness and variety to consumption patterns in American society. Rather, the concept refers to certain types of persons who have something in common even though they may never have met.

Indeed, according to one authority, it has become intellectually stylish to discover subcultures everywhere in national and international life (Valentine, 1968). Thus we have replaced neighborhood groups with national groups, such as the subculture of poverty, the black subculture, the youth subculture, and social class or status subcultures. In the remaining part of this section we examine the most frequently discussed of these—black consumers.

Black Consumers

The simple fact is that blacks have become a major force in the American marketplace. Accounting for 11 percent of the United States population, blacks are growing in number at a faster rate than white Americans and are beginning to attain higher levels of affluence than blacks of previous decades.

Blacks have not attained an economic status equivalent with whites, however. According to the Census Bureau, which collects data on persons by race, white Americans had median family incomes of slightly over $10,000 in 1970; black Americans, in contrast, had a median family income level of slightly over $6,000. Moreover, about 1 out of every 3 blacks lived in poverty, as against less than 1 out of every 10 white Americans.[1]

On the average, then, blacks are relatively poor. But it is the fact that the black market is expanding very vigorously that accounts for the increasing attention that is being given to blacks by marketers of consumer goods. This expansion, while lagging that of whites, in absolute terms, is showing up in both economic and educational terms.

Economically, two trends stand out. One, the poor or poverty sector of the black population has shrunk. While slightly over 25 percent of blacks now live in poverty, this is considerably below the 1959 figure of 48 percent. The second and more important trend is the expanding proportion of affluent blacks. Over the decade of the 1960s, the proportion of nonwhite families with annual incomes over $12,000 jumped from 8 to 21 percent—a percentage increase of 162 percent.

Educationally, blacks lag whites by about one decade in overall educational attainment. Nevertheless, blacks as well as whites are continuing a massive move to college. In 1960, about 10 percent of black persons 20–24 years of age

[1]In 1969 the Social Security Administration's definition of *poverty* was a family of four with an income of less than $3,721. In 1959, the corresponding figure was $2,943.

had completed at least one year of college; the figure increased to 24 percent in 1970 and is expected to reach 40 percent in 1980.

Traditionally, higher levels of income and educational attainment (which usually go together) have meant increased expenditures among white Americans. The same is the case with black Americans. As blacks have become more affluent, their consumption expenditures have increased dramatically as compared with the United States population as a whole. To illustrate, household ownership of electric ranges increased by 1.2 percent for the population as a whole during the period 1968–1972; the corresponding increase among blacks was 31.2 percent. This relative growth pattern has shown up across a wide variety of consumer products and services including expensive watches, luggage, foreign travel, boats, golf equipment, power lawn mowers, and color television. As one black commentator summarizes the increased expenditure pattern:

> The primary explanation for this spurt naturally is that the great majority of blacks who have become members of the "affluent society" have gained this status only fairly recently and over a shorter period of time than their white counterparts. One can think of the black demand for consumer goods as more compressed and therefore bound to be released with more explosive force (*Black Enterprise,* 1973).

To reiterate, black consumers are making their presence known in the marketplace. A crucial question remains, however: Do blacks really constitute a group of consumers who differ from whites in important ways other than their relative socioeconomic standing? To many people this question has had an obvious and often stereotyped answer; nevertheless, students of consumer behavior have attacked the question with vigor.

Consumption Patterns Even with the recent "expenditure explosion," blacks on the average consume less than whites simply because on the average they have less to spend. Thus, to obtain more revealing answers to the question concerning black versus white behavior, scholars have concentrated on doing comparative analyses of expenditure patterns of whites and blacks of *similar* income. By controlling for income, researchers have found some interesting and (to some) surprising answers to the basic question. In an early review paper on the subject, for example, Alexis (1962:27) concluded:

1 Total consumption expenditures of blacks are less than those of comparable whites, or blacks save more out of a given income than do whites with the same income.

2 Black consumers spend more for clothing and nonautomobile transportation and less for food, housing, medical care, and automobile transportation than do whites with comparable income.

3 There is no consistent racial difference in expenditures for either recreation and leisure or home furnishings and equipment at comparable income levels.

While Alexis based these conclusions on a review of the then existing literature, Stafford, Cox, and Higginbothom (1968) conducted a survey in the Houston area to determine via self-report if any consumption differences emerge in five product categories—food and soft drinks, liquor, personal hygiene products, home appliances, and home ownership—covering twenty products.

Dramatic differences were found for two products (butter and Scotch whiskey). As the following data show, a larger percentage of blacks than of whites reported purchasing these items during a designated time period regardless of income class:

	Annual family income							
	Less than $3,000		$3,000-5,999		$6,000-7,999		$8,000 or more	
Product	Whites	Blacks	Whites	Blacks	Whites	Blacks	Whites	Blacks
Butter	6.6	23.3	8.0	31.2	7.7	26.9	14.1	45.4
Scotch	3.3	9.3	4.2	22.1	7.7	34.6	19.7	27.3

Source: Stafford et al. (1968).

But for most of the products studied, Stafford and his associates found either no significant differences in consumption or that the differences were explainable by characteristics other than race.

In general, then, while there are some differences in consumption expenditures attributable to race, there is more similarity than difference, particularly where the effects of income are controlled. Expressed another way, as blacks move up the income or status scale, they behave increasingly the way whites do.[2]

Shopping Patterns Shopping behavior, as opposed to consumption behavior has become important in consumer research, notably from a public policy standpoint. The reasons are the geographical location and income levels of blacks in general. In 1969, 70 percent of the blacks lived in metropolitan areas as compared with 64 percent of the whites in the United States. While these figures are somewhat similar, 55 percent of all blacks lived in central cities and 15 percent in suburbs. For whites, 16 percent lived in central cities and 38 percent in the suburbs (Bureau of the Census, 1969).

Furthermore, the areas where blacks live offer them shopping outlets

[2]Other studies suggesting this generalization include Bullock (1961), Bauer, Cunningham, and Wortzel (1965), and Sommers and Bruce (1968).

featuring higher prices, inferior merchandise, high-pressure selling, hidden and inflated interest charges, and a generally degrading environment for shopping (Sturdivant, 1968). The question, of course, is, "Do blacks shop in these areas?"

Studies in New York, Chicago, Los Angeles, Pittsburgh, and Tuscaloosa, while differing somewhat in their mix of findings, all seem to indicate that whether or not blacks patronize the ghetto stores depends to a large extent on their incomes and their ownership of automobiles.[3] In general, those who are not "locked into" the neighborhood by the lack of private or public transportation and income tend to shop frequently outside their areas of residence.

Reaching Black Consumers While there is a great deal of similarity in the consumption and shopping behaviors of blacks and whites of comparable incomes, it would be a mistake to assume that all blacks are alike just as it would be to assume that all whites are alike.

As we have already shown, more affluent blacks behave differently from poor blacks. The black market can be segmented in other ways as well. Indeed, most of the bases of segmentation discussed in the adulthood chapters apply to blacks as well as to other groups in society. And for the producer and marketer of branded merchandise, it is important to have a rich description of the subsegments of the black market in order to reach them.

Most research on how to reach blacks, however, has dealt with their response to advertising. One basic conclusion is that blacks are more responsive to advertising than whites are (Petrof, 1968). Also, blacks can be reached either by general media, particularly with all-black or integrated models in the ads, and/or through black-oriented media (Petrof, 1968; Barban, 1969; Tolley and Goett, 1971).

Blacks, however, do not endorse media, advertisers, or advertisements without criticism (*Black Enterprise,*1973). A frequent criticism is that blacks shown in ads are rarely portrayed in higher-income roles. This criticism is somewhat surprising in view of a study which found that while the number of black models in advertising had not increased in the time period of 1946–1965, the social status of blacks had increased (Kassarjian, 1969). Perhaps the status increase has not kept pace with the expectations of blacks. Another criticism relates to the use of black jargon in ads. While its use is attention-getting, blacks object on the grounds that excessive use of jargon may create an image of blacks as persons unable to speak English correctly.

Blacks are also conscious of their perceptions of the advertiser. If blacks feel that a company discriminates against blacks, many will try to avoid its products; the opposite also appears to be true. Marketers appealing to blacks, then, must have specific knowledge of how they are perceived by blacks.

[3]Feldman and Starr (1968), Caplovitz (1963), Sturdivant (1969), Mason and Madden (1971), and Gensch and Staelin (1972).

SOCIAL CLASS

Consumers also differ on a dimension that incorporates but extends beyond the loosely woven relationships that characterize ethnic groupings. In every society, people look upon themselves, and others, as belonging to one or another of several social classes that are thought of as ranking, in some sense, from "high" to "low." Social scientists working in many different kinds of communities, both in the United States and in other countries, have found it easy to get informants to name individuals, or types of individuals, who are "above me" or "below me" or "just like me."

One of the ways to investigate the class structure of a community is to ask people to classify themselves. For instance, in one study of social classes, interviewers asked respondents to place themselves on the following scale (Social Research, Inc., 1965):

I *The Upper Class*—3 percent of the population. The "400," the "Country Club Crowd."

II *The Upper Middle Class*—10 percent of the population—top executives and business owners, professionals.

III *The Lower Middle Class*—30 percent of the population—lower management and white-collar personnel and skilled worker families.

IV *The Upper Working Class*—40 percent of the population—families of average workers with steady jobs and reasonably good incomes.

V *The Lower Working Class*—15 percent of the population. Families of workers in less skilled jobs, or with unsteady jobs. They often don't have enough money to make ends meet comfortably.

VI *The Lower Class*—2 percent of the population. People who are really "down and out."

This scale is only one of several used for self-classification, and the percentages assigned to the various categories are not necessarily correct either for any single community or for the United States in general; but this ordered set of categories illustrates the concept of social class, at least as a first approximation.

Since people within any one social class regard other people in the same class as being on their level, and people in other classes as being either "above" or "below" them, they tend to associate with each other more than they associate with people in other classes. This difference in amount of personal contact reinforces any already existing differences in attitudes, needs, tastes, values, and consumption patterns.

In studies that use the self-designation method, some informants tend to be pretentious and some tend to be overly modest in their self-evaluations. Students of social class have therefore sought more objective methods of identifying class position.

The best of these more objective methods requires participant observation. When the investigator can live within the community for extended periods of time, he can learn the community class structure for himself and can learn the place of community members within it. By asking about friends and neighbors and social contacts, he can find out what community members associate with each other and which are considered "upper," "middle," and "lower" by the community in general.

But participant observation is so time-consuming that it cannot be employed in more than a handful of communities, and it is obviously impractical in the large-scale surveys that are often used in studies of consumer behavior. Social scientists have therefore sought quick, inexpensive ways of designating class position that do not demand extended personal contact and do not demand that respondents rank themselves.

When social scientists looked for dimensions that could be used as substitutes for participant observation, they found that social class rankings obtained through extended personal contact could be reasonably well predicted from knowledge of the respondent's occupation, education, and type of dwelling. In other words, some combinations of these characteristics come remarkably close to ranking people in the same order as the costly and time-consuming participant observer method. This knowledge has proved useful to students of consumer behavior.

In studies of consumer behavior it is common practice to collect demographic information about the respondents, including information on education, family income, and occupation of the head of the household. This information can be used to show how well the sample of respondents corresponds to the population from which it was drawn, and it can be used to help describe selected groups of consumers.

In studies that employ the social class concept, separate pieces of demographic information are often combined to produce a single score, or index, to represent the respondent's class position. These composite scores do a better job of predicting the results of participant observation than do any of the separate pieces.

Two somewhat different indices have been used in many studies of consumer behavior. One index, developed by Lloyd Warner (1949), combines occupation, income, source of income, house type, dwelling area, and education. Called the "Index of Status Characteristics" (ISC), it produced a correlation of .98 with social class scores determined by participant observation.

The other major social class index, developed by August B. Hollingshead (1958), combines occupation, dwelling area, and education. This index was found to correlate .89 with social class scores derived from long, wide-ranging narrative interviews. A "two-factor" version of this index, combining occupation and education, does almost as well and has become widely used in studies of consumer behavior, primarily because respondents can be assigned scores on the index in an inexpensive and straightforward manner with data originating via phone or mail surveys as well as with personal interviews.

Hollingshead's procedure combines occupation and education in the following manner to produce an "Index of Social Position" or ISP score. Respondents are assigned a score ranging from 1 to 7 on each of the two scales.

I Occupation scale:
- **1** Executives and proprietors of large concerns and major professionals
- **2** Managers and proprietors of medium concerns, lesser professionals, and minor officials
- **3** Administrative personnel of large concerns, owners of small independent businesses, and semiprofessionals
- **4** Owners of little businesses, clerical and sales workers, and technicians
- **5** Skilled workers
- **6** Semiskilled workers
- **7** Unskilled workers

II Education scale:
- **1** Graduate professional training
- **2** Standard college or university graduation
- **3** Partial college training
- **4** High school graduation
- **5** Partial high school
- **6** Junior high school
- **7** Less than seven years of school

Each respondent's scores are then multiplied by a weight (7 for occupation and 4 for education) and the products are summed to produce the person's ISP. A physician, for example, would be scored as follows:

Factor	Score		Weight		
Occupation	1	×	7	=	7
Education	1	×	4	=	4
			ISP	=	11

After the persons' ISP scores are computed, each individual is assigned to a social class based on these ISP score ranges:

Social class	Ranges of computed scores
I	11–17
II	18–27
III	28–43
IV	44–60
V	61–77

It is of course no accident that education and occupation should turn out to be closely related to class rankings made by participant observers. Higher education opens doors to positions of authority and prestige in the community; and it can and often does lead to command of substantial purchasing power. Moreover, as Hollingshead assumed, men and women who possess similar educations tend to have similar tastes and attitudes and tend to exhibit similar behavior patterns.

Furthermore, occupation is itself one of the major determiners of social class position. Occupations differ in prestige, and these prestige differences are used as cues when community members rank themselves and others. Occupations differ in prestige primarily because different occupational functions imply that persons occupying them exercise varying degrees of control over the pursuits and destinies of other persons.

The high-prestige occupations require extended periods of formal training. They require "brain work" rather than "hand work," and they carry the power to make decisions that have major impact on the lives of other people.

The low-prestige occupations require little formal training. They require "hand work" or "back work" rather than "brain work," and they carry little responsibility for the conduct of others. The occupants of these occupations are the bossed rather than the bosses.

When members of a community are asked to name people who are "above" them or "below" them or "just like" them, it is considerations of this kind that determine rankings. Therefore from a communitywide or nationwide perspective, social class and status or prestige are closely related.

But the relationship breaks down when we look within reference groups. Since a person's reference groups are almost always composed of members of his own social class, he can attain status and prestige by doing well in comparison with them even though he may not be near the top of the occupational-educational hierarchy.

When simple indices of social class, like the ISC and the ISP, became available, it became possible to think of social classes as extending beyond the confines of individual communities. An index like the Hollingshead index, for example, could be applied to any household in the United States.

With this step the concept of social class was broadened and made more generally useful, but it also lost some of its original meaning. When defined this way, the term "social class" no longer refers to a specific group of persons who interact freely with each other and who rank acquaintances as being "above" them or "below" them in the class structure. Rather, it refers to certain types of persons who have similar attitudes, values, and experiences, and who therefore have something in common even though they may have never met.

Some of the original meaning remains, however. For instance, when people move from community to community, they size up neighborhoods, and one of the criteria they use is whether they think they would fit in with the people who already live there. But more importantly from a marketing perspective, the broadened concept has become a useful basis for identifying market segments, as we will discuss in this chapter and those to follow.

Before proceeding, however, it is important to note that social classes differ greatly in size. While the exact proportion of the population assigned to each class depends upon which index the investigator uses and upon exactly where he draws the dividing lines, all the ways of dividing households into social classes agree that there are far more households in the "working" class than in the "upper" class, and most agree that there are substantially more households in the "working" class than in the "middle" class. The two distributions of the population by social class shown in Figure 8-1 illustrate these generalizations.

Social Class and Media Use

When social class is measured by education and occupation, class position is strongly related to amount and type of exposure to the mass media of communication.

The "upper" classes—Classes I and II in the Hollingshead index, for example—spend more time reading than "lower" classes do; and when they read magazines, the magazines they read are different.

W. R. Simmons & Associates, one of the research organizations that measure magazine audiences, routinely tabulates magazine readers by social class groupings as determined by Hollingshead's two-factor index. Table 8-1 shows how the audiences of selected magazines differ in social class, first for men, then for women.

The selectivity of magazines can most easily be seen by comparing the magazines on the left side of the table with the magazines on the right side. Among men, for instance, 150,000 men from ISP Class I are readers of the *Saturday Review,* while only 59,000 ISP Class I Males are readers of *True.* For Classes IV and V, however, the corresponding figures are 107,000 for the *Saturday Review,* and 483,000 for *True.* Note that while the relationship

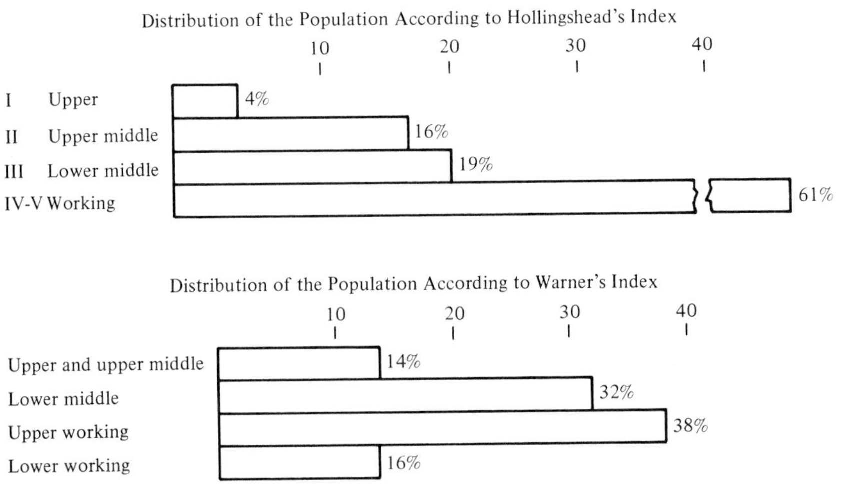

Figure 8-1 Distribution of the population by social class. *Source:* Hollingshead (1958) and Social Research, Inc. (1965).

Table 8-1 Social Class Differences in Magazine Audiences

Average issue, adult male audience (in home reading) (in thousands)

ISP Class	Saturday Review	Harpers Atlantic	Time	Life	Mechanix Illustrated	TV Guide	True	Total U.S.
I	150	130	704	539	73	330	59	1,925
II	114	144	1,156	1,817	233	730	327	5,080
III	135	193	1,204	2,503	443	1,836	617	9,219
IV and V	107	106	1,662	5,879	1,546	7,002	1,438	42,771
Total	506	573	4,726	10,738	2,295	9,961	2,441	58,995

Average issue, adult female audience (in home reading) (in thousands)

ISP Class	Saturday Review	American Home	Better Homes & Gardens	Life	Family Circle	TV Guide	True Story	Total U.S.
I	118	188	344	532	234	219	6	1,443
II	119	641	1,421	1,810	1,322	1,134	17	6,183
III	80	1,236	2,205	2,308	1,837	2,234	176	9,862
IV and V	92	3,509	5,762	6,975	5,621	8,757	4,200	45,478
Total	409	5,574	9,732	11,625	9,014	12,344	4,399	62,966

Source: Simmons (1966).

between social class category and readership of these magazines is fairly strong, it is far from perfect. Some Class IV and Class V males are readers of the *Saturday Review,* and some Class I males are readers of *True,* despite the general trend.

The "Total U.S." column on the far right reemphasizes a point already made in the text: The upper social classes are much smaller, numerically, than the lower classes.

In general the magazines favored by the upper social classes feature comment on national and world affairs and news of developments in science, art, music, literature, and the theater. By comparison with other magazines, the material in them is more abstract and wider-ranging. It covers the world and beyond and extends both forward and backward in time. In many ways the upper-class magazines serve to extend and reinforce the attitudes, tastes, ideas, and values that are developed and encouraged in a liberal arts college education.

The magazines favored by the lower social classes are literal rather than literary. The men's magazines are full of concrete information about hunting, fishing, camping, home maintenance, car repair, and sports. The fiction in them features action and adventure, graphically portrayed.

The women's magazines favored by the lower social classes give instruction in cooking, sewing, shopping, and child care. When they turn to fiction, they almost always focus on interpersonal relationships, especially relationships through which women learn how to handle men. Even the movie magazines, ostensibly about the activities and careers of movie and television personalities, are largely concerned with who is or is not in love with whom.

The social classes also differ in attitude toward and exposure to television. Television programs are scrapped if they fall too far behind in the competition for a large share of the viewing audience, and programs that attract large audiences are widely imitated. Because Classes III, IV, and V are so much larger numerically than Classes I and II, survival of the fittest in the contest for audience size produces programming that is slanted toward the tastes, interests, and values of the lower social classes. As a consequence, members of Class I are apt to regard many television programs as "low in quality" (meaning not tailored to their cultivated tastes and special interests), and on the average they spend somewhat less time in front of the television screen.

The amount of time devoted to the television—both daytime and evening—is related to social class, when social class is defined by occupation and education.

The first set of data in Table 8-2 shows how the amount of time spent viewing television in the evening is related to the way an adult male earns his living. Note that the difference is not as great as one might expect in view of the negative attitudes toward television programming frequently expressed by viewers with higher-level occupations.

The relationship with education shown in the lower set of data in the table is somewhat stronger and is most marked for daytime viewing by housewives. Again, the relationship while clearly present, is not strong. Compared with special-interest magazines, TV is a very "blunt medium" covering huge audiences and reaching consumers with a wide range of interests.

Table 8-2 Social Class and TV Viewing

Average amount of weekday viewing after 6 P.M.	Male viewing by occupation				
	Operatives	Craftsmen	Clerical	Business owners	Professional and technical
4 hours	16	13	12	11	9
3 hours	17	19	19	18	14
2 hours	26	31	30	30	27
1 hour	24	24	27	34	38
None	17	14	11	8	12

Average amount of weekday viewing before 6 P.M.	Female viewing by education					
	Grade school or less	Some high school	Graduated high school	Some college	Graduated college	Some post-graduate
4 hours	4	3	2	2	1	—
3 hours	3	2	3	1	1	—
2 hours	8	8	6	5	4	1
1 hour	23	20	22	23	18	17
None	62	67	68	70	76	81

Source: Starch (1969).

It is by no means certain that members of the upper classes would spend much more time watching television if the programming were different. Members of Classes I and II experience many demands on their time from a wide variety of interesting and attractive options. While members of these classes typically have more discretionary time, the time devoted by choice to community and cultural activities, to entertaining friends and business associates, and to recreation and travel scarcely leaves time to watch the relatively few television programs that attract their interest. Members of the lower classes, on the other hand, have little to do with their spare time that is more engaging than watching television. They do not like to read. They have few social contacts outside the family. And they have neither the opportunity nor the inclination to explore the wider world, either mentally or in person.

Television takes homemakers of the lower classes as far beyond their immediate environment as they ever get or want to go. It tells them more than they want to know about national and international affairs. It shows them a parade of colorful and glamorous personalities. It tells them stories that help them understand and cope with their problems. And it shows them that money, worldly success, prestige, and power do not necessarily lead to happiness.

Members of Classes I and II have another complaint about television: it is "too passive." Trained in achievement motivation from childhood, they believe that time is a precious and perishable commodity that should be used constructively and creatively, not merely squandered. They want their children to be active and inventive even when they are playing. They believe that leisure (even vacations) should be educational. And they believe that sitting passively in front of a television set is a waste of time, unless the set is teaching something useful. Consequently they try to put limits on viewing, especially when it interferes with such worthwhile activities as raking leaves, practicing for Saturday's piano lesson, doing homework, collecting for the Red Cross, or painting the kitchen.

Members of Classes IV and V experience no such pangs of guilt when they find themselves or their children enjoying television. Television supplies information and entertainment—all of it free—in a form that is easy to understand and therefore not dull or boring. For many of the people in Classes IV and V it is much easier to learn something from a television program than to learn anything at school.

So television programming, and the interests and needs of Hollingshead's Classes III, IV, and V, are locked in a circle. As long as television programs survive only by attracting larger audiences than competing programs, and as long as Classes III, IV, and V account for the bulk of the population, television programs will reflect Class III, IV, and V's needs and values. The behavior of television programmers is shaped by the positive reinforcement of large audiences. In the world of television, the majority rules.

Social Class and Income

As would be expected from the relationships between social class and occupation and between social class and education, there is a strong positive relationship between social class and income. But because the wages of some skilled workers are substantially higher than the salaries of some white-collar workers, there is a considerable overlap in the income levels of the classes, especially between the incomes of the lower middle class and the upper working class. For instance, a study by Social Research, Inc., that employed the Warner Index of Stratification showed the following distribution:

	Class			
Income	% Lower working	% Upper working	% Lower middle	% Upper middle
$10,000 and over	—	5	22	60
8,000 to $9,999	5	10	20	22
7,000 to 7,999	6	14	20	6
6,000 to 6,999	6	19	15	3
5,000 to 5,999	14	21	15	3
4,000 to 4,999	21	14	6	3
Under 4,000	47	17	2	—

Source: Social Research, Inc. (1965).

In this study, about 6 out of 10 men in the lower middle class had incomes over $7,000, but about 3 out of 10 men in the upper working class also had incomes above that level.

But there is another income difference between the classes, and this difference influences not only the amount of income available at one point in time but also attitudes toward money—and toward work—throughout the family life cycle. In white-collar occupations, especially upper-middle-class occupations that require extensive formal education, income reaches its top level comparatively late in life and then remains relatively stable. In blue-collar occupations, income reaches its peak and levels off comparatively early. This difference contributes to a class difference in attitudes toward jobs, and most especially to a difference in achievement motivation; persons in early-ceiling jobs, recognizing they have reached a peak, tend to turn to collective action to protect their jobs and to obtain increased benefits.

Thus social classes differ in their outlook on life, and this attitude influences their attitudes toward money and their use of services associated with money.

Not only do the higher classes tend to have higher incomes, they are also more apt to use the income they have with an eye to the future. The upper classes tend to use charge accounts and credit as a matter of convenience, keeping charge accounts paid monthly and minimizing finance charges. The lower classes tend to use time payment plans and "revolving charge" accounts to acquire goods as rapidly as possible (Mathews and Slocum, 1969, 1970). This practice permits the family to enjoy the use of goods while the goods are being paid for, but it adds substantially to the total cost of many items and it puts the family in a precarious financial position. If the family's regular income is curtailed for any reason, or it new financial demands are suddenly added, it can create a financial catastrophe.

The future-versus-present attitude toward life also influences other aspects of consumer behavior, as other chapters will show. Specifically, in future chapters the concept of social class will be shown to relate to and to aid in an understanding of consumers' perceptions of products and stores, product positioning, and innovative behavior.

GEOGRAPHY

Consumers differ from each other on several major characteristics, such as income, age, and ethnic and class identification. Spanning many of these variables is a basic characteristic of consumer behavior: almost all consumer behavior is seasonal; and the influence of seasons is moderated by geography: where people live.

Seasons

Holidays play an important role. Department stores expand their toy departments before Christmas and contract them after the holiday is over. Candy stores stock up for Valentine's Day, Mother's Day, Christmas, and Easter. A large proportion of the turkeys sold are sold just before Thanksgiving.

Even more important are the roles played by seasonal variations in daylight and temperature. The increased daylight and warm temperatures of summer spur the consumption of soft drinks, beer, light clothing, suntan lotion, sports equipment, and air conditioners. The dark hours and cold temperatures of winter encourage consumption of fur coats, snowmobiles, home heating fuel, electricity for light, hot chocolate, and television sets.

Suppliers try to foresee these seasonal variations in demand and to dampen them as much as possible. The tactics they most often use are to lower prices during the "off" season so as to borrow sales from the past or the future, and to conduct special "clearance" sales during the "on" season just after the season has reached its peak.

Many suppliers keep careful records of sales month by month and use this accumulated past experiences as the basis for future planning. This method usually works, for seasonal variations in aggregate consumer behavior are surprisingly stable.

Sometimes, however, past records for specific products are unavailable, and sometimes the marketer is more interested in knowing when consumers begin to "think Spring" than when they actuually begin to engage in Spring-associated behavior.

One way to find out when the seasons change in consumers' minds is to ask for word associations: "I am going to read you a list of words one at a time, and I want you to tell me the very next word you think of. Any word is all right; the main thing is speed. For example, if I said 'paper,' you might say 'book.' Do you understand?"

When this technique was used week by week with national samples of consumers, the stimulus word "season" evoked the responses shown in Figure 8-2.

This chart shows that Spring began to rise in the thoughts of consumers at the beginning of calendar Winter and began to decline very early in calendar Spring. Psychological Summer began its rise in early April, held fairly steady from mid-June until Labor Day, when it suddenly lost its share of the mind to Fall and Autumn. Psychological Winter had the shortest duration. It began its rise in mid-November, peaked just before Christmas, and dropped steadily until it began a long low in mid-March.

In mid-January, when the snow is still on the ground in much of the country, spring fashions appear in department store windows and tulips appear on magazine covers.

Location

While uniformly affected by seasons, consumers are unevenly affected by them because they live in different parts of the country, and where consumers are located—see Figure 8-3—affects the way they live.

Midwest winters are long and cold and, compared with the Southeast, the growing season—from the last frost to first frost—is short. The longer, colder winters in the East North Central mean that home heating takes a larger portion of the household expenditures of consumers living there and biases their choice of fuel away from electricity toward natural gas. The shorter growing season means that locally raised fresh fruits and vegetables are less available, and this difference in turn affects both what a Midwest housewife pays for food and how she plans her menus. Two or three fresh vegetables per meal—standard fare in Halesboro, Georgia—is unusual in Indianapolis.

The water in much of the Midwest, including the area around Indianapolis, is much harder than the water in southeast Georgia. This difference in mineral content makes a home water softener a highly desirable appliance in Indiana but almost unheard of in Georgia. Water hardness influences the sudsiness of detergents, toothpaste, shaving cream, and soap, so products that produce too little lather in unsoftened Indianapolis water produce too much in Halesboro. This difference in turn influences the relative popularity of brands that differ in ability to make lather and suds. The minerals in water influence brand choice in still another way: they alter the taste of instant coffee and other dried and powdered products, and they affect the readiness with which such products dissolve. Thus brands that are perfectly satisfactory in one region are less than satisfactory in another.

Finally, geography affects consumption through the action of local social norms. For instance, consider beverages. An Indianapolis family might drink scotch or bourbon during an evening on the porch. A Halesboro family would have soft drinks or iced tea. The Indiana family would serve champagne as a matter of course at their daughter's wedding reception. In Halesboro, the proper beverage would be fresh fruit punch, unspiked.

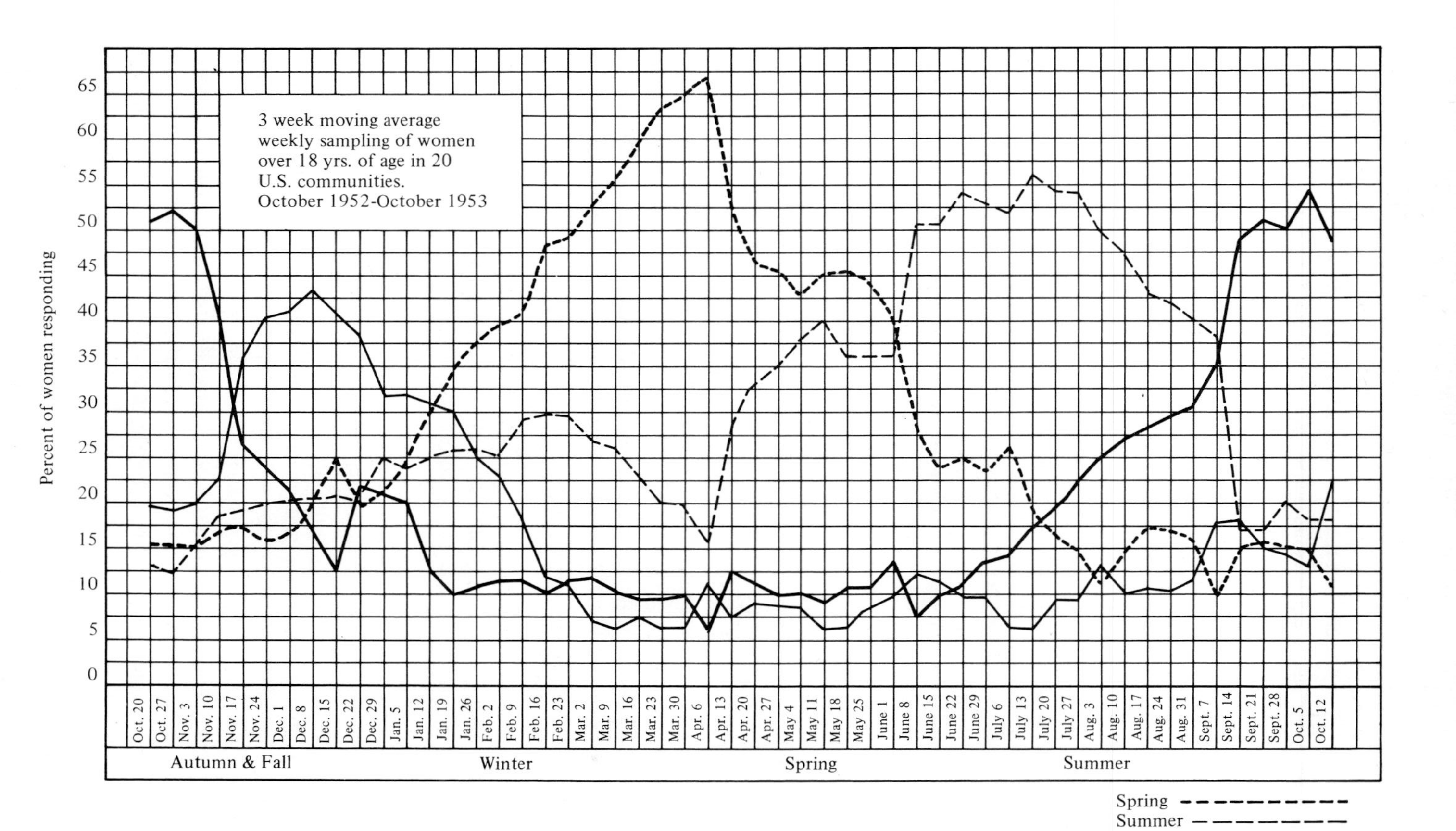

Figure 8-2 Psychoseasonal trends in the U.S. *Source:* Vicary (1955).

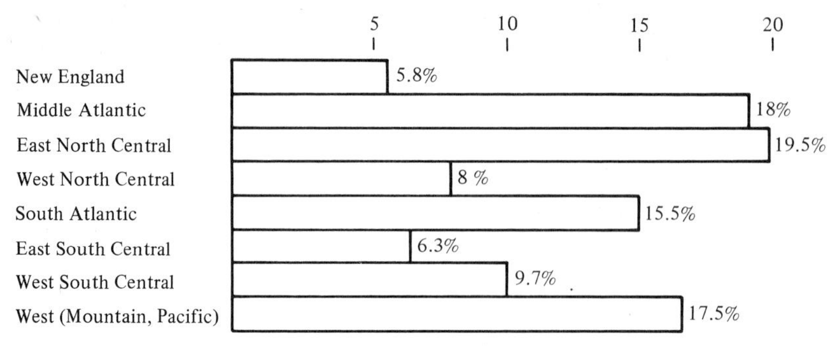

Figure 8-3 Population location by geographic region. *Source:* Data calculated from Linden (1974).

Climate and social norms can be so pervasive an influence that major geographical regions of the United States can be characterized as having their own cultures. Tables 8-3 to 8-6 show many of the marked differences among five major regions (East, South, Midwest, West, and Southeast) in life style, product usage, product ownership, and media usage. These differences are described as follows:

East Easterners, when compared with those living in other regions, portray themselves as cosmopolitan travelers. They are most apt to like to visit places that are totally different from their homes, to want to spend a year in a city like London or Paris, and to have actually taken a trip outside the United States during the past year. Their activities and consumption patterns reflect this cosmopolitan orientation. Easterners are most likely to have a cocktail or drink before dinner (blended whiskey or scotch), to cook outdoors, and to drink hot tea. They are above the United States average in having wine with dinner. They prefer "All in the Family" but are least apt to prefer a traditional marriage and are below average on frequent church attendance. Furthermore, they are least likely to chew gum, go hunting, or listen to country and western music.

Moreover, Easterners are most likely to ride a bus and, along with westerners, to use a bank charge card in spite of their above-average concern with getting jobs in a tight economy. They view themselves as routined and settled, stating that their days seem to follow a definite routine; this opinion probably reflects the need to schedule their lives around a mass-transit schedule. In keeping with this self-view, they report the highest level of readership of the daily evening paper and an above-average readership of the Sunday paper. Easterners are more likely than persons of most regions to go bowling and least likely to be thinking of buying life insurance. They are least apt to have meat at breakfast, to own a freezer, or to own a garbage disposal, and they are below average in the ownership of a water softener. Also, they are below the United States total for weekly consumption of soft drinks and potato chips and cottage cheese.

Table 8-3 Regional Life Style Profile

Item	Percentage agreeing					
	Total	East	South	Mid-west	West	South-west
Prefer a traditional marriage with the husband assuming the responsibility for providing for the family and the wife running the house and taking care of the children.	52	39	52	59	45	61
When making important family decisions, consideration of the children should come first.	52	49	62	51	48	50
Every vacation should be educational.	48	49	54	52	38	47
I am considering buying life insurance.	19	14	30	17	17	21
I nearly always have meat at breakfast.	29	14	52	22	26	34
Went out to breakfast instead of having it at home at least once last year.	57	57	42	61	71	61
Worked on a community project at least once during the past year.	35	39	50	34	31	34
Attended church 52 or more times last year.	28	23	37	31	20	30
I like to visit places that are totally different from my home.	72	79	63	72	75	65
I would like to spend a year in London or Paris.	33	40	36	27	38	24
Went on a trip outside the U.S. last year.	14	24	8	12	19	15
Rode a bus at least once last year.	32	49	26	28	40	24
It is hard to get a good job these days.	77	82	83	77	65	80
Used a bank charge card at least once last year.	43	52	43	41	52	50
Returned an unsatisfactory product at least once during the past year.	65	67	52	70	65	64
Used a "price off" coupon at a grocery store.	63	67	50	72	60	53
My days seem to follow a definite routine – eating meals at the same time each day, etc.	62	68	66	58	53	64
Cooked outdoors at least once last year.	81	86	82	84	80	84
Went on a picnic at least once last year.	75	78	65	79	79	73
Had wine with dinner at least once during the past year.	60	70	38	62	72	49
Had a cocktail or drink before dinner at least once last year.	70	78	59	75	77	53
I am interested in spice and seasoning.	43	46	44	41	54	35
Visited an art gallery or museum from 1 to 4 times in the past year.	30	29	27	32	40	34
Went bowling at least once last year.	36	42	20	44	34	24
Went hiking at least once during the past year.	46	49	47	43	59	45
Went backpacking at least once last year.	6	8	7	4	16	5
Went hunting at least once last year.	32	18	43	29	32	40

Source: Needham, Harper & Steers, (1975).

Table 8-4 Regional Consumption Differences

Product	Percentage reporting using once a week or more					
	Total	East	South	Mid-west	West	South-west
Regular chewing gum	26	17	40	30	24	26
Mouthwash	51	48	62	47	40	54
Men's cologne	61	58	72	61	55	71
Shaving cream in a can	55	55	54	55	45	54
Toothpaste	88	89	92	89	90	82
Regular coffee (nondecaffeinated)	62	59	63	58	72	66
Instant coffee (nondecaffeinated)	36	40	33	36	31	24
Hot tea	29	44	14	30	30	24
Iced tea (summer)	69	73	84	69	52	76
Regular soft drinks	53	46	67	53	35	63
Artificial sweetener	18	19	30	19	11	21
Nondairy powdered creamer (Coffee-mate, Cremora, etc.)	23	23	33	23	20	15
Potato chips	35	21	48	41	26	43
Fresh sausage	18	15	30	15	11	22
Bologna	33	30	23	36	31	28
Cottage cheese	32	27	17	41	40	30
Yogurt	5	9	2	4	11	3
Vitamin tablets	35	36	21	36	44	35
Domestic wine	14	15	5	16	28	8
Blended whiskey	11	16	4	13	13	7
Scotch	7	12	5	7	8	2

Source: Needham, Harper & Steers, (1975).

South Southerners, frequently characterized as political conservatives, can be characterized as church-, children-, and community-oriented. People of the Southern region report substantially higher levels of church attendance and participation in community projects. Also, they are least apt to drink wine with dinner or drink domestic wine and blended whiskey, and they are below average in having a drink before dinner. They appear to be especially interested in children, in considering children when making important decisions, in

Table 8-5 Appliance Ownership by Region

Product	Percentage owning					
	Total	East	South	Mid-west	West	South-west
Automatic dishwasher	43	44	42	42	56	56
Garbage disposal	28	11	8	35	50	44
Freezer	58	48	68	62	58	60
Water softener	13	6	1	21	14	9
Room air conditioner	41	45	45	42	28	37
Color TV set	77	79	65	83	83	77

Source: Needham, Harper & Steers, (1975).

Table 8-6 Regional Media Differences

Category	Total	East	South	Mid-west	West	South-west
	Percentage exposed					
Newspapers						
Sunday newspaper (read 4+ issues in past 4 weeks)	68	73	63	69	65	74
Daily morning (read 9+ issues in past 10 days)	31	34	31	30	30	37
Daily evening (read 9+ issues in past 10 days)	45	54	48	52	35	39
Radio station types						
Popular music — top 40	46	47	51	52	46	35
All talk — telephone discussion/news	40	43	51	44	38	24
country and western	53	38	70	56	42	54
Magazines						
TV Guide	37	41	47	28	49	38
National Geographic	33	37	30	31	42	44
Penthouse	17	19	7	15	24	14
TV programs[a]						
"Hawaii Five-O"	35	36	41	31	26	35
"Sanford and Son"	40	37	48	38	32	41
"All in the Family"	46	55	47	34	40	40

[a]Rated "very good" to "one of my favorites."
Source: Needham, Harper & Steers, (1975).

ensuring that vacations are educational, in serving meat (fresh sausage, commonly) at breakfast, in having breakfast at home, and in providing for the material future through life insurance.

In contrast to Easterners, Southerners do not view themselves as cosmopolitan, at least in their activities. They are least apt to want to visit places totally different from their homes and to have traveled outside the United States during the past year. They do hunt, chew gum, drink soft drinks, and eat potato chips, and they prefer country and western music. Also, they are most apt to listen to radio talk shows, read *TV Guide,* and prefer "Hawaii Five-O" and "Sanford and Son" but probably not view them on a color set. They are least apt to read the Sunday paper and *Penthouse* magazine.

Climate affects Southerners in obvious ways. They are least apt to own a water softener or to drink hot tea; they are most likely to own a freezer, to drink iced tea, and to use mouthwash and cologne.

Although Southerners are most apt to say, "It is hard to get a good job these days," they are least likely to return an unsatisfactory product or to use a price-off coupon in the grocery store. And while in the grocery store, they are least likely to buy bologna or cottage cheese but mostly likely to buy artificial sweetener and powdered creamer. After each meal, they are least likely to turn on a garbage disposal but may be listening to popular music.

Midwest As the data in Tables 8-3 to 8-6 indicate, Midwesterners more than people of any other region may claim to be "typical" or "average" Americans. When compared with the United States total, they are most apt to reflect that total. But Midwesterners also have their subculture, traits of which result from preference as well as season and climate. They are most likely to return an unsatisfactory product and to use a price-off coupon in the store, perhaps suggesting a more rigid decision-making characteristic than other regions.

Although most likely to own a color TV, Midwesterners are least likely to read *TV Guide* and to prefer "All in the Family." They are most likely to listen to popular music and to go bowling, to eat cottage cheese, and to own a water softener. They are above average on readership of the evening paper, in preference for a traditional marriage, in the consumption of potato chips, in the ownership of a garbage disposal, and in baving a cocktail before dinner; and they are below average in having meat with breakfast and in wanting to spend a year in London or Paris.

West In contrast to Easterners, and even though Westerners report an above-average level of bus riding, they say they are least likely to follow a definite routine. Their flexible orientation to life is demonstrated in a number of activities and opinions. They are least apt to read the evening daily paper, to feel that every vacation should be educational, or to attend church every week; they are most likely to go out to breakfast and above average in their desires to spend a year in London or Paris.

Westerners appear to be especially interested in unique forms of recreation. They are most apt to visit an art gallery or museum and to go hiking and backpacking, and they are above-average readers of *National Geographic*. In keeping with the "natural" aspects of their activities, Westerners report the highest levels of consumption of cottage cheese and yogurt, vitamin tablets, domestic wine (frequently with dinner), and regular but not instant coffee; they report the lowest levels of usage of artificial sweetener, regular soft drinks, iced tea, mouthwash, cologne, and shaving cream from a can. Fresh sausage and potato chips do not fit their consumption preferences, however; but they are interested in spice and seasoning.

To aid the maintenance of a unique and flexible life style, Westerners use time-saving appliances, such as automatic dishwashers and garbage disposals, and convenient credit forms, such as the bank charge card. They feel secure: they are least apt to report it is hard to get a good job these days.

Westerners are most likely to own a color TV and to read *TV Guide*, but they are not apt to watch "Hawaii Five-O," "Sanford and Son," and "All in the Family." Nor are they apt to consider country and western music to be for the Westerner.

They tend to be more liberal than their Southwestern neighbors, as shown in their relatively high readership of *Penthouse*, in above-average consumption of cocktails before dinner, and in below-average preference for a traditional marriage arrangement.

Southwest Southwesterners emerge from the data in the tables as traditionalist, sharing many traits with Southerners, although not to the same degree. Nevertheless, the Southwest has its own characteristic style of life.

Persons in the Southwest are most apt to prefer a traditional marriage and least likely to have a cocktail or to drink before dinner or to drink scotch; less likely to have wine with dinner or to drink domestic wine; least apt to want to spend a year in London or Paris and less apt than the "average" American to want to visit places totally different from their homes. They are most likely to read the daily morning paper,. the Sunday paper, and *National Geographic;* they do not care particularly for All Talk shows, the Top-40, the evening paper, or "All in the Family." All in all, they give a portrait suggesting a traditional, conservative, and routine style of life.

Southwesterners share with their Western neighbors a penchant for time-saving appliances (dishwashers and disposals) and bank credit cards, but not the inclination for spice and seasoning (despite their proximity to Mexico). They exceed the Westerners' dislike for instant coffee. Like Southerners, but to a lesser degree, Southwesterners enjoy having meat at breakfast, going hunting, and drinking regular soft drinks and eating potato chips. Also, they are not apt to consume hot tea or bologna or to use a price-off coupon; but, unlike their Southern neighbors, they are likely to avoid nondairy powdered creamer. Yet, like the Southerner, the Southwesterner is above average in the usage of cologne.

Compared with other regions, persons in the Southwest are least likely to ride a bus, to go bowling, or to use toothpaste.

SUMMARY

In addition to life periods, other factors, such as subculture and geography, are important in determining consumer behavior. Subcultures are discussed in terms of ethnic groups and social classes, and geography is discussed in terms of seasons and location.

Ethnic groups are composed of people with the same racial and/or national origin who can be readily identified by their distinct behavior patterns, customs, and values. Such groups affect consumer behavior both within and beyond their own social or regional boundaries as a result of the gradual process of diffusion. Many "ethnic" foods and products are eventually accepted and enjoyed by Americans who are not of the same ethnic group. Because blacks are an important ethnic group, we compare the income levels, consumption patterns, and shopping patterns of these consumers with those of their white counterparts. Except for a few products, differences between blacks and whites seem to be the result of income effects rather than racial effects.

The concept of social class is useful from a marketing perspective because it serves as a basis for identifying important market segments. Consumers belonging to different social classes exhibit marked differences in media habits, income levels, and attitudes about life and money. People in each group can be identified with the use of such measures as Warner's "Index of Status Characterisitcs" and Hollingshead's "Index of Social Position."

Consumer behavior is also influenced by geography, since basic needs for clothing and shelter are modified by climate considerations and since the availability, as well as the price, of many foods depends on consumer's locations. Much consumer behavior is seasonal, and this factor is modified by geography. In addition, regional customs are important in determining behavior, as illustrated in the discussion of five regions. Easterners have a characteristic style of life described as routine cosmopolitanism. Persons in the South appear to have their focus on church, children, and community. Midwesterners are "middle-Americans" but are somewhat more rigid deciders than others. Western Americans have a penchant for flexibility, and Southwesterners a penchant for a more traditional, conservative style of life.

REVIEW QUESTIONS

1 Identify and discuss the two different ways in which the ethnic origins of Americans influence consumption of products and services.
2 Blacks have become a major force in the American marketplace. Why?
3 In general, differences in consumption expenditures between blacks and whites are attributable to income rather than racial effects. What products seem to be exceptions to this general rule? Why?
4 Hollingshead found that social class rankings can be predicted from a knowledge of three demographic characteristics. Identify these and indicate which ones are used in computing the ISP score.
5 Discuss the differences between Warner's ISC and Hollingshead's ISP in terms of the proportion of the total population each index assigns to the different social classes.
6 The concept of social class has become a useful basis for identifying market segments. Discuss the differences in media usage between the different social classes.
7 Is there a perfect correlation between income and social class? Why or why not?
8 How does the future-versus-present attitude toward life differ among the various social classes? How does this attitude affect consumer behavior?
9 In addition to social class, there are several other factors which affect consumer behavior. Identify these and give specific examples illustrating the effect of each factor on behavior.

EXERCISE

Two very successful regional magazines are *Sunset* and *Southern Living.* Examine several recent issues of these magazines and prepare an outline or report showing the compatibility of the contents of each to the life styles of the region being served. Using these successful magazines as a model, develop a proposal for a regional magazine for the East and one for the Midwest. In your proposal, show how the contents would differ and how they would be similar for the various regions. Also, develop a priority marketing plan for advertisements the magazines should "go after"; this plan should show a ranking by product types and a justification for that ranking.

REFERENCES

Alexander, Milton. "The Significance of Ethnic Groups in Marketing." In L. H. Stockman (ed.), *Advancing Marketing Efficiency.* Chicago: American Marketing Association, 1959.

Alexis, Marcus. "Some Negro-White Differences in Consumption." *American Journal of Economics and Sociology,* 21 (January 1962), 11–28.

Barban, Arnold M. "The Dilemma of 'Integrated' Advertising." *Journal of Business,* 42 (October 1969), 477–496.

Bauer, Raymond A., Scott M. Cunningham, and Lawrence H. Wortzel. "The Marketing Dilemma of Negroes." *Journal of Marketing,* 29 (July 1965), 1–6.

Black Enterprise. "The Black Consumer." *Black Enterprise* (November 1973).

Bullock, H. A. "Consumer Motivations in Black and White." *Harvard Business Review,* 39 (May–June and July–August, 1961), 80–104 and 110–124.

Bureau of the Census and Bureau of Labor Statistics. *The Social and Economic Status of Negroes in the United States.* Washington, D.C.: U.S. Department of Commerce and U.S. Department of Labor, Series p. 23, No. 29, 1969.

Caplovitz, David. *The Poor Pay More.* New York: The Free Press, 1963.

Feldman, Laurence P., and Alvin D. Starr. "Racial Factors in Shopping Behavior." In Keith Cox and Ben Enis (eds.), *A New Measure of Responsibility for Marketing.* Chicago: American Marketing Association, 1968.

Gensch, D. H., and Richard Staelin. "Making Black Retail Outlets Work." *California Management Review,* 15 (Fall 1972), 52–62.

Hollingshead, August B., and Frederick C. Redlich. *Social Class and Mental Illness.* New York: Wiley, 1958.

Kassarjian, Harold H. "The Negro and American Advertising: 1946–1965." *Journal of Marketing Research,* 6 (February 1969), 29–39.

Kluckhohn, Clyde, and H. A. Murray. *Personality in Nature, Society, and Culture.* New York: Knopf, 1949.

Linden, Fabian. "The Changing Topography of Demand." *The Conference Board RECORD* (September 1974), 47–51.

Mason, J. Barry, and C. S. Madden. "Food Purchases in a Low-Income Negro Neighborhood: The Development of Socio-Economic Behavioral Profile as Related to Movement and Patronage Patterns." Unpublished paper. Graduate School of Business, University of Alabama, 1971.

Mathews, H. Lee, and John W. Slocum, Jr. "Social Class and Commercial Bank Credit Card Usage." *Journal of Marketing,* 33 (January 1969), 71–78.

Needham, Harper & Steers Advertising, Inc. *Life Style Survey,* 1975.

Petrof, John V. "Reaching the Negro Market: A Segregated vs. a General Newspaper." *Journal of Advertising Research,* 9 (April 1968), 40–43.

Sexton, Donald E., Jr. "Do Blacks Pay More?" *Journal of Marketing Research,* 8 (November 1971), 420–426.

Simmons, W. R., and Associates. "Selective Markets and the Media Reaching Them." New York: 1966.

Slocum, John W., and H. L. Mathews. "Social Class and Income as Indicators of Consumer Credit Behavior." *Journal of Marketing,* 34 (April 1970), 69–74.

Social Research, Inc. *The Working Class World.* Chicago, Ill.: Social Research, Inc., 1965.

Sommers, Montrose, and Grady D. Bruce. "Blacks, Whites, and Products: Relative Deprivation and Reference Group Behavior." *Social Science Quarterly,* 49 (December 1968), 631–642.

Stafford, James E., Keith Cox, and J. B. Higginbotham. "Some Consumption Pattern Differences between Urban Whites and Negroes." *Social Science Quarterly,* 49 (December 1968), 619–630.

"Starch Profile of Market Segments," Mamaroneck, NY: Daniel Starch & Staff, Inc., 1969.

Steele, A. T. "Weather's Effect on the Sales of a Department Store." *Journal of Marketing,* 15 (April 1951), 436–443.

Sturdivant, Frederick D. "Better Deal for Ghetto Shoppers." *Harvard Business Review.* 46 (March–April 1968), 130–139.

———. *The Ghetto Marketplace.* New York: The Free Press, 1969.

Tolley, B. Stuart, and John J. Goett. "Reactions to Blacks in Newspaper." *Journal of Advertising Research,* 11 (April 1971).

Valentine, C. A. *Culture and Poverty.* Chicago: University of Chicago Press, 1968.

Vicary, James M. "The Psychology of Seasons." In Edmund Wooding (ed.), *The Changing Consumer.* Ann Arbor, Mich.: University of Michigan, 1955, 74–83.

Warner, Loyd W., Marchia Meeker, and Kenneth Eells. *Social Class in America.* Chicago: Science Research Associates, 1949.

Wells, William D., and Fred D. Reynolds. "Psychological Geography." Unpublished paper. Needham, Harper & Steers Advertising, Inc., 1976.

Wheatley, J. J. "The Use of Black Models in Advertising." *Journal of Marketing Research,* 8 (August 1971), 390–393.

Yudkin, John. "Man's Choice of Food." *Lancet* (May 12, 1956), 645–649.

Part Three

The Analysis of Consumer Stimuli and Responses

Chapter 9

The Role of Product Perceptions and Preferences

To consumers, products represent an assortment of means needed to maintain and/or extend patterns of behavior—to live a particular style of life (Alderson, 1965). To consumer advocates and sometimes to public policy administrators, some products are potentially hazardous objects—objects that may cost too much, wear out too fast, not perform as advertised, or create dangers to health or to life itself.

To marketers, products represent the dominant element of the marketing mix. More often than not, product decisions take precedence over other marketing decisions and tend to dictate decisions regarding distribution, promotion, and price.

> A common problem marketing consultants are asked to solve is determining the market for a new product. Someone in a white coat has come out of an industrial laboratory with something in a test tube. The marketing consultant is told that the firm has a compound or artifact which will do thus and such. He is asked whether there is a market for this "thing," how big the market is, where the market is, what it is like, what promotional, pricing, and place strategies are appropriate, given *this* product and *this* market? (Reynolds, 1969:6).

Note that while product decisions initially dominate, market decisions gradually assume an equal and ultimately superordinate role in the decision-making process. Products and markets are inseparably interwoven. Marketers must have some idea of how people interact with products and how this interaction affects sales.

PEOPLE AND PRODUCTS

When the marketing consultant ponders the question, "Is there a market for this 'thing,' " he is asking himself, "Is there a demand for it?" Demand exists in the person, not in the product itself. To the coffee drinker, coffee is more than just black liquid in a cup. It is stimulating; it does things to people. When the coffee lover gets up in the morning, coffee ends the night and starts the day. Coffee has "strength," a quality that distinguishes it from tea. It can be a sedative, even when it is a stimulant. People use it to renew their energies; it is both relaxing and invigorating. It also has a number of social meanings. While people can and do drink coffee alone, it serves especially as a sign of sociability, hospitality, friendliness, and equality. Coffee drinking is a ritual, a part of American life, a habit adhered to, like eating three meals a day (Martineau, 1957). Thus, the "demand" for coffee rests upon a complex set of attributes, some of which are intimately related to physical properties of the product, and some of which are not. Coffee "is" all of these attributes in the minds of some consumers, and it "is" few or none of them in the minds of others. It is a complex stimulus with a meaning that varies from person to person. Even within the same person its meaning varies from time to time.

In general, every product has an aura of subjective as well as objective meanings that help determine how much of a product people will want. It is not surprising, then, to find that marketers are interested in learning how people view products—what people believe about them, what benefits or functions they expect, what beliefs are important in reaching a decision to buy or not to buy, and how people develop the attitudes, opinions, and beliefs they hold.

Whenever students of consumer behavior begin to think about these questions, they invariably think about consumers' cognitions—literally, about what consumers know. Through cognitive activities people reduce environmental complexity, facilitate the identification of things, lessen the need for instant learning, and anticipate the results of a given response to a given situation.

PERCEPTION

Throughout the book reference has been made to the notion that people interact with aspects of their environs. Such interaction is accomplished through information handling processes by which consumers acquire, interpret, and decide on responses to stimuli. The importance of perception as a concept in the study of consumer behavior stems from the fact that it is the information handling process whereby people attach *meanings* to aspects of their environment. As the coffee example has indicated, the behaviors of consumers—their responses to stimuli and situations—are shaped by the meanings they attach to things.

Several persons can and do attach virtually the same meaning to the same object. But most of the time, the complex set of meanings that makes up the person's cognitive world is personal and unique, and it may not be congruent with objectively defined reality. Several noted psychologists have emphasized the individuality of cognition by referring to the human being as a "nonrepresentational artist" and as "man the scientist."

Krech (1962) has stressed the notion that the meanings we attach to the world are not necessarily valid. He points out that the cognitive map of the individual is not a photographic representation of the physical world, but is a partial, personal construction in which certain aspects are selected out for major roles while others are ignored. He views the human being as a nonrepresentational artist, painting an internal picture of the world that expresses the human's own particular view of reality.

Another psychologist, George Kelly, developed an elaborate theory of human behavior based on the notions of personal constructs and anticipatory behavior. According to Kelly (1955), human beings may be thought of as "scientists" in the sense that the aspirations of the scientist are basically those of all people. Each person is assumed to be concerned with the prediction and control of that individual's universe. To accomplish these aims, individuals represent their world by creating "constructs" or patterns to help them interpret the events happening in nature. Each person develops an individual repertoire of constructs—the person's own theories—and uses them to interpret, conceptualize and predict events occurring in the individual's universe.

Both Krech and Kelly emphasize that perception is invariably an individual matter. It is never a "sure thing," an absolute representation of "what is." Rather, it is a prediction, a personal construction developed in the light of past experiences to provide the perceiver with the best possible basis for directing behavior. Translated into marketing terms, this view would hold that consumers' decisions and resulting behaviors are made on the basis of the consumers' views of products in the context of the use they anticipate making of them. When the consumer shops for and buys a new shirt or a new or used car or leaves a sweater to be dry-cleaned, these acts are based on the belief that these products or services will satisfy some need or set of needs that happen to have arisen in this consumer's interaction with the world. In short, the consumer has a personal "theory" of the way the product or the service will work. The theory may or may not be the same as the comparable theory held by someone else.

Product Perceptions

Because they are generally aware of the importance of perceptions, marketing managers express concern about "images." Take, for example, the case of a large savings and loan association located in a major metropolitan area in the Southwest. Throughout its history, this company had maintained a position of steady growth and leadership in its market area. In 1972, however, management became concerned about the increasingly aggressive policies of its competitors and decided to reformulate its marketing plans to reassert its dominant position. As part of its new policy, the management set three objectives:

1 Generate an influx of new and active savings accounts—accounts that maintain a regular and stable savings regimen.
2 Attract younger savers to expand the base of operations for the future.
3 Establish a strong and positive image for the association.

A consumer research project was undertaken to aid in the development of strategies for the achievement of these objectives and to establish bench marks for the future evaluation of the effectiveness of the marketing program later implemented. One aspect of the study was a series of choice questions designed to determine the existing image of the association and those of its two major competitors:

Which of the three do you *think* has the most savings account customers?
Which of the three do you *think* has the most branches?
Which do you *think* pays the highest rate of interest?
Which do you *think* provides the most services?
At which one do you *think* it is easiest to obtain a loan?
At which do you *think* it is most difficult to obtain a loan?
Which do you *think* has the best financial advisors?
Which do you *think* advertises the most?
Which do you *think* appeals most to younger people?
Which do you *think* appeals most to older people?
Which do you *think* has the friendliest personnel?
In which savings and loan do you *think* your money is most safe?

The pattern of answers to the full set of twelve "what do you think" questions gave management the opportunity to see the "images" of the three institutions. One of the associations was described by consumers as having the most customers, as being safest, and as offering the most services, the best financial advice, and the highest interest. However, it was also seen as appealing to older people and as being the most reluctant to grant loans. All in all, in the minds of the association's present and potential customers, it appeared to be successful, conservative, and professional but impersonal and somewhat unsympathetic to people in need of loans.

While many consumers held this image, others did not. About 20 percent of the people surveyed described the institution as having the friendliest personnel, easiest to get a loan from, and appealing to young people. These consumers saw the association as open, cooperative, aggressive, and helpful, not as an impersonal and unsympathetic organization.

This illustration underscores the contention that different consumers have different "theories" of reality. It also serves to emphasize that a retail outlet—a store or a bank—is a lot more than a place to buy things or to invest money.

Through its design and decor, its advertising, the range and price level of its merchandise, and the appearance and behavior of its personnel, it conveys an "image" of the kind of place it is and, by implication, of the kind of person who shops there. Consumers are sensitive to these images; and, along with other factors, these images guide their behavior.

The image of a retail outlet has two components that interact with each other but that can be measured separately. The first component consists of the characteristics or attributes of the outlet itself: its size, location, parking facilities, advertising, displays, credit and return policy, price range and price level, variety and depth of merchandise, behavior of clerks and others who come into contact with the public, and so on. The second component consists of the patrons who use it—the human environment that will make any one consumer feel ill at ease or at home.

Images of Products and Brands

Products and brands also acquire images, sometimes through a carefully calculated campaign on the part of the manufacturer and sometimes almost by accident. Like images of retail outlets, product and brand images have two separable but interacting components, one consisting of the attributes of the object, the other consisting of the characteristics of the user. In both cases, it is more accurate to say "perceived" characteristics, because a perceived characteristic can influence consumer behavior even when the perception is inaccurate.

Figure 9-1 lists over sixty attributes that can be ascribed to particular automobile makes or brands. People do not use all possible perceptions to evaluate the desirability of a product. Rather, they perceive selectively and make their evaluations on the basis of a limited number of attributes selected from the total possible set. The attributes may be very specific in nature or quite abstract; i.e., they might be concepts that capture the essence of a number of specific attributes. For example, one buyer might evaluate automobiles in terms of interior roominess, durability, gasoline economy, warranty coverage, and price, while another might compare cars in terms of styling, comfort, performance, and prestige.

Because people do not use all possible perceptions of a product to establish its meaning and desirability, marketers are naturally interested in finding out which perceptions are used and by whom. The search is for the "determinant attributes," a phrase suggestive of the notion that certain features of a product are closely associated with preference, while any remaining features, whether perceived or not, are immaterial (Myers and Alpert, 1968).

One simple and direct approach to isolating determinant attributes is "aided recall." Recent purchasers of a product are provided a lengthy list of attributes and asked to check which were reasons why they chose the brand they purchased rather than some other brand. When provided with a lengthy list, consumers often check a fairly large number. After completing the attribute list, respondents are then asked to select the three or four attributes

Figure 9-1 Automobile Attributes

Comfort and convenience
- Heater comfort
- Ventilation comfort
- Air conditioning
- Interior roominess
- Front seat comfort
- Rear seat comfort
- Instrument legibility
- Convenience of controls
- Ashtray accessibility
- Exterior door handle operation
- Interior door handle operation
- Front visibility
- Rear visibility
- Ease of getting in and out — front
- Ease of getting in and out — rear
- Front head room
- Rear head room
- Front leg room
- Rear leg room
- Luggage capacity

Operation
- Transmission
- Brakes
- Ease of handling
- Freedom from breakdown
- Durability

Performance
- Drivability
- Acceleration from standstill
- Passing acceleration
- Starting ease
- Riding quality
- Handling ease
- Highway stability
- Gasoline economy

Styling
- Overall exterior appearance
- Front end appearance
- Appearance of grill
- Front bumper appearance
- Side appearance
- Wheel appearance
- Rear end appearance
- Tail light appearance
- Appearance of rear bumper
- Overall interior styling
- Instrument panel styling
- Steering wheel styling
- Appearance of seats
- Upholstery appearance

Workmanship
- Overall body workmanship
- Exterior moulding fit
- Fit of doors
- Paint finish
- Quality of chrome trim
- Window operation
- Freedom from leaks
- Overall interior workmanship
- Instrument panel
- Overall quietness
- Road noise level
- Wind noise level
- Level of engine noise
- Squeaks and rattles

Other
- Prestige of car
- Reputation of car
- Warranty coverage
- Future resale value
- Final cost at dealer
- Safety features

they feel were "most important" in their selection of the brand purchased. A frequency count of the "most important" is made and the attributes are ranked according to the total number of mentions. The highest-located attributes in the summary ranking are considered "determinant."

One problem with this approach is the assumption that consumers know why they do what they do. In fact, as we noted in Chapter Two, consumers make many decisions for many reasons, and they are not always fully aware of their own motivations.

Another problem with this approach is the assumption that consumers will reveal their true motivations when asked. It seems especially likely that a respondent to an attribute list will emphasize those attributes that make the respondent appear to be a sensible, rational decision maker and deemphasize attributes that make the respondent appear to be foolish, gullible, or vain.

Despite these limitations, attribute lists frequently provide helpful clues as to what consumers consider important and what they do not. Such lists are also useful for classifying consumers into groups that set different priorities on what is important and what is not.

Another technique used to isolate determinant attributes is "item analysis" (Corey, 1970). In this approach, consumers are asked to describe both their belief about the existence of an attribute in a product and the degree to which they hold that belief. A score is assigned to the degree of belief for each feature, and then these scores are summed for each respondent to develop an overall perception score. Each attribute is then correlated with an adjusted total score (the score on the attribute being correlated with the total is subtracted from the total to avoid double counting or inflated correlations). The correlation coefficients are then used to select the most important attributes.

To illustrate, Corey (1970) administered the rating scale shown in Figure 9-2 to a sample of housewives. For scoring purposes, he assigned weights of 6,

Figure 9-2 Rating Scales for Instant Milk

On the left, circle the *one* phrase that *best* describes *your* feelings about Instant Non-Fat Dry Milk and then check the *one* box that shows *how much* you feel that way.

	Extremely	Quite	Slightly
Uneconomical *or* economical	☐	☐	☐
Convenient *or* inconvenient	☐	☐	☐
Low nutrition *or* high nutrition	☐	☐	☐
Kids dislike it *or* kids like it	☐	☐	☐
Good tasting *or* bad tasting	☐	☐	☐
Best with snacks *or* best with meals	☐	☐	☐
Artificial *or* real	☐	☐	☐
Appetizing *or* unappetizing	☐	☐	☐
Better than skim milk *or* worse than skim milk	☐	☐	☐
Adults dislike it *or* adults like it	☐	☐	☐

Source: Corey (1970:42). Reprinted from the *Journal of Advertising Research*, © 1970 by the Advertising Research Foundation.

5, and 4, respectively, to degrees of positive belief, and weights of 1, 2, and 3 to degrees of negative belief. Ratings on each attribute were then correlated with the sum of ratings on the remaining nine features combined. From the results of the item analysis, the ten instant milk attributes were ranked according to their correlation coefficients (r), as shown in Table 9-1. Notice that the analysis resulted in a wide range of values, thereby clearly differentiating degrees of correlation between each feature and the adjusted overall score for all features. From the results in the table one might conclude that "better than skim milk" and "economical" are more determinant than the other eight attributes and should, therefore, be incorporated into marketing plans for the product.

The item analysis approach provides consumer researchers with more refined data than does the simple frequency count. Its major disadvantage is that it measures association rather than causation. The researcher cannot be sure whether the consumers' evaluation of a product on a given attribute (such as "better than skim milk" in Table 9-1) *caused* the favorable overall evaluation or whether a favorable overall evaluation prompted the consumer to give the product a favorable rating on the dimension. Moreover, one cannot be sure that an apparently unimportant dimension—such as"kids like it" or "best with snacks"—could not be made extremely important through some change in product formulation or some change in advertising.

These two examples of attempts to discover and measure "determinant" attributes illustrate how difficult and hazardous that enterprise can be. Marketers are continually seeking ways to find out how they can change their products to make them more appealing to consumers. But this task is more complex than it at first appears to be.

To illustrate, consider beer. To construct a multidimensional map of beer brands, several items of information are needed:

1 Consumers' perceptions of the brands in the product class
2 What attributes of the brands discriminate among them

Table 9-1 Item Analysis of Ten Instant Milk Attributes

Attribute	r	r^2	Average rating
Better than skim milk	.90	.8100	3.6
Economical	.76	.5776	4.9
Convenient	.70	.4900	4.5
Good tasting	.57	.3249	3.3
Appetizing	.49	.2401	3.0
Adults like it	.39	.1521	3.3
Real	.36	.1296	3.4
High nutrition	.31	.0961	4.8
Kids like it	.25	.0625	3.1
Best with snacks	.17	.0289	3.1

Source: Corey (1970:43). Reprinted from the *Journal of Advertising Research*, © 1970 by the Advertising Research Foundation.

3 The preferences of the consumers toward these attributes, i.e., what they ideally would like to have

Figure 9-3[1] illustrates the information for the first two items. The figure is a geometric construction of a product space along two dimensions (*body,* ranging from "light" to "heavy," and *taste,* ranging from "bitter" to "mild") which represents the consumers' perceptions of the eight brands on the two attributes.[1] With data such as those shown in the figure, one can readily see where the brands are positioned with respect to each other in consumers' minds. By examining the axes jointly, we can determine how consumers view each brand on the two dimensions. Miller's, for instance, is perceived as a relatively light and mild beer, whereas Blatz is viewed as highly bitter and somewhat neutral in body—neither light nor heavy. Such "maps" show which brands are seen as quite similar and which as dissimilar. In general, similar brands can be thought of as competitive brands and dissimilar brands as noncompetitive.

The data shown in Figure 9-3 are incomplete for planning purposes. The manager also needs to know which consumers prefer which combinations of the two attributes. To obtain such data, consumers are clustered in terms of their attribute preference—their "ideal" brands. A clustering of this sort is shown in Figure 9-4. In the study, Johnson found that the ideal points cluster in certain distinct parts of the map. The clusters of market segments are shown as circles of varying size. The size of a circle roughly corresponds to the size of the market segment. We can now examine the complete map for marketing planning.

Note that the largest segments are near the best-selling brands, but that none of the best-selling brands is located in the center of a circle (the most-intense-preference location). Several implications for these brands could be suggested. Miller's, for example, could be repositioned to the center of segment 2 and thereby increase its share of the market. It could be repositioned by convincing consumers through advertising that it really is not as light as it is

[1]This illustration is adapted from Johnson (1969, 1971).

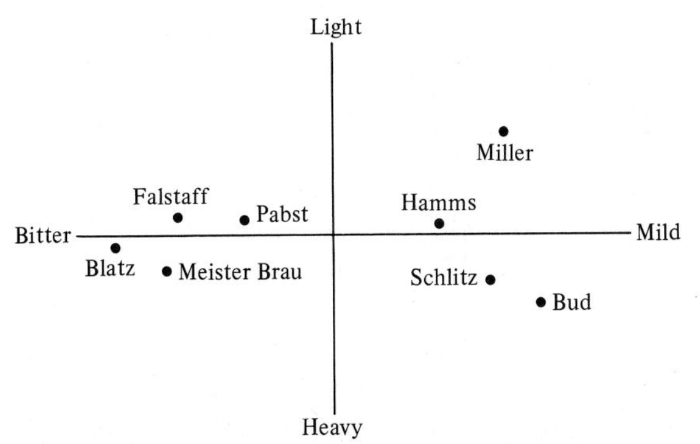

Figure 9-3 Consumers' perception of the beer market. *Source:* Adapted from Johnson (1969 and 1971).

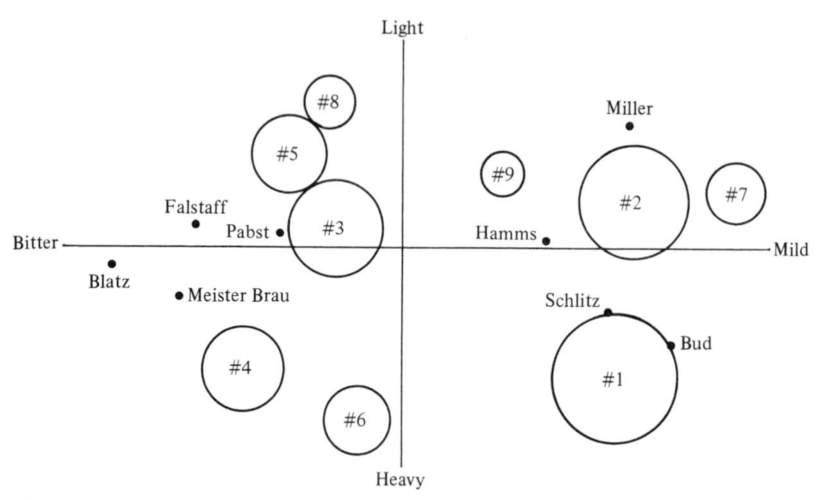

Figure 9-4 Distribution of ideal points in product space. *Source:* Adapted from Johnson (1969 and 1971).

perceived, or by changing the physical attribute and then promoting the change. In a similar vein, the data suggest that beer drinkers would prefer Budweiser to be slightly heavier and a little less mild. For existing brands, then, the analysis can yield insights on how to improve their competitive positions through product repositioning.

The data in the figure also show possibilities for new market entries. Segments 6 and 8, for example, are far removed from any of the existing brands. Assuming these segments are large enough to justify mass marketing, their positions indicate opportunities for two brands of beer, since existing needs are not being met by existing brands. A heavy-bodied beer of a slightly bitter taste could be developed and promoted to occupy a position near the center of segment 6 and a light, slightly bitter beer could be developed to meet the needs of segment 8.

A classic example of repositioning occurred in the 1950s when the Philip Morris Company deliberately set out to change the status image of Parliament cigarettes. Before that time Parliament had been a premium-priced brand. This image was encouraged by the price level and was deliberately reinforced by advertising that consistently portrayed elegantly dressed men and women in country club settings, at the opera, or at the ballet. If multidimensional scaling methods had been available at that time, a multidimensional map of cigarette brands would surely have shown that Parliament was perceived as being at the "high-priced" end of a "high-priced–low-priced" dimension and quite distinct from most other brands.

Aware that there are far more people (and therefore far more smokers) in the middle and working classes than in the upper classes, the manufacturer set out to "democratize" Parliaments. The price was lowered, the elegant package was made plainer, and for about a year the advertising showed upper-class people interacting with middle- and working-class people, with Parliament cigarettes as the coin of exchange. In one advertisement, the owner of a Rolls-Royce conversed with the mechanic repairing it, while the Rolls-Royce owner smoked one of the mechanic's "new" Parliaments. In another, a well-dressed couple stopped at a diner for a cup of coffee on the way home from the theater. Being out of cigarettes, they accepted (and of course enjoyed) the "new" Parliaments offered by the counter hand. As the year went by, image measurements showed a steady movement of Parliaments out of the exclusive (and therefore small) upper-class region into the much larger territory of the average man.

ATTITUDES AND INTENTIONS

Consumers' perceptions of products and brands ultimately consolidate into attitudes and intentions. An attitude is a generalized disposition to respond, positively or negatively, to an object or class of objects. "Object," as it is used here, is a very broad term. It can refer to a specific object, such as one particular automobile or a feature of an automobile. Or it can refer to a class of objects, such as a product (e.g., cigarettes) or a brand, such as Parliament.

Marketers have shown considerable interest in people's attitudes because they have assumed that attitudes will accurately predict consumer behavior. They have also been interested in attitudes because psychologists and other social scientists have developed a variety of techniques that make it possible to locate people, at least roughly and temporarily, on attitude dimensions.

Attitude Scales

Reports of Behavior One way of measuring attitudes depends on inferences made from behavior—or reports of behavior. For instance, if a teenage boy buys and reads motor magazines, visits the auto show, and spends a lot of time talking with his friends about cars, it seems reasonable to infer that he maintains a strong favorable attitude toward automobiles. Similarly, if a housewife buys and reads *Good Housekeeping* and *Ladies' Home Journal,* spends much of her day cooking, polishing windows and furniture, and exchanging recipes and shopping tips with neighbors and friends, it seems reasonable to suppose that she has a strong favorable attitude toward the traditional homemaker role. One way to construct an attitude scale, then, is to collect a number of examples of the attitude in action and to find out how often the respondent has engaged in the behaviors on the list.

The following question, used in a study of innovative behavior, is a typical example of the way reports of behavior are used to measure attitudes:

> Which of the following food items have you purchased at least once?
>
> Spaghetti-O's
> Instant breakfast

Flavored rice
Instant casserole mixes
Toast'em Pop-ups
Bugles, Whistles, and Daisies
Boneless, frozen turkey roasts
Shake 'n Bake seasoning
Dry roasted nuts
Instant oatmeal
Gourmet soups
Whip & Chill
Frozen, ready-to-bake bread
Cereal with freeze-dried fruit

At the time the study was conducted, each of the items in the question was relatively new, so the purchase of an unusually large number of them was taken as an indication of a favorable attitude toward new grocery products (Robertson, undated).

One problem with this approach is that any set of behaviors may mean several different things. A record of having purchased many new grocery products may mean that the respondent has a strong favorable attitude toward new brands, but it may also mean that the respondent has a relatively high income and a large family to feed, so—compared with respondents who have low incomes and medium-sized or small families—this customer purchases many brands, both new and old. A record of having purchased mostly secondhand furniture and inexpensive clothes may mean that the respondent has a negative attitude toward accumulating material things, but it may also mean that the respondent is poor. A record of having been a faithful precinct worker in every election may mean that the worker has a strong positive attitude toward the party; but it may also mean that if the worker does not turn out for every election, the job will be forfeited.

The Thurstone Method The difficulties of inferring attitudes from behavior have encouraged the practice of asking about attitudes directly, or asking about thoughts, feelings, and opinions instead. One of the best-known techniques of using thoughts, feelings, and opinions to measure attitudes was introduced by L. L. Thurstone in 1928 and has since been widely used.

To apply Thurstone's method of attitude scale construction, the investigator first collects or invents a set of statements that seem to indicate varying degrees of favorableness or unfavorableness of attitude toward an object or an object class. The researcher then asks a group of judges to sort the statements into (usually) about eleven categories ranging from "extremely favorable" through "neutral" to "extremely unfavorable." If the judges disagree about where a statement belongs, it is considered ambiguous and is dropped. The scale itself is constructed by selecting, from among the remaining statements, a set of statements spaced as equally as possible along the "favorable–unfavorable" continuum.

The scale in Figure 9-5, developed to measure attitudes toward trading stamps, was constructed by the Thurstone method. In using this scale to measure attitudes toward trading stamps, each statement is assigned a "scale score" depending upon the degree of favorableness or unfavorableness it represents, and each respondent in the population being studied would receive an attitude score determined by the scale score (or scores) of the statement (or statements) with which he agrees.

The Likert Method A somewhat different method of attitude scale construction, first proposed by Rensis Likert, has also been widely used in studies of consumer behavior.

Like the Thurstone method, the Likert method starts with a collection of statements about the object or object class, but instead of being sorted along a "favorable–unfavorable" continuum, the statements are put into a questionnaire and a preliminary group of respondents are asked to indicate their degree of agreement or disagreement (usually on a six- or seven-step scale) with each statement. If the statements are all tapping approximately the same dimension, respondents with a favorable attitude will tend to agree with the favorable statements and to disagree with the unfavorable statements, while respondents with an unfavorable attitude will do the opposite. The scale can be "refined" by dropping the statements that are inconsistent with the others. If most of the original statements tapped the right dimension, dropping the inconsistent statements will produce a scale that measures the desired dimension.

The scale in Figure 9-6, intended to measure attitude toward an advertisement, was constructed by the Likert routine. The scale is scored in the following way. The number of agreements with items 1, 3, 4, 7, 8, and 10 (the favorable items) *plus* the number of disagreements with items 2, 5, 6, 9, 11, and 12 (the unfavorable items) is divided by 12 and multiplied by 100 to produce a number between 0 and 100. (The multiplication by 100 is simply to remove the decimal.) To obtain a single score for an individual advertisement, the scores received from all respondents are averaged.

Figure 9-5 An Attitude Scale Constructed by the Thurstone Method

Scale score	Statement
9	Trading stamps are really great!
8	I wish all stores would give trading stamps.
7	Trading stamps are a bonus to the shopper.
6	Trading stamps are all right.
5	Trading stamps are both good and bad.
4	Trading stamps are hardly worth the effort of saving them.
3	Trading stamps cause higher prices.
2	Trading stamps are a nuisance.
1	I hate trading stamps.

Source: Udell (1965:48). Reprinted from the *Journal of Marketing*, published by the American Marketing Association.

Figure 9-6 An Attitude Scale Constructed by the Likert Method

1. This ad is very appealing to me.
2. I would probably skip this ad if I saw it in a magazine.
3. This is a heart-warming ad.
4. This ad makes me want to buy the brand it features.
5. This ad has little interest for me.
6. I dislike this ad.
7. This ad makes me feel good.
8. This is a wonderful ad.
9. This is the kind of ad you forget easily.
10. This is a fascinating ad.
11. I'm tired of this kind of advertising.
12. This ad leaves me cold.

Source: Wells (1964:46). Reprinted from the *Journal of Marketing*, published by the American Marketing Association.

The Likert method of attitude scale construction has much in common with the "item analysis" approach to discovering determinant attitudes. The Likert method singles out and focuses upon those attitude statements that are most highly correlated with overall favorability toward the object being studied. The item analysis approach singles out and focuses on those attributes that are most highly correlated with overall favorability toward the product. In the former case the assumption is that those statements most synonymous with overall favorability, when pooled, yield an adequate measure of overall favorability. In the latter case, the assumption is that those attributes most synonymous with overall favorability are in some sense the cause of that favorability. For reasons noted earlier in the discussion of attempts to discover "determination" attributes, it is easier to defend the assumption underlying the Likert method of attitude scale construction than it is to defend the assumptions underlying the "content" analysis approach to the discovery of determinant attitudes.

Bipolar Graphic Rating Scales Attitudes are often measured simply by asking respondents to indicate their attitude toward an object by checking the appropriate slot in bipolar graphic rating scales like these:

Like ____ ____ ____ ____ ____ Dislike
Nice ____ ____ ____ ____ ____ Awful
Great ____ ____ ____ ____ ____ Lousy

Considerable research has been devoted to such questions as: How many steps should the scales contain? Should they be horizontal or vertical? Should the steps be defined by numbers, letters, words, or nothing?

This research shows that five to nine steps are about right for most purposes, that it does not make much difference whether the scales are vertical or horizontal, and that labeling the steps has a slight tendency to discourage using only the extreme categories.

Comparisons of results obtained from these simple graphic rating scales with results obtained from scales constructed by the much more elaborate Thurstone and Likert methods have usually shown a degree of agreement that is surprisingly high. As a consequence, they are often used instead.

Thurstone and Likert scales are still used when the investigator decides that the added precision of measurement is worth the added effort of constructing them. Together with the graphic rating scale, they show what they term *attitude* means.

Multiattribute Method In recent years consumer researchers have focused considerable attention on measuring and evaluating attitudes by means of multiattribute attitude models. These models, which have their genesis in the work of Rosenberg (1956) and Fishbein (1967), resemble the more traditional single-scale evaluative methods in the acceptance of the concept of attitude as one of most important variables in consumers' decision processes. They depart from the traditional one-scale measures in that they employ multiple dimensions that are measured separately and then combined to provide an overall measure of affect (Pessemier and Wilkie, 1972).

Formally, the model is specified as (Pessemier and Wilkie, 1972):

$$A_{jk} = \sum_{i=1}^{n} I_{ik} \cdot B_{ijk} \qquad (9\text{-}1)$$

where i = attribute
j = brand
k = consumer

such that: A_{jk} = consumer k's *attitude score* for brand j.
I_{ik} = the *importance weight* given to attribute i by consumer k.
B_{ijk} = consumer k's *belief* as to the extent to which attribute i is offered by brand j.

An example of a multiattribute model in use can be found in a study by Sheth (1973) of Carnation Instant Breakfast and Sego. Sheth measured beliefs about both products on the following attributes, using a seven-point bipolar rating scale:

1 Very easy to use—a little trouble to use
2 Poor substitute for a meal—good substitute for a meal
3 Low in calories—high in calories
4 Delicious tasting—not delicious tasting
5 Somewhat nutritious—very nutritious
6 Very good for a snack—not good for a snack
7 Low in price—high in price

8 Very filling—not very filling
9 Does not dissolve easily—dissolves easily
10 Provides lots of energy—provides little energy
11 Good buy for the money—not a good buy for the money
12 Has a real flavor—has an artificial flavor
13 Good source of protein—not a good source of protein

To obtain importance weights, Sheth used a three-point scale:

In general, in deciding whether or not to buy ____, how important to you is each of the characteristics below? For each characteristic, please check whether it matters a great deal, matters somewhat, or matters very little.

To develop an attitude score for an individual, each attribute belief score was multiplied by its corresponding importance weight and then the products were summed. This procedure was repeated for each respondent. The following hypothetical data illustrate the computation of an attitude score toward Sego of a single person, using Eq. (9-1):

Attribute	Belief score	Importance weight	$B \cdot I$
1.	1	1	1
2.	6	3	18
3.	2	2	4
4.	2	1	2
5.	7	1	7
6.	7	3	21
7.	3	2	6
8.	3	2	6
9.	3	3	9
10.	2	1	2
11.	2	2	4
12.	2	1	2
13.	1	2	2
			$A_{jk} = 84$

In this example, a person's attitude score could range from 13 to 273, with 13 representing the most favorable and 273 the most unfavorable ends of the continuum.

Sheth compared the results obtained from the multiattribute method with those obtained from a single bipolar graphic rating scale ("In general, I like it very much—In general, I don't like it"). The degree of agreement between the two methods, while not low, was not high. However, Sheth demonstrated other approaches to calculating the attitude score under the multiattribute method which did produce high levels of agreement. The multiattribute method still is being used separately from single-scale evaluations because it seems plausible that consumers might like some object but not assign any real importance to it.

Attitudes and Behavior

Attitudes are important in the study of consumer behavior because they influence the ways consumers employ resources to obtain benefits. In the S→C→R formula, attitudes are relatively enduring but modifiable characteristics of C, the consumer. Consumers bring their existing attitudes to a given information handling situation. The attitudes interact with stimuli, and with other consumer characteristics, to produce responses. Hence, marketers attempt to use measures of consumer attitudes to predict consumer behavior.

One example of the relationship between attitudes and behavior is shown in Figure 9-7. The figure shows that product use is directly related to attitude toward the brand in each of the four products studied: where attitude is highly favorable, there is a high incidence of product usage; where attitude is poor, there is a low incidence of usage. In the study, Achenbaum (1966) also found that when people have highly unfavorable attitudes toward a brand, they are likely to stop using it. A relationship, even one as direct as that shown in Figure 9-7, does not prove that favorable attitude toward a brand caused use of the brand. The converse could also be true: use of the brand could have caused a favorable attitude toward it. Cause-and-effect relationships can be uncovered only through carefully designed and implemented experiments.

One controlled field experiment which examined, among other things, the role of attitude in behavior was conducted in the 1960s by Benton and Bowles

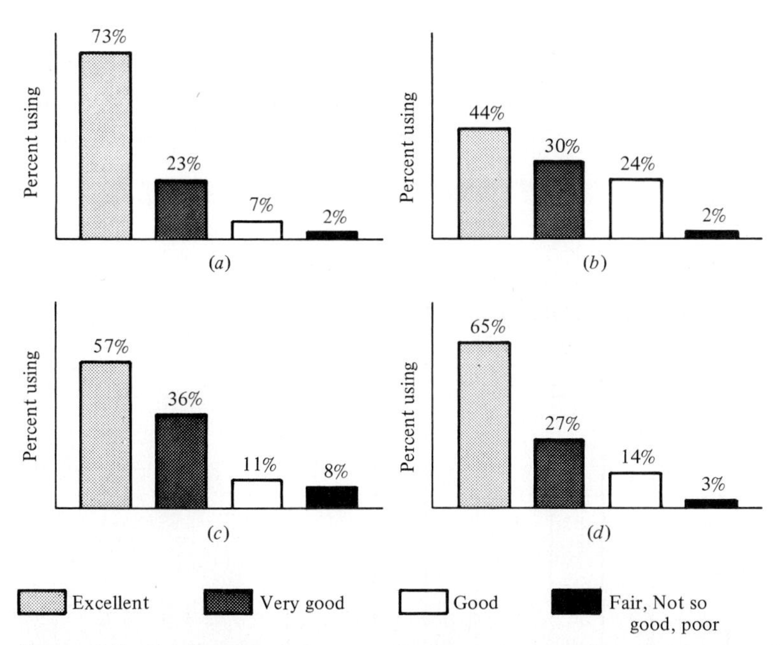

Figure 9-7 Relationship between attitudes and usage for selected brands of consumer products: *(a)* cigarette *(b)* deodorant *(c)* gasoline *(d)* laxative. *Source:* Achenbaum (1966:113). Reprinted from *Attitude Research at Sea,* published by the American Marketing Association.

(Appel, 1966). The purpose of the experiment was to measure the effectiveness of two dollar-equivalent advertising plans relative to each other and relative to a control condition in which all advertising was withheld during the period of the experiment.

The study demonstrated quite clearly how consumers' attitudes interact with stimuli such as advertising to produce responses. Figure 9-8 presents the data relevent to this discussion. The data in the figure repeat the overall positive relationship between attitude and product use shown in Figure 9-7. More importantly, however, the data indicate that the level of attitude is closely related to whether or not the advertising had any effect on product use: among those consumers with the least favorable attitude there was virtually no change attributable to the presence of advertising—only 1.2 percentage points; among those with a more favorable attitude, there was an increase of 5.6 percentage points; and among those with the most favorable attitude, the increase in use was 7.8 percentage points. In other words, the attitudes consumers initially held toward the advertised brand were extremely important in predicting changes in brand use as a result of exposure to advertising.

Modifying Influence Attitudes do not always predict behavior. Other influences can modify, cancel, or even reverse them. The S→C→R model suggests that all consumer responses are influenced both by the characteristics of the consumer and by the *stimuli present at the time the response is made.* When situational stimuli are strong enough, they can overrule consumer characteristics that would otherwise carry the day.

In the grocery store an unexpectedly low price or an especially prominent and attractive display can divert choice to a competing product, canceling the

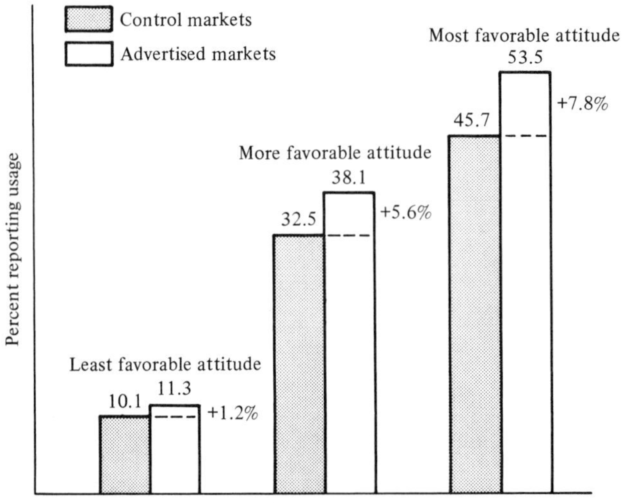

Figure 9-8 Attitude as a moderator of advertising effectiveness. *Source:* Appel (1966:113). Reprined from *Attitude Research at Sea,* published by the American Marketing Association.

effect of a favorable attitude. Similarly, if the favored item is unexpectedly high in price or temporarily out of stock, an established attitude may fail to be acted out.

In the automobile or appliance showroom, a favorable attitude toward one product may be overcome by unanticipated features of the other products on display. In the furniture store, a model room may present an article of furniture in a whole new light.

The stimuli that influence the consumer at the response point can also come from other people seeking their own ends. A father's offer to pay part of the cost of a new conservative sedan could be decisive in overturning his son's strong favorable disposition toward a souped-up secondhand hot rod.

Attitude Change Although attitudes are by definition relatively permanent characteristics of the consumer, attitudes change. If a favored brand proves disappointing, or if a favored retail outlet changes its image, a positive attitude may weaken or even turn negative.

An attitude may also change when new information pits one attitude against other, more strongly held attitudes. If consumers find that a manufacturer engages in practices of which they disapprove, they may alter their attitudes toward all of the manufacturer's products. If consumers are suddenly informed that some of the products they like and use contribute to waste disposal problems or to water pollution, they may alter their attitudes toward these products if their attitudes toward conservation of the environment are sufficiently strong.

Changes of this type are attributed to the operation of "cognitive dissonance." Dissonance theory holds that it is uncomfortable to maintain conflicting attitudes, and that new information that brings attitudes into conflict will produce a strain toward consonance (Festinger, 1957).

Attitudes change when reference groups change, provided that members of the new reference group have attitudes different from the attitudes consumers bring to the group with them. Consumers know that attitude differences between themselves and their associates are uncomfortable, so when they are forced to change reference groups—when moving from one community to another, for instance—they seek out new reference groups that will have attitudes similar to those they brought with them. White-collar families seek out white-collar neighborhoods, blue-collar families seek out blue-collar neighborhoods, Puerto Ricans seek out Puerto Ricans, and so on. Such behavior maintains the effectiveness of attitudes by reinforcing them. When such behavior is impossible—when consumers are forced by circumstances into an environment in which the prevailing attitudes are different from their own—their attitudes are apt to change.

Finally, attitudes change when behavior changes, if the behavior is contrary to the attitude. After Vince La Motta signed a contract for ten years of family photographs, one would expect him to have a more favorable attitude toward family photographs than before he signed it. If an airline pilot is fired because of an energy crisis and takes a more routine nine-to-five job, one might expect some alteration in the pilot's attitudes toward types of employment. Such changes can also be attributed to the action of cognitive dissonance. The behavior is a public fact. If it continues, the probability is high that dissonant attitudes will change to meet it.

Because dissonance theory seems to explain many after-the-decision changes in human behavior, consumer researchers have made many attempts to apply the theory to predicting consumer behavior. These studies have shown that making specific predictions about consumer behavior on the basis of dissonance theory is a risky business. Dissonance can be reduced in many ways, and it is extremely difficult to foresee—let alone measure—all of them. But the weight of the evidence suggests that people do find dissonance uncomfortable and do employ various strategies to reduce it or avoid it. For this reason, the theory has been said to explain a number of actions even when it cannot be used for predicting those actions.

Resources Another of the reasons why attitudes do not predict behavior perfectly is that the consumer may not have the resources to carry out the favorable disposition.

Often the resources required are financial. A consumer may have a strongly favorable attitude toward a Cadillac or a mink coat without having the financial resources to buy one. Even in much smaller purhcases—the choice of a regular brand instead of a premium brand of coffee, for instance—a favorable attitude toward a brand may be overcome by its higher cost.

Sometimes the required resource is time or energy. Consumers who believe strongly in shopping around to get the best buy may have so many other demands on their time that they are unable to do it. Similarly, visting widely scattered retailers takes a certain amount of mobility, and if consumers are old or ill or do not have ready access to an automobile, they may not be able to do much comparison shopping despite a favorable attitude toward getting the most for their money.

Resources can also be psychological. A mother who has a negative attitude toward television may find herself unable to keep her children from watching "too much" television simply because the children exert so much pressure on her that she feels the need to conserve her authority for more important issues. In the same way, favorable attitudes toward certain foods—like vegetables—and certain services—like music lessons—may fail to be carried over into purchasing behavior because the parent is not prepared to put up the fight that would be required.

Intentions

Just as consumers are aware of many of their own attitudes, they are also often aware of many of the circumstances that determine whether or not the attitudes are apt to be carried over into behavior. They are aware, at least approximately and temporarily, of their financial resources, of their capacity to spend time and

Figure 9-9 Time Dimension Scale

Which of the following statements best describes your intentions with respect to (name of product)?

____ I plan to buy ( ) within the next seven days.
____ I plan to buy ( ) sometime within the next 30 days, but not within the next 7 days.
____ I plan to buy ( ) within the next six months but not within the next 30 days.
____ I plan to buy ( ) within the next year but not within the next six months.
____ I plan to buy ( ) within the next five years, but not within the next year.
____ I might buy ( ) sometime, but not within the next five years.
____ I will probably never buy ( ).

energy, and of the needs and wishes of others who may have important influences on their purhcasing of products and use of media.

They can often weigh these influences to express *intentions* that can be measured or scaled along a time dimension or a probability dimension. Figure 9-9 is a time dimension scale for measuring consumers' intentions.

The specific time periods can be altered to suit the product or service in question, with shorter time periods for drug and grocery products and longer time periods for major purchases like automobiles, furniture, and appliances. In either case, the purpose of the scale is to locate the purchase on the consumer's time horizon.

A probability dimension intention scale would look like one shown in Figure 9-10.

When the purchase is very remote, or when consumers have no way to assess the specific conditions that will influence their purchasing, intention scales become generalized attitude scales. But occasionally consumers know enough about their own affairs to be able to predict other influences and to weight them, along with generalized attitudes, in stating their intentions. Under those conditions, intention scales predict better than attitude scales do (Juster, 1960).

Figure 9-10 Probability Dimension Scale

Taking everything into account, what do you think would be the chances that you would buy this product?

____ Certain, practically certain (99 in 100)
____ Almost sure (9 in 10)
____ Very probably (8 in 10)
____ Probably (7 in 10)
____ Good possibility (6 in 10)
____ Fairly good possibility (5 in 10)
____ Fair possibility (4 in 10)
____ Some possibility (3 in 10)
____ Slight possibility (2 in 10)
____ Very slight possibility (1 in 10)
____ No chance, almost no chance (1 in 100)

Source: Gruber (1970).

SUMMARY

Products are physical objects with certain measurable characteristics, but they also have subjective meanings, and these subjective qualities influence behavior.

Consumers, as individuals, perceive things differently; that is, they attach different meanings to the same object. Thus, objects have different "images." The image of a retail store is composed of the perceived attributes of the store itself and of the customers who patronize that store. Similarly, images of products and brands are based on perceived product attributes and on the perceived characteristics of product users. Not only do different people perceive the same object differently, but different attributes of objects are important to different groups of people. The attributes which are most influential on consumer behavior are called "determinant attributes," and they vary among the buyers of the same product or brand.

One technique used to isolate determinant attributes is aided recall. When this approach is used, respondents are required to identify and rank the attributes responsible for their choice of one brand over another. A second technique is item analysis, an approach which requires respondents to relate their beliefs about the presence of particular attributes in specific products and the degree to which they hold those beliefs. Although item analysis provides researchers with useful data, it deals with association rather than causation. As a result, identifying determinant attributes is a difficult process. In order to offer products which are appealing and satisfactory to consumers, however, marketers must know which attributes are determinant ones for their products and consumers.

This process becomes even more difficult when we recognize that determinant attributes affect consumer behavior on several levels. Considerations include consumers' perceptions of all the brands within a product class, which attributes distinguish one brand from another, and consumers' preferences toward these attributes. Perceptual mapping is a multidmensional approach which attempts to discover how these three factors interact to define a product class.

Consumer perceptions of product attributes are generalized into attitudes toward products and product classes. Attitudes are important because they influence consumer behavior and may be used to predict consumer behavior. The relationship is considered so strong that researchers have attempted to measure attitudes by observing behavior. Since an observed set of behaviors can be interpreted as indicating several attitudes, it is very difficult to obtain conclusive results from direct observation of behavior, and researchers have turned to alternative approaches such as the Thurstone method of attitude scale construction, the Likert method, bipolar graphic rating scales, and multiattribute models in order to measure attitudes.

The Thurstone method involves asking a group of impartial judges to sort statements which indicate attitudes into eleven categories ranging from "extremely favorable" to "extremely unfavorable." Scale scores are assigned to each statement, and respondents receive an attitude score based on the statements with which they agree. The Likert method requires respondents to indicate the degree of agreement of disagreement they experience toward several statements on a six- or seven-point scale. The resultant scale is refined by dropping those statements which do not seem to measure the desired attitude or dimension, and subsequent respondents are scored on the basis of the number of agreements they exhibit toward favorable items and the number of disagreements toward the unfavorable items.

A simpler approach to attitude measurement is the bipolar graphic rating scale, which requires respondents to indicate their attitude about a product in terms of several personal judgments, such as "like/dislike." In contrast, the multiattribute method attempts to measure attitude by first measuring the multiple dimensions of an attitude in terms of the respondents' beliefs and the importance of the product to the respondents and then combining the results to produce an overall score.

The study of attitudes is important because consumer behavior is influenced by positive or negative attitudes, although to actually prove a cause-and-effect relationship between the two is a demanding task. Furthermore, attitudes can act as a modifying influence between the stimulus (advertising, promotion, interpersonal communication) and the response (purchasing).

Other factors, such as the point-of-purchase situation, can also act as modifying influences. An exceptionally low price on a competing brand, or an out-of-stock condition for a preferred brand, may influence consumers to behave inconsistently in terms of their attitudes. Attitudes themselves are subject to modifying influences and may change when new information and/or actual experience causes cognitive dissonance. Changes in reference groups, or behavior, often precede changes in attitude. Lack of resources in terms of time or disposable income may result in attitudes not being translated directly into consistent behavior.

Intentions represent the influence of attitudes and other "modifiers" on future behavior. Consumer intentions are measured by time or probability scales and are better predictors of behavior than are attitude scales in cases where the future purchase will take place in the short run.

REVIEW QUESTIONS

1 Define perception and discuss the importance of this concept to consumer behavior.
2 Identify the two components of store image. How do they interact with each other? Are the same components important to product and brand image? Why or why not?
3 Why are marketers interested in identifying "determinant attributes"? Why is this enterprise difficult?
4 Discuss the notions of product positioning and repositioning. Define the concept of product positioning. What items of information are needed to employ this concept?
5 Define attitude. Can studying behavior be used to indicate consumers' attitudes accurately? Why or why not?

6 Discuss the different steps involved in constructing the Thurstone, Likert, and Bipolar graphic attitude scales. Do the results obtained from these three scales generally agree? When would the Thurstone or Likert scale be preferred to the bipolar scale?
7 How does the multiattribute method differ from other methods of measuring attitudes? In what way is it similar?
8 Achenbaum found a high positive correlation between attitudes and usage for several products. Does this indicate a causal relationship between attitudes and behavior? Why or why not?
9 How can attitudes toward a brand be helpful in predicting consumers' responses to marketing efforts?
10 Identify and discuss the factors which can modify the influence of attitudes on consumer behavior.
11 How do intentions differ from attitudes? Do attitude scales always predict behavior better than intention scales?

EXERCISE

Consult several magazines published in 1970 and 1975 for advertisements of these brands: Lady Remington (shaver) and Pinto (automobile). For each brand, which attributes were promoted during each time period, and how were they communicated in tone and setting? Prepare a brief report documenting the stability or change in attributes promoted. Discuss whether or not the advertisers were trying to reposition the brands and the reasons justifying your conclusion.

REFERENCES

Achenbaum, A. A. "Knowledge is a Thing Called Measurement." In L. Alder and I. Crespi (eds.), *Attitude Research at Sea.* Chicago: American Marketing Association, 1966.

Alderson, Wroe. *Dynamic Marketing Behavior.* Homewood, Ill.: Richard D. Irwin, 1965.

Appel, Valentine. "Attitude Change: Another Obvious Dubious Method for Measuring Advertising Effectiveness." In L. Adler and I. Crespi (eds.), *Attitude Research: At Sea.* Chicago: American Marketing Association, 1966.

Corey, Lawrence G. "How to Isolate Product Attributes." *Journal of Advertising Research,* 10 (August 1970), 41–44.

Edwards, Allen L. *Techniques of Attitude Scale Construction.* New York: Appleton-Century-Crofts, 1957.

Festinger, Leon. *A Theory of Cognitive Dissonance.* Stanford, Calif.: Stanford University Press, 1957.

Fishbein, Martin. "Attitude and the Prediction of Behavior." In M. Fishbein (ed.), *Readings in Attitude Theory and Measurement.* New York: Wiley, 1967.

Gruber, Alin. "Purchase Intent and Purchase Probability." *Journal of Advertising Research* (February 1970), 23–27.

Johnson, Richard M. "Market Segmentation: A Comparison of Techniques." paper presented at the International Meeting of the Institute of Management-Sciences, March 1969.

———. "Marketing Segmentation: A Strategic Management Tool." *Journal of Marketing Research,* 8 (February 1971), 13–18.

Juster, F. Thomas. *Consumer Buying Intentions and Purchase Probability: An Experiment in Survey Design.* National Bureau of Economic Research, Occasional Paper 99. Distributed by Columbia University Press, 1966.

Kelly, George A. *The Psychology of Personal Constructs.* Vol. I. New York: Norton, 1955.

Krech, David, Richard S. Crutchfield, and Egerton L. Ballachey. *Individual in Society.* New York: McGraw-Hill Book Co., 1962.

Martineau, Pierre. *Motivation in Advertising.* New York: McGraw-Hill Book Co., 1957.

Myers, James H., and Mark I. Alpert. "Determinant Buying Attitudes: Meaning and Measurement." *Journal of Marketing,* 32 (October 1968), 13–20.

Pessemier, Edgar A. and William L. Wilkie. "Multi-Attribute Choice Theory: A Review and Analysis." Paper No. 372, Herman C. Krannert Graduate School of Industrial Administration, Purdue University, 1972.

Reynolds, William H. *Products and Markets.* New York: Appleton-Century-Crofts, 1969.

Robertson, Thomas S. *Questionnaire for Innovation Study.* Unpublished.

Rosenberg, M. J. "Cognitive Structure and Attitudinal Affect." *Journal of Abnormal and Social Psychology,* 53 (1956), 367–372.

Sheth, Jagdish N. "Brand Profiles from Beliefs and Importances." *Journal of Advertising Research,* 13 (February 1973), 37–42.

Steffire, Volney. "Market Structure Studies: New Products for Old Markets and New Markets (Foreign) for Old Products." In F. Bass, C. W. King, and E. A. Pessemier (eds.), *Applications of the Sciences in Marketing Management.* New York: Wiley, 1968.

Udell, Jon G. "Can Attitude Measurement Predict Consumer Behavior?" *Journal of Marketing,* 29 (October 1965), 46–50.

Wells, William D. "EQ, Son of EQ and the Reaction Profile." *Journal of Marketing,* 28 (October 1964), 45–52.

Chapter 10

The Influence of Advertising

With the emergence and widespread acceptance of major newspapers, magazines, radio, and television, the mass media have become one of the most ubiquitous and inescapable facets of our society.

To some, the mass media represent powerful forces influencing and shaping our values, tastes, and quality of life. Others view mass media more as reflecting our culture than as shaping it. Still others maintain that the true relationship lies somewhere in between.

To marketers, the mass media provide the vehicles for advertising. Advertising, an essential ingredient in almost every marketing mix, represents a principal means for making products known to potential buyers, for keeping consumers informed, and for persuading many customers to buy.

To accomplish these tasks marketers must have some idea of how advertising operates. This in turn requires an understanding of how consumers interact with various media, how this interaction shapes the nature of advertisements, how people react to different types of messages, and how one might assess the impact of various messages.

PRINT MEDIA AND ELECTRONIC MEDIA

Consider the following situation: A young mother is sitting at the kitchen table finishing her morning coffee and supervising the breakfast of her three-year-old son. A portable television set, temporarily in the kitchen, is turned to "Captain Kangaroo," while the mother leafs through the morning newspaper.

In this situation, which is surely not uncommon, the young mother would have been "exposed" to two of the most important advertising media: newspapers and TV.

On her way through the paper, the mother might have examined several advertisements that attracted her attention, and she probably would have glanced briefly at others. She might not have been watching the television screen with any consistency or any great interest, but a series of messages, half heard, would have come from the set while she was reading. Occasionally, if her son directed her attention to the television set, she might have both seen and heard some of the commercials.

Selective versus Intrusive

This vignette illustrates an important difference between newspapers and television, and between print media and electronic media in general. The consumer's use of print media is, for the most part, selective. A reader can browse through a newspaper or a magazine, glancing at editorial material and advertising, skipping that which is of little interest, and concentrating on what is deemed important.

Electronic media are more intrusive. The viewer cannot skip the commercial and go on to the program, and so he is exposed to many commercials whether he wants to be or not. Sometimes, as in the situation described above, the "viewer" may be exposed to television fare that he did not select for himself, and television messages intrude into the midst of other activities.

From the advertiser's point of view, this intrusiveness has both advantages and disadvantages. The principal advantage is that it exposes consumers to commercial messages they would otherwise skip, and so it brings the message to a wider audience. On the other hand, viewers resent being "forced" to view commercials that they would not seek out voluntarily, and some of this resentment may spread to the product or to television in general.

Transience versus Permanence

Another important difference between electronic media and print media is that the messages delivered by electronic media disappear as soon as the advertisement is over, while the messages delivered by print media have a certain degree of permanence. When a radio or television commercial is over, it is gone, except insofar as it is stored in the memory of the listener or viewer. But messages delivered via print stay around at least for a while.

One consequence of this difference is that radio and television commercials usually focus on making a few simple points and on making them as vividly as possible. There is no time for long, detailed explanations; even if there were, the probability is very high that the consumer would not remember them anyway. To consumers who want to make decisions based on careful examination of detailed information, advertising broadcast over the airwaves is apt to be unsatisfactory.

Another consequence of the relative permanence of printed advertisements is that printed advertisements make comparisons relatively easy. If any important decision is to be made—especially an important decision that is made over an extended period of time—the consumer can collect advertisements from different magazines or different newspapers and make comparisons among them. Women who are thinking of buying rugs, furniture, or draperies sometimes save advertisements for this purpose. Some especially careful grocery shoppers even make systematic comparisons among the advertisements of local grocery stores before beginning the weekend shopping.

Finally, the relative permanence of printed advertisements makes them candidates for repeat and "pass-along" readership. Long after the original reader has seen the advertisement for the first time, subsequent readers may see it, or the original reader may see it again. The degree of repeat and pass-along readership is much more difficult to measure than is the degree of original exposure; and, as a consequence, this aspect of print advertising's influence is often ignored even though it may be very important.

Children

A third important difference between print media and electronic media is that electronic media make it easy to appeal directly to children. Starting at about age two—long before they can read—children begin to pay some attention to television commercials; and by the time they are ready to enter first grade, children have already acquired a large fund of information about products they find interesting.

This information has at least two effects. The most direct and obvious effect is that it encourages children to ask their parents to buy special products, especially toys and food items. Children quickly learn that these requests, like other requests, are not all granted, and that even when requests are granted, the product does not always live up to the advertising. By age six or seven almost all children have become selective about when they ask for what, and most can describe a time when something they managed to get did not live up to expectations(Ward, 1974).

The more subtle effect of exposure to television advertising is that it associates the brand name with a variety of appealing characters and pleasant experiences. While remaining skeptical of any specific claims made for what is seen advertised, the child can still prefer certain brands because of their favorable associations. If all brands are about equal as far as the mother is concerned, and if the child takes to one more readily than to another, that brand has an advantage even in the absence of strong direct child pressure.

HOW ADVERTISING WORKS

Announcement and Display

In its simplest and most primitive form, advertising *announces* the availability of services and articles for sale. "Classified" advertisements in the newspaper, such as an advertisement for a garage sale, are typical examples of announcement advertising, as are listings in the classified section of the telephone directory and many types of signs and posters.

When announcements are expanded to contain pictures and descriptions of the articles for sale, advertising's announcement function merges imperceptibly into the *display* function. For instance, a simple announcement of a house for sale may be expanded to include a picture of the house, or at least an enthusiastic description of its better points. An announcement of a clothing sale may show samples worn by attractive models, along with verbal descriptions and prices.

When display advertising is accurate, it is helpful to consumers, for it presents an array of products for inspection without requiring that the prospective purchaser visit each place where one of the products might be. Catalogs and brochures sent by mail, and many of the display advertisements in newspapers and magazines, are designed to work in this way.

This service is so useful that consumers rate advertising near the top when asked to name the features of the newspaper they value most; and some magazines, like *Vogue,* are purchased as much for their advertising as for the editorial matter they contain.

On television, the counterpart of the display function is *demonstration.* Here the product (or, occasionally, a service) can be shown in use, and the consumer can see both how the product or service operates and what the results of using it might be.

The trouble with display and demonstration advertising is that the sponsor of the advertisement has an irresistible urge to present his product in the best possible light. Just as the job applicant puts on his best suit and sits up straight when he appears before a prospective employer, the advertiser describes and displays his product at the peak of its attainable perfection—and a bit beyond when he thinks he can get away with it. Thus a modest three-bedroom bungalow becomes a "lovely California ranch-type house." The plastic toy racing car is photographed against a background that makes it look almost real and twice its size. And advertisements for a computer dating service feature testimony from its three most satisfied customers.

In advertising's early days, this urge to present one's product in the best possible light frequently produced wildly false claims, especially for foods and medicines. Predictably, the wildly false claims produced demands for reform and regulation, and finally false advertising became a violation of federal law.

With blatantly false advertising a violation of federal law, some advertisers turned to other tactics. One favorite tactic was (and is) to imply superiority without telling a lie, by claiming that a product was "unexcelled" or "more effective (than it was before)." Another favorite tactic was to use such exaggerated hyperbole that no one would mistake the advertisement for a literal claim. This tactic produced a galloping white knight with a white lance that whitened sweatshirts, a washing machine with a giant inside, and an after shave lotion that rendered its wearer a target for assault by young and beautiful girls.

Consumers react to such tactics by discounting most of the advertising they hear or see, reserving judgment until they can give the product a try ot get advice from someone they can trust. As a result, display and demonstration advertising is less effective than it would be if all advertising provided dependable information.

Some advertisers have used a different tactic. Instead of stressing only superiority, they have said both good and bad things about their products, with the bad points made tongue-in-cheek and the good points made in a straightforward manner. This idea of using "two-sided" messages is congruent with the results of communication experiments conducted by Hovland et al. (1948). In these experiments on propaganda and opinion change, it was found that two-sided messages were more effective than one-sided messages when members of the audience were well educated, initially opposed to the position advocated, and later exposed to counterpropaganda. Similarly, Faison (1961) found that two-sided approaches were more effective than one-sided approaches in an experiment using messages about automobiles, ranges, and floor waxes.

The foregoing discussion is not intended to imply that all advertising, or even most, is dishonest, guileful, or untruthful. Much advertising is strictly accurate, and many individual advertisers insist upon strict rules of self-regulation. Self-regulation helps produce truthful ads in good taste, ads which conform to rules considerably more strict than those proposed by government agencies. Both self-regulation and governmental regulation of advertising are discussed in more detail later in this chapter.

Need Arousal

Some advertising is intended not so much to direct consumers to products or services that meet existing needs as to arouse a need—to move a particular need up the consumer's motive hierarchy, and then to show how the advertised product or service can satisfy it.

Anxiety and Fear The need for safety, security, and esteem is so strong that any real or imagined threat to their continued satisfaction is apt to arouse anxiety or, in some cases, outright fear. Insurance advertisers and advertisers for security devices such as fire extinguishers or burglar alarms have at times attempted to arouse anxieties or fears by showing the dire consequences of being unprepared. Government and social service agencies, attempting to persuade consumers to use seatbelts, to quit smoking, or to stay away from harmful drugs, have also followed the strategy of presenting advertisements that show tragedies in graphic detail.

On a milder level, the arousal of anxiety has also been attempted through threats to self-esteem. Much toothpaste and mouthwash advertising and much toilet soap advertising have focused on the negative social consequences of not using the advertised product. Diet soft drinks and filling, low-calorie foods have depended upon advertising that shows the unattractiveness of being overweight.

The danger of such advertising—from the advertiser's point of view—is that it may go too far. It may be so fearful or so conducive to anxiety that the recipient may avoid it, distort it, or forget it rather than come to grips with the situation the advertising protrays. The response to a positive appeal is apt to be positive. The response to a negative appeal may be the response that the advertiser desires, but it may be just the reverse (Janis and Feshback, 1953; Ray and Wilkie, 1970).

Prestige Another motive that advertisers have frequently tried to move up the motive hierarchy is prestige. Since expensive products serve so well as status symbols, advertisers have been careful to dramatize the favorable consequences of wearing expensive jewelry and beautiful clothes, or of driving a new and fashionable car and of living in an elegant house.

It should be noted that advertisers did not invent prestige. Prestige is an important motive even in societies where advertising does not exist, and vehicles, houses, clothes, and jewelry were status symbols long before advertising came on the scene. Advertisers did not invent status symbols, but advertisers of prestige-related products make continuous efforts to make prestige needs prepotent and to keep them near the forefront of the consumer's mind.

Advertisements intended to arouse fear or anxiety and advertisements intended to appeal to the prestige motive have been special targets for advertising's critics. No one likes to be reminded of the misfortunes and dangers of life, no matter how real these misfortunes and dangers might be, and no one likes to be reminded of the various human imperfections that make the person less than ideal. The most lurid of the advertisements that follow this line are frequently considered to be in bad taste.

The criticism of advertisements that appeal to the prestige motive is on a somewhat different plane. Critics of this kind of advertising assert that consumers do not "really" need prestige products. In their view, consumers "really" need wholesome food, adequate protection from the elements, and some minimal, inexpensive way of getting around. Anything beyond that is "unneccessary" and therefore a waste.

Advertisers argue that psychological needs, such as self-esteem and self-actualization, are just as "real" as the more basic physiological needs, once the physiological needs are satisfied. They argue that the proper course is to offer a range of products and services that satisfies all sorts of needs—from the most basically physiological to the most evanescent—to advertise such products and services vigorously, and to let the consumer make the choice.

Brand Awareness

In addition to its announcement, display, and need arousal functions, advertising serves to keep the brand name toward the front of the consumer's mind. Whether or not the advertisement can furnish a convincing demonstration or an attractive display, whether or not it can arouse an otherwise latent need, the repeated calling the brand name to the consumer's attention gives the brand an advantage over an "unknown" brand when a choice must be made. Sheer number of messages has this effect, quite independently of what the messages have said.

Common sense suggests that simple, primitive awareness must be an important function of advertising, especially advertising of established brands. Some brands are so well known that just about everthing that can be said about them has been said many times. A major function of their advertising, then, must be to keep the brand name salient in the consumer's mind in spite of the consumer's tendency to forget and in the face of a continuous onslaught of competing messages.

Advertising and Other Influences

Most announcement and display advertising is intended to influence intentions. At any one point in time only a very small proportion of the consumer population is "in the market" for a given product, and it is these immediate prospects whom announcement and display advertising is, as a rule, intended to affect.

Selective Attention But before advertisements can have their intended effect, they must penetrate the consumer's selective attention screen. Hundreds of advertisements reach individual consumers each day,[1] and if the consumers attended to every advertisement reaching them, they would have little time for anything else. Fortunately, consumers are selectively tuned to pick up relevant messages and dismiss others. For the most part, this tuning is the product of the consumers' current needs, so that the relatively few consumers who are "in the market" for a given product will be especially likely to attend to its advertising.

This tuning mechanism does not work perfectly. Sometimes the advertisement's physical properties are so strong that it demands at least some attention. Sometimes, as when a baby picture in a baby food advertisement attracts a grandmother's eye, the advertisement's content draws attention even though the message is not immediatley relevant. But in general consumers exposed to advertising, like consumers shopping in supermarkets, select out those messages that are most relevant to their concerns.

While this process is especially noticeable in consumers' reactions to print advertising, it also affects reactions to television commercials. Television commercials are more intrusive than print advertisements, but they still must compete for the consumer's attention against other distracting stimuli. Not every viewer pays close attention to every commercial that comes along.

Source Credibility and the Sleeper Effect Even when the consumers do pay attention to an advertisement, they consider its source. From the time they

[1]Britt et al. (1972) estimate that the range of TV, radio, newspaper, and magazine advertising exposure for males is between 117 and 285 messages per day, and between 161 and 484 for females.

first become aware of advertising as children, the consumers are told, first by adults and then by their own experience, that "you can't believe everything they say." As a consequence, consumers know that advertisements are far from trustworthy, and they continually check what they see and hear in advertising against their own experience and the experience of others.

Advertisers try to overcome the credibility filter by using communicators such as national celebrities who are thought to be perceived by consumers as credible (trustworthy and competent) persons. In mid-1976, for example, American Express used a commercial which began with an incident of purse snatching and ended with an actor from a popular detective show announcing that money, if stolen, is lost; but traveler's checks, if stolen, are quickly replaceable without loss. In this case a person related (fictionally) to crime prevention is used as a "credible" communicator for the company.

Advertising's low credibility would be even more of a filter if it were not for a phenomenon known as the "sleeper effect." Some of the earliest studies of attitude change demonstrated that the credibility of an information source has an important influence on the source's ability to influence attitudes and opinions. As would be inferred from the motivation behind the traveler's checks advertisement, trusted sources have great impact; suspected sources have little or none. It came somewhat as a surprise, then, to find in subsequent studies that this effect fades with the passage of time. After a while, the message seems to become "detached" from the source, at least in some cases, and the influence of the credibility of the source becomes much less strong (Hovland and Weiss, 1951; Schulman and Worrall, 1970).

It is quite probable that a similar phenomenon occurs in the case of messages delivered by means of advertising. Consumers discount advertising messages because they know advertising cannot be trusted. With the passage of time, however, some of this distrust may become "detached" from the message, allowing the message to be more effective than it would have been if the source had been kept in mind.[2] The effect of the credibility (or lack of credibility) of the source undoubtedly persists, but the sleeper effect weakens it.

Attitudes and Intentions If an advertisement gets past the selective attention filter and the source effect filter, its influence can be altered—either enhanced or reduced—by existing attitudes and intentions. Messages that are consonant with existing attitudes and intentions reinforce them. But when existing attitudes and intentions are strong, messages that contradict them are most often suppressed, distorted, or ignored (Sherif and Hovland, 1961).

Some attitudes—and, especially, some intentions— are much less resistant to change than others. If an attitude is not strongly articulated with important aspects of the self concept—if it is simply a casual favorable or unfavorable

[2]In an experiment on the effects of pleasant versus irritating radio commercials, Silk and Varva (1972) found that soft-sell or pleasant deliveries initially produced more favorable reactions, but with the passage of time no significant differences were found between the lasting effects of soft-sell and hard-sell messages.

disposition toward an object or a class of objects—new information in the form of advertising messages may change it. Intentions are especially alterable because a change in intention does not even require a change in attitude. If new information—say, an especially low price on an acceptable brand, or an announcement of a new brand's arrival in the marketplace—is conveyed by advertising, intentions may change without altering existing attitudes toward established products.

Advertising messages do not fall on empty organisms. Consumers attend to them or ignore them selectively, and they consider the source. When advertisements do gain attention and credibility, they are differentially effective depending upon the attitudes and intentions that consumers hold.

Events between Perception and Action Even when an advertising message gets past the selective attention filter, and even when it is strong enough to alter existing attitudes and intentions, its effect can be modified by events that take place between the time the message is received and the time it is acted upon.

One important class of such events is messages received from other people in the consumer's environment. Other family members, friends and neighbors, and members of important reference groups may make requests, render opinions, or set examples that countermand the advertisement's influence before the influence can be carried over into behavior.

Another important class of intervening events is other advertising. A consumer who has been "set" by the influence of an advertising message can be "reset" by conflicting messages from other advertisers. Advertisers with large budgets have a great advantage over advertisers with small budgets because, on the average, they have the greatest probability of getting in the last word.

Stimuli at the Point of Purchase When the consumer arrives at the point of purchase, still other stimuli come into play. An attitude or intention established at least in part by advertising may be foiled by an unexpectedly high price, by especially attractive packaging of a competing product, by some difficulty in locating the preferred brand, or by any other point-of-purchase influence.

Advertising is one of the influences that affect C in the S-C-R formula, but it is only one of the influences. Along with the other influences on C, it interacts with stimuli at the decision point to produce the consumer's response.

Company Images

Announcement and display advertising attempts to create a favorable image of the product in the mind of the prospective purchaser. Other advertising focuses less on the attributes of specific products than on the attributes of the sponsoring organization.

Some company image advertising is not intended to produce retail sales, but rather to achieve some other purpose. At the close of World War I, for instance, DuPont and other munitions manufacturers were widely accused of being "merchants of death." In subsequent years, DuPont invested heavily in campaigns that described its activities as "better things for better living through chemistry." More recently, companies that have been singled out as major contributors to air and water pollution have turned to advertising to describe their antipollution efforts.

But much company image advertising is intended to produce a generalized favorable attitude toward the company on the assumption—congruent with dissonance theory—that a favorable attitude toward the company will encourage favorable attitudes toward the company's products. "You can be sure if it's Westinghouse" and "You can put your confidence in General Electric" are typical examples.

An important function of company image advertising is the elementary one of making the company "well known." Consumers believe, with some justification, that a company which invests heavily in advertising will produce good products because bad products destroy an expensive reputation. They therefore tend to choose brand names that are familiar over brand names that are strangers, even when the branded item is somewhat more expensive. Moreover, this tendency seems to exist whether or not the branded item is that of a national manufacturer or the "private" brand of a large retail organization.

There is some evidence that companies come to be regarded as especially competent in specialized areas, and that these highly specialized images are even more important than generally favorable attitudes or a general reputation for being "well known." The following study is an example.

A well-known manufacturer of consumer electric appliances wished to introduce a new low-priced calculator for office use. As part of the pre-introduction testing, the calculator, and a calculator made by a company already preeminent in the office machine field, were placed in offices under three conditions: (1) appropriate brand labeling—both machines with their correct company names; (2) reversed brand labeling—brand names reversed; and (3) neutral labeling—machines identified as X and Y.

Under condition (1) the new machine was rated as somewhat *inferior* to its competitor. Under condition (2) the new machine was rated *far superior* to its competitor. And under condition (3) the new was rated *somewhat superior* to its competitor.

Even though the maker of the new machine had a generally favorable image, its generalized image was not as influential as the specialized image of a company that was already well established and highly regarded as a maker of the product in question (White, 1966).

Product User Images

Because people use products as props when enacting social roles, products that are visible in use tend to acquire "user images." The terms "white-collar worker" and "blue-collar worker" show how easily clothing can acquire symbolic value. A diamond ring worn on the third finger of the left hand, a corncob pipe, a rocking chair, a hard hat, a dozen red roses, a black leather motorcycle jacket, a sports car—all have widely shared connotations.

Some user images develop spontaneously when a product is adopted by an identifiable group of people. For many years, white-collar workers did in fact wear white collars; rich men did in fact (and still do) smoke expensive cigars, drink expensive wines, and travel in chauffer-driven Cadillacs. These products, then, became associated with high social and financial status.

User images that develop spontaneously may be undesirable from the manufacturer's point of view, and at times advertisers have tried to change them. Before Clairol, artificial haircoloring was commonly associated with low social status and dubious moral character. In a long series of advertisements showing beautiful young mothers with beautiful young children, Clairol made artificial haircoloring as acceptable as any other cosmetic to the masses of consumers.

It should be noted that attempts to change user images are not always successful. In the United States, hot tea has long been associated with being sick and little old ladies: In spite of well-financed attempts to convince consumers that hot tea is "brisk," "robust," and "hearty," hot tea is still widely associated with being sick and little old ladies.

Because user images develop spontaneously when the product is visible in use, and because a user image, once developed, may be very difficult to change, marketers make strenuous efforts to "position" products when they introduce them. They define the market as broadly as possible in view of the product's uses, features, and price; and, within the limits set by this definition, they seek to induce trial by everyone. No manufacturer wants to see his product preempted by a limited group that other potential customers are disinclined to copy.

Brand User Images

Advertising is also used to generate, alter, or maintain brand user images. Demonstration and display advertising contributes to the user image whenever it shows both the user and the product, and much advertising is designed to say something about both the product and the user at the same time. Automobile advertising, for instance, usually shows what the car looks like, describes one or two of its most significant characteristics, and implies—by the setting in which the car is shown and by the human models displayed with it—what sort of person the car is "for." The advertising for Hallmark Greeting Cards usually shows a few samples of an extensive product line, and it thus displays and demonstrates the product, but it also always strives to make the point that Hallmark Cards are "for those who care enough to send the very best."

In some advertising, the user image is the major message and little emphasis is given to display or demonstration. Clairol, for example, advertised its Long and Silky hair conditioner to the teen market of 1973 by showing three attractive long-haired teenage girls wearing jeans with pocket patches. One of these patches proclaimed, "Long is beautiful," another featured the Long and

Silky logo. The caption on the ad stated: "Long & Silky . . . Because the only important things you wear are your jeans and your hair." The idea, of course, was to help the reader associate the brand with a life style in which fashion—or the absence of it—plays a large part.

Even the most cursory examination of consumer magazines will show that advertisers believe that consumers use conspicuous brands of conspicuous products to maintain and enhance self-esteem. Automobile and cigarette advertising and advertising for cosmetics, home furnishing, and home appliances contain many examples of attempts to position brands as symbols of success, good looks, or youth and vitality. In general, advertisers attempt to position or reposition a brand so that it is perceived to be highly compatible to the self-concepts of persons in a target market.

In a study (Ross, 1971) designed to test the assumption that self-concept is strongly related to brand preferences, 247 coeds were asked to rate themselves on the 15 bipolar rating scales shown in Figure 10-1. They were then asked to rate, on the same set of scales, "the kind of girl who would most prefer to read" each of six magazines (*Look, Mademoiselle, Reader's Digest, Saturday Evening Post*, *Seventeen*, and *Vogue*) and "the kind of girl who would most prefer to own" each of seven automobiles (Cadillac, Chevrolet, Corvair, Dodge Dart, Ford Falcon, Imperial, and Lincoln). Finally, they were asked to rank-order the magazines and the automobiles according to their own personal preferences.

The results of the study were analyzed by computing, for each respondent, a set of statistics that showed the degree of correspondence between the respondent's self-image and the user image she held for each automobile and each magazine. This analysis showed that similarity between self image and the user image of preferred brands was much greater than the similarity between self-image and user image of nonpreferred brands, both for magazines and for automobiles.

Figure 10-1 Bipolar Rating Scales Used in Product Image Study

excitable	___	___	___	___	___	___	calm
simple	___	___	___	___	___	___	complicated
graceful	___	___	___	___	___	___	awkward
conservative	___	___	___	___	___	___	liberal
humorous	___	___	___	___	___	___	serious
follower	___	___	___	___	___	___	leader
dominating	___	___	___	___	___	___	submissive
popular	___	___	___	___	___	___	unpopular
extravagant	___	___	___	___	___	___	economical
mature	___	___	___	___	___	___	immature
unsuccessful	___	___	___	___	___	___	successful
informed	___	___	___	___	___	___	uninformed
weak	___	___	___	___	___	___	strong
interesting	___	___	___	___	___	___	dull
conformist	___	___	___	___	___	___	nonconformist

Source: Ross (1971).

This study did not answer the question of cause and effect. There is no way to know whether the respondents preferred brands because the brands reflected their self-images, whether they imputed congruent user images to brands they already preferred for other reasons, or some of both. The study therefore does not prove that changing a nonpreferred brand's user image would change its preference ranking.

The study does show that—at least for this sample of respondents and at least for these two products—the agreement between self-image and brand user image of favored brands is very close.

Image advertising has not been as subject to government regulation as announcement and display advertising has. If a false claim is blatantly false, or if the product pictured in an advertisement is not the product offered for sale, enforcement agencies find it relatively easy to establish a case in court. But if the advertisement is designed to imply rather than to state, to lead to a vague inference rather than to a demonstrably false conclusion, the case against the advertisement is much more difficult to prove. As a result, image advertising has been widely adopted by advertisers who need to differentiate their brands from their competitors' and who cannot legally claim superiority on any dimension that is intrinsic to the product itself.

REASONS FOR LIKING AND DISLIKING ADVERTISING

In a study sponsored by the American Association of Advertising Agencies (Bauer and Greyser, 1968), a cross section of American adults were asked the following questions (among many others):

> "Some people we've talked to say they like advertising very much and feel very favorable toward it. Why do you think they feel this way?"
>
> "Some people we've talked to say they don't like advertising and feel very unfavorable toward it. Why do you think they feel this way?"

The results of the study are shown in the tables on pages 259 and 260. Note that information related reasons are by far the most numerous of the reasons given for liking advertising. It is worth noting also that intrusiveness and untruthfulness were the most common reasons given for negative reactions.

REGULATION OF ADVERTISING

Government Regulation

In response to demands for more honest advertising, *Printer's Ink*, an advertising trade publication, proposed a "model statute" in 1911 that has formed the basis for much state legislation. This model statute states that anyone responsible for an advertisement that ". . . contains any assertion, representation or statement of fact which is untrue, deceptive or misleading shall be guilty of a misdemeanor." Forty-six states have adopted some version of this statute, but

Reasons Why People Like Advertising

Information-related reasons		57%
Advertising is informative, educational (nonspecific); it shows what is on the market; gives a better understanding of the products sold; keeps people informed on products; people can learn a lot from it.	35%	
It provides information on new products; it introduces people to new products; keeps them up to date on what is new on the market; helps introduce new things.	17	
It provides information on prices; it gives a person a chance to compare prices; tells how much things cost; shows where the cheapest place to buy is.	5	
Invidious reasons for liking advertising		22
Some people live on it; they must be employed in advertising; businessmen must like it; they must see the gain business makes from it; must be an advertising agency.	22	
Entertainment-related reasons		13
Advertising is enjoyable, entertaining, amusing. Some commercials are entertaining; there are many clever ads; ads are often very colorful; they may like the ads themselves.	9	
Advertising pays for entertainment. Someone has to sponsor what we see on TV; advertising pays more freight.	4	
Miscellaneous reasons		11
It helps improve product quality; provides information on product quality. Competition in advertising keeps product quality up. It helps in getting a better product; provides information on how products hold up.	2	
Other answers.	9	
No good reason		4
There is no good reason. Cannot see why they would like it; there isn't any reason why anybody should like it.	4	
		107%
No opinion; don't know.		12%
N = 1,846.		

Source: Bauer and Greyser (1968:131–135).

the vigor with which laws are enforced varies considerably, both from state to state and from time to time within the same state.

At the federal level, responsibility for regulation of advertising is distributed among several agencies:

- Food and Drug Administration (labeling of foods and proprietary drugs)
- Post Office Department (lotteries, fraud, obscenity via the mails)
- Federal Communications Commission (obscene or fraudulent advertising, or advertising in bad taste over the air)
- Alcohol and Tobacco Tax Division of the Internal Revenue Service (advertising of tobacco and of alcoholic beverages)
- Securities and Exchange Commission (advertising related to sale of securities)

Reasons Why People Do Not Like Advertising

Advertising's intrusiveness — its amount, frequency, and interruptive nature.		40%
There is too much advertising; too many advertisements. There is far too much; magazines are full of it; they spend too much time trying to sell their wares.	19%	
It interrupts entertainment; it cuts in right at the most interesting part of the show; they cut programs off to advertise.	12	
It is repetitious; there is just too much of the same thing over and over; they repeat the same commercial so often; you see or hear many of them so often you could scream.	6	
Commercials are too loud or long; the commercials come on louder than the show; you wonder whether some will ever end.	3	
Advertising is untruthful or exaggerated.		26
Advertising is false, misleading; ads are not quite truthful; trying to fool the public; they don't give a true picture; I've found it was false, or at best misleading.	21	
Exaggeration; products can't do all they say; they make them sound as though they were the last word.	5	
Advertising is silly, insults people's intelligence.		11
It is silly, irritating, or annoying (general); some advertising is irritating; a lot of nonsense; it's a nuisance, it's ridiculous.	6	
It is patronizing, insults people's intelligence; it talks down to people; it's geared to reach people with a low level of intelligence; people are smarter than advertising gives them credit for being.	5	
Advertising is offensive or bad for children.		8
It is objectionable or offensive (product itself or advertisement); some things should not be advertised; they are often in poor taste; some are immoral.	5	
Advertising exerts a bad influence on children; it makes kids want everything they see advertised; children should not know about some of the things they see advertised.	3	
High-pressure selling.		6
It is "high pressure"; some of it is shoved down your throat; trying to force people to buy things they don't need.	6	
Advertising increases prices.		3
Advertising increases product prices; if there were fewer ads, prices would be lower; the consumer pays the cost of advertising in higher prices.	3	
Miscellaneous reasons.		11
No good reason.		9
There is no good reason. I don't know why they should feel that way; there's nothing wrong with advertising.	9	114%
No opinion; don't know.		15%
N = 1,846.		

Source: Bauer and Greyser (1968:131–135).

In addition, the legislation that created the Federal Trade Commission in 1914 gave the Commission authority to act when dishonest advertising injured competition. Initially the Commission was uncertain about its power to act in cases where possible injury to the consumer rather than direct injury to competition was the issue. The Wheeler-Lea Amendment to the Federal Trade Commission Act, passed in 1938, settled the matter. It said, in part, "Unfair methods of competition, in commerce, *and unfair or deceptive acts or practices in commerce,* are hereby declared unlawful," and it gave the Commission power to seek contempt of court citations against advertisers who did not comply with final cease-and-desist orders.

Self-Regulation

An example of an advertiser's efforts to regulate its own behavior is provided by General Foods' written policy for food commercials:

> **1** Food will be photographed in an unadulterated state—product must be typical of that normally packed with no preselection for quality or substitution of individual components.
>
> **2** Individual portions must conform to amount per serving used in describing yield.
>
> **3** Package amounts shown must conform to package yield.
>
> **4** Product must be prepared according to package directions.
>
> **5** Recipe must follow directions and be shown in same condition it would appear when suitable for serving.
>
> **6** Mock-ups may not be used.
>
> **7** Props should be typical of those readily available to the consumers.
>
> **8** Theatrical devices (camera angles, small-sized bowls and spoons) may not be used to convey attributes other than those normally seen in use.

According to the testimony of Ms. Peggy Kohl before the FTC's hearings on modern advertising practices, the intent of this policy is to ensure that consumers are provided with correct visual impressions of the quality, attributes, and amount of product they will receive. She noted that this policy prevents photographing some foods because mock-ups cannot be used: "Every now and then there is a great tasting recipe which is downright ugly in an honest photograph" (Howard and Hulbert,1973).

The advertising industry as a whole is also involved in self-regulation. As noted earlier, most state legislation dealing with the regulation of advertising had its genesis in an industry-proposed statute; more recently a National Advertising Review Board has been organized to receive and evaluate complaints. Organized by the Council of Better Business Bureaus and three major advertising trade associations in 1971 to provide a formal program of self-regulation, the board has the responsibility for reviewing complaints about the honesty of advertising and judging whether or not complaints are valid.

Self-regulation, of course, is limited in its effectiveness. Since it depends almost entirely on voluntary compliance, an advertiser is free to defy the board's rulings if he considers that action to be in his best interest. It is likely, then, that the regulation of advertising will continue to be a combination of governmental and industry control (Cohen, 1972).

MEASURING ADVERTISING'S EFFECTS

Immediate Results

It might seem that the easiest and best way to measure the effect of an advertisement would be to run it for a while and see if consumers act in any way different from the way they acted when it was not running.

Mail-order advertising can be tested this way. If the advertisers keep careful records of the orders received from each advertisement, they can establish exact links between advertising and consumer responses. Similarly, advertising intended to elicit inquiries can be tested by printing a coupon in the body copy and counting the coupons that come in.

Sometimes mass media advertisements intended to produce immediate results get immediate results. Once, through a typographer's error, a New York discount store advertised, $240 television sets for $24, and the following morning 600 customers were waiting at the door. When Pan American ran a newspaper, direct-mail, and TV campaign to introduce its 747 aircraft, it published a picture of the new plane with the headline, "The world's first 747s have orders to report to the world's most experienced airline. Reservations, anyone?" The campaign produced 2,500 reservations in one week—fourteen months before the first flight was scheduled to be made (*Marketing Insights*, 1968).

Occasionally, even mass media campaigns get immediate results measurable in terms of sharp changes in brand share. In 1972, R. J. Reynolds introduced Winchester cigars with a heavily television-oriented campaign resembling the Marlboro Man campaign of the TV-cigarette years. As the data in Table 10-1 show, Winchester captured over 60 percent of the little-cigar market in one year.

But aside from such special cases, the effects of an advertisement are not easy to gauge. Even department store announcement and display advertising, which for the most part is designed to affect intentions, is hard to link unequivocally to consumer behavior because so many other factors interfere. An otherwise effective advertisement may produce few customers if the weather is bad or if a major competitor is running a special sale. A weak advertisement might pass the cash register test of subsequent sales if store traffic has been built by advertising from other departments or if customers passing on the street are stopped by an especially attractive window display.

Experiments

If the advertising is not intended to arouse immediate intentions but rather to modify attitudes or enhance images, the problem becomes much more difficult. Now, many experiences intervene between exposure to the advertisement and its effect (if any) on behavior, and the impact of the exposure becomes exceedingly hard to trace.

The only known way to handle this problem is to conduct a controlled experiment. In the ideal controlled experiment one group of consumers is

Table 10-1 The Sudden Success of Winchester
(In millions of units)

	1969		1970		1971		1972	
	Units	% of market	Units	% of market	Units	% of market	Units	% of market
Reynolds								
Winchester	—	—	—	—	—	—	2,500.0	63.6%
Lorillard								
Omega (85mm and and 100mm-F)	106.0	14.4%	161.0	17.9%	221.5	20.5%	297.4	7.5
Between the Acts (80mm)	102.0	13.8	97.0	10.8	109.9	10.1	109.3	2.8
Madison (80mm)	106.0	14.4	99.0	11.0	109.8	10.1	109.6	2.8
Total	314.0	42.6	357.0	39.7	441.2	40.7	516.3	13.1
American Cigar								
Roi-Tan (85mm and 100mm-F)	69.0	9.4	83.0	9.2	139.0	12.8	156.0	4.0
Antonio Cleopatra (100mm-F)	68.0	9.2	123.0	13.7	134.0	12.4	164.0	4.2
Deringer	—	—	—	—	—	—	155.0	3.9
Total	137.0	18.6	206.0	22.9	273.0	25.2	475.0	12.1
United States Tobacco Co.								
Tall N' Slim (100mm-F)	68.0	9.3	105.0	11.7	110.0	10.1	90.0	2.2
Little Nippers (100mm-F)	71.0	9.6	80.0	8.9	74.1	6.8	50.0	1.3
Sano (85mm and (100mm-F)	12.0	1.6	4.0	0.4	3.0	0.3	2.0	0.1
Little Nippers (Mini-tip)	—	—	—	—	7.3	0.7	(f)	0.0
Zig Zag	—	—	—	—	—	—	65.0	1.7
Total	151.0	20.5	189.0	21.0	194.4	17.9	207.0	5.3
Stephano Bros.								
Trend (85mm)	38.0	5.2	38.0	4.2	16.5	1.6	15.9	0.4
Herald (85mm-F)	20.0	2.7	22.0	2.4	13.5	1.2	13.0	0.3
Action (100mm-F)	—	—	21.0	2.3	17.5	1.6	16.0	0.4
Kingston (85mm-F)	17.0	2.3	20.0	2.2	13.5	1.2	13.0	0.3
Total	75.0	10.2	101.0	11.1	61.0	5.6	57.9	1.4
M&N Cigar Manufacturers								
St. Regis	11.0	1.5	12.0	1.3	14.0	1.3	16.0	0.4
Others	18.5	6.6	30.1	4.0	100.8	9.3	160.7	4.1
Total	736.5	100.0%	901.1	100.0%	1,084.4	100.0%	3,932.9	100.0%

Source: John C. Maxwell Jr., Maxwell Division, Wheat First Securities.

exposed to the advertising which another, identical group is not. The groups are truly matched to begin with, and the only difference in the way they are treated is the advertising. In this ideal case any difference in behavior must be attributed to the advertising.

A large-scale field experiment sponsored by the American Newspaper Publishers' Association illustrates both the logic and the special value of experimental design and the many problems such experiments entail.

In this experiment advertisements for seven durables and twenty-four frequently purhcased drug and grocery store items were inserted into morning newspapers delivered in Amarillo, Los Angeles, Pittsburgh, Providence, Roanoke, and Wichita. In each city, the home delivery routes were divided into two matched samples, and consumers in each sample received somewhat different versions of the paper. For each of the products included in the study, the consumers in one sample received a paper containing an advertisement for one brand while the consumers in the other sample received a paper containing an advertisement for a competing brand; or the consumers in one sample received a newspaper containing an advertisement for the "test" brand while the consumers in the other sample received a newspaper containing no advertisment for any brand in that product category. The advertisements were carried on specially prepared newspaper pages that were virtually indistinguishable from ordinary advertising and editorial matter.

The day after these doctored papers were delivered, 2,438 home interviews were conducted with housewives in the six cities. Each respondent was asked what stores she had been in or phoned "yesterday" or the day of the interview, whether she had bought any brand in any of the test product categories, what brands she had bought, and her attitudes and purchase intentions with respect to the test brands and their major competitors.

The essence of the experiment was that the *only* systematic difference between the two prematched groups of consumers was the advertising in the morning paper, so any statistically significant difference between them, in attitude or in behavior, could be attributed to the advertising and to the advertising alone.

Comparison of the "test group" (respondents exposed to an advertisement for the brand) with the "control group" (respondents exposed to an advertisement for a competing brand, or to no brand in the product category), averaging over all the products covered in the study, is shown in Table 10-2.

Table 10-2 What One Little Ad Can Do

	Control		Test		
	Percent	Base number of instances	Percent	Base number of instances	Difference
24 packaged goods					
Purchases of test brand today or yesterday	0.44%	(22,603)	0.5%	(22,548)	+14%
Brand share of test brand	10.6	(938)	11.7	(958)	+10
6 nonpaired packaged goods					
Purchases of the test brand today or yesterday	2.9	(4,955)	3.3	(4,905)	+15
All 31 brands in test					
Would pick brand "next time I buy product"	19.2	(26,858)	20.0	(26,855)	+ 4

The figures in Table 10-2 show how "thin" most markets are—only a very small proportion of the population buys a product on an average day. They also show that, on the average, the advertisements worked. Even though the proportion buying the product during the time of the experiment was very small, it was measurably higher among the "test group" consumers than among the "control group" consumers.

The authors of this study note that even though the averages were higher in the test group than in the control group, for some individual brands the results were the reverse. Some of the advertisements were counterproductive.

One problem with this experiment as a measurement of advertising effect was that it was sensitive to behavior change only among the small proportions of the sample who happened to be "in the market" for the test products during the thirty hours between exposure and interview. Any post-interview effect would go unmeasured, except insofar as it was picked up by the attitude and intentions scales.

Another problem was the enormous cost of the experiment. Consider the logistics of designing the test advertisements, preparing them in the proper style and format for each newspaper, seeing that the right advertisements in the right combinations were inserted into the right newspapers on the appointed day, conducting 2,438 personal interviews in six widely scattered cities, and assembling this vast amount of data in such a way as to demonstrate a tiny but significant effect. A study of this size is far beyond the capabilities of all but the largest advertisers, and even the largest advertisers could not afford to use this method to evaluate the many advertisements they employ in the course of a year.

The large-scale field experiment is the *only* way to demonstrate the effect of an advertising campaign on consumer behavior, because it is the only way to rule out other influences that operate at the same time. Unfortunately for those who need good information on advertising's effects, large-scale field experiments are exceedingly expensive, exceedingly cumbersome, and exceedingly difficult to arrange. The administrative problems of making sure that the right advertisements get to the right people (and only to the right people) are enormous, as are the problems associated with getting accurate measurements of sales. If the experiment interferes with an ongoing program—increasing advertising in some areas and cutting it in others, as required by some experimental designs—the experiment is apt to meet stiff resistance from those in the "low advertising" areas who depend on advertising to stimulate buyer activity. And even when the experiment is conducted and analyzed with maximum speed, the results may arrive too late to be of any immediate use.

Because of these drawbacks, field experiments are rare, and advertisers are forced to rely on other techniques that depend on the notion of "hierarchy of effects." The *hierarchy of effects* hypothesis holds that advertising leads the consumers through an orderly psychological sequence: first it makes the consumers aware of the product, then it interests them in it, then it creates a desire to buy it, and finally it inspires buying action. In other words, advertising functions in much the same way as a personal salesperson, as exemplified by the interaction between the La Mottas and the salesman in Chapter One.

If advertising does work this way, it is possible to get at least a partially satisfactory measure of advertising effectiveness by tapping into this sequence at some point prior to the actual act of purchasing. If sales effects cannot be measured because measurement of sales effects would be too expensive or too unwieldy or would take too long, the advertiser can measure the degree to which the message has made consumers aware of the product, has provided some memorable information about it, has created a favorable attitude toward it, or has inspired an intention to buy it. While not as fully convincing as a sales measure, a measurement taken at some intermediate point in the effect sequence could be used to demonstrate that the advertising is capable of doing at least part of what it was designed to do.

Attitude Change Measures

One of the methods most often used to evaluate the effectiveness of television commercials taps into the hierarchy of effects at the "desire" stage. Consumers are invited to a theater to view and express their opinions about "programs that might be shown on television next year." Before the program begins, the audience is told that door prizes in the form of substantial supplies of various products will be awarded, and they are asked to list the brands they would like to receive if they win. At the end of the program, which consists of an entertaining film and commercials for some of the door-prize products, audience members are asked to evaluate the film, and (on the rather shaky excuse that some of the preprogram brand-choice ballots were improperly filled out) they are again asked to list the brands they would like to receive if they are door prize winners. Any difference between the proportion choosing a brand at the beginning of the program and the proportion choosing the brand after exposure to the commercial is ascribed to the commercial's persuasive power. This is a test of attitude change.

Recall Measures

Another technique used to evaluate television commercials is "day-after recall." The commercial to be tested is cut into the commercial segment of an on-the-air program in selected cities. The next day consumers who saw the program are located by telephone. After making sure that the respondent was watching the program at the time the test commercial was shown, the interviewer asks a series of questions designed to determine what, if anything, the respondent remembers about the specific commercial.

This technique differs from the theater test in two important ways. First, the advertisement is exposed in a natural setting where it must compete for the viewer's attention against the many distractions that occur during normal viewing. It seems reasonable to suppose that commercials that attract and hold the viewer's attention to an unusual degree will be more memorable than less attention-getting commercials, and, other things being equal, that these more memorable commercials will also be better at delivering a persuasive message.

A second difference between the theater test and the recall test is that the recall test taps into the effect hierarchy at the earlier "interest" stage. In general, commercials that say something about the product that is of real interest to the consumer are better remembered than commercials that do not say anything about the product that is relevant to the consumer's concerns. Belief in the value of the recall test depends in part upon the assumption that commercials that are interesting enough to be remembered are also interesting enough to have been effective.

Recognition

Finally, advertisements—especially print advertisements—are also tested by the "recognition" method. Respondents are contacted by personal interview some time after they have received a regular issue of a popular magazine. Going through the magazine page by page, the interviewer asks a series of standardized questions about each advertisement, inquiring whether the respondent remembers having looked at it, having read most of it, and having read the part of the advertisement that contains the advertiser's name. This method seeks to tap into the effect sequence at the very earliest stage. Its purpose is to determine whether the advertisement made any impression on memory at all.

Some Problems

Each of these methods of measuring the effects of advertising has its own set of obvious faults. Consumers who can be persuaded to attend "television previews" may differ from the bulk of a product's purchasers in many important ways. Furthermore, the artificial attention created by the theater setting makes it impossible to measure the commercial's ability to attract attention against the many distractions that occur during normal home viewing.

The day-after recall test is sensitive to the advertisement's ability to attract and hold attention, but there is no guarantee that being able to deliver a memorable message is a is a valid index of the commercial's ability to influence sales.

Because it taps into the effects hierarchy at the earliest stage, the recognition method is farther removed from sales than either attitude change or recall. Experiments with this method suggest that it favors advertisements that are attractive and well liked, but the relationship (if any) between attractiveness and subsequent consumer behavior is unknown.

IS HIERARCHY OF EFFECTS A VALID MODEL OF THE WAY ADVERTISING WORKS?

Finally, all three of these commonly used methods depend to some degree upon the validity of the assumption of "hierarchy of effects." The question that users of these methods must answer is: Does advertising operate by making the consumers aware of the product, then interesting them, then creating desire, then precipitating action?

This model has considerable intuitive appeal as a way of thinking about demonstration and display advertising for products that are new to the consumer, although in such cases the first three steps—awareness, interest, and desire—may be so fused that they cannot be measured separately. But the model does not seem to fit advertising for long-established, well-known brands, where the function would seem to be reinforcement of the brand image and maintenance of awareness of the brand name (Palda, 1966). It seems especially inappropriate as a model for brand user image advertising, where the object is to surround the brand with a subtle aura, to confirm its congruence with an attractive self concept, or to evoke a mood. It is hard to believe, in any of these cases, that the consumer moves from awareness to action through any orderly sequence of gradually unfolding, separately measurable steps, and it is doubly hard to believe that the advertisement's effectiveness is adequately measured by its ability to produce an immediate change in intentions or to elicit high recognition or recall.

It might seem that this question could be settled by a straightforward empirical test: measure the sales effectiveness of a representative sample of advertisements by means of a proper experiment, measure the ability of each advertisement to produce attitude change, recognition, or recall, and then find out to what degree, if any, attitude change, recognition, or recall predicts sales effect.

But because it would be so immensely complex and expensive, this grand experiment has never been, and probably never will be, done. When bits and pieces of it have been tried (Appel, 1966; Bogart et al., 1970), the results have not been encouraging for those who think that recognition, recall, or attitude change scores are reasonably good measures of an advertisement's ability to encourage sales. Nevertheless, because these substitute measures are within the range that advertisers can afford, while proper experiments as a rule are not, recognition, recall, and attitude change continue to be used as ways to evaluate the advertisements that reach consumers every day.

SUMMARY

Advertising in electronic media differs from advertising in print media in three important ways. Advertising in electronic media is intrusive, while advertising in print media is more often deliberately sought out. Advertising in electronic media is transient, while advertising in print media is more permanent. And advertising in electronic media is much better suited than advertising in print media to communicating with preschool children.

One of the ways advertising works is by announcing and displaying articles for sale. When announcement and display advertising is accurate, it is helpful because it saves the consumer energy and time. Often, however, announcement and display advertising has been inaccurate, and these inaccuracies have brought both punitive legislation and calls for further government regulation and industry self-control. When consumers are asked what they like about advertising, they mention its informative function most often. When they are asked what they dislike about advertising, they refer most often to intrusiveness and untruth.

Some advertising is intended to arouse needs and then suggest products or services that fill them. Two needs often employed in this way are the need for freedom from fear or anxiety and the need for self-esteem or prestige.

In addition to announcing and displaying products, advertising serves to keep the name of the brand near the forefront of the consumer's mind.

The influence of advertising is mediated by several factors. Advertising messages must pass the filter of selective attention. They must pass the source credibility filter. They may be distorted or ignored if they conflict with important attitudes and intentions. Their effects may be canceled or reversed by events that occur between receipt of the message and the relevant action. And their effects may be canceled or reversed by stimuli at the response point.

Some advertising is primarily intended to create company images, product user images, or brand user images. Most advertising intended to create company images is based on the assumption that a favorable attitude toward a company will generalize to the company's products. Advertising intended to create product user images or brand user images is based on the assumption that consumers will purchase those products and those brands that are perceived as enhancing the self.

Except for rare cases in which the effects of an advertisement can be easily and immediately observed, the only way to measure an advertisement's effect on consumer behavior is by means of a controlled field experiment. Because controlled field experiments are costly and difficult to arrange, advertisers have sought less expensive substitute measures: attitude change, recall, and recognition.

Although each of these measures has its own shortcomings, and although the hierarchy of effects hypothesis upon which they are all based has not been verified and may well be false for many important kinds of advertising, these methods continue to be widely used and continue to exercise a major influence over the advertising to which consumers are exposed.

REVIEW QUESTIONS

1. Identify the major differences between print media and electronic media. How do these differences affect the nature of advertisements placed in each type of media?
2. Why do many advertisements aimed at young children attempt to associated brand names with appealing characters? Is this an effective approach? Why or why not?
3. Describe the announcement and display functions of advertisements. Which seems more useful for consumers?
4. What are the drawbacks to sponsors of advertising which is false or highly exaggerated?

5 Some advertisers say both good and bad things about their own products. Why is that a useful procedure?
6 Describe the points of view of advertisers and their critics concerning need arousal through advertising. Can advertisers actually create consumer needs or motives?
7 How does the sleeper effect modify the importance of source credibility in advertising?
8 Several consumer filters and external stimuli must be overcome before advertisements can have their intended effect. Identify and discuss each of these factors.
9 What is the purpose of image advertising? What types of images can this tactic be utilized to influence?
10 List each step in the sequence implied in the hierarchy of effects hypothesis. Is this hypothesis equally valid for all types of advertising?
11 Although a large-scale field experiment is the only way to accurately demonstrate the effect of an advertising campaign on consumer behavior, such studies are seldom used. Why? What substitute measures are used to approximate advertising effects on consumer behavior?

EXERCISE

Make a list of several consumer magazines, each having a different editorial focus (e.g., *Time, Good Housekeeping,* and *Vogue*). Select two years (e.g., 1966 and 1976) representing two decades and for which the magazines are available in your library. Then examine the specific ads and answer the following questions:

1 How do the appeals to consumers vary, if they do, by type of product and editorial focus? Why?
2 Have the appeals changed for specific products during the ten-year period? If so, in what ways? Why have the appeals changed or not changed?
3 Has there been a shift in proportion from announcement-and-display ads to need-arousal ads during the ten-year period? If so, describe the nature of the shift. Explain why you think such a shift has or has not occurred.
4 Document and explain any changes in the occupational roles of women shown in ads.

REFERENCES

Appel, Valentine. "Attitude Change: Another Dubious Method for Measuring Advertising Effectiveness." In Lee Adler and Irving Crespi (eds.), *Attitude Research at Sea.* Chicago, Ill.: American Marketing Association, 1966, 141–152.
Bauer, Raymond A. and Stephen N. Greyser. *Advertising in America: The Consumer View.* Boston: Division of Research, Graduate School of Business Administration, Harvard University, 1968.
Bogart, Leo, B. Stuart Tolley, and Frank Orenstein. "What One Little Ad Can Do." *Journal of Advertising Research,* 10, No. 4 (August 1970), 3–13.
Britt, Stewart Henderson, Stephen C. Adams, and Allan S. Miller. "How Many Advertising Exposures per Day?" *Journal of Advertising Research,* 12 (December 1972), 3–10.

Cohen, Dorothy. "Surrogate Indicators and Deception in Advertising." *Journal of Marketing,* 36 (July 1972), 10–15.

Faison, E. W. "Effectiveness of One-sided and Two-sided Mass Communications in Advertising." *Public Opinion Quarterly,* 25 (1961), 468–469.

Hovland, Carl I., A. . Lumsdaine, and F. D. Sheffield. *Experiments on Mass Communication.* Vol. 3. Princeton, N. J.: Princeton University Press, 1948. Chap. 8.

——— and Walter Weiss. "The Influence of Source Credibility on Communication Effectiveness." *Public Opinion Quarterly,* 15 (1956), 635–650.

Howard, John A. and James Hulbert. *Advertising and the Public Interest.* A staff report to the Federal Trade Commission, 1973.

Janis, Irving and Seymour Feshbach. "Effects of Fear-Arousing Communications." *Journal of Abnormal and Social Psychology,* 48 (January 1953), 78–92.

Marketing Insights. "Ad Power." *Marketing Insights* (November, 1968), 6.

Ray, Michael L. and William L. Wilkie. "Fear: The Potential of an Appeal Neglected by Marketing." *Journal of Marketing,* 34 (January 1970), 54–62.

Ross, Ivan. "Self Concept and Brand Preference." *Journal of Business,* 44, No. 1 (January 1971), 38–50.

Sherif, M. and C. I. Hovland, *Social Judgement: Assimulation and Contrast Effects in Communication and Attitude Change.* New Haven: Yale University Press, 1961.

Shulman, Gary I. and Chrysoula Worrall. "Salience Patterns, Source Credibility, and the Sleeper Effect." *Public Opinion Quarterly,* 34 (Fall 1970), 371–382.

Silk, Alvin and T. Varva. "Pleasant/Unpleasant Appeals to Create Awareness and Evaluation." Paper presented at the Association for Consumer Research Workshop on Buyer/Consumer Information Processing, November 1972.

Sternthal, Brian and C. Samuel Craig. "Fear Appeals: Revisited and Revised." *Journal of Consumer Research,* 1 (December 1974), 22–34.

Ward, Scott. "Consumer Socialization." *Journal of Consumer Research,* 1 (September 1974), 1–14.

White, Irving S. "The Perception of Value in Products." In Joseph W. Newman (ed.), *On Knowing the Consumer.* New York: Wiley, 90–106.

Chapter 11

The Effects of Interpersonal Communication

In the preceding chapter we examined advertising, one of the most visible and one of the most criticized types of consumer stimuli. We reiterated our assertion from Chapter 2 that consumers interact with and are influenced by advertising, along with a host of other stimuli, including those resulting from personal relationships.

Students of consumer behavior have been intrigued for years by the effects of interpersonal communications. Marketers, public administrators, and consumers all recognize the need to understand this phenomenon and have begun to probe for answers to such questions as: Under what circumstances do consumers turn to others for advice in preference to or to the exclusion of advertising? What determines how many sources of information consumers consult before they buy or reject a product? and What sources are consulted for what products?

SOURCES OF INFORMATION

To whom do people turn when they need information for reaching a purchasing decision? One recent study asked this question in a nationwide survey of households which had purchased a new car or a new major appliance (Newman and Staelin, 1973).

Table 11-1 shows the answers to the survey questions.[1] The data show that consumers vary both in the number of sources they use and in the type of source they use. While the majority of the respondents reported they consulted more than one type of source before buying, a large number (44 percent) said they used only one source—or none at all. Some of the variation in the number of sources appears to depend upon the source type. When buyers reported consulting retail outlets, or when they reported consulting friends and neighbors, they tended to rely on a smaller number of sources. On the other hand, when they reported using advertising and other mass media, the number of sources consulted tended to be substantially higher.

Why the variation? Why do buyers who use advertising in books, pamphlets, and articles also tend to use friends and outlets, while those who use friends and retail outlets tend not to use the mass media? There are two plausible and probably interrelated reasons. One deals with the characteristics of the sources themselves and the other is related to differences among people.

Mass Media versus Personal Media

The advertiser communicating with consumers through mass media is constantly trying to establish, or trying to deepen, a relationship with consumers (Bogart, 1967). However, the physical separation of the source of the message from the receiver of the message creates several distinctive differences in the efficiency of the communication, the nature of the message, and the influence of the message on consumer actions.

Relative to interpersonal sources, the mass media can communicate messages more quickly and with less effort and cost (Cox, 1963, and Howard and Sheth, 1969). But, as we saw in the previous chapter, this very characteristic shapes the nature of the message that can be communicated (Howard and

[1]The data understate consumer use of information sources for two reasons: (1) the number of individual sources used within a given type of decision was not measured and (2) no questions were asked regarding family members as sources.

Table 11-1 Type of Information Sources Used, by Total Number of Sources Consulted

	Number of types consulted			
Type of source used	One	Two	Three	Four
Advertising (newspaper, TV, magazine)	9.0%	34.7%	72.9%	100.0%
Books, pamphlets, articles	5.5	27.0	66.1	100.0
Friends, neighbors	22.0	58.1	73.7	98.7
Retail outlet	60.0	75.4	83.9	100.0
Other	3.5	4.8	3.4	1.3
Number of respondents	(199)	(167)	(118)	(77)

Source: Newman and Staelin (1973: 21).

Sheth, 1969). The message must be designed for a "typical" person, and so it may be too simple for some people, too complex for others. Since the mass media provide only one-way communication, the consumer has no chance to clarify any ambiguity. In two-way communication, the consumer can ask questions about anything he does not understand. Because the message delivered via a mass medium is restricted in content, it may not contain some item of information the consumer needs. In the two-way situation, the give-and-take of the conversation can often produce the relevant information.

These differences imply a superiority of personal sources, at least for major purchases. They help explain why the respondents shown in Table 11-1 seldom found it necessary to supplement mass media information with information from sources they considered more complete or more trustworthy.

Individual Differences

Newman and Staelin also examined individual differences in the use of information. They determined which of twenty-nine consumer characteristics discriminated between consumers who used many sources and consumers who used few sources. Their conclusion was that two general conditions explained the variations in number of sources used: (1) the buyer's ability to seek and use information; and (2) the buyer's perceived need for prepurchase information.

Ability to seek and use information was related to educational differences among the buyers in a somewhat complicated fashion. Both higher- and lower-educated respondents reported the use of fewer sources than did those with medium levels of formal schooling. Presumably, those with less education lack the ability or the desire to use many sources, while those with a great deal of education are either more confident in their ability to judge products or less concerned about the consequences of a poor decision. Those of medium levels of education both have the ability to use information and feel the need to obtain as much information as possible in order to minimize the risk of making the wrong choice.

The perceived need for information prior to purchase was related to several other variables. Lesser need for information was indicated when a buyer thought mainly of one brand or had purchased the same brand as before. Thus, prior experience, when successful, allows consumers to anticipate consequences without additional information. Conversely, a greater need for information was found where consumer characteristics indicated less experience with the brand, i.e., when consumers were switching brands, considering several brands, planning to buy several major appliances, or planning to purchase higher-priced products. Greater need for information was also found among younger families, which would be expected to have relatively little experience with appliance purchasing.

Importance of Sources

The preceding discussion implies that personal sources of information are more important than mass media in affecting consumer behavior. A substantial amount of research has addressed the question of relative effectiveness for a variety of products, including food, fashions, and major durables. Most of these studies have supported the notion of personal source superiority.[2] It should be noted, however, that the question of relative importance is extremely difficult to answer categorically. The answer can vary by type of person, by type of product, by buying situation, and even by the nature of the question put to respondents. The remainder of this chapter illustrates this complexity by describing three interpersonal communication situations that have received considerable attention in the literature: interpersonal communication among friends, interpersonal communication between members of the nuclear family, and interpersonal communication between customers and sales personnel.

INTERPERSONAL COMMUNICATION AMONG FRIENDS

Personal Influence: The Part Played by People in the Flow of Mass Communications, by Elihu Katz and Paul F. Lazarsfeld (1955), is one of the most important published studies in consumer behavior. This study showed, as had been suspected, that interpersonal communication among friends plays a major role in a great many consumer decisions, and that some consumers—the "opinion leaders"—have a more central role in this process than others.

Opinion leadership refers to the degree to which a person is able to influence informally other peoples' behavior in a desired way (Rogers and Shoemaker, 1971). Opinion leaders are those persons who seem to possess an unusual degree of this ability. They are leaders. They can affect the behavior of others toward products favorably or unfavorably. If they are cold to an idea or a new product, they can fight successfully against its adoption. If they like a new product, they can almost assure its success. Opinion leadership is, however, *informal* leadership. Opinion leaders rarely go about attempting to control the actions of others. Rather, opinion leadership is subtle; persons interacting with each other are not always aware that they are influencing or being influenced (Arndt, 1967b, and Reynolds and Darden, 1972). Moreover, it is not even necessary for persons to talk to others to influence them; their actions, if visible, can result in others' imitating their behavior. However the influence takes place—verbally, visually, or both—it is nonetheless real. In extreme cases, it can make or break a firm's product or a political party's candidate.

This knowledge had both theoretical and practical appeal to students of consumer behavior. From the theoretical point of view, the prospect of being able to identify and study opinion leaders and their followers offered new opportunities to understand the process by which information and influence are transmitted to product users. From a practical viewpoint, the fact of opinion leadership was important because it suggested that marketers might concen-

[2]See, for example, Katona and Mueller (1955), Katz and Lazarsfeld (1955), Beal and Rogers (1957), Arndt (1967a), Engel et al. (1969), and Reynolds and Darden (1972).

trate their efforts on opinion leaders and depend on this relatively small number of key individuals to persuade the rest of the population.

Mancuso (1969) reported a dramatic illustration of the practical usefulness to marketers of concentrating efforts on informal leaders. His field experiment dealt with the problem of how to popularize a record by unknown rock singers in an environment where more than 200 rock records are introduced each week. The traditional marketing approach in this industry is to try to push the product through the distribution channel by influencing disc jockeys and record stores. Mancuso tried to pull the record through the channel by trying to get informal leaders to influence their friends to demand the recording.

Mancuso obtained names and addresses of social leaders among the target market segment—class president, sports captains, cheerleaders, etc.—from high schools in the test cities. These social leaders then were contacted by mail and invited to join a "select panel" to help evaluate rock records. The introductory letter stressed to the student leader these points:

1 The student leader had been carefully selected, and the panel sponsors felt that the student, as a leader, should be better able to identify potential rock hits than the person's fellow students.

2 In return for the student's help, the student would receive free records in appreciation for this cooperation.

3 The student was encouraged to discuss these choices with friends and to weigh their opinions before submitting a final vote.

4 The student would be told something about each specific record and the recording artist. Also, *Billboard Magazine* and record stores were suggested as sources of information to verify the student's opinions and eventual choices.

5 The student was a member of a panel of leaders, and after the panel members voted would be informed of the outcome.

6 The student was under no obligation to join the panel and could withdraw from it at any time.

7 The student would be informed of any expected or unexpected results.

8 An informal two-way atmosphere was encouraged and any new ideas or suggestions would be welcomed and, if appropriate, adopted.

9 The student would be asked to answer a few simple questions each month; the results of the previous month's questionnaire would be made available to panel members.

The results? Mancuso reported that several records distributed to panel members reached the "top ten" charts in the trial cities. These hit records did not make the "top ten" selections in any other cities. Thus, the power of interpersonal communications among friends produced a hit.

The rock record example suggests more than the effectiveness of interpersonal communications. It also raises the two basic questions: (1) Can opinion leaders be identified and do they differ in other ways from the remainder of the population? (2) Can opinion leaders be reached efficiently through deliberate selection of specific promotional media? If, as in the rock record example, these questions can be answered in the affirmative, marketers can indeed concentrate their efforts on opinion leaders.

Can Opinion Leaders Be Identified?

Opinion leadership is a deceptively simple concept. It is easy to discuss but hard to measure.

When studying opinion leadership within small groups, such as the doctors associated with a single hospital, researchers often use the "sociometric" technique. Each doctor is asked to name those doctors who influenced specific decisions under specific circumstances. Doctors receiving the most mentions by other doctors are classified as influential.

When studying large groups of consumers, this approach is impractical, especially if leaders and led are distributed throughout a wide geographical area. Under these conditions, researchers usually resort to a questionnaire that asks the respondent to report his own leadership activity. This approach suffers from the tendency of some respondents to exaggerate or to minimize their own importance or simply to forget relevant transactions. Despite these handicaps, accuracy checks have indicated that the self-designation questionnaire technique is correct enough for most purposes.

Once opinion leaders have been isolated or measured, the question becomes that of identifying consumer characteristics on which they differ from the remainder of the population. From a practical point of view, one of the most basic questions to ask deals with the notion of generalized opinion leadership. That is, are consumers who are opinion leaders with respect to one product also opinion leaders with respect to others? If generalized opinion leaders exist, the job of further defining them is simplified and the task of concentrating marketing efforts tailored to this group is made less difficult.

After analyzing their data on opinion leadership in public affairs, fashion, and marketing, Katz and Lazarsfeld came to the conclusion that there is little if any overlap in opinion leadership among these three areas. A person who is an opinion leader in public affairs is neither more nor less likely to be an opinion leader in fashion or marketing. Subsequent attempts to answer this question, some of which took a second look at the original Katz and Lazarsfeld data (Marcus and Bauer, 1964), have suggested that the amount of overlap may not be exactly zero. But all research in this field has indicated that overlap in opinion leadership among areas as different as public affairs, fashion, and marketing is small.

What about within the area of marketing? A study by King and Summers (1970) that focused on opinion leadership with respect to packaged food products, women's clothing fashions, household cleansers and detergents, cosmetics and personal grooming aids, large appliances, and small apliances showed that about 13 percent of the homemakers interviewed could be classified as opinion leaders in four or more of these areas. This finding confirmed the previous research that suggested that generalized opinion leaders, if they exist at all, are few in number. However, this study also showed that overlap between some *pairs* of areas was much higher than overlap between other pairs. For instance, overlap between opinion leadership with respect to food products and opinion leadership with respect to household cleansers was much greater than overlap in opinion leadership between appliances and cosmetics. Overlap between cosmetics and fashions was much higher than overlap between cosmetics and packaged food products. And overlap between large appliances and small appliances was higher than overlap between either of these categories and any of the others. The opinion leadership scale used in the King and Summers study is shown in Figure 11-1. Their results are shown in Table 11-2.

The product categories for which overlap was found suggest "spheres of influence," in which opinion leaders expose themselves to sources of information about their areas of special interest and pass this information on to others.

A large number of subsequent studies across a large variety of consumer product areas has tended to substantiate the overall conclusion that within a

Figure 11-1 Opinion Leadership Scale

1 In general, do you like to talk about _____ with your friends?
Yes___ No___

2 Would you say you give very little information, an average amount of information, or a great deal of information about _____ to your friends?
You give very little information ___
You give an average amount of information ___
You give a great deal of information ___

3 During the past six months, have you told anyone about some _____?
Yes___ No___

4 Compared with your circle of friends, are you less likely, about as likely, or more likely to be asked for advice about _____?
Less likely to be asked ___
About as likely to be asked ___
More likely to be asked ___

5 If you and your friends were to discuss _____, what part would you be most likely to play? Would you mainly listen to your friends' ideas or would you try to convince them of your ideas?
You mainly listen to your friends' ideas ___
You try to convince them of your ideas ___

6 Which of these happens more often? Do you tell your friends about some _____, or do they tell you about some _____?
You tell them about some ___.
They tell you about some ___.

7 Do you have the feeling that you are generally regarded by your friends and neighbors as a good source of advice about _____?
Yes___ No___

Source: King and Summers (1970:45). Reprinted from *Journal of Marketing Research*, published by the American Marketing Association.

Table 11-2 Correlation Matrix of Opinion Leadership Scores

Product category	Packaged food products	Women's clothing fashions	Household cleansers and detergents	Cosmetics and personal grooming aids	Large appliances	Small appliances
Packaged food products		.32	.50	.27	.29	.32
Women's clothing fashions	.32		.33	.51	.23	.24
Household cleansers and detergents	.50	.33		.35	.31	.33
Cosmetics and personal grooming aids	.27	.51	.35		.19	.24
Large appliances	.29	.23	.31	.19		.66
Small appliances	.32	.24	.33	.24	.66	

Source: King and Summers (1970:49). Reprinted from *Journal of Marketing Research*, published by the American Marketing Association.

given sphere of influence a number of characteristics separate opinion leaders from nonleaders. For instance:

1 Opinion leaders have greater exposure to topic-relevant mass media than do their followers. Two studies of women's fashion leadership (Summers, 1970, and Reynolds and Darden, 1971) found that opinion leaders reported proportionately higher exposure to fashion-oriented media than did nonleaders, but leaders and nonleaders were about the same on exposure to other forms of mass media. This makes sense: if opinion leaders are influential, their ability to influence is in part related to their knowledge and experience about the product area. People will follow them because they perceive their advice to be sound, based on superior knowledge.

2 Opinion leaders tend to be more gregarious than nonleaders. If opinion leaders are to be effectively heard or seen, it stands to reason that they must have some direct contact and/or dialogue with those influenced. Thus, opinion leaders have been found to demonstrate their gregariousness by being more active in social and community projects and in seeking out other persons for information exchanges.

3 Opinion leaders are more interested in the area of influence than are nonleaders. Leadership, of course, is not just a matter of interest. Rather, it is interrelated to other characteristics which differentiate leaders from nonleaders. Interest, for example, might lead to higher media exposure, and interest combined with new information and a gregarious personality might lead to the initiation of conversation about the topic with persons who are also interested in the area.

4 Opinion leaders tend to interact with persons of similar but slightly lower status positions. The old adage about "birds of a feather" applies to the types of friends who will and will not interact with each other. This does not mean that people of substantially different social positions never influence each other; they obviously do. Such influence, however, is infrequent and pertains more to visual imitation than to word-of-mouth interactions.

Can Opinion Leaders Be Reached?

The second question—Can opinion leaders be reached efficiently through deliberate selection of specific advertising media?—is related to the first. Since generalized opinion leaders, if they exist at all, are few in number, there seems to be little reason to suppose that they will be more than a small proportion of the opinion leaders for any one product. However, since there is some overlap in opinion leadership among some products, it might be possible to identify the opinion leaders for closely related groups of products and attempt to select media that reach them efficiently. Even this strategy is so difficult to implement in practice that it is seldom followed.

In cases where products have an abundance of specialty media keyed to them (women's clothing fashions or sports cars, for example) opinion leaders can be reached more effectively. But for most products with broad markets and low consumer interest, marketers must use broad media schedules and trust the proclivity of the opinion leaders to seek out the information they need.

INTERPERSONAL INFLUENCE IN FAMILIES

Probably the single most influential consumer stimulus is other family members. Members of a family live together and rarely fail to talk to each other to express their views about life and the artifacts that go with it, including, of course, consumer goods.

When the consumer activities of families are considered, it is readily evident that the situation is quite complex. Breadwinners shop for and buy some products, homemakers others, children still others, and some products are bought as joint purchases involving the homemaker, the breadwinner, and sometimes the children. Moreover, in many families there is considerable interpersonal communication and influence about products regardless of who buys or who, on the surface, appears to make the decision about what to buy.

Marketers, of course, are highly interested in family members' influences on each other. It is one thing to know the characteristics and locations of the best potential families for a product. It is quite another to know to whom within these families marketing efforts should be directed. Consider, for example, the purchase of a sports jacket by the husband. One of his children might have brought up the idea that Father's coats are out of style; his wife might suggest some appropriate colors and patterns; she might even accompany him on the shopping trip and help him look around; and he might finally go back to a store to make the purchase. To whom, in this situation, should marketers direct their advertising?

The Ties That Bind

One way to approach the study of intrafamily influences is to first determine which types of families engage more frequently in mutual exchanges of information and then focus on the nature of influence by type of product within those families.

The variability of family interaction is related to the norms for behavior that family members establish to guide their decisions in recurring situations. These ties-that-bind are reflected in roles assigned to the various members of the family. Traditionally, men have played the role of "breadwinner" and have been responsible for making decisions about employment, the purchase of lawn mowers, snow shovels, car tires, and other "instrumental" things; women traditionally have taken on the household role of purchasing agent for food and items for the children and as the decider on such things as draperies for the living room windows, the style of home furnishings, and other "expressive" items; children can make certain decisions with respect to products they themselves use or own. Not all family roles, of course, are so simple or clear-cut. For example, a study of the relative influence of husbands and wives on the purchase of automobiles and living room furniture found that role structure was not an either-or situation (Davis, 1970). Responses by the husbands and wives to a series of relative-influence questions showed substantial variation within each of the product categories (see Table 11-3). These data indicate that any conclusion about "who makes the decision" depends upon exactly which decision one is talking about. The data also suggest that a considerable amount of "equal influence" interaction must take place.

A number of dimensions have been explored by consumer researchers to determine the types of families who interact more frequently and those who seemingly adhere to more rigorously defined norms for behavior. Two characteristics—stage in the family life cycle and social class—seem particularly useful in identifying interacting and noninteracting families. There is a negative relationship between interaction and stage in the life cycle. In general,

Table 11-3 Marital Roles in Selected Purchase Decisions as Perceived by 97 Wives

	Patterns of influence (percent)		
Who decided	Husband has more influence	Have equal influence	Wife has more influence
For the automobile			
When to buy it?	68%	30%	2%
Where to buy it?	59	39	2
How much to spend for it?	62	34	4
What make to buy?	50	50	—
What model to buy?	47	52	1
What color to buy?	25	63	12
For furniture			
How much to spend?	17	63	20
When to buy?	18	52	30
Where to buy?	6	61	33
What furniture to buy?	4	52	44
What style to buy?	2	45	53
What color and fabric to select?	2	24	74

Source: Davis (1970:170). Reprinted from *Journal of Marketing Research*, published by the American Marketing Association.

as the family gets older, its members tend to engage in less interaction before making decisions. Apparently, as a marriage matures, husbands and wives get to know each other and become more willing and able to establish more and firmer norms than they could during the early or "getting to know all about you" years (Blood and Wolfe, 1960; and Granbois, 1963).

There is a curvilinear relationship between family interaction and social class. Specificially there is greater interaction in middle-class families than in either lower-class families or upper-class families. In lower-class families, lack of interaction is attributed to the difficulties family members have in expressing and dealing with their problems. Upper-class families can afford to make mistakes; they can, therefore, forego extensive consultation. Middle-class families seem to represent democracy in action, with every member of the family having a vote (Komarovsky, 1961; and Wolgast, 1958).

Family Influences[3]

To illustrate the complexity of family decision making, this section explores the nature of family influence on a variety of consumer activities ranging from food shopping to vacations.

Food Shopping The homemaker frequently is depicted as the family purchasing agent. This is likely to be true for family food supplies and, as we shall see, a number of other purchase categories.

When homemakers describe their trips to the grocery store, they depict themselves as wary shoppers trying to make ends meet by shopping in a systematized, highly practical fashion. When their accounts of their activities are examined in detail, however, they emerge as sensitive compromisers working hard to keep their families happy and healthy, and quite willing to spend more than the bare minimum to achieve those goals. As a result, food shopping behavior tends to be erratic and situation-dependent—an overt manifestation of the flexibility of the pragmatist.

The mother's mix of authority and flexibility varies by family size. Mothers in large, economy-oriented families buy food preferred by the majority of family members and avoid short-order cooking. They plan their meals around the budget and their family's nutritional needs and are not easily influenced to change their practical shopping habits. In smaller families, homemakers are more careful to give everyone in the home, except themselves, a turn at having their favorite foods.

In general, family members have veto power over foods they "hate," and mothers seldom force their own food tastes on other family members. The influence of family members' preferences vary; however, women pay very close attention to their husbands' likes and dislikes. The family dinner menu in particular is very frequently planned around the father's food preferences.

[3]The material in this section is a summary of results of proprietary studies in the respective produce areas.

Meals are seldom dictated by children's food preferences, but many mothers try to serve each child his or her favorite once in a while out of a sense of fairness.

Most women seem to prefer to go grocery shopping alone. They find that when they are accompanied by either their children or their husbands they shop in a less organized manner and spend more than they had intended. Children seem to enjoy grocery shopping because they have an opportunity to exert point-of-purchase influence. They know that their requests will be successful at least some of the time, particularly when the requests are for cereals and snack foods.

The homemaker's mood on shopping day appears to be a factor in the success or failure of family members' attempts at influencing purchases. Homemakers say that fewer concessions are made when they feel tired or harassed. If, however, it has been a "leisure day," requests are granted more easily and more frequently. Many children sense the importance of this mood and know when to ask for something and when to keep quiet.

The family's influence on food choice is, of course, not limited to direct requests. While mothers sometimes choose to exert power (for a variety of reasons) by denying explicit requests, almost all of them buy products they know their families enjoy (Coulson, 1966). The idea that "I know what my family likes without being told" seems to give a woman a feeling of expertise and to reveal the summary effects of her family's influence.

Clothing Influences When asked about family influence on their clothing purhcases, women claim they dress for their husbands. Actually, the husband's influence is most usually in the form of an anticipated veto rather than a positive pressure on choice. Women seem to dress so as to avoid complaints, and beyond that they follow their own preferences. A few style-conscious, upper-middle-class men make suggestions based upon what they see women in the office or on the street wearing, but even in these cases the wives generally get what they themselves like and want even if they have to resort to gameswomanship to avoid conflict.

Children, especially teenaged girls, exert or attempt to exert a moderating force on their mothers' wardrobes. They are especially concerned that their mothers not look old-fashioned or out of style. Most teens seem to feel that they are ineffective, but they continue to make suggestions in the hope that they may have some influence.

Children exercise some influence on the choice of their own clothes. As discussed in Chapter 4, parents tend to give younger children a relatively free rein in picking their own clothing, whereas they are forced to exert more pressure to prevail with teen-age children.

Cosmetic and Toilet Articles Husbands seem to take a direct part in choosing their own toilet articles such as shampoo, after-shave lotion, shavers, and cologne. The wife will often do the actual purchasing, but the final decision seems to be based on the husband's choice, and very often the choice is based on his strong brand preference. Occasionally the product choices will be experimental, but the husband (and in some cases the son also) determines the trial products. Even with toothpaste, husbands show a greater desire to change brands than do their wives (Jaffe and Senft, 1966). Occasionally the husband's choice of product meets with resistance from his wife. Generally, however, the husband's preference results in indulgence on the wife's part. Her purchase of a requested product is calculated to fit in with her role of making her husband feel important and "special."

As with clothing, teens try to influence their mothers' choice of cosmetics. There is considerable interest in trying to change Mother's "old-fashioned" ideas. Teens seem to have more success influencing their mothers to buy face and hair care products than makeup. Again, the comparison with the purchase of clothing is clear. Eye makeup, like flashy or fad clothing, has connotations of the daughter's growing up—a process many parents wish they could retard. But interest in hair and complexion care products indicates an interest in healthy good grooming and cleanliness—traits all parents encourage, just as they encourage an interest in good taste and value in clothing.

Appliances As a rule, women play the major role in purchasing appliances. Typically, for smaller appliances such as broilers or toasters, the women will shop without their husbands. Some will discuss the decision to purchase an appliance with their husbands beforehand. However, this is usually the extent of the men's involvement.

When a large, relatively expensive item is to be purchased, most women say they would prefer having their husbands shop with them, and men show greater willingness to participate. Commercial studies have yielded many instances where husbands were present at the point-of-purchase for large appliances. Various reasons are given for the man's participation in major-appliance shopping, but the underlying reason seems to be connected with the traditional concept of the masculine role. That is, it should be up to the man to make the "big" decisions. Hence, women operate rather independently for small appliances but as a rule seek their husbands' opinion before buying expensive things.

Some women rely rather heavily on their husbands for guidance and advice in purchasing appliances. They allow their husbands to determine the brand or price of the item or even the department store at which they shop. However, most women prefer to limit the husbands' influence on appliance purchases. They enjoy having their husbands present so that they can share in the responsibility for the purchase (e.g., take the blame should something go wrong); yet they also jealously guard the prerogative to make the appliance selection. As primary users, they feel they are better judges of what will be suitable.

Part of the men's role in the appliance purchase decision is to evaluate the mechanical quality of the machine. However, the man may not make any evaluation until after his wife has made some preliminary selections. In other words, his function often is simply to apply the "seal of approval."

Women like to have their husbands along on an appliance purchasing expedition to provide the encouragement necessary to spend that "little extra" for a better appliance. They have found that their husbands say, "Get the best," or "Be sure you get the one that does everything you want it to."

In some households men serve as stumbling blocks to purchases. Resistance from the man must be broken down before the item is purchased. Hence, the male's negative or restraining influence may be just as important a consideration as, and in some cases more important then, his positive influence on purchases.

Several additional influences on the purchase of appliances should be mentioned. These influences include recommendations of *Consumer Reports* and similar publications as well as those of friends, relatives, and neighbors. It seems commonplace for people to consider information from any or all of these sources before making a final decision on a brand.

Appliances are popular gift items. In fact, some families make a practice of buying appliances only when a gift-giving occasion arises, such as Mother's Day, Christmas, or a birthday. As one women has commented, "Usually everything is a fight, unless an appliance breaks down."

Vacations Vacations are unique among the "product areas" explored in our discussion, because the concept of a vacation differs among different people. Further, more than with most other products, the planning of such a "purchase" is considered a family activity characterized by family members exerting influence on each other.

A *vacation* is generally considered to be a trip to a destination some distance from the family's home. Some people also use the term "vacation" to mean time off from their regular jobs, regardless of whether travel is involved. But, in general, a "real" vacation means going somewhere.

Who decides to take a vacation? Who plans it, where do they go, and how do they get there? What do families expect a vacation to give them? What needs does it fulfill? And, finally, who benefits most?

Both vacations and the planning that goes into them seem to be joint family decisions. Occasionally the vacation, from the first idea to the final bill, is arranged by either the husband or the wife. But as a rule vacations are negotiated. Disagreements arise, compromises are made, and only then is a final decision reached.

The types of vacations planned seem to be as individual as people themselves. The vacation appears to be a time to try to do what you have wanted to do for a long time. This is also a time to get together with families and relatives—to get families together again—a time to relax and "let down one's hair," and/or a time to see new places and have new experiences. But, as varied as their reasons are for taking a vacation, without exception most people seem to expect a vacation to be a pleasurable, happy family activity.

It is essential that all members of the family benefit from the vacation. The families that cannot decide on a single place to satisfy everyone have different methods of working out a compromise. Some allow children to pick one trip with the parents picking another. Others exclude the children from one vacation and take a second which includes the children.

It is safe to assume that no one happily chooses not to go on a vacation. And yet, each year, that decision is reached by many families. Several studies provide an insight into a few of the many reasons why families choose (or are forced) to postpone vacation plans. Some vacations are postponed by unexpected financial reversals. Others are postponed by scheduling difficulties: at the time Father gets his vacation, the children may be in school. At the height of the gasoline shortage produced by the oil producers' embargo in 1974, vacations were postponed by doubts as to the availability of fuel.

Some families have developed "vacation substitutes." Although they are unable to actually go *away* on a trip, they try to make the best of it by engaging in more local attractions. Perhaps a vacation is only a state of mind.

When vacations are taken, automobile travel is favored over air travel by young families, probably because the cost of air travel is too great and because viewing the country from an automobile is considered part of the educational aspect of a vacation. Since the auto is the frequent vacation vehicle, the gasoline shortage and Sunday closing of gasoline stations during 1974 caused a serious economic blow to facilities catering to the vacationing family.

Some Problems in Measurement

As we discussed in the previous section, information on family purchase influences can be helpful to marketers, particularly in the selection of appropriate advertising appeals—how helpful depends on the ability of researchers to measure the influencers and their influences accurately.

The most frequently used procedure for measuring influence involves asking one member of the family who in the family has the most influence or who decides what. This self-report procedure has several built-in problems: (1) Who in the family is most knowledgeable about the relative amount of influence within the family? (2) Will this person willingly and truthfully describe variations in influence? (3) Is the person able to recall accurately how influence was distributed during some previous set of family interactions? and (4) Should the person be asked general or specific questions about influence? (Ferber, 1955: Kenkel, 1961; and Davis, 1971).

Students of consumer behavior have examined the first problem by interviewing husbands and wives at the same time but in different locations and then measuring the degree of similarity of their responses. Such studies show that the responses of husbands and wives are very similar when compared on an aggregate basis but dissimilar on a within-family basis (Davis, 1971). That is, data collected from husbands agree with data collected from wives when all the husbands are considered together and compared with all the wives considered together, but there is likely to be substantial disagreement within individual husband-wife pairs. Most marketers are interested in the general question of degree of influence because they wish to know where they should direct their marketing efforts. They are therefore encouraged by the aggregate-level agreement between data obtained from husbands and data obtained from wives. On the other hand, students of consumer behavior who are interested in untangling the process of husband-wife interaction, and therefore need to know which individuals are influential and which are not, find the within-pair disagreements discouraging.

Why do within-pair disagreements occur? Since family members willingly admit to variations in influence, they probably answer truthfully as they perceive the truth. The problem appears to be a matter of perceptions. Moreover, the environment surrounding the interview may affect respondents' perceptions of reality. O'Rourke (1963), for example, who measured family interactions both in the home and in a laboratory, found that husbands were ascribed more power in the more insecure environment than in the home.

The third question—the question of accuracy of recall—has not been examined formally in the context of family interactions. But, as with most recall questions, the nearer in time to the interaction, the better the recall. And since relatively few persons are in the market on a given day, it is necessary to use fairly large samples to find families that recently made a given purchase.

The fourth problem has been explored by Davis (1971). He concludes that more specific questions are better than general influence questions. Thus, instead of asking,

> When important purchasing decisions have to be made in your family, how do you make these decisions?
>
> **a** I usually decide without consulting my wife (husband).
> **b** My wife (husband) and I discuss the situation and then I make the final decision.
> **c** My wife (husband) and I discuss the situation and then we both make the final decision.
> **d** My wife (husband) and I discuss the situation and then she (he) makes the final decision.
> **e** She (he) usually decides without consulting me.

ask,

> Who decided:
>
> **a** When the car would be purchased?
> **b** How much money would be spent for the car?
> **c** What make of car would be purchased?
> **d** What model to get?
> **e** What color to get?
> **f** Where the car would be purchased?
> **g** Who made the initial suggestion to buy a new car? (Davis, 1971:308).

CUSTOMER-SALESPERSON INTERACTION

Among the stimuli that influence consumers, some of the most powerful come from personal contacts with salespersons. The stimuli delivered by advertising, packages, or displays may or may not be appropriate to the individual decision, but the stimuli delivered by salespeople can always be tailored to meet the needs of the moment.

Because of this trait, salespersons are an important element of our society and in our economy. They play a significant role in our lives in that they directly affect our standard of living, influence the structure of our society, and help determine what directions we will follow in the future (Woolman, 1970). Salespersons are particularly important to those firms who need the personal touch to reach consumers.

Salespersons have evolved styles and techniques that follow two related but somewhat different patterns.

In the "stimulus and response" approach, illustrated in Chapter 1 by the contact between the La Mottas and Peter Marks, the salesperson is carefully trained to follow a sequence of steps designed to get attention, arouse interest, stimulate desire, and get buying action. The salesperson is allowed to deviate from the memorized presentation to take advantage of customers' remarks and to answer questions, but the presentation itself is not the salesperson's creation. Rather, it is painstakingly designed, polished, and tested to bring the prospect through the AIDA steps—attention, interest, desire, and action. This approach is more frequently employed when the product is standardized, when large numbers of salespeople must be trained to sell it, and when an immediate sale can be expected.

The second approach is sometimes called "need satisfaction." Following this approach, the salesperson attempts to identify the customer's needs and to show how the product in question can meet these needs better than the products offered by competition. The need satisfaction approach is most frequently used when the product can be tailored to suit the consumer's needs, when a very limited group of potential customers require technical information about an expensive product, and when there is a good chance that the purchasing decision will be carefully considered over an extended time period.

Regardless of the approach used, the salesperson typically has the initiative in the actual sales interview. Usually the salesperson opens the interview and the prospective customer responds in some way (including silence). The salesperson then finds it necessary to reply; and so the process goes, with the customer and salesperson interacting with each other.

The acid test of a salesperson's ability is the person's degree of maintaining the initiative—of controlling the sales interview without seeming to. In one carefully conducted study of the interactions between customers and retail appliance salespersons, it was found that salespersons acting within the context of their selling environment do appear to control the interaction: "Whether he is aware of it or not, by virtue of his patterning of interaction and his response to customer interaction" (Willett and Pennington, 1966:611). This does not mean that the buyer is a passive respondent to the salesperson. If that were the case, there would be a much higher closing rate and probably a lot fewer salespersons. Rather, the salesperson's ability to control the sales process is related to the ability to pay attention to what the customer says and does and how the customer says it and does it and to understand why the consumer is reacting so. After correctly observing and interpreting the customer's reaction, the salesperson must do and/or say something which will influence the prospect to move toward the close. Again, this must be accomplished subtly, for the salesperson usually cannot "tell" the customer; it is necessary to get the prospective buyer to say the things the salesperson would like to say (Cash and Crissy, 1969).

This covert control is modified to some extent by the selling environment and the corresponding expectations consumers have about salespersons behavior. Whyte (1948) demonstrated this point in his classic study of human relations in restaurants. He concluded that the customer-waitress relationship varied with the standing of the restaurant. In lower-standard restaurants, the relationship was highly informal. The waitresses "put the customer in his place" if he did not conform to standards of behavior acceptable to the waitresses. Relations were more formal in higher-standard restaurants: waitresses had to supress their desire to "talk back" to customers.

Tucker has also noted that the nature of the customer-salesperson relationship varies with the selling environment. He classified furniture stores into three classes (the "borax," which appeal to lower-class customers; the "fashionable," which appeal to upper-middle-class consumers; and the "high fashion," which are characterized by offering the services of interior designers) and commented on the variation in relations with each class:

> In the first type of store, the salesman is apt to be forceful, dynamic, and just a bit brusque. He may play the part of a tipster on price or be obsequious. In order to speed up the customer's reaction, he may rely heavily on the role of a busy businessman who is impatient with a relatively unimportant sale. He is quite likely to let the customer know that he has superior information and taste and that his word should, therefore, be taken as law on the matter. . . .
>
> The salesman in the second type of store is much more likely to be friendly, treating his customers as equals, deferring to their opinions. He is probably less certain of his own ability to judge what is in good taste than is the salesman in either the high-fashion or the "borax" store, because a number of his customers look down on the kind of furniture he has in his own home. . . . He is much more likely than a "borax" salesman to talk about matters unassociated with furniture, discovering what the customer's job is, and discussing events of common interest. He wants to be liked and makes a point of finding some common ground with the customer.
>
> The salesman in the high-fashion shop generally knows furniture construction, fabrics and current fashion better than do his customers, and has complete confidence in his own judgments. If a lower-class customer enters the store by mistake, he will be warned off rapidly but subtly. Unlike the salesman in the middle-class store, the high-fashion salesman does not attempt to establish casual

> friendship with the customer. His talk is all of furniture and decoration, with emphasis on the esthetic rather than on the practical elements of construction. He wishes to be regarded as a specialist and makes his expertise known (Tucker, 1964:74–75).

The effectiveness of the salesperson during the interaction process is also related to the degree the customer and the salesperson are similar in certain relevant characteristics. Probably the most significant study in this regard is Evans's study of insurance agents. He examined the characteristics of insurance agents, of 168 purchasers of insurance, and of 183 unsold prospects. He concluded:

> The more alike the salesman and his prospect are, the greater the likelihood for a sale. This is true for physical characteristics (age, height), other objective factors (income, religion and education) and variables that may be related to personality factors (smoking, politics). It is also important to note that the perceived similarity for religion and politics is much higher and of greater importance than the true similarity (Evans, 1963:79).

It should be emphasized that salesperson effectiveness is related to similar characteristics relevant to the buying situation. These characteristics obviously vary by products, environments, and a host of other factors, including the personalities of the consumers themselves. Substantial research is required to isolate the relevant characteristics for various situations before this generalization can be useful for salesperson selection on a wide scale. Until such research is conducted, the knowledge that customer-salesperson similarity leads to more effective selling should prove at least intuitively useful for personnel selection.

Truth in Selling

The manager of a local office of a major stock brokerage firm once said, "The only thing I can't offer my account executives that the vice-presidents of the bank across the street have is prestige. But my men make a . . . lot more money." This statement reflects a widespread sentiment among people that personal selling as an occupation, regardless of the titles sales personnel are given, has low prestige relative to other "white-collar" and some "blue-collar" occupations.

Salespersons often are depicted as using misinformation or as withholding relevant information in their attempts to make a sale. In other words, salespersons are denounced for not telling the truth or, at best, for not telling the whole truth. The untrustworthiness of salespersons shows up quite clearly in the bipolar adjective profile of door-to-door salespersons in Figure 11-2.

There is little doubt that consumers tend to have negative attitudes toward salespersons, particularly high-pressure and door-to-door persons who employ "stimulus-response" selling. And, as Jolson (1971) has pointed out, some of the charges against salespersons are justified: "The findings indicate that some direct selling firms train their representatives to misrepresent." Not all of the

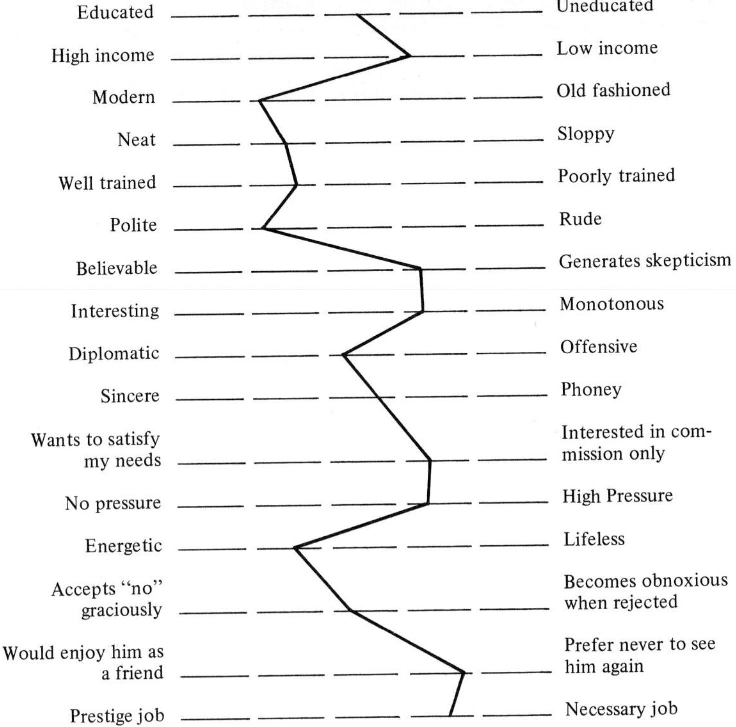

Figure 11-2 Profile of the direct salesperson as perceived by the consumer. *Source:* Jolson (1971:177).

charges are justified, however: "Most direct salespeople are trained by their firms to transmit only true, correct statements to the consumer." Unfortunately, though, even when a salesperson makes no statement that is literally false, the AIDA steps may be so designed as to create a wholly false impression, as in the La Motta illustration in Chapter 1.

Because "stimulus-response" selling is so frequently deceptive, and because it works best among those members of the consumer population who are least capable of seeing through the deception (and least able to help themselves if they eventually do see through it), attempts are frequently made to regulate salespersons' activities by legal means. Enforcement is extremely difficult, however, even in the most blatant cases, and some twenty-two states have therefore passed "cooling-off period" laws which permit a consumer to disown a contract he has signed if he thinks better of it within a specified time period—usually, within one to four days (see Table 11-4). Even this measure is frequently ineffective. Having been persuaded that a purchase is desirable, the consumer may avoid all contrary evidence, and may go on believing that he was fortunate indeed to "have been selected." And even if the consumer could be expected to make effective use of his cancellation privilege, there are many ways unscrupulous firms can avoid the provisions of the law: in using written

Table 11-4 Contract Recision Statutes Enacted: July 1, 1969[1]

State and year enacted	Length of cooling-off period	Applicable to cash sales as well as installment sales	Notice to buyer required in contract	Registered or certified mail required to notify seller	Delivery negates right of recision	Penalty for cancellation
Connecticut: 1967 (Amended, 1969)[1]	Three business days	No	Yes	Yes	No	Yes
Georgia: 1967	One business day	No	No	Yes	No	Yes
Hawaii: 1967 (Amended, 1969)	Three business days	No	Yes	Yes	No	Yes
Illinois: 1967	Three business days	Yes ($50 minimum)	No	No	No	No
Indiana: 1969	Two business days	Yes ($50 minimum)	Yes	No	No	No
Maine: 1969	Three business days	Yes ($25 minimum)	Yes	No	No	No
Massachusetts: 1966	One business day	No	Yes	Yes	Yes	No
New Hampshire: 1969	Four days	No	Yes	Yes	No	No
New Jersey: 1968	Two business days	No	No (Notice to appear on "receipt")	Yes	No	No
Oklahoma: 1969 (UCCC)[2]	Three business days	No	Yes	No	No	Yes
Pennsylvania: 1968	Two business days	Yes ($25 minimum)	No	No	No	No
Rhode Island: 1968	Three business days	No	Yes	Yes	No	Yes
Utah: 1969 (UCCC)[2]	Three business days	No	Yes	No	No	Yes
Vermont: 1967 (Amended, 1969)	One business day	Yes	No	Yes	Yes	No
Washington: 1967	One business day	No	Yes	Yes	Yes	Yes

[1] All statutes and amendments will be in effect on or before October 1, 1969.
[2] The recision statutes are a part of the Uniform Commercial Credit Code adopted by these states.

Source: Walker and Ford (1970:54). Reprinted from *Journal of Marketing*, published by the American Marketing Association.

sales contracts, making immediate delivery, delaying delivery until after the cooling-off period, and taking the customer to a "temporary store" to sign the installment contract (Walker and Ford, 1970).

The Federal Trade Commission can hold firms accountable for the misrepresentations of their sales personnel. This is true even for cases where the company either does not condone or does, in fact, condemn such practices. As with deceptive advertising, the FTC can employ any of three procedures to bring a deceptive selling practice to a halt: (1) voluntary compliance, (2) consent order, and (3) full adjudication. It may even become possible for the FTC to issue Trade Regulation Rules which require door-to-door salespersons to tell consumers orally and in writing that they have three days to obtain a full refund if they change their minds about a purchase. Whether or not the Commission has the authority to issue such regulations, however, has not yet been decided in federal courts.

On a more positive side, the adoption of the marketing concept by many firms has tempered many of these problems. In one study, for example, a national sample of business executives from *Fortune's* "500" companies were asked their opinions about the marketing concept. Over 70 percent of the 203 respondents agreed with the statement, "The marketing concept has forced advertising and personal selling to become more informative and helpful to consumers" (Barksdale and Darden, 1971).

Measuring Sales Performance

Although salespeople typically do not have subordinates, they almost always have superiors who are responsible for their behavior during the sales interview. One such monitoring program is the one used by Montgomery Ward to encourage better performance of their store salespersons. Each month, Ward's gives sixty women $25 each to use in making purchases in a Ward's store. Their instructions are to (1) avoid the busiest periods, (2) be nice and not look for trouble, and (3) ask for the lowest-priced items in each department to see if the salespeople will try to trade them up. At the end of their shopping "spree" the women make a written report to the district manager of Ward's on each salesperson with whom they interacted. The reports are published in a monthly magazine. In each report, salespersons are graded on courtesy and helpfulness (which are attributes Ward's feels are good for the customer) and on their attempts to sell higher-quality items and to suggest related items (attempts which are good for Montgomery Ward). Salespeople with perfect scores get a ten dollar prize; those who fall short receive caustic comments in the monthly house organ. Some typical reports, grades, and managerial comments:

> The saleslady asked, "May I help you?" I inquired about men's shorts. She explained the three grades of merchandise and explained why the best quality was worth buying. I selected them and she asked if I needed T-shirts or socks. She asked if I was putting the items on my charge and when I said I didn't have one, she asked if I would like to open one. She gave me a form to complete, thanked me and said, "Come again."
> Grade: 100 percent. Comment: It is superfluous to comment on perfection.

> The salesman was very friendly. I asked for some good car wax and he showed me a brand telling me how good it was and how easy to apply. I said I would try it and

he rang up the sale and thanked me. He failed to suggest related merchandise or credit. He was very polite and helpful.

Grade: 50 percent. Comment. How can the shopper describe this salesman as helpful? Car wax needs an applicator. You can't apply car wax with some old toothbrush. If the shopper were really going to use this on her own car, she would be furious with the salesman, after she started to work on the car, because he had failed to suggest the additional equipment necessary to apply the car wax. Always remember that you are doing the customer a favor when you suggest merchandise that he needs to complete his job.

The saleslady asked to help me. I picked out some washcloths and said I would take them. She said, "Will that be all today?" When I said, "I guess so," she asked if the sale would be cash or charge. I said, "Cash, I don't have a charge." She rang up the sale and thanked me.

Grade: 40 percent. Comment: This "selling" effort does not rate more than 10 percent, if that. This is the type of "salesmanship" which causes the operators of our company (and all companies) to study the feasibility of coin-operated dispensers.

I looked around and no one approached me. I finally selected a pair of socks and took them to the salesman. He told me the amount of the sale, rang it up and thanked me. Did not greet me, suggest better merchandise or related items or credit.

Grade: Zero. Comment: This salesman is an experienced department manager. Everyone should study his technique. But do not consider this technique as a method to follow for advancement in the company. We do not promote people into department managers because of their pretty brown eyes or because they play golf with the boss. Then just how did this guy make it to department manager?

The saleslady was talking to a friend and after about ten minutes she asked to help me. I asked for a pair of ladies' briefs. She got them for me and said, "Will that be one pair?" I said, "Yes, " she rang up the sale and thanked me. She didn't suggest related items or credit. We seemed to be interrupting her visiting.

Grade: Zero. Comment: And it rated zero. With the economy the way it has been, how can any of us be so thoughtless as to ignore a customer? We need all the customers we can bring into the store and we can't have anyone irritate a potential customer. Remember, when we ignore a customer in one department, she will be mad all day and if she remained in the store she could be mad at 44 different departments. Does any one person have the privilege of making all of her fellow employees unhappy because she chose to insult one customer? (Herndon, 1972: 127–129).

A method of evaluation such as Ward's Courtesy Shopper Program has an intuitive appeal in that it measures consumers' perceptions of salespeople during the sales process.

Most sales research, however, does not examine the sales process, even in a rudimentary manner. Rather, typical "sales" research is actually research which focuses on the results of the sales processes—the transactions—and seeks to develop sales goals or standards of performance with which the actual performance of salespersons is compared for purposes such as redefining sales territories, determining the number of customers per day a salesperson should call upon, and so forth. While standards of performance are necessary to sales managers, research that is limited to measuring standards provides little insight into customer-salespersons interaction as a dyadic process.

SUMMARY

Consumers vary in the types and number of sources of information they consult when they need information for reaching a purchasing decision. Because of the nature of information sources, consumers seldom find it necessary to consult the mass media after personal sources have been consulted, and they often find it necessary to supplement mass media information with information from sources they consider more complete or more trustworthy. Variations in information seeking also depend on consumers' abilities to seek and use information and their perceptions of the need for prepurchase information.

Because of the important role played by personal sources of information, considerable attention has been devoted to three interpersonal communication situations. Interpersonal communication among friends focuses on the concept of opinion leadership and on opinion leaders. The concept recognizes that friends interact, informally, and influence takes place. Opinion leaders can be located in the population by the sociometric or the self-designation technique. Their influence is limited to one or a few related topics of interest about which they expose themselves to sources of information. Opinion leaders differ from nonleaders on a number of important dimensions: they are more exposed to topic-relevant mass media; they are more gregarious and more interested in the area of influence; and they usually interact with persons of similar but slightly lower-status positions.

In examining interpersonal influence in families, it is useful to first determine which types of families engage more frequently in mutual exchanges of information and then to focus on the nature of influence by type of product within those families. The variability of family interaction is related to norms for behavior as reflected in roles assigned to the various members of the family. Some families adhere to rigorously defined norms and interact less frequently, while others interact more frequently. In general, younger families tend to interact more frequently than older families, and lower- and upper-class families tend to interact less frequently than middle-class families. The context of family influence was demonstrated in the chapter by discussing family decision making on a variety of consumer activities. While information on family purchase influences can be helpful to marketers, there remain several problems in measuring this influence.

Some of the most powerful stimuli that influence consumers come from personal contacts with salespersons. Salespersons use different styles and influence strategies, such as the "stimulus-response" and the "need satisfaction" approaches, to maintain the initiative in a sales situation. The salesperson's ability to maintain the initiative is modified by the selling environment, consumers' expectations of the salesperson's behavior, and the degree of customer-salesperson similarity on certain relevant characteristics.

REVIEW QUESTIONS

1 How do the differences between mass media and interpersonal communication affect the efficiency of communication, the nature of the message, and the influence on consumer behavior?
2 Consumers turn to different information sources and use different numbers of information sources. Discuss two general consumer conditions which help explain these variations in information seeking behavior.
3 Define opinion leadership. Would the individual who is an opinion leader in the area of food products be expected to be an opinion leader in the area of cosmetics? Why or why not?
4 Describe the techniques used to identify opinion leaders. In what situations are the techniques applicable? How do opinion leaders differ from nonleaders?
5 In what situations is the strategy of reaching opinion leaders likely to be effective and feasible?
6 Discuss the effects that family life cycle and social class have on interaction between family members. Which types of families exhibit the most interaction between members?
7 The influence of individual family members on buying decisions is related to product class. Identify the product classes which are the "respective spheres of influence" of mothers, fathers, and children. Do most product decisions involve the wishes of more than one family member, at least on an implicit basis? Using food purchases as an example, illustrate how this is, or is not, the case.
8 What procedure is most frequently used to measure influence within the family? Identify the problems inherent in this method and tell how they have been resolved by students of consumer behavior.
9 Why is the influence of salespersons so powerful when compared with other consumer stimuli, such as advertising? What are the two basic approaches used by salespersons to influence consumers? Are they equally effective in every situation? Why or why not?
10 Does the selling environment influence customer-salesperson interaction? If so, how? Why does "truth in selling" offer advantages for the marketer as well as the consumer?
11 Discuss the method discussed for measuring sales performance. Do you agree that better methods are needed? Why or why not?

EXERCISE

Below are some decision areas and consumer activities. Select those you have been involved in recently and report your perceptions of the major consumer stimuli affecting the specific decisions that had to be made. Compare your perceptions with those of other students in the class—do any patterns emerge that would indicate to whom marketers should address their efforts? (To simplify comparisons, it would be useful to develop a checklist of questions for each decision with a place to code the influential stimulus.)

Decision Areas and Activities

1 New or used car purchase
2 Shoes
3 Jeans
4 Hairspray
5 Stereo
6 TV
7 Vacation
8 Cookies
9 Fast-food restaurant
10 Odd jobs
11 Meal preparation
12 Attending a movie

REFERENCES

Arndt, John. "Role of Product-Related Conversations in the Diffusion of a New Product." *Journal of Marketing Research*, 4 (August 1967a), 291–295.

———. *Word of Mouth Advertising*. New York: Advertising Research Foundation, 1967b.

Bales, Robert F. *Interaction Process Analysis: A Method for the Study of Small Groups*. Reading, Mass.: Addison-Wesley, 1950.

———. "Some Uniformities of Behavior in Small Social Systems." In G. E. Swanson, T. M. Newcomb, and E. L. Hartley (eds.), *Readings in Social Psychology*. 2d ed. New York: Holt, 1952.

Barksdale, Hiram C. and Bill R. Darden. "Marketers' Attitudes toward the Marketing Concept." *Journal of Marketing*, 35 (October 1971), 29–36.

Beal, George M. and Everett M. Rogers. "Information Sources in the Adoption Process of New Fabrics." *Journal of Home Economics*, 49 (1957), 630–634.

Blood, Robert O., Jr., and Donald M. Wolfe. *Husbands and Wives: The Dynamics of Married Living*. Glencoe, Ill.: Free Press, 1960.

Bogart, Leo. *Strategy in Advertising*. New York: Harcourt, Brace & World, 1967.

Cash, Harold C. and W. J. E. Crissy. "Strategy *vs.* Tactics in Selling." In R. F. Gwinner and E. M. Smith (eds.), *Sales Strategy: Cases and Readings*. New York: Appleton-Century-Crofts, 1969.

Cotham, James C., III. "Selecting Salesman: Approaches and Problems." *MSU Business Topics*, 18 (Winter 1970), 64–72.

Coulson, John S. "Buying Decisions within the Family and the Consumer-Brand Relationship." In J. W. Newman (ed.), *On Knowing the Consumer*. New York: Wiley, 1966.

Cox, Donald L. "The Audience as Communicators." In S. A. Greyser (ed.), *Toward Scientific Marketing*. Chicago: American Marketing Association, 1963.

Davis, Harry L. "Dimensions of Marital Roles in Consumer Decision Making." *Journal of Marketing Research*, (May 1970), 168–177.

———. "Measurement of Husband-Wife Influence in Consumer Purchase Decisions." *Journal of Marketing Research,* 8 (August 1971), 305–314.

The Editors of *The Wall Street Journal, How They Sell.* New York: Dow Jones & Co., 1965.

Engel, James F., Roger D. Blackwell, and Robert J. Kegerreis. "How Information Is Used to Adopt an Innovation." *Journal of Advertising Research,* 9 (December 1969), 3–8.

Evans, Franklin B. "Selling as a Dyadic Relationship: A New Approach." *American Behavioral Scientist,* 6 (May 1963), 76–79.

Ferber, Robert. "On the Reliability of Purchase Influence Studies." *Journal of Marketing,* 19 (January 1955), 225–232.

Granbois, Donald H. "The Role of Communication in the Family Decision-Making Process." In S. A. Greyser (ed.), *Toward Scientific Marketing.* Chicago: American Marketing Association, 1963.

Herndon, Booton. *Satisfaction Guaranteed.* New York: McGraw-Hill, 1972.

Howard, John A. and Jagdish N. Sheth. *The Theory of Buyer Behavior.* New York: Wiley, 1969.

Jaffe, Lawrence J. and Henry Senft. "The Roles of Husbands and Wives in Purchasing Decisions." In L. Adler and J. Crespi (eds.), *Attitude Research at Sea.* Chicago: American Marketing Association, 1966.

Jolson, Marvin A. "Consumer and Sales Force Perceptions of Direct Selling: Is Conflict Inevitable?" *Proceedings,* 2d Annual Conference, Association for Consumer Research, 1971.

Katona, George C. and Eva Mueller. "A Study of Purchase Decisions." In L. H. Clark (ed.), *Consumers' Behavior: The Dynamics of Consumer Reactions.* Vol. 1. New York: New York University Press, 1955.

Katz, Elihu and Paul F. Lazarsfeld. *Personal Influence.* Glencoe: Free Press, 1955.

Kenkel, William F. "Family Interaction in Decision-Making on Spending." In N. F. Foote (ed.), *Household Decision-Making.* New York: New York University Press, 1961.

King, Charles W. and John O. Summers. "Overlap of Opinion Leadership across Consumer Product Categories." *Journal of Marketing Research,* 7 (February 1970), 43–50.

Komarovsky, Mirra. "Class Differences in Family Decision Making on Expenditures." In N. F. Foote (ed.), *Household Decision-Making.* New York: New York University Press, 1961.

Mancuso, Joseph R. "Why Not Create Opinion Leaders for New Product Introductions?" *Journal of Marketing,* 33 (July 1969), 20–25.

Marcus, Alan S. and Raymond A. Bauer. "Yes: There Are Generalized Opinion Leaders." *Public Opinion Quarterly,* 28 (Winter 1968), 628–632.

Montgomery, David B. and Alvin J. Silk. "Clusters of Consumer Interests and Opinion Leaders' Spheres of Influence." *Journal of Marketing Research,* 8 (August 1971), 317–321.

Nelson, John L. "The Low Prestige of Personal Selling." *Journal of Marketing,* 29 (October 1965), 7–10.

Newman, Joseph W. and Richard Staelin. "Information Sources of Durable Goods." *Journal of Advertising Research,* 13 (April 1973), 19–30.

O'Rourke, John F. "Field and Laboratory: The Decision-Making Behavior of Family Groups in Two Experimental Conditions." *Sociometry,* 27 (December 1963), 422–435.

Reynolds, Fred D. and William R. Darden. "Mutually Adaptive Effects of Interpersonal Communication." *Journal of Marketing Research,* 8 (November 1971), 449–454.

——— and ———. "Why the Midi Failed." *Journal of Advertising Research,* 12 (August 1972), 39–46.

Rogers, Everett M. and F. Floyd Shoemaker. *Communication of Innovations: A Cross-Cultural Approach.* New York: Free Press, 1972.

Summers, John O. "The Identity of Women's Clothing Fashion Opinion Leaders." *Journal of Marketing Research,* 7 (May 1970), 178–185.

Tucker, W. T. *The Social Context of Economic Behavior.* New York: Holt, 1964.

Walker, Orville C., Jr. and Neil M. Ford. "Can 'Cooling-off Laws' Really Protect the Consumer?" *Journal of Marketing,* 34 (April 1970), 53–58.

Whyte, William F. *Human Relations in the Restaurant Industry.* New York: McGraw-Hill, 1948.

Willett, Ronald P. and Allan L. Pennington. "Customer and Salesman: The Anatomy of Choice and Influence in a Retail Setting." In R. M. Haas (ed.), *Science Technology and Marketing.* Chicago: American Marketing Association, 1966.

Wolgast, Elizabeth. "Do Husbands or Wives Make the Purchasing Decisions?" *Journal of Marketing,* 23 (October 1958), 151–158.

Woolman, Lewis H. *Salesmanship: Concepts and Strategies.* Belmont, Calif.: Wadsworth, 1970.

Chapter 12

New Product Purchasing Behavior

From the marketer's point of view, one of the most critical aspects of consumer behavior is the acceptance or rejection of new products. New products often fail, and failures are so expensive that a series of unsuccessful new product ventures can put a company out of business.

With new products so risky, it might seem that the safest course would be to stand pat with a successful product line. But if a company does stand pat, the probability is very high that competitors will introduce enough improvements to capture its market. Producers of consumer goods and services must innovate to survive.

Consumers are not affected as suddenly or as drastically by new product failures or successes, but they have a stake in this process, too. Unsuccessful new products add to the cost of doing business, and thus ultimately to the prices consumers pay. Successful new products add to the customer's range of choice; sometimes they fill an important and previously unfilled need.

THE DEFINITION PROBLEM

One of the problems that plague research on the introduction and diffusion of new products is the problem of definition. Just what is a new product, and what is not? Is a new detergent with "magic whiteners" a new product? How about toothpaste with flouride? Was color television a new product, or merely a variation of black-and-white TV? How about the wristwatch when it supplanted the pocket watch? Or the steel plow, which gained acceptance gruadually as farmers became convinced that a steel blade would not poison the soil? Several authorities (Rogers, 1962; Zaltman and Stiff, 1973) define a *new product* as anything consumers perceive as new. While this definition is essentially correct, it omits a number of important considerations.

As a partial answer to the definition problem, students of the diffusion process have attempted to classify innovations according to the amount of change they bring about (Alderson, 1965). The impact of an innovation on consumer behavior can be thought of in terms of a continuum ranging from innovations like the wheel, which have changed the lives of all mankind, to innovations that have little or no impact except for a small segment of society. Robertson (1969) has attempted to represent this continuum by dividing it into three categories:

1 *Continuous innovations.* Innovations that have little effect on consumption patterns other than encouraging consumers to switch from brand to brand. New brands of established grocery products, new cigarette brands, and the annual new-model automobile change-overs are examples.

2 *Dynamically continuous innovations.* Innovations that encourage a different way of using an existing product. Electric toothbrushes, videotelephones, lightweight cassette tape recorders are innovations of this type.

3 *Discontinuous innovations.* Innovations that require or produce new behavior patterns that affect other areas of the consumer's life: retirement communities, checking accounts, the automobile, the mobile home, in-home shopping via TV.

These categories are not entirely satisfactory, for a product that is continuous for one consumer may be discontinuous for another; but they do serve to identify a dimension that provides some help in predicting how readily a new product will be accepted. In general, the more discontinuous the innovation, the harder its introduction will be.

Another part of the definition problem is: At what point in the development of a new product is the product to be considered "a product"? Is it a product when it is at the "seriously considered idea" stage? When prototypes have been made? When it is in test market?

If "continuous" innovations are counted as new products, and if a product is counted as a product even when it is at the "seriously considered idea" stage, the failure rate for new products is exceedingly high. One careful study of product innovation in the food industry, for example, showed that out of every 1,000 new product ideas:

810 are rejected at the idea stage
135 are rejected on the basis of production tests

12 are discontinued after test marketing
43 are introduced to the market
36 remain on the market after introduction (Buzzell and Nourse, 1967).

With a failure rate like this, it is easy to see why so much attention has been paid to the consumer's acceptance of new ideas.

THE ORIGIN OF NEW PRODUCTS

New product ideas come from a variety of sources, all of which have contributed some notable successes and some rather spectacular flops.

Independent Inventors

The classic source is the independent inventor. At one time the American dream of Horatio Alger—the man with the idea that will make him rich—was frequently realized, and a large number of new products came into being this way. Over the past few decades, however, this dream appears to be dying. In 1950, for example, figures from the U.S. Patent Office show that 45 percent of all patents were issued to individuals. By 1970, this figure had dropped to 22 percent, with the remainder of the patents going to companies, corporations, and the government.

Jacob Robinow, Director of the U.S. Office of Invention and Innovation, has suggested two reasons for the relative decline of the individual inventor and the rise of the corporate inventor. In the first place, the individual who has an idea usually does not have the money for research and development necessary to get the idea translated into a marketable product. Secondly, the cost of obtaining a patent is becoming prohibitive. Robinow said: "The more complicated the machine, the more it will cost. It could realistically be $1,500 to $2,000 and if the inventor runs into interference (e.g., court litigation), it could run into many thousands of dollars" (Cimons, 1973).

Company Laboratories

Most large companies maintain extensive research laboratories dedicated to new product development. Occasionally the laboratory produces a technological improvement on an established product that does not degrade its other desirable qualities and does not increase its cost. If the innovation is continuous—if it does not require restructuring of significant habit patterns—it is almost assured of success. Nylon, synthetic detergents, long-playing micro-groove phonograph records, ball-point pens, transistorized radios, and plastic laminated counter tops are innovations of this kind.

A second, more common, laboratory contribution is a technological improvement that either increases the product's cost or degrades its quality of some dimension consumers consider important. Stereo records, sanitary napkins, the automatic transmission for automobiles, and color television sets are familiar examples of increased-cost innovations; cakes made from prepared mixes, "simulated leather" photograph album covers, artifical Christmas trees, and stainless steel "silverware" are examples of innovations that are inferior in some respects to the products they are intended to replace. In general, if an increased-cost innovation is to gain acceptance, it must provide some feature that is so desirable to consumers that they are willing to "trade off" the higher price for the feature. Some innovations of this type become so widely adopted that they become the accepted standard and the less expensive items they replaced pass from the scene. When there is a genuine degradation in some desirable attribute, however, the most common outcome is that the old product and the new product continue to exist, with adoption of the new never quite complete.

Ivory Soap: A Company "Invention" In 1878 White Soap, the forerunner of Ivory, was one of the twenty-four varieties manufactured by Procter and Gamble. One day the worker in charge of a blending machine forgot to turn off the steam power when he went to lunch, and an unintended amount of air was shipped into the mixture. Customers who received the accidental batch began to call for more of "that soap that floats," and thereafter the accident was deliberately repeated.

The first batch was an accident, but the rest of the invention of the product was not. Buoyancy was a product advantage, for in 1878 wash water piped in from rivers was often murky, and a sunken cake of soap was hard to find. But Harley Procter felt that he also needed a dramatic statement for advertising and a more interesting name for the brand. The statement appeared with samples sent to chemical laboratories for analysis produced reports that the product was "$99^{44}/_{100}\%$ pure"; the name came from the Bible, Psalms 45:8: "All thy garments smell of myrrh, and aloes, and cassia, out of the ivory palaces, whereby they have made thee glad."

The final element was added to the Ivory image when the company used verse and humor and art work by first-rate illustrators to place the brand into a warm and friendly context—at a time when most advertisers were still using small-space, small-print announcement.

Thus Ivory was a modest continuous innovation—a technological improvement on an existing product that did not increase its cost. Note, however, that the physical change in the product was not the only ingredient (and maybe not the major ingredient) in the brand's success.

Conjectural Interdependence

Another source of new products—or, at least, new styles—is "conjectural interdependence" among designers and producers. Because of the long lead times required by the manufacturing process, product designers are continually on the alert for the first signs of any change in consumers' preferences. When such signs do appear, and when designers and producers assume that their competitors are also reading the same signs, they may all react in the same way, and consumers are confronted with an abrupt change in the products offered for sale.

One example of this phenomenon is the rapid diffusion through the automobile industry of the "wide C-post" style (Reynolds, 1965). The roof and glass area of an automobile are ordinarily supported by three posts or pillars on each side, designaged "A," "B," and "C" from the front to rear. Except for luxury limousines designed to provide privacy for the rear passengers, the first postwar cars with wide C-posts were the 1955 two-passenger Thunderbird and the 1956 Continental Mark III. During the 1958 model year, Ford management became alarmed by rumors that the 1959 Chevrolet would be completely restyled, and, seeking a means to counter this threat, they used the wide C-post on the 1959 Ford *Galaxie.* The *Galaxie* was a great success, despite its relatively high price, and by 1961 the wide C-post had appeared on the 1961 Chevrolet four-door hardtop and on luxury Buicks, Oldsmobiles, and Pontiacs. By the mid 1960s it had become the accepted style.

The speed with which this innovation spread from a single high-priced, low-volume model in the mid-1950s to virtually all American cars in the mid-1960s can be attributed at least in part to the "conjectural interdependence" of Ford and its competitors. Ford put the wide C-post on the *Galaxie* in response to a rumored styling change by Chevrolet. Ford's competitors adopted the wide C-post in response to what they perceived to be a successful trend in Ford design. These interdependent conjectures then become self-fulfilling prophecies, for by 1965 some variant of the wide C-post was nearly the only American design.

Need Recognition

Still other innovations come from the recognition of an unfulfilled consumer need. Sometimes through deliberate, systematic search, and sometimes through fortunate inspiration, a creative entrepreneur recognizes a gap in the array of products offered to consumers and proceeds to fill it. Book clubs, community antenna television, life and fire insurance, mutual funds, supermarkets, and mass-produced, medium-cost housing were innovations that depended less upon laboratory developments or upon conjectural interdependence than upon recognition of consumers' needs.

This approach has its hazards. It is easy to misread consumer needs, and if such misreading is combined with enough financing and enough bad luck, it can lead to a very expensive dead end.

Need Association

The fifth type of innovation is the most controversial. Innovations sometimes succeed when the innovator attaches his product to a set of needs that had not been associated with that product before. In Alderson's terminology, the innovator converts an existing need or need pattern into a "want" for a specific brand. Products that allegedly increase sexual attractiveness, enhance status, or make the user more acceptable by eradicating such maladies as bad breath, body odors, and dandruff are often introduced this way.

Innovations of this fifth type draw criticism on the grounds that they fulfill—or even create—needs that are not "real." Their sponsors are often charged with exploiting human foibles and weaknesses, with creating problems and anxieties where none existed before, and with persuading consumers to buy products that do them no real good.

The introduction of the Edsel by the Ford Motor Company represents both an attempt to find and fill an existing gap in the products offered to consumers, and an attempt to attach a brand to a need pattern that had not been associated with that brand before.

Shortly after the close of World War II Ford executives began considering the addition of a new car to the three-car Ford lines so that Ford could compete more effectively with General Motors, which was then offering five cars, and Chrysler, then offering four. The go-ahead decision was made in April 1955, largely on the basis of three considerations: (1) the outlook for the automobile market as a whole was very favorable, both on the basis of immediate past performance and on the basis of predictions about the future course of consumer spending; (2) there was good reason to believe that the medium-price segment of the automobile market would expand faster than the high-priced or low-priced segments because many consumers had been "trading up" from low-priced cars; and (3) Ford had only one relatively weak entry (Mercury) in the medium-priced field. As a consequence of this situation, many Ford owners who traded up bought Chrysler or GM products, while Chevrolet or Plymouth owners who traded up tended to stay within the family.

Research designed to identify the ideal image for the new medium-priced Ford product, then called the "E-car," produced the following prescription:

> The most advantageous personality for the E-car might well be THE SMART CAR FOR THE YOUNGER EXECUTIVE OR PROFESSIONAL FAMILY ON ITS WAY UP.
>
> Smart Car: recognition by others of the owner's good style and taste.
>
> Younger: Appealing to spirited but responsible adventurers.
>
> Executive or Professional: Millions pretend to this status, whether then can attain it or not.
>
> Family: Not exclusively masculine; a wholesome good role.
>
> On Its Way Up: "The E-car has faith in you, Son; we'll help you make it!" (Brooks, 1961)

The search for a name for the E-car featured a contest among employees of the advertising agency and some intriguing correspondence with poet Marianne Moore. The agency contest produced over 18,000 entries, including *Corsair, Citation, Pacer,* and *Ranger,* the names later assigned to the four series in the Edsel line. The correspondence with Miss Moore produced, among other suggestions, *Intelligent Bullet, Utopian Turtletop, Pastelogram, Mongoose Civique,* and *Andante Con Moto.* This experiment proved, if nothing else, that advertising copy writers and poets do not think alike.

The Edsel was introduced in late 1957, with Ford proudly announcing that it had invested more than a quarter of a billion dollars before the first car was sold. By mid-1958 the pace of sales made it obvious that the Edsel was not going to succeed, and in November 1959 the brand was discontinued.

Why did the Edsel fail? Some observers blamed the consumer research, claiming that it prescribed the wrong image. But more searching postmortems revealed the following network of decisions and guesses which, in retrospect, can be seen to have been wrong:

Nineteen fifty-eight was a recession year—not a boom year, as had been predicted in 1955 when the go-ahead decision was made—and the medium-priced segment of the car market was particularly hard hit. General Motors and Chrysler suffered, too, and Chrysler was forced to retire one of its medium-priced brands (DeSoto) shortly after Ford withdrew the Edsel.

Ford decided to establish a separate dealer network for the Edsel. Inexperienced and underfinanced in the face of a recession, many of the new Edsel dealers never really got started, and the Edsel was not as available as it should have been.

By establishing a separate Edsel division, the company increased expenses at a critical time and spread its management and staff so thin that none of the divisions was properly manned.

Ford decided to introduce the Edsel in four series and a wide variety of models, to create the impression of an established product as quickly as possible. As a result, quality control problems were greater than they would have been with fewer models, and many of the early Edsels were defective. By the time the early defects could be corrected, it was too late.

The early quality control problem was made much worse by the introductory publicity that created great interest in the car and focused attention on anything about it, good or bad. This campaign was also credited with creating such great expectations for the Edsel that no product could have lived up to what consumers had been led to expect.

A campaign by the National Safety Council against the advertising of power and speed led to a decision in 1957 by the Automobile Manufacturers Association to stop using racing as a promotional theme. This decision, which aborted Ford's plan to use racing themes to position the Edsel as the "hottest car on the road," was later rescinded.

For all these reasons, and perhaps others, the Edsel failed. Ford had attempted to analyze consumers' needs and build a product to fill them, and had attempted, in constructing the Edsel image, to make use of the powerful self-respect needs associated with social class. But change in the economic climate, major problems with distribution and quality control, and an unforeseen reaction against power and speed on the highway created a situation which no amount of image building could overcome.

Less than ten years later, Ford made another attempt to analyze consumers' needs and build a product to suit them. None of the mistakes (and none of the misfortunes) associated with the Edsel were repeated, and the Mustang was a great and widely imitated success.

NEW PRODUCT ACCEPTANCE AND REJECTION

Students of the innovation diffusion process have found that some innovations diffuse with much more rapidity than others, that innovations follow different patterns of acceptance over time, and, of course, that some innovations fail to receive any wide degree of acceptance at all. Students of consumer behavior have examined the variations of diffusion patterns and have attempted to identify factors that make rapid diffusion probable.

Patterns of Diffusion

As already noted, classifying new products according to the impact they have on familiar behavior patterns serves to identify a dimension that provides some help in predicting how readily a new product will be accepted. Further help is provided by general trends in how diffusion usually proceeds. Armed with the knowledge of the diffusion pattern of a product, the marketer can use the early results in the market to predict the remainder of the diffusion in the future.

Figure 12-1 shows two generalized patterns of diffusion along with two special cases of these patterns—the fad, the fashion growth curve, an exponential new product growth curve, and a logistic new product diffusion pattern. Of the four, the logistic or S-shaped diffusion curve has received the most attention. A number of studies have suggested that many different kinds of innovations follow this form, including farming innovations (Rogers, 1962),

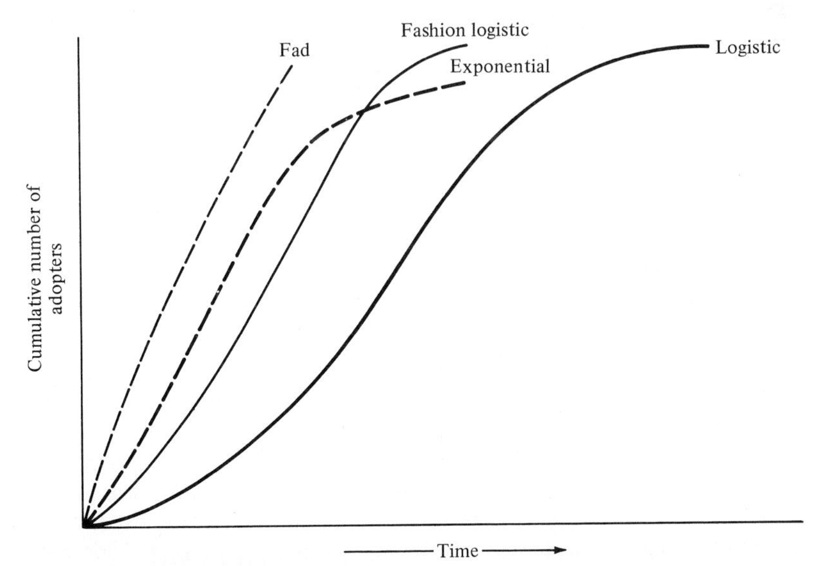

Figure 12-1 Generalized diffusion patterns.

new drugs (Coleman et al., 1966), certain new food products (Buzzell, 1966), informational messages (Dodd, 1955), mass media (De Fleur, 1970), and supermarket promotional games (Allvine, 1968). This S-shaped curve is produced by a diffusion process in which acceptance is initially slow, then grows rapidly, and then tapers off. It is the process whereby people successively interact with each other and influence each other's behavior. The spread of influence in this process is analogous to the spread of infectious diseases.

Not all new products diffuse according to the S-shaped pattern. For some products the period of rapid growth occurs almost immediately, i.e., without the initial period of slow growth exhibited by the logistic curve. Such growth curves are "exponential." A generalized exponential curve is shown in Figure 12-1, along with a fad growth curve. The fad growth curve is viewed as a special case of a more generalized rapid growth pattern but in the context of a briefer time frame. Fads, unlike fashions, have little durability. While they exhibit rapid acceptance, they tend to be discontinued very rapidly.[1]

If marketers have prior knowledge of the type of pattern an innovation will follow, they can use the growth curve with early market results to predict the rate and extent of diffusion in a market segment. With the generalized exponential growth curve in mind, Fourte and Woodlock (1960) and Anscombe (1961) have specified such a functional statement for a new product growth or penetration model:

$$rx(1-r)^{i-1}+k$$

where r = the rate at which the level of penetration approaches the ceiling of penetration

x = the ceiling of penetration

I = the number of time periods passed

k = a constant representing the rate at which new customers are added once the product reaches maturity

This functional statement is illustrated in Figure 12-2.

To determine how well the function could predict diffusion from early market results, Kelly (1966) conducted a field test using a new dairy products store as his lab. Each shopper was identified on each occasion of entering the test store during the first twelve weeks of store operations. Promotional practices and price levels were held constant during that period. The *actual* penetration data for the first twelve weeks are presented in Table 12-1.

To test the function described above for predicting ultimate diffusion, Kelly used the first three weeks' data. Table 12-2 and Figure 12-3 show a comparison between actual penetration based on customer counts and Kelly's estimates.

In this test, the difference between estimated and actual diffusion at the

[1]For a more exhaustive discussion of diffusion patterns, see Robertson (1971).

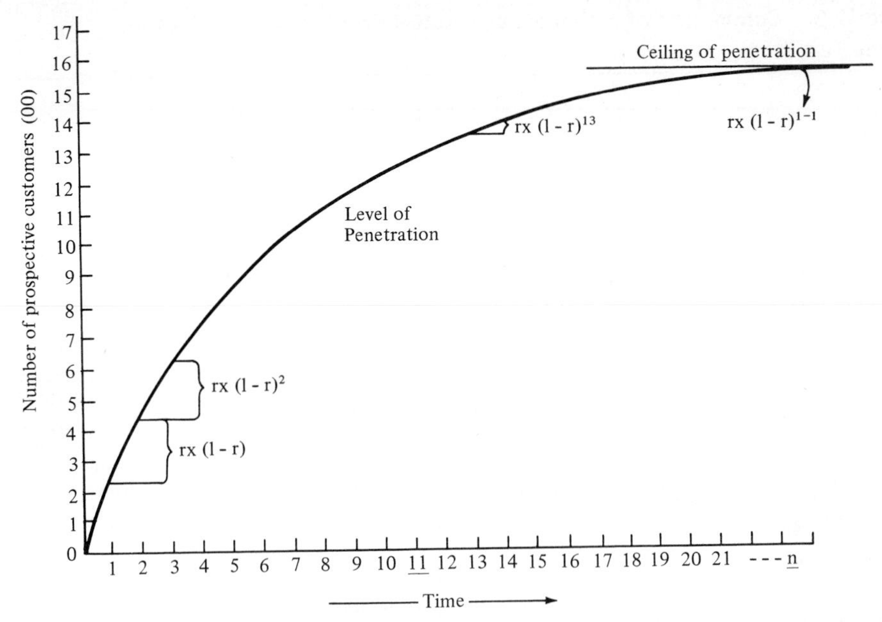

Figure 12-2 The penetration function $[rx(1-r)^{i-1}+k]$. *Source:* Kelly (1966:742). Reprinted from *Science Technology and Marketing*, published by the American Marketing Association.

end of the test period was about 2.5 percent—making the estimate quite useful for operational purposes.

Although the study of diffusion patterns can be helpful for predicting the success of new products and for planning marketing programs over a product's life cycle, the prediction is not simple and automatic. Some hard decisions must be made based on assumptions that may or may not be true. One crucial assumption concerns the pattern that the growth of a new product of a given type can be expected to follow. In order to specify a mathematical function to

Table 12-1 Actual Penetration Data from the Test Store

Time period	Penetration increment	Penetration level
1	300	300
2	280	580
3	172	752
4	118	870
5	85	955
6	31	1,006
7	70	1,076
8	54	1,130
9	45	1,175
10	27	1,202
11	21	1,223

Source: Kelly (1966:743). Reprinted from Science, *Technology & Marketing*, published by the American Marketing Association.

Table 12-2 Comparison of Estimated and Actual Penetration Data for the for the Test Store

Time period	Actual penetration		Estimated penetration	
	Increment	Total	Increment	Total
1	300	300	322	322
2	280	580	243	565
3	172	752	184	749
4	118	870	140	889
5	85	955	106	995
6	31	1,006	80	1,075
7	70	1,076	61	1,136
8	54	1,130	46	1,182
9	45	1,175	35	1,217
10	27	1,202	26	1,243
11	21	1,223	20	1,263

Source: Kelly (1966:744). Reprinted from Science, *Technology & Marketing*, published by the American Marketing Association.

represent future diffusion, one must forecast the shape of the curve. In general, it is believed that discontinuous innovations tend to follow the S-shaped growth curve and that continuous innovations tend to exhibit an exponential growth curve. Empirical evidence documenting this belief is sparse, however.

Another crucial assumption is the assumption that the new product will diffuse. As we have already seen, this frequently is not the case. To cope with

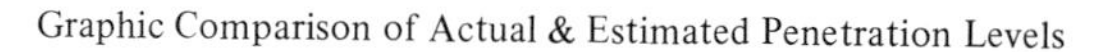

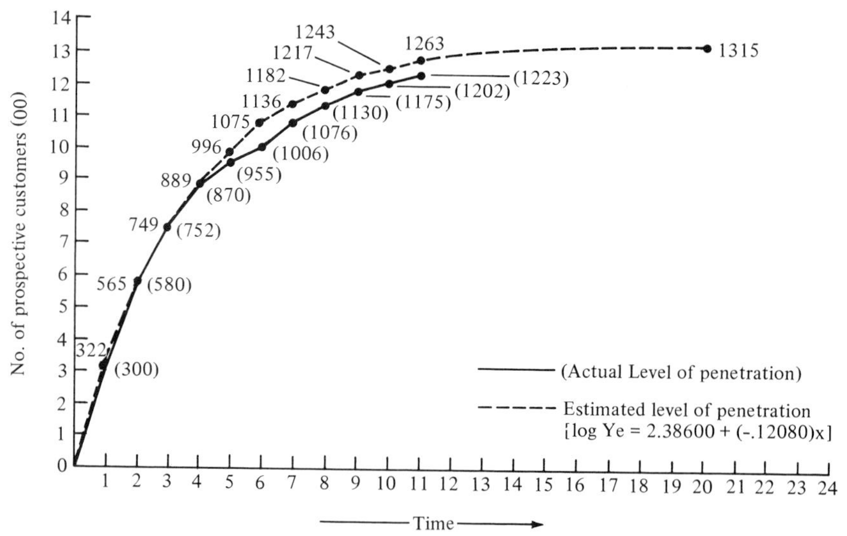

Figure 12-3 Graphic comparison of actual and estimated penetration levels. *Source:* Kelly (1966:744). Reprinted from *Science Technology and Marketing*, published by the American Marketing Association.

this problem and to cope with the more basic question of whether the product should be introduced at all, students of the diffusion process have attempted to identify determinants of acceptance and rejection of new products. Among the most important of determinants of acceptance and rejection are five general product attributes: *compatibility, relative advantage, perceived complexity, trialability,* and *communicability* (Rogers, 1962, and Zaltman and Stiff, 1973). By focusing on these attributes researchers hope to establish a standard classification scheme for describing perceived attributes in universal terms (Rogers and Shoemaker, 1971).

Compatibility is the degree to which the new product is perceived as consistent with established beliefs and ways of doing things. The great resistance that has greeted important discontinuous inventions makes it obvious that new products or services requiring new forms of consumer behavior are much harder to introduce than those that fit easily into established ways.

Another attribute that influences the rate of diffusion is *relative advantage,* the degree to which the innovation is perceived as being better than the product or service it is intended to replace. Jet airplanes are obviously superior to propeller-driven aircraft for many purposes, and within five years of introduction they were adopted by all major airlines. By contrast, the advantage of an aerosol can over the conventional toothpaste tube is not at all obvious, and this innovation has never been widely accepted in spite of several well-financed attempts to introduce it.

The *perceived complexity* of a product or service influences both rate and extent of diffusion. Innovations that are easy to understand and easy to use diffuse rapidly if they are both continuous and demonstrably superior. Innovations that are so complicated that they cannot be used or appreciated without specialized training diffuse slowly and may never penetrate more than a limited segment of the population. Bridge and chess are complex games, and although they have been widely known for many years, they have never been as popular as poker and checkers. Similarly, complexity retards the diffusion of scientific literature and classical music, while simplicity speeds the diffusion of best-seller novels and popular songs.

Trialability refers to the degree to which an innovation can be tried out or experimented with on a limited scale. Inexpensive, frequently purchased grocery and drugstore items can be given a provisional try at low risk. A home permanent is less triable, since one must live with the results at least for a while, and an automobile is even less triable. The "free home trial" period sometimes offered for furniture or appliances, and the demonstration ride sometimes offered by automobile dealers, are attempts to make such products more triable than they otherwise might be.

Finally, an innovation is easiest to introduce if its advantages are readily *communicable*—easy to observe, easy to show, and easy to describe. A gelatin dessert that separates into three layers as it cools is easier to demonstrate than a margarine that tastes somewhat better than competing products. A kitchen appliance that compresses trash is easier to demonstrate than a toothpaste that reduces cavities. The possibility of winning a lot of money at the races is easier to demonstrate than the advantages of life insurance. And "outer" clothing items are more socially visible than undergarments.

Compatibility, relative advantage, simplicity, triability, and communicability all help pave an innovation's way. The degree to which these elements are present, or can be created, will determine how difficult the introduction job will be.

The role of each of these general attributes can be seen in the failure of the midi style.

In July 1970 Reynolds and Darden (1972) conducted a study of a number of fashion topics, including reactions to the midi style, among 300 middle-class homemakers in Athens, Georgia. Their analysis and interpretation of that data led them to predict that the midi would be rejected. In May 1971 a follow-up survey of 103 persons of the original sample confirmed the prediction (Reynolds and Darden, 1973) and provided the basis for a postmortem. In the follow-up survey, respondents were asked to recall the content of the discussions they had with friends about the midi. Over 80 percent of the sample responded to the question, providing 233 negative comments, which could be classified into six themes:

Recurrent theme. Thirty-nine comments related to the recurrence of an old fashion. Women perceived the midi as a recurring style from yesteryear. They expressed a belief that the midi would make them feel "older" or "old-fashioned"—a feeling incompatible with their life styles and/or, perhaps youth value. This theme suggests that the midi was not perceived as compatible.

Economic theme. Seventeen comments related to the need for buying a "whole look." Women perceived a necessity to buy accessories to complement the look. This, they claimed, was too expensive. Thus, the midi was not perceived as triable.

Mirror theme. Seventy-one comments related to appearance of wearer as she saw "herself" in the midi. These women used comments such as "I am less feminine-looking in it," "It isn't flattering," "My legs are too pretty to cover," "I am too short to look well in it," "I wouldn't look attractive in it," "It would look sloppy on me," and "It would make me look chubbier." Clearly, the midi presented a relative disadvantage rather than a relative advantage and one obviously easy to communicate.

Poor design theme. Eighteen comments were about design features excluding "length." These women perceived the design itself to be poor, i.e., heavy, bulky, uncomfortable; there were too few suitable fabrics for the style; it was too hot for the Southern summer; it was not versatile for daily wear. It had an unfinished look, and movement was inhibited—again, a disadvantage for those who desire comfortable and versatile styles.

Fashion prediction theme: fad element. Eight comments were on the faddish nature of the midi. These persons perceived it as a fad—something "too shocking to stick"—much like the granny dress of a few years ago. Another relative disadvantage.

Fashion prediction theme: risk element. Eleven comments related to whether or not it would be accepted. These women apparently perceived greater risk in the midi than others did. They were concerned about whether or not others would wear it and cause their own styles to become "obsolete" or "out of fashion." For them, the difficulty of prediction made the innovation too *complex.*

Other. Sixty-nine comments were too superficial to assign to a theme. The most typical were, "I just don't like it" and "Length."

Note that when the content themes were translated into general product characteristics, all five postulated by diffusion researchers emerge:

Attribute	Number of comments
Relative advantage (disadvantage, in this case)	97
Compatibility	39
Trialability	17
Complexity	11
Communicable	71*

*Also included in relative advantage component.

In summary, homemakers viewed the midi as *in*compatible, as having several *dis*advantages, as difficult to put to a low-risk trial, and as complex in the sense that acceptance by others was difficult to predict. In general, the study reinforces the importance of perceived attributes in determining how difficult an introduction job will be.

INNOVATORS

In addition to trying to understand varying rates of acceptance, and in addition to attempting to identify attributes underlying acceptance or rejection of innovations, students of consumer behavior have examined the characteristics of consumers who are innovators. The thrust of the examination has been to identify segments of consumers who can be expected to be early purchasers of innovations so that marketing programs can be tailored and targeted to these segments.

Agents of the U.S. Department of Agriculture, anxious to get farmers to use improved farming methods, have found that their work goes much easier once they can get even a small number of farmers in a community to follow scientific advice. If a few farmers try a new hybrid seed corn, or a new fertilizer, and their fields look a lot better than their neighbors', it is not long before the neighbors are adopting the innovation, too.

The trick is to get the first triers. Farmers who are doing reasonably well with established methods are understandably reluctant to risk the fruits of a growing season on some crackpot scheme that may not work any better than what they have been doing all along.

A similar problem confronts the marketer of a new consumer product, especially if, as was the case with the midi, buying or using the product entails more than trivial risk. Many consumers wait until others lead the way, preferring to be the followers, not the leaders, in the adoption parade. Because of this obvious behavior, the concept of *consumer innovativeness* has emerged as the main focus of research dealing with first purchase responses. It refers to the degree to which a person is earlier than other persons in a market segment to purchase a new product. Since it is difficult to think in terms of a large number of persons individually, diffusion researchers have evolved a set of "innovativeness" categories to designate consumers who enter the diffusion process at different stages. The first 2.5 percent who try the new product or new method are called the "innovators"; the next 13.5 percent, the "early adopters"; the next 34 percent and the following 34 percent, the "early majority" and the "late majority," respectively; and the last 16 percent, the "laggards" (Rogers, 1962).

There is no magic in these percentages, of course. They are arbitrary divisions of a continuous distribution and could equally well be somewhat different. But the divisions and their names have been widely accepted as standard, and they have served to focus attention on consumers who enter the diffusion process early or late.

One of the reasons why innovators are so important is that they break the ice; i.e., they represent the origin of diffusion. As in the agricultural studies, if a few consumers in a community can be persuaded to adopt the innovation, and if the innovation is highly visible, the mere act of adoption encourages others who are less bold.

If the innovator is a respected member of an important reference group, his influence is stronger than if he is not. Studies of the diffusion of new clothing fashions (Baumgarten and King, 1970; Darden and Reynolds, 1973), for instance, show that new fashions diffuse rapidly once they are adopted by a relatively small and identifiable fashion leader group. Similarly, studies of the adoption of new prescription drugs show that the use of new drugs spreads rapidly once they are adopted by "influential" doctors—men named by their associates as colleagues they "look to for information and advice" (Coleman, Katz, and Menzel, 1957).

Another reason innovators are important is that they are often, although not always, gregarious opinion leaders. In a famous study of the way room air conditioners diffused through a Philadelphia neighborhood, Whyte (1954) found that diffusion proceeded up and down streets and across narrow alleys, where the "web of word-of-mouth" would be most likely to connect, rather than across major thoroughfares. In the drug study mentioned above, earliest adopters were often named as colleagues seen socially and colleagues with whom cases were frequently discussed. And in a study of the introduction of a new detergent brand (Pessemier, Burger, and Tigert, 1967), 40 percent of the early buyers, as opposed to 32 percent of the late buyers, and 22 percent of the nonbuyers responded "yes" to the question, "Have you recently been asked your opinion on detergents or have you volunteered any information on detergents to anyone?" Innovators are often opinion leaders, either by setting the example or by spreading the word.

It is important to note that innovators are not always opinion leaders, and opinion leaders are not always innovators. Sometimes innovators, like the first buyers of the Edsel and the midi, are not followed by a sizable adopter group. Sometimes opinion leaders work against innovations, exercising their influence on behalf of the tried and true. While opinion leadership and innovation often go together, especially when the innovation turns out to be successful, innovativeness and opinion leadership are not the same.

Can Innovators Be Identified?

One important question to ask about innovators and early adopters is, "Are they identifiable in any way other than by their first purchasing behavior?" For instance, do persons high on innovativeness differ from the remainder of the population in age or personality or social class? If they do, marketers have an additional dimension of analysis to help them anticipate whether or not a new product will diffuse, since innovators represent the origin of diffusion when their example influences less innovative persons to purchase. In general, if innovators are identifiable in terms of certain characteristics, marketers can assess favorable and unfavorable reactions to new product ideas in terms of these characteristics without having to wait for actual behavior to occur. If those persons expressing favorable opinions or intentions about a new product concept turn out to have the characteristics associated with previous highly innovative behavior, marketers might expect diffusion to be rapid and widespread (Reynolds and Darden, 1973).

In a review of diffusion studies covering a wide range of products, ideas, and practices, Rogers and Stanfield (1966) discovered that innovators and early adopters had often been found to differ from the remainder of the population in education, literacy, standard of living, and income—four characteristics that help to define or are strongly correlated with social class. Education and income were also found to differentiate innovators from noninnovators in studies limited to household products.

For all these reasons—greater financial resources, greater ability to absorb a loss, wider horizons, and more self-confidence—consumers near the top of the social class ladder are more apt to be innovators and early adopters than are consumers near the bottom.

Within social classes, innovators and early adopters are often found to have a generalized "attitude" that has been labeled "innovation proneness." An attitude is a disposition to respond, either favorably or unfavorably, to a particular object or class of objects. In social psychology, where the study of attitudes originated and is now most highly developed, the objects of attitudes are often members of racial or religious groups. When such attitudes are negative, they are called "prejudices."

In the study of consumer behavior, attitudes studied are often positive rather than negative. If the object of a positive attitude is a brand or a store, and if this favorable attitude is repeatedly carried over into purchasing behavior, the result is brand or store loyalty.

The object of a favorable attitude may also be a class of objects, like "new things" or "old things" or "things that come from the Far East." If the object class is "new things" or "new ideas," and if the attitude is favorable, the consumer holding the attitude is said to be "innovation prone."

Attitudes can be inferred from behavior or from expressed intentions. If examination of a homemakers' purchase diaries show that they consistently try new brands soon after they are first offered, it seems reasonable to infer that they have a generally favorable attitude—one might say a positive prejudice—toward new grocery products. Similarly, if homemakers are shown a list of plausible products not yet on the market, and they say they would be willing to give most or all of them a try, it is reasonable to make the same inference about a favorable attitude toward newness—at least, with respect to the kinds of items included in the list.

Both of these methods have been used to measure "innovation proneness." Purchase diary records and reports of having purchased new products (such as electric toothbrushes or touch-tone telephones) when they were first introduced have been used to indicate innovativeness by purchasing behavior; self-assessed willingness to try hypothetical new products, or new products in general, has been used to indicate innovativeness by intentions (Bell, 1963; Robertson, 1969).

Although a favorable attitude toward newness has usually been found to be positively related to indices of social class, and although both these dimensions have often been found to discriminate between innovators and laggards, these two variables are not always the most important. Sometimes an innovation is especially suited to consumers at a particular stage of the life cycle or to consumers who live in a particular geogrphical area; in such cases, age or location, or some other set of variables, may provide the key. The importance of compatibility between an innovation's characteristics and the characteristics of the adopting group is demonstrated in a classic study by Saxon Graham. Graham determined via telephone interviews whether each of 150 Connecticut families had accepted or rejected each of five innovations. When he divided the families into social strata on the basis of the family head's occupation, he found the relationships shown in Table 12-3.

This table shows that at the time of the study there was a pronounced relationship between class standing and acceptance of television (ownership of a receiving set), with acceptance being higher in the lower classes. Further investigation of this relationship showed that rejecters differed from accepters in that they preferred active, creative recreational activities, such as participation in sports (as opposed to passive watching), get-togethers with friends, and serious reading. In reading, the rejecters of television preferred serious fiction and nonfiction, while the accepters confined their reading to "fiction, a cursory inspection of the newspaper, or to no reading at all."

Table 12-3 Innovation Acceptance and Social Class

Innovation	Proportion of each class accepting the innovation					
	I	II	III	IV	V	VI
Television	24%	44%	48%	52%	84%	72%
Canasta	72	72	44	20	32	12
Supermarkets	52	80	56	80	52	48
Blue Cross hospital insurance	88	96	100	88	92	76
Prepaid medical insurance	20	48	40	24	36	20

Source: Graham (1956).

The trend for canasta was in the opposite direction, with highest acceptance in the upper classes. Here the critical difference was the greater interest among the upper classes in all kinds of complex, abstract games and the greater and more varied social contacts of upper-class respondents. With more social contacts, members of the upper classes had more opportunity to meet and interact with canasta players who could teach them how to play.

The other three innovations showed no strong class-related acceptance pattern. Accepting (doing more than half the grocery shopping at) supermarkets was irregularly related to social class. Accepting supermarkets depends upon the ease with which a supermarket can be reached, and when this particular study was done, accessibility of a supermarket may well have had no direct relationship to class position.

The strong acceptance of Blue Cross in all classes except the very lowest precluded a strong class-related acceptance pattern. Conceivably, if the study had been conducted before adoption of this innovation was so nearly complete, some pattern would have been detected. Acceptance of prepaid medical insurance shows a curvilinear relationship with class position. One might speculate that members of the highest class found it reasonable to insure themselves against future doctor bills, since as a result even substantial bills would have less impact, while members of the lower classes lacked not only the money to meet the premiums but also the disposition to do that much advance planning.

These plausible explanations may not be complete or entirely correct. Even so, the study demonstrates four different relationships—and one nonrelationship—between acceptance of innovation and social class.

Can Innovators Be Reached?

The marketer of a new product would like to be able to identify the potential innovators and concentrate on persuading them. If the innovators can be persuaded, they will set an example for others to follow, and if they are also gregarious opinion leaders, they will facilitate the flow of communication—from the marketer to the innovators and from the innovators to the public at large.

Because in general there is a positive relationship between innovativeness and social class, some mass communication media—especially some magazines that attract middle- and upper-class audiences—have tried to show that they are especially efficient carriers of messages to the innovator group. "Advertise here," they say, "and you will influence the influentials."

The marketer who follows this strategy encounters two problems. First, the relationships between innovativeness and social class, and between social class and magazine readership, are so far from perfect that many innovators will not be in the audience of the selected magazines, and the magazine audiences will contain many consumers who are not innovation prone. Second, as the Graham study indicated, acceptance of the specific innovation may be negatively related to social class or not related to social class at all. In either case, confining introductory advertising to magazines that attract the "influentials" will miss many of the consumers whom the advertiser most wants to reach.

If the innovation is continuous, it is sometimes possible to reach potential innovators by making use of the "heavy user" concept. A heavy user of grocery store items is apt to be a pretty good bet for almost any new grocery store brand, provided that it helps solve the problem of feeding a large family. A heavy user of electrical gadgets is apt to be an early adopter of the next new electrical gadget that comes along. These different usage patterns reflect different sets of interests and needs; and to the degree that the need patterns also mediate exposure to media, specific media audiences will contain unusual numbers of the heavy users of specific types of products.

Sometimes it is possible to identify innovative opinion leaders by asking group members questions about each other. If the consumer decision is important enough—if it is a decision about adopting a fashion that might set a trend, or adopting a new farming technique or a new medical treatment—the marketer may find it worth the trouble to identify opinion leaders within relatively small groups and to make special efforts to see that they are convinced.

Efforts to reach innovators and opinion leaders are facilitated by the fact that consumers who are most apt to be either innovators or opinion leaders, or both, seek out the communications media that carry information about innovations in their fields of interest. Homemakers who are especially likely to try new food brands and to talk with others about their experiences are also especially likely to be readers of home- and family-oriented magazines and to be unusually attentive to food commercials on television. Avid picture takers, who are most apt to try new cameras and new photographic supplies, are also most apt to read photographers' magazines. Physicians who are most influential in disseminating information about the effectiveness of new treatments are also the readers of medical journals.

Potential innovators can be reached by identifying and seeking out the heavy user of the product type, or by asking members of small local groups to say which group members lead the way. In either case, attempts to reach innovators are facilitated by the innovator's proclivity to seek out information about the products with which he is involved.

NEW PRODUCT INTRODUCTIONS

By the time a new consumer product is placed in national distribution, it represents an investment of millions of dollars in research and development, manufacture, and promotion. Because of the size of this investment, most new products undergo a series of tests designed to weed out failures at the earliest possible date.[2]

Concept Testing

Once a new product has reached the "seriously considered idea" stage, the first hurdle it must pass is some form of *concept testing.* In principle, a concept test is easy. An accurate description of the new product is presented to a representative sample of consumers, and respondents are asked to say whether they would buy such a thing if it were offered for sale.

In practice, however, concept testing presents some serious problems. One problem is that it is often surprisingly difficult to prepare a full and accurate description of a new product. "A white soap that floats" is an accurate description of Ivory, but the product introduced to the public in 1879 included the name "Ivory," the "$99^{44}/_{100}$ percent pure" slogan, and a new form of large-space, family-oriented advertising. "A white soap that floats" was less than $99^{44}/_{100}$ percent of what the product was.

An accurate description of a new product is even more difficult if the product is discontinuous, for then product acceptance depends upon a behavior change that may be difficult to foresee. A reasonably accurate description of prepared baby food might be, "baby food that is ready to serve except for warming, that saves hours of tedious hand work in the kitchen, and that is very much more expensive per ounce than baby food prepared at home." Confronted with this description in 1900, many mothers would have said that such a product would be too costly. Now, even though the cost difference between prepared baby food and homemade baby food is just as great as it ever was, mothers can hardly believe that their grandmothers and great-grandmothers spent hours straining peas. The general acceptance of the product makes it a different product.

Even when the product is not discontinuous and the description is accurate and complete, consumers sometimes mispredict what they will do. Surveys show that consumers "want" cereal boxes that will not tip over easily and catsup bottles with wide mouths, yet products packaged in accordance with these findings have not sold well. Interviews with automobile buyers regularly show that many drivers want a small, simple, economical car that will not attain

[2]For more complete discussions of these tests, see Worcester (1972).

high speeds and will not use much gasoline. When such products have been offered, manufacturers have found that few consumers buy them, and those who do buy them often order such extra-cost options as the higher-horsepower engine, power steering, and mag wheels.

Product Testing

The hazards of evaluation are reduced when samples are available for test. Major food companies maintain testing centers where products of experimental kitchens can be compared with products off the grocery shelf. Manufacturers of automobiles and large appliances sponsor "clinics" in which consumers examine and appraise models of new design.

While models and samples eliminate some of the problems associated with providing accurate descriptions, they cannot provide the full context in which the new product will eventually be seen. Because of the lead time required by the manufacturing process, new automobile styles must be "locked up" eighteen to twenty-four months in advance, and a design that appeared to be riding the crest of a style trend in 1956 may appear gaudy and ostentatious in the social and competitive climate of 1958. Similarly, because "conjectural interdependence" often drives competitors along parallel lines, a food product or a drugstore product that appears to be a substantial improvement at the testing stage may turn out to be a "me too" brand by the time it can be manufactured in quantity and distributed to retail stores.

The problems of product testing are increased by differences between prototypes tested in the laboratory and the products that finally arrive at the retail store. Cookies that were rated "like very much" when they were warm from the test-kitchen oven may be rated "dislike very much" after they have spent two months in the wholesaler's warehouse and two weeks on the grocer's shelf. An instant drink mix that made a tasty beverage when mixed with spring water in the laboratory may receive an exceedingly low rating when mixed with the high-mineral, chlorinated water that comes from city taps. A dress prototype, lovingly hand-sewn, may produce an unrecognizable offspring by the time all the "minor" changes required by mass production have been made.

Pair Comparison and Single-Stimulus Testing

Pair Comparisons One of the methods most often used in product testing is the method of "pair comparison." Samples of the product to be tested and samples of the product with which it is to compete are presented to consumers, and the consumer judges are asked to say which they like better. Usually, the products are unlabeled except for code letters, and often the pairs are presented several times with the order of presentation systematically reversed so as to balance out the effect of being tried first.

One of the problems that arise in pair comparison testing is the interpretation of ties. If 50 percent (or near 50 percent) of the judges prefer one product and 50 percent (or near 50 percent) prefer the other, the experimenter cannot tell whether half the judges really prefer one product and half really prefer the other or whether they simply cannot tell them apart.

One of the ways to handle this problem is to present the two products in a "triad." Two samples of one product and one sample of the other are presented two at a time, with each sample having a different code label. If the judges can discriminate, they will rank the two samples of one product consistently above or consistently below the other. If they cannot discriminate, the comparisons will show a random mix.

The pair comparison method can be expanded to include more than two products by presenting a whole selection of products, each differently labeled, in all possible pairs. Then, by examining the number of times each product is preferred over every other product, it is possible to develop a "scale" that shows both how the products rank with respect to each other and how far they are apart.

Single-Stimulus Testing An alternative approach is to present the products one at a time and ask the judges to rate each product on a scale defined by numbers or words. If each set of judges sees only one product, the frame of reference for the rating is the judges' previous experience with products of that type rather than the specific group of products that happen to be under test.

Considerable research has been devoted to questions like, "How many steps should the scale contain?" and "How should the steps be labeled?" In one especially thorough investigation of the question (Jones, Peryan, and Thurstone, 1955), the scales in Figure 12-4 were tested for ability to discriminate among samples of various foods.

Using the criteria of time required for completion, reliability, and amount of information transmitted, the two eight-step scales (numbers 7 and 8 in the figure) were judged the best.

The pair comparison method is usually more discriminating than the single-stimulus rating scale method because in the pair comparison method judges are forced to make a choice between the products being tested even when the difference between them is so slight that both would be placed in the same slot on the rating scale. On the other hand the single-stimulus method is more realistic in the sense that consumers usually evaluate products against their previous experience with similar products rather than against a present product array. Therefore, the pair comparison method is often used when the experimenter wants to know whether the difference between two products is detectable, while the single-stimulus method is often used when the investigator wants to know whether the new product is noticeably superior or inferior to products the consumer has tried in the recent past.

Home Use Tests

Evaluation can be made more accurate by *home use tests* of samples drawn from production lines. Here the problems of context are much less formidable than they are in the testing laboratory, and it is reasonable to assume that the

Scale for measuring food preferences

Scale number	Number of intervals	Phrases defining successive intervals								
1	9	Dislike extremely	Dislike very much	Dislike moderately	Dislike slightly	Neither like nor dislike	Like slightly	Like moderately	Like very much	Like extremely
2	9	Dislike extremely	Dislike very much	Dislike	Mildly dislike	Neutral	Mildly like	Like	Like very much	Like extremely
3	7	Dislike extremely	Dislike very much	Mildly dislike	Neutral	Mildly like	Like very much	Like extremely		
4	6	Dislike extremely	Dislike very much	Mildly dislike	Mildly like	Like very much	Like extremely			
5	5	Dislike extremely	Dislike	Neutral	Like	Like extremely				
6	9	Dislike extremely	Dislike very much	Dislike fairly much	Dislike slightly	Neither like nor dislike	Like slightly	Like moderately	Like very much	Like extremely
7	8	Dislike extremely	Dislike very much	Dislike moderately	Dislike slightly	Like slightly	Like moderately	Like very much	Like extremely	
8	8	Dislike extremely	Strongly dislike	Mildly dislike	Neither like nor dislike	Like slightly	Like moderately	Like very much	Like extremely	
9	7	Dislike extremely	Strongly dislike	Mildly dislike	Mildly like	Like fairly well	Like quite a bit	Like very much		

Figure 12-4 Some scales used to rate food samples. *Source:* Jones, Peryan and Thurstone (1955).

product being evaluated is much like the product that the consumer will eventually be asked to buy. Note, however, that the research and development costs and the manufacturing costs of a new product failure have already been incurred. By this time so much has been invested, both in money and in hope and fear, that the course now set may be pursued to the end even in the face of very bad test results. There is always the possibility that bad signs are wrong.

In home use tests, product samples (usually unlabeled) are delivered to consumer either in person or by mail. The testers are asked to use the product in the normal way and to give their reactions on a follow-up questionnaire.

One particularly thorough home use test, which incorporated an unusual extra dimension, was conducted in the process of introducing Pledge. Before Pledge was introduced, the manufacturer was undecided as to whether to portray it as a new spray furniture polish (which it was) or a new product that would permit housekeepers to polish surfaces as they dusted them.

In this test half the test containers were distributed with "new spray polish" advertising attached, and half were distributed with advertising that attemped to convey the then novel "polish as you dust" idea. At the end of the trial period, the test containers were collected and consumers were asked to rate how ready they would be to buy the product on a scale like the one on p. 323.

If this product were available in the store—

I would certainly buy it.
I probably would buy it.
I might buy it.
I probably wouldn't buy it.
I certainly wouldn't buy it.

Examination of the partly empty containers showed that consumers in the "polish as you dust" group had used significantly more of the product than consumers in the "new spray polish" group, and tabulation of the ratings showed that the "polish as you dust" respondents had a stronger inclination to purchase the product if it were available at the store. Thus the physical product and an important element of the brand's "image" were tested under realistic home use conditions at the same time.

Test Markets

The final hurdle a new product must pass is the *test market.* In test marketing, the product is distributed through regular retail channels in selected cities, usually with an accompanying advertising and promotion campaign, and sales are carefully monitored to assess initial trial and repurchase rates.

By this time investment is great. Plants have been built, large quantities of the product has been manufactured, packages and advertisements have been designed and made, and careers have been staked on the product's success. Nevertheless, the process can still be stopped if test market results indicate that the product is bound to fail. If failure is to be the eventual outcome, the sooner the process is stopped, the better.

Even test markets—the closest possible approximation to a full-scale introduction—do not produce infallible signs. No one knows for sure how representative the test market areas of the market that will eventually develop for the brand under test. No city or group of cities is representative of the United States in all respects, and the differences between test markets and the national market—in demographic characteristics, in amount and nature of retail distribution that can be attained, and in kinds and amount of advertising and promotion that can be employed—may produce a false picture of what would happen if the test product were to be introduced on a national scale.

With all their faults, test markets are the best (and the most expensive) insurance a marketer can buy. They are the last and the most realistic preintroduction opportunity the marketer will have to submit his product to the consumer vote.

Mathematical Models for Use in Test Markets

In test markets, time is of the essence. Now the marketer's product, and his plans for its promotion, are all revealed, and his competitors have solid information for making counterplans. Interdependence is no longer conjectural but very real.

Time is even more crucial in view of the expenses being incurred. Manufacture, distribution advertising, and promotion are costly, even in test markets. It is essential that readings be made as early as possible, to permit rapid expansion if the product is to be a success, or to shut off the financial drain if the product is to fail.

The high stakes in test markets have encouraged the development of mathematical models of consumer behavior that permit forecasts of what consumers in general will do. If early results can be used to project the outcome, it is not necessary to wait for the final outcome before deciding on the next step.

A key element in these models is the notion of "brand loyalty."[3] Before the introduction of a new brand, if none of the competitors has been engaging in any unusual marketing activity, brand shares as measured by store audits change little from one time period to another. Such a market is said to be in a "steady state," and a record of brand switches, obtained from consumer purchase diaries or from special surveys, will produce a "brand switching matrix" like the matrix shown in Figure 12-5.

This matrix says that 50 percent of the consumers who bought Brand A in period 1 stayed loyal in period 2, while 20 percent of them switched to Brand B and 30 percent switched to Brand C. It also says that Brand B enjoyed more "loyalty" than Brand A: 60 percent of its period 1 customers remained loyal, while 15 percent and 25 percent of its period 1 customers switched, respectively, to Brands A and C.

When an important new brand is introduced, a previously steady market is thrown into "disequilibrium," producing a matrix that might look like the matrix shown in Figure 12-6.

This matrix shows that the new Brand D drew some customers from all three of the original brands, as would be expected. It also shows that Brand D is a greater threat to Brand B than to the other brands, because it has attracted more of Brand B's customers.

The most crucial phase in the test market occurs when the innovators who tried Brand D deplete their stocks and are ready to buy the product again. Will a substantial proportion of them repurchase Brand D, or will they revert to their earlier habits? The matrix in Figure 12-7 shows what might happen then.

[3]This element advances these models beyond simple diffusion growth curves by explicitly account for repeat-purchase behavior in addition to first-purchase behavior. This addition is particularly important in the analysis of frequently purchased new products.

Figure 12-5 A Brand Switching Matrix

		Period 2		
	Brand	A	B	C
Period 1	A	50%	20%	30%
	B	15%	60%	25%
	C	17%	25%	58%

Source: Lipstein (1970:6). Reprinted from the *Journal of Advertising Research* © 1970 by the Advertising Research Foundation.

Figure 12-6 A Matrix Showing Disequilibrium

	Brand	Period 3 A	B	C	D
	A	40%	20%	30%	10%
Period 2	B	10%	30%	25%	35%
	C	17%	10%	58%	15%
	D	—	—	—	—

Source: Lipstein (1970:6). Reprinted from the *Journal of Advertising Research* © 1970 by the Advertising Research Foundation.

A matrix like this would be a bad omen for the new brand, for it shows that a very small proportion of those who tried Brand D remained loyal for even one repurchase, while most of them switched back to the older brands, especially to Brand B.

A finding like this would be especially valuable if it became available while total sales and brand share for the new brand are still on the rise. Not all customers try a new brand the first moment it is offered. Since a new brand can continue to draw substantial members of triers from present users of the established brands for quite a long time, its total sales curve can continue to rise longer after a low repurchase rate has told Brand D's managers that they are in serious trouble, and a high switchback rate has told the managers of Brand B that they can relax, at least until the next crisis.

As the market settles down after the disturbance produced by the entry of the new brand, the figures in the period-to-period transition matrix show less and less change, and it becomes possible to predict, by mathematical manipulation of the matrices, the "steady state" shares that the new brand and the established brands will eventually reach (Lipstein, 1970). At this point, long before the final returns are in, the sponsor of the innovation, and the sponsors of the products to which the innovation is a threat, will know whether the innovation has made the grade.

Pretest Market Models

Because test markets require such a great commitment of resources, marketers are continually searching for ways to provide relatively accurate predictions of

Figure 12-7 A Matrix Showing a Return to Equilibrium

	Brand	Period 4 A	B	C	D
	A	40%	20%	30%	10%
Period 3	B	10%	30%	25%	35%
	C	17%	10%	58%	15%
	D	15%	50%	30%	5%

Source: Lipstein (1970:6). Reprinted from the *Journal of Advertising Research* © 1970 by the Advertising Research Foundation.

market results without actually going through the test market phase. The mathematical formulations mentioned earlier normally cannot be used in this manner. They are, in essence, models for forecasting equilibrium levels of brand shares from data obtained during the early phases of a test market.

In recent years, a number of models have been developed for the purpose of predicting product performances before test marketing or market introduction. These models include DEMON (Charnes et al., 1966), the Ayer Product Model (Claycamp and Liddy, 1969), SPRINTER (Urban, 1969), and COMP (Burger, 1972, and *Marketing Today*, 1973).

COMP (A Comprehensive System for Predicting Sales of New Products) is an interesting example of models useful as a final new product test before test marketing. It incorporates a variety of research procedures normally conducted separately. Introduced in 1971 by Elrick and Lavidge, Inc., COMP was designed to:

1 Predict sales (or market shares) of new products.
2 Diagnose competitive strengths and weaknesses of products tested.
3 Describe the characteristics and attitudes of the most likely purchasers.
4 Measure repurchase rates and show which product attributes attract or discourage repeat purchases.

The COMP system employs nine basic steps divided into three phases: Prelaboratory, Controlled Laboratory Sales Experiment, and Postlaboratory Analysis.

Prelaboratory

1 Respondent Screening Screening interviews are conducted to select individuals who are logical prospects for the test product. Prospective respondents are screened individually in high-traffic locations—normally, suburban shopping centers.

2 Initial Interview The selected consumers are interviewed to obtain measurements of their brand awareness, perceptions of the importance of product benefits and attributes, ratings of the competitive brands being used in the experiment, prior purchase and use of current brands, brand purchase intentions, and appropriate demographic characteristics.

Controlled Laboratory Sales Experiment

3 Advertising Exposure The participants are exposed to advertising messages for the test product and its major competitors. Print or television advertising (or both) may be used. An "advertising evaluation" questionnaire is administered to reinforce recall of the messages.

4 Shopping Next, participants are given an opportunity to purchase the test product and/or any competing brands at low but realistic prices, using money paid to them previously for their participation. For consumer package goods, products are normally displayed on standard grocery or drugstore shelving units set up at the interviewing locations.

5 Postshopping Interview After the purchasing opportunity. participants rate the new product and competitive products on selected product benefits and attributes. At this point, ratings of the new product are based on the advertising message and product appearance only.

Postlaboratory

6 Home Use Consumers who do not purchase the test product are each given a free sample of it so that their attitudes toward the product after use can be obtained. Thus a home use test is included as part of the COMP system.

7 Repurchase Opportunity When sufficient time has passed for the participants to try the products purchased in the laboratory, they are contacted by telephone and given an opportunity to purchase any or all of the products which were available in the laboratory.

8 Follow-Up Interview After a few days or weeks, depending on the product usage cycle, participants are interviewed about their satisfactions and dissatisfactions with the products they have used, future purchase intentions, and attitudes toward all the brands in the experiment. Each brand is again rated on the list of product attributes and benefits, this time on the basis of experience with the new product in use.

9 Sales Prediction and Explanation The information developed through this series of experiments and interviews serves as the basic input for the COMP model. The responses are examined one person at a time through an analytic procedure that predicts the purchase behavior of each individual test participant. The model adjusts the data to reflect real-world marketing conditions. Market share is computed at each possible level of awareness and distribution which can be expected for the new product if it is marketed.

Attitudinal data provide diagnostic information which gives reasons for the market share estimate and may indicate ways in which the product or positioning can be improved.

"How well does COMP work?" According to releases from Elrick and Lavidge, "COMP has accurately predicted market share in every case where validation was possible." Two cases released by the company are quoted below.

1 Children's OTC Drug Product
Product: A new children's OTC Drug product, designed to compete with several different kinds of products already on the market. A really new product, combining the benefits of many others.
Purpose: The prime purpose of the COMP experiment was to validate the

sales prediction power by testing the product at the same time it was in test markets. One of the test areas was in the Southeast, the other in the Pacific Northwest. The COMP experiment was conducted in the Chicago area.
Procedure: The COMP experiment was conducted with a sample of 500 homemakers who had children three through twelve years of age. An additional qualification was that at least one of the children in the family must have had the symptoms for which the product was designed within twelve months prior to the experiment.
Results: The COMP sales prediction was within one percentage point of actual market share achieved in the test results. Moreover, the information about consumers' attitudes toward and perceptions of the new product showed how the level of sales could be increased above that which had been achieved and predicted.
Supplement: Because of the success of COMP in this instance, the product was retested at a higher price. The results indicated that the same market share would be achieved at the higher price, thus providing the client with an opportunity for greater profit potential.

2 Womens' Toiletries Product
Product: A new version of a womens' toiletries product with product attribute and benefit claims designed to segment the market in a unique way.
Purpose: To demonstrate the validity of COMP by comparing the results with an earlier sales prediction test using a different and much costlier procedure (the cost is three to five times that for COMP).
Procedure: The product was tested using the COMP procedure among 300 women, ages fifteen and older, who were known users of the product type. Quotas were established by age and information was obtained about such major marketing questions as:

a Characteristics of the best prospects for the new product.
b The attributes and benefits of the product which have greatest appeal to those who were most likely to use it.
c The nature of brand switching which would occur because of the new product entry, particularly the degree to which there would be cannibalism from the company's existing products.

COMP provided, at a much lower cost than the competitive system, the same levels of predictions about share of market plus substantial additional information to assist in improving the marketing plans and tactics. (Elrick and Lavidge, Inc., 1973).

SUMMARY

This chapter has examined the relationships between new products and people's reactions to them. It was shown that companies introduce a variety of new products each year in hopes of maintaining or increasing their market position. These products come from a variety of sources, including independent inventors, company laboratories, and design centers. These sources have originated new product ideas through planned technological programs, accidental discovery, conjectural interdependence, and the recognition of unfulfilled consumer needs and wants.

Because of the high failure rates of new products and the detrimental consequences for consumers and marketers, a substantial amount of research has been conducted to help firms improve their new product success rates. Presumably, a greater understanding of why people accept or reject new products can lead to improved new product development and marketing programs.

Several dimensions that provide insight into product acceptance and rejection were discussed. When innovations were classified in terms of their effect on behavior patterns, it was noted that a number of innovations, particularly discontinuous ones, follow the S-shape curve, while more continuous innovations tend to follow a more rapid growth pattern, such as an exponential curve. Although predictions based on general diffusion patterns have sometimes been quite accurate, they depend greatly upon an accurate forecast of the general curve the new product will follow.

Diffusion researchers also have attemped to identify general product attributes that lead to acceptance or rejection of new products. In general, the degree to which a new product is perceived to be compatible, superior, easy to understand and use, communicable, and triable on a limited basis will greatly influence the ease or difficulty of gaining its acceptance.

In addition to product attributes, diffusion research have examined the characteristics of innovative consumers in order to identify segments which can be expected to exhibit early purchasing behavior. Identification of these groups would allow industry to tailor their marketing programs to these segments, which is important since innovators are often opinion leaders who influence other consumers. Research indicates that innovators tend to be members of the higher social classes. However, in the designing of marketing programs, the compatibility between the product's characteristics and the characteristics of the adopting group is sometimes more important in determining diffusion patterns than social class or other variables.

Because of the magnitude of the investment in product introductions, most new products undergo a series of tests designed to weed out failures as soon as possible, starting with concept testing, through product and home use testing, and finally test marketing. Mathematical models have been developed to permit rapid feedback from marketing situations which predict success or failure at an early stage. Recently, a number of models have been developed for use in pretest market situations in an attempt to cut down the great expense incurred during the test marketing stage.

Pretest market models, and all new product testing techniques discussed in this chapter, are aimed toward decreasing the amount of uncertainty and risk involved in introducing a new product. The variables which determine the success and failure of a new product range from the attributes of the product itself to the characteristics of the consumers who will buy the product and the interrelationships between the two, as well as external factors such as the state of the economy. It is only through a thorough understanding of all these factors that new product introduction can become less traumatic and failure-ridden for marketers and more satisfying for consumers. Several of the factors and concepts which affect new product success are responsible for the success (and failure) of promotional campaigns designed to boost sales of older products and for brand shares of older products. We examine how these factors affect the market strength of established brands in the next chapter.

REVIEW QUESTIONS

1 The definition of a new product as anything consumers perceive as new omits a number of important considerations. Identify and discuss those omissions. Why are they important from a marketing viewpoint?
2 New product ideas come from a variety of sources. Discuss each source and its relative importance in terms of new product contributions.
3 List the two generalized patterns of diffusion along with the two special cases of these patterns. Discuss the major differences between the diffusion patterns. Which patterns has received the most attention? Why?
4 How are diffusion patterns used to predict the rate and extent of diffusion in market segments?
5 List the five most important determinants of product acceptance and rejection. How does each product attribute affect the diffusion process?
6 Define consumer innovativeness. Discuss the differences between the innovativeness categories developed by diffusion researchers. Which categories are most important during the introduction of a new product?
7 Discuss the relationship between innovators and opinion leaders. Are the two always positively related? Why is this association important in understanding new product behavior?
8 How does social class relate to innovativeness? Does this relationship hold true for all types of products? Why or why not?
9 Compare each of the new product tests designed to weed out failures at the earliest possible date. Discuss the advantages and limitations of each type of test and the corporate investment levels which occur at each testing stage.
10 Why are mathematical models used in conjunction with test marketing? Describe the "brand switching matrix" and discuss the information it provides.
11 In recent years a number of pretest market models have been developed. Why is there a need for such models? Have they been used to successfully predict eventual market share for new products?
12 Examine the COMP model. Discuss the three phases of research explicit in this model, and indicate how the information obtained from each phase is used to predict the success or failure of a new product.

EXERCISE

The long, steep slide in United States auto sales that began in October 1973 started to bottom out and turn around in the Summer of 1975. Nevertheless, the slump left automakers shaken and uncertain.

Within this climate of uncertainty, executives of VMW (Vehicle Motor Works) of Bavaria wanted to assess the feasibility of introducing a new line of compact imports into the American market. The executives of VMW formulated the following objectives and method for a study of the United States market:

I Objectives
- **A** To develop an authoritative body of knowledge of the United States market in general and in suitable segments based on regional and metropolitan locations, demographic tabulations, and socioeconomic trends and forecasts.
- **B** To develop similar definitive material for the United States automobile market, with special emphasis on changes in marketing practices for domestic and imported vehicles and consumers' views of automobiles and other forms of transportation.
- **C** To formulate a strategic (five-year) marketing plan which offers the most likely route to succesful diffusion in the United States market by VMW if the decision is made to introduce its new line of cars.

II Method
- **A** To meet the objectives, the analysis should follow the following pattern
  - **1** Study of the United States market in general via readily available official and commercial research reports.
  - **2** Study of the automotive market via surveys of industry observers, dealers and distributors, and consumers, with stress on attitudes and buying habits.
  - **3** Integration of the results of (1) and (2) and formulation of a strategic marketing plan.

You have been hired as marketing counsel to VMW. Your job is to develop a list of specific areas of inquiry for steps (I) and (II) above. The list should show what areas and what kinds of data would be needed to complete the study and formulate a marketing plan.

REFERENCES

Alderson, Wroe. *Dynamic Marketing Behavior.* Homewood, Ill.: Richard Irwin, 1965.

Allvine, F. C. "Diffusion of a Competitive Innovation." In *Proceedings,* Fall Conference of the American Marketing Association, 1968.

Anscombe, F. J. "Estimating a Mixed Exponential Response Law." *Journal of the American Statistical Association* (September 1961), 493–502.

Baumgarten, Steven A., and Charles W. King. "A Study of Fashion Adoption among College Students." *Broadening the Concept of Marketing.* Chicago: American Marketing Association, 1970.

Bell, W. E. "Consumer Innovators: A Unique Market for Newness." In S. A. Greyser (ed.), *Proceedings of the American Marketing Association,* 1963, 85–95.

Brooks, J. *The Fate of the Edsel and Other Business Adventures.* New York: Harper and Row, 1961.

Burger, Philip C. "COMP: A New Product Forecasting System." Unpublished paper. Northwestern University, 1972.

Buzzell, R. D. "Competitive Behavior and Product Life Cycles." In J. Wright and J. Goldstucker (eds.), *New Ideas for Successful Marketing. Proceedings of the American Marketing Association,* 1966.

——— and R. Nourse. *Product Innovation in Food Processing: 1954–1964.* Boston: Division of Research, Harvard Business School, 1967.

Charnes, A., W. W. Cooper, J. K. Devoe, and D. B. Learner. "DEMON: Decision Mapping Via Optimum Go-No Networks—A Model for Marketing New Products." *Management Science,* 12 (July 1966).

Cimons, Marlene. "Are Inventors a Dying Breed?" *The Atlanta Journal and Constitution* (Mar. 4, 1973), 14-D.

Claycamp, H. J., and L. F. Liddy. "Prediction of New Product Performance: An Analytical Approach." *Journal of Marketing Research,* 6 (November 1962), 414–420.

Colemen, J., E. Katz, and H. Menzel. "The Diffusion of an Innovation among Physicians." *Sociometry* (December 1957), 253–270.

Darden, William R., and Fred D. Reynolds. "Male Apparel Innovativeness and Social Context: An Application of Multivariate Analysis of Variance." *Proceedings,* Association for Consumer Research, 1972.

DeFleur, M. L. *Theories of Mass Communications.* New York: McKay, 1970.

Dodd, S. C. "Diffusion Is Predictable: Testing Probability Models for Laws of Interaction." *American Sociology Review,* 20 (December 1955), 392–401.

Elrick and Lavidge, Inc. "COMP System Successful in Predicting Sales of New Consumer Products." *Marketing Today,* 11, No. 1, 1973.

Fourt, A., and J. W. Woodlock. "Early Prediction of Market Success for New Grocery Products." *Journal of Marketing,* 25 (1960), 31–38.

Graham, S. "Class and Conservatism in the Adoption of Innovations." *Human Relations,* 9, No. 1 (1956), 91–100.

Jones, Lyle V., David R. Penyam, and L. L. Thurstone. "Development of a Scale for Measuring Soldiers' Food Preferences." *Food Research,* 20, No. 5 (1955), 512–520.

Kelly, R. F. "The Diffusion Model as a Predictor of Ultimate Patronage Levels in New Retail Outlets." In R. M. Haas (ed.), *Science, Technology and Marketing.* Chicago: American Marketing Association, 1966.

Leo Burnett Company, Inc. "The Procter and Gamble Company." *Hello* (February–March 1970), 7–9, 14–15.

Lipstein, B. "Modelling and New Product Birth." *Journal of Advertising Research,* 10, No. 5 (October 1970), 3–11.

Pessemier, Edgar A., Philip C. Burger, and Douglas J. Tigert. "Can New Product Buyers Be Identified?" *Journal of Marketing Research,* 4 (November 1967), 349–354.

Reynolds, Fred D., and William R. Darden. "Fashion Theory and Pragmatics: The Case of the Midi." *Journal of Retailing,* 49 (Spring 1973), 51–62.

——— and ———. "Why the Midi Failed." *Journal of Advertising Research,* 12 (August 1972), 39–44.

Reynolds, W. H. "The Wide C-Post and the Fashion Process." *Journal of Marketing,* 29 (January 1965), 40–54.

Robertson, Thomas S. *Innovative Behavior and Communication.* New York: Holt, 1971.

———. "The New Product Diffusion Process." In B. A. Morin (ed.), *Marketing in a Changing World.* Chicago: American Marketing Association, 1969, 80–86.

Rogers, Everett M. *Diffusion of Innovations.* New York: Free Press, 1962.

——— and Floyd Shoemaker. *The Communication of Innovations.* New York: Free Press, 1971.

——— and David Stanfield. "Adoption and Diffusion of New Products: Emerging Generalizations and Hypotheses." In Frank M. Bass, Charles W. King, and Edgar A. Pessemier, *Applications of the Sciences in Marketing Management.* New York: Wiley, 1968.

Urban, G. L. "A Mathematical Modeling Approach to Product Line Decisions." *Journal of Marketing Research,* 6 (February 1969), 40–47.

Whyte, W. H., Jr. "The Web of Word of Mouth." *Fortune,* 50 (November 1954), 146 ff.

Worcester, R. M. (ed.). *Consumer Market Research Handbook.* London: McGraw-Hill, 1972.

Zaltman, Gerald, and Ronald Stiff. "Theories of Diffusion." In Scott Ward and Thomas S. Robertson (eds.), *Consumer Behavior: Theoretical Sources.* Englewood Cliffs, N.J.: Prentice-Hall, 1973.

Chapter 13

Repeat-Purchasing Behavior

Chapter 2 began with an example of consumer behavior obtained through two methods of studying behavior: direct observation and direct interviewing. The sequence of events observed in the supermarket revealed some of the complexities of buyer behavior and some contradictory patterns of behavior. Why, for example, did the homemaker ignore price specials on particular brands of bleach and detergent and purchase the special on Dial? Some of the ambiguity was lessened when the homemaker answered a direct question to the effect that the reduced-price brands of detergent and bleach were not her "regular" brands. Her answer implied that Dial is a regular brand or one that she would have purchased even if it had not been on sale at a reduced price.

The example, of course, was but one of thousands of supermarket episodes taking place every day. Figuratively, it was a snapshot of one person's purchases. Now, by way of contrast, suppose we are interested only in Dial and would like to know how many of a large number of consumers purchase it on a regular basis. One way to obtain an answer would be to repeat the direct observation for a number of consumers at a number of stores and count the number of persons who purchased Dial. But if the concern is with the regular purchasers of Dial, the observations would need to be repeated over time with the same consumers. This approach of course, would present some large-scale administrative problems and in general would not be practical.

Nevertheless, the study of consumers' purchases of established products is concerned primarily with their purchases over time. Analysis over time is important because the actions of people over time are often a better reflection of their true behavior than observed and/or reported behavior at a single point in time. To illustrate, a motion picture conveys more information than a snapshot. A "snapshot" of 100 women at a supermarket featuring a special on Dial might show that 20 of them had purchased Dial; a snapshot of 100 at another supermarket where Dial was offered at the regular price might show the same thing. Do we conclude that 20 percent of the shoppers purchase Dial regularly and 80 percent do not? A motion picture of the women in each group taken over a six-month period might show that they all purchase Dial but only 20 percent of the time. This finding is consistent with those from the snapshots, but it leads to a different conclusion, one that might be particularly important to marketers of Dial—a point that will become evident later in the chapter.

Major marketers of consumer products like Dial spend a substantial proportion of their market research budgets obtaining "motion pictures" of the purchases of their brands, particularly their established brands, since most month-by-month sales come from these. In essence, monitoring markets—keeping track of market changes and competitive and own-brand performance—is to the marketer what blood pressure monitoring is to the physician trying to keep his patients healthy.

MARKET MONITORING

Marketers can monitor the ongoing activities in markets by subscribing to one or both of two types of services offered by several consumer research agencies: (1) store audits and (2) consumer panels.

Store Audits

One way marketers can keep track of retail sales is by means of "store audits" conducted by firms such as the A. C. Nielsen Company, the same company that rates television programs. The store audit is a method of indirect observation of consumer behavior since it tracks product movement through retail outlets instead of watching the actual purchases of products by consumers themselves. Every week, auditors check drug and grocery stores scattered throughout the United States to determine the sales of major brands. Sales can be calculated each period by a fairly simple formula:

$$\text{Previous-period stock} + \text{purchases received} - \text{present stock} = \text{sales}$$

Once sales are determined, each brand's share of the total sales in its product category is computed. These brand shares are the principal barometers of a brand's success or failure in the marketplace. Since even a small shift in brand share can mean a difference in income of millions of dollars to the manufacturer, marketing executives watch brand share changes with the same alertness that speculators watch stock market reports.

Brand shares are in fact surprisingly stable. Except when a major new brand is being introduced, such as Winchester in 1972 (see Table 10-1), brand shares for the nation as a whole seldom change more than a few percentage points from month to month. But since even these small shifts represent substantial sales and profit changes, marketing managers use audit data to help them evaluate the causes of the brand share changes. Evaluation is accomplished by comparing audit data with data on marketing efforts. For example, marketers can compare brand share shifts with their own or their competitors' recent promotional activities and get some idea of the types of activities that are likely to be effective on a short-term basis and which activities to avoid. In essence, the comparison of audit data with marketing data allows marketers to assess quickly competitive activities and own-brand performance. It is an application of an aggregate stimulus-response model.

Audit data can also be useful in gauging market changes of a long-term nature. Simple observations of audit data over extended time periods can reveal certain trends in the basic nature of the market that call for serious review of a firm's position with respect to the various elements of its marketing mix and even its productive capacity. For example, if a competitive brand with certain characteristics is found to be slowly but steadily gaining an increasing share of an increasing market, this trend would indicate a need for an in-depth review of the company's own marketing program, particularly its product line. Another instance might call for a strategic review of distribution policy, as in the case where product category sales are shifting within retail outlets; that is, a new form of retail outlet may be making dramatic inroads as the outlet for a product class. In cases such as this—reflecting an underlying shift in consumer patronage—a company must redirect its distribution policy and ensure that its brands are receiving adequate placement in the growth outlets.

There is always an inherent danger, however, in reading long-term trends from audit or any other type of aggregate data. Trends that stand out so clearly in hindsight may be obscured in a welter of signals at the time decisions are made for the future. During January and February of 1974, for example, small cars outsold large cars for the first time in automotive history, partly as a result of a trend among consumers for smaller cars and as a result of the dramatic decline in large-car sales. The sales decline was more traumatic for General Motors than for other United States auto manufacturers because GM was locked into production of large cars, particularly the Buick-Oldsmobile-Pontiac lines, where GM had always dominated the mid-price market segment. The fuel crisis, of course, was an unanticipated and major factor contributing to the greater than expected automotive sales slump. But even so, there was an underlying trend toward smaller cars long before the energy crunch, particularly among the more affluent segments of the population—the innovators. A 1970 "snapshot" illustrates the trend: 44 percent of the new cars registered in one of

California's most affluent counties were compact or subcompact imports. How could GM executives misread the trend? Actually, it was probably very easy—the automobile industry launched their 1974 models on the wake of one of the biggest sales years in United States auto history, a year in which both large and small cars were selling well and a year in which GM's Vega was not selling as well as expected (*Newsweek*, 1974).

Correctly reading the trends, however, can lessen the consequences of a major crisis. Executives at Ford, for example, may have read the trend toward smaller cars more accurately than GM and consequently suffered less during the gasoline crisis. Ford had introduced the Mustang II prior to the gasoline problem, thereby having an additional small-car entry. More significantly, however, the company's president was able to announce in January 1974 that 60 percent of Ford's 1975 model production would be devoted to small cars—an amazing production feat in an industry where three-year model lead times are common, but not so amazing if Ford executives had anticipated the underlying trend correctly and had planned for the changes to come in the auto market (Dahlquist, 1974). Ford executives made the decision to retain the Maverick-Comet and add the Granada-Monarch as a separate brand in the summer of 1973. By late 1976, with Granada the third largest selling auto brand in the United States, it appeared Ford executives made the right decision.

Consumer Panels

Another way to keep track of retail sales is to follow the purchasing behavior of individual homemakers. Several major research companies, including the Market Research Corporation of America, maintain national "consumer panels" for this purpose. *Consumer panels* are composed of a representative sample of individuals or households from the population. Every time a drugstore or grocery store purchase is made, the panel member records it in a "purchase diary," showing the amount purchased, the price, and the brand. When the reports of panel members are added together, they show how much of the purchasing in each product category was accounted for by each brand.

When the records of the panel families are added together, the share of sales accounted for by individual brands is seen to be quite stable, just as it is in the Neilsen store audit reports. Indeed, the analysis derived from the data of consumer panels to show the condition of the market and of its principal brands is quite consistent with that derived from store audit data. Both methods of market monitoring have been shown to provide accurate brand share and trend data over a wide range of product categories. Both provide information to marketers on such important questions as: How much of my brand was purchased? Who are my strong competitors? How strong are they? Is my brand gaining, losing, or holding its own? Is my brand or any brand reponsive to price cuts or special promotions? And does my brand have regional or store-type strengths or weaknesses?

In other words, data from consumer panels provide a broad picture of the market, and this is essential information to marketers. But this is not the sole reason for using consumer panels. As noted, brand shares derived from audit or panel data are quite stable. This apparent stability led rather naturally to acceptance of the notion of "brand loyalty." As the executive in charge of a nationally advertised brand might put it, "We have our customers, and our competitors have theirs; the way to increase our share the market is to lure their customers away." A corollary of this proposition is that, from the marketers' point of view, it is an exceptionally good idea to find out who these loyal customers are and to do whatever is necessary to convert them. It is in this corollary that the import of the consumer panel is found: panel data put the C back into the S→C→R model. Since panel data are obtained from individual consumers or families, these consumers' characteristics also can be measured and subsequent analyses can show the anatomy of the characteristics of consumer purchasing behavior as well as the aggregate results of behavior.

MARKET DYNAMICS

Anyone who looks at the purchasing records of individual panel families or members can see immediately that the apparent stability of the brand share conceals a great deal of consumer trading or brand switching—a family that switched from Brand X to Brand Y from one time period to the next is balanced by some other family that switched from Brand Y to Brand X. Thus the notion that "we have our customers and our competitors have theirs" turns out to be a great oversimplification.

The three market situations shown in Figure 13-1 clearly demonstrate the need for a fuller and more detailed understanding of market dynamics—of putting the C back into the S→C→R model. The figure depicts three brand share trends that could be revealed by either audit or panel data. Yet a variety of different consumer purchase patterns could bring about each of the trends (Lipstein, 1959).

The first graph in the figure shows a level trend of brand share. This trend could result from a fixed group of consumers purchasing the brand at regular intervals, but it could also be the result of a constant entrance and exit of consumers purchasing the brand.

The second graph depicts a trend of increasing brand share of market. Such a trend could arise because the brand has: (1) a fixed group of buyers plus new buyers switching to the brand at a regular rate; or (2) a greater number of buyers switching to than away from the brand, plus those that remain using the product at an increasing rate.

The third graph shows a declining brand share of market. This trend could result from: (1) a fixed rate of consumers switching from the brand; (2) a greater rate of consumers switching out than in; or (3) a declining rate of usage.

In each case the differing causes of the trend in brand share might call for different marketing efforts. And for every case that can be attributed to brand loyalty, there is at least one other possible explanation.

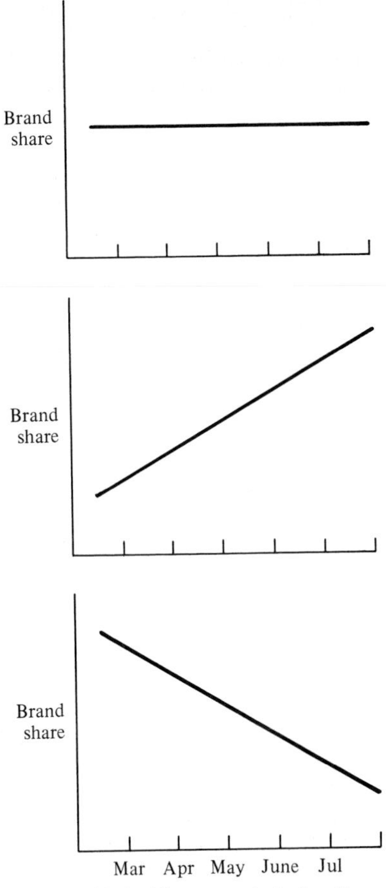

Figure 13-1 Three market situations. *Source:* Lipstein (1959:101). Reprinted from *Proceedings: 5th Annual Conference* © 1959 by the Advertising Research Foundations.

Repeat-Purchasing Patterns

Is there then no such thing as "brand loyalty"? Granted that consumers will seldom be perfectly consistent, do they not show some purchasing pattern other than random switching from brand to brand? Investigations of this question show that consumers in fact show several different patterns of repeat-purchasing behavior.

One of the earliest studies of repeat-purchasing behavior was conducted by George H. Borwn (1952–53), who followed the purchasing behavior of 100 members of a consumer panel maintained by the *Chicago Tribune.*

Brown identified four "loyalty" patterns:

1 *Undivided loyalty.* A panel member buys only one brand in a product category. This is the classic instance of "We have our customers, and our competitors have theirs."

2 *Divided loyalty.* A panel member divides her purchases between two, or sometimes among three or four, brands in a product category. A divided loyalty purchase pattern looks like this: ABAABABBABA. Or like this: ABACBACCABACBABCAB.

3 *Unstable loyalty.* A panel member purchases brands A and B in the following order: AAAAABBBBB. This pattern is an indication that the consumer has switched undivided loyalty from brand A to B.

4 *No loyalty.* The brands in a product category are purchased in a completely random order.

Brown found that the amount and type of loyalty vary greatly from one product category to another. For instance, the proportion of panel families showing undivided loyalty to a single brand varied from 12 percent to 73 percent, depending on the product, and the proportion showing some form of loyalty varied from 54 percent to 95 percent. Later studies have indicated that these differences are at least in part a function of the number of brands the product category contains—the more brands in a category, the less loyalty. Differences among product categories in amount of loyalty also seem to depend upon the extent to which the product category is dominated by only a few brands and upon the amount of dealing and price activity.

Another important brand loyalty study was conducted by Ross Cunningham (1956, 1961), who also used the *Chicago Tribune* panel. Like Brown, Cunningham found strong evidence for loyalty in some product categories. For each of the products he studied, at least half the panel members gave 43 percent or more of their patronage to a single brand. And, like Brown, he found very substantial differences in loyalty levels from product to product.

Cunningham raised the further question, Are some consumers generally more brand-loyal than others—i.e., if a consumer shows strong brand loyalty in one product category, is she also apt to show strong brand loyalty in others? In general, the answer to that question was "no," and the same answer has come from later investigations of the same topic. This finding suggests that the analysis of consumers' repeat-purchasing behavior should be examined within a single product category or even within a single brand in a category in order to provide meaningful insights for marketing decisions. And when purchases of frequently bought products have been studied in this context, students of consumer behavior have found that repeat-purchasing behavior tends to follow a common pattern for a brand irrespective of what the brand is or the product class the brand is in (Ehrenberg, 1972).

Use of Repeat-Purchase Patterns In the preceding chapter it was noted that the high stakes in test markets have encouraged the development of mathematical models of consumer behavior that permit forecasts of what consumers in general will do. It was also noted that the models usually incorporate repeat- as well as first-purchase behavior because the ultimate success of any brand depends on the willingness of consumers, once having tried it, to continue purchasing it. One use of repeat-purchase data, then, is to help determine the ultimate fate of a new product long before it becomes apparent from simply observing historical sales or brand share trends.

New product introductions, though, are but one type of competitive activity. Marketers also change other elements of the marketing mix for established products. New advertising campaigns are launched and special promotions and price cuts are offered to induce consumers to switch. Sometimes these changes succeed in increasing brand share and at other times they flop. Thus the need to be able to anticipate the ultimate outcome of a change in marketing effort for an established brand is just as real as for a new brand. Students of consumer behavior have found that mathematical models developed to predict brand share for new brands also work fairly well for established brands, particularly those of the frequently purchased type. At one point in time it was thought that the conditions existing for first-purchase and repeat-purchase behavior when a new brand was launched were somewhat different from those applying to an established brand. It has since been demonstrated, however, that market dynamics of an established brand differ only in degree rather than kind from those present at the launch of a new brand. Hence it is possible to predict fairly accurately the effect on established-brand share of changing a marketing effort, in the same manner as predicting new product performance; the only technical difference in the analysis is that an arbitrary time is picked to begin the analysis for an established brand (Parfitt and Collins, 1968).

One basic method for predicting brand share is the product of three measures calculated from the continuous purchasing records of panel members: (1) ultimate penetration, (2) repeat-purchasing rate, and (3) buying rate index.

Ultimate penetration, discussed in detail in Chapter 12, refers to the ultimate cumulative proportion of new buyers of a brand. For established brands, these "new" buyers may be persons switching from another brand, new buyers in the market, or both. *Repeat-purchase rate* is a measure representing the proportion of the total purchases a brand receives in its product class from repeat buyers. Table 13-1 shows the calculation of repeat-purchasing rates for Brand T at two-week intervals for seven consumers. The calculations are made after a person has first tried the brand. As shown in the table, in each of the two-week periods the seven buyers made ten purchases in the product class, of which successively 60 percent, 50 percent, and 40 percent were repeat purchases of Brand T. In this example, a repeat-purchasing rate of 40 percent would be selected, since it is at this proportion that the rate leveled off or became fairly steady.

The *buying rate index* is calculated to compare the rate of purchasing in the product class of the repeat buyers with the average rate of all buyers in the product category. The average buying level is expressed as 1.0; thus a heavy buyer might have an index of 1.20 and a light buyer an index of 0.75.

Once these three measures have been estimated, brand share can be predicted in a straightforward manner: ultimate penetration × repeat-purchasing rate × buying rate index (Parfitt and Collins, 1968).

Weeks		1	2	3	4	5	6	7	8	9	10	11
Buyer:	1	T	T	R	T	R	R	R	R	T	R	R
	2	T		S		S		S		S		S
	3		T	T	T	T	T	T	T	T	T	T
	4		T		T		R		T		R	
	5			T		T		T		T		T
	6			T	T	R	T	R	R	S	R	R
	7			T	S		S		S		S	
Cumulative buyers		2	4	7								
Repeat-purchasing rate					$\frac{6}{10}$ = 60%		$\frac{5}{10}$ = 50%		$\frac{4}{10}$ = 40%		$\frac{4}{10}$ = 40%	

Table 13-1 Illustration of repeat-purchasing rate calculation from a hypothetical example. *Source:* Parfitt and Collins (1968: 132). Reprinted from *Journal of Marketing Research, published by the American Marketing Association.*

An example to illustrate the use of this formula is shown in Table 13-2. Brand L is an established brand of household detergent which normally captures about 5 percent of the market. A 50 percent price cut is initiated as a competitive tactic, and management needs to know the results of the promotion. The data in the table show that the promotion produced a substantial change in brand penetration (from 20 percent to 31 percent), which means that a number of buyers switched to L from other brands and/or came into the market after the price cut. This also would mean a relatively large increase in brand share at the time of the offer, but not necessarily one that would hold over the long run. The data also show that the repeat-purchasing rate of the 11 percent new buyers was only 4 percent after the offer was completed. The low repeat-purchasing rate at an average level of buying would mean a modest increase in long-term brand share (less than 1 percent of the market). Whether or not this long-term result is satisfactory would depend upon other measures, such as total sales and costs to the firm. But satisfactory or unsatisfactory to management, the results can be predicted.

Explaining the Patterns

The tendency for most consumers to develop habits or consistent patterns of repeat-purchasing behavior provides the basis for the ability to use these patterns to predict market changes. And generally the prediction models work well for a wide range of practical situations. But the models do not work in all situations—there are exceptions or cases that cannot be predicted with reasonable accuracy. Moreover, the prediction models are based on *how* people buy, not *why*. Hence there has been and continues to be a great deal of consumer research and speculation trying to explain the patterns of repeat-purchasing behavior. The thrust of most of this research has been to identify consumers who can be expected to be loyal to one or a combination of brands—those who exhibit undivided and those who show divided or "multi-brand" loyalty. At one time or another these patterns have been attributed to characteristics of buyers other than their purchasing characteristics, to characteristics of products, and to stochastic or random decision processes.

Consumer Characteristics In spite of the finding by Cunningham that a generalized brand-loyal consumer does not appear to exist, some students of consumer behavior have attempted to identify the "brand-loyal consumer" by asking such questions as, "Are brand-loyal consumers different from nonloyal consumers in age, in level of education, in personality?" As might be expected, the answers to this question have turned out to be contradictory, because they have depended upon the particular mix of products covered by each study. Not surprisingly, in some studies that used an index of brand loyalty that combined loyalty to many varied products, no correlates of loyalty were found at all (Frank, 1967).

Yet when researchers have focused on a single product category, the results have been more promising. Carman (1970), for example, used a special-purpose consumer panel (that allowed for more measures of consumers' characteristics than is typical in commercial panel studies) to explore individually the correlates of loyalty to food stores, regular ground coffee, canned fruit, and frozen orange juice. Not surprisingly, when his data were examined across the four categories, the usual contradictory results were found, particularly with respect to demographic and general personality characteristics. There were, however, some highly significant consistencies that suggest a relationship between personal characteristics, the shopping process, and brand loyalty. Based on his findings, Carman suggested:

1 The single most important predictor of brand loyalty is store loyalty.
2 Consumers who are not "shopping-prone" will shop in a very small number of stores and, within those stores, will remain loyal to a very small number of brands rather than make careful choices between the values offered by those stores.
3 Personal characteristics of consumer will explain differences in store loyalty.

Carman's findings, should they be found fairly regularly in future studies

Table 13-2 The Results of a 50-Percent Price Cut

Brand L	Ultimate penetration	X	Repeat-purchasing rate	X	Buying rate index	=	Ultimate brand share
Before price cut	20%	X	25%	X	1.03	=	5.15%
After price cut	11%	X	4%	X	1.01	=	0.45%
							5.60%

Source: Adapted from Parfitt (1972).

of brand loyalty, have significant implications for marketers trying to reach brand-loyal buyers of frequently purchased products. Specifically, his results suggest: (1) identifying the store-loyal consumer, (2) identifying retail outlets with the highest proportion of store-loyal buyers, and (3) ensuring that a particular brand is available in those stores. This implication will be explored further in the next chapter under the discussion of store loyalty.

Product Attributes In Chapter 9 we discussed the role of product perceptions and predispositions on people's behavior. Not surprisingly, students of consumer behavior have attempted to determine the relationship between consumers' attribute perceptions and preferences and their repeat-purchase behavior. Several studies have demonstrated the usefulness of brand-specific measures in predicting brand choice. Using the multiattribute model discussed in Chapter 9, for example, Kraft, Granbois, and Summers (1973) found the summated score to be highly related in the aggregate to brands purchased by consumers over the sixteen-week study period of a specially designed consumer panel. And on the basis of individual respondents, the index predicted the brand most frequently purchased in about two-thirds of the cases for each of the three product categories studied (coffee, orange juice, and paper towels). Other more specific consumer measures, such as brand bought last and favorite brand, however, performed about as well as the summated index in predicting brand purchases.

It would seem, then, that for purposes of prediction, particularly for the pattern of undivided loyalty, the behavioral pattern itself is sufficient. The examination of consumers' perceptions and preferences is not meaningless, however. Rather, its value may be more diagnostic than predictive, along the lines of our discussion in Chapter 9.

Another pattern of repeat-purchasing behavior identified by Brown was called "divided loyalty," meaning that persons exhibiting this behavioral pattern buy a relatively stable mix of brands within a product category. More recently students of consumer behavior have labeled such a pattern "multi-brand loyalty." Whatever we call it, however, the crucial question is, "Why do some consumers switch their purchases among a limited set of brands and not switch across the entire product category?"

One plausible explanation is that the chosen brands are perceived as close substitutes for one another. In other words, consumers have certain attribute preferences and perceive only a subset of brands in a product class as having similar sets of these attributes.

Some evidence to support this notion is found in an experiment conducted by Bass, Pessemier, and Lehmann (1972). Using eight brands of soft drinks as the product category, the authors required panel members to select a 12-ounce can four days a week for three weeks. The subjects also were measured on certain characteristics, such as their attribute perceptions of each brand. To test the hypothesis that consumers switch to similar brands, the authors not only examined the overall repeat-purchasing patterns but also employed "forced brand switching" by withholding certain brands on selected days and thereby simulating an out-of-stock condition. The results? The major beneficiary of an out-of-stock condition was the brand most similar to the unavailable brand. For instance, in normal purchasing periods the authors found that 15 percent of people who selected Coke one time selected Pepsi the next time (Coke and Pepsi were perceived by the subjects to be quite similar on the eight attributes measured). When Coke was denied, however, the switching figure to Pepsi increased to 53 percent!

Overall, the authors concluded that the predominant switching to similar brands tends to confirm the notion that choice is influenced by attitudes which derive from beliefs and values for specific attributes of brands.

Bass and his colleagues also noted a tendency for some panel members to switch to dissimilar brands, a pattern of behavior similar to Brown's "no loyalty" category. The authors found, for example, that 10 percent of the persons who chose Coke most often chose 7-Up second most often. The amount of switching to dissimilar brands led them to reject a completely deterministic view of the choice processes of consumers and to postulate that there is also a random component in choice which arises because of consumers' need for variety.

IMPULSE BUYING

Another concept that has proved to be important in the study of consumer behavior is "impulse buying." To what degree do consumers plan their purchases in detail before they go shopping, and to what degree to they buy on impulse, picking up things that they had not planned to get and perhaps do not really need?

The answer to this question depends on exactly how impulse buying is defined, and impulse buying turns out to have at least four definitions (Stern, 1962):

1 *Pure impulse buying.* The "novelty or escape purchase which breaks a normal buying pattern."

2 *Reminder impulse buying.* "A shopper sees an item and remembers that the stock at home is exhausted or low, or recalls an advertisement or other information about the item and a previous decision to buy."

3 *Suggestion impulse buying.* A shopper sees a product for the first time and visualizes a need for it, even though he or she has no previous knowledge of the item. This type of impulse buying is distinguished from reminder buying in that the consumer has no previous experience with the product to serve as a guide. Rather she must evaluate the product at the point of sale.

4 *Planned impulse buying.* "The shopper enters the store with some specific purchases in mind, but with the expectation and intention to make other purchases that depend on price specials, coupon offers and the like."

A series of studies by E. I. DuPont Company (see Table 13-3) has shown that American homemakers are increasingly transferring their purchase planning from the home to the store, entering the store with a general set of

Table 13-3 Unplanned Purchases as a Percentage of Total Purchases in Supermarkets

Type of purchase	1945	1949	1954	1959
Specifically planned	48	33	29	31
Generally planned	11	27	21	16
Substituted (change from a specifically or generally planned item)	3	2	2	2
Unplanned	38	38	48	51

Source: *DuPont Consumer Buying Habits Studies*, as cited in Stern (1962).

expectations but making a great number of the actual buying decisions at the point of purchase. Studies of this kind have sometimes been interpreted as showing that consumers are becoming less rational in their decision making—that instead of being guided by the intrinsic merits of products, the modern American consumer is frequently trapped into bad decisions by such superficial lures as attractive packaging and inviting displays.

This interpretation of the increase in impulse purchasing is not necessarily correct. Even though most grocery buying decisions are made at the point of purchase rather than at home, and most of them fit one of the definitions of impulse buying given above, the behavior is not necessarily foolish or impetuous and it is not dominated by meaningless, superficial influences. Rather, considering the number of homemakers who are working spouses and/or the number who must get their shopping done quickly in the company of one or more distracting children, considering that they have to make many rapid decisions among hundreds of marginally different brands, and considering the requirements imposed by other family members and a flexible but finite budget in an inflationary economy, their behavior is for the most part realistic and efficient.

Nevertheless, the connotation of the general term *impulse buying*, along with the growing number of decisions made in the stores, has led to increased efforts by many marketers to design eye-catching packages, to develop and promote special in-store displays, and to offer inducements to retailers to place their brands in preferred store locations. The effectiveness of efforts of this nature is discussed in the following section.

IN-STORE MERCHANDISING

Monotony is sleep-inducing; counting sheep is a popular remedy for insomnia. Similarly, monotonous stores—stores where all packages were the same size and color and where fixtures, lighting, and other elements of store design tended toward the drab and dull—would be highly effective in "putting customers to sleep." But stores are not monotonous. Take a casual stroll down detergent lane or snack alley in a typical supermarket: packages of all shapes, sizes, colors, and descriptions seem to almost jump from the shelves to catch your eye; and if you are not somewhat cautious in rounding an aisle, you may walk into or trip over special display while listening to piped-in music inviting a mood to "stay and shop a while longer."

Marketers, particularly in self-service stores, spend millions each year on in-store merchandising trying to increase sales of potentially profitable items and trying to get consumers to switch brands and to remain loyal to their favorite brands. Most in-store merchandising principles have been developed from experimental research conducted in the context of self-service stores—the supermarket and the drugstore. The relevancy of these principles in other contexts has generally not been examined. Hence the discussion in this section is limited primarily to the effectiveness of various in-store merchandising tactics in the context of the self-service type of retail outlet. Only the discussion on pricing moves beyond this contextual situation.

Special Display

> Special display is the showpiece of all in-store merchandising techniques. Used correctly, it can increase sales dramatically, can add visual excitement to the store's aisles, can help shape the store's image and can be a shopping aid to customers (*Progressive Grocer,* 1971).

"Used correctly" means that while special displays can be effective in-store stimuli, they are more effective in some situations than in others. In an attempt to determine the situation-specific effects of special displays and other in-store merchandising tactics, *Progressive Grocer,* with the cooperation of the Great Atlantic & Pacific Tea Company, conducted a series of in-store experiments during a five-month period in mid-1970 in a panel of supermarkets. In the supermarket panel, both test and control stores were matched in volume, layout, size, and demographics. Merchandising experiments were conducted in parts of stores, with comparison control stores retaining normal operating procedures during the length of each specific experiment.[1]

Effect of In-Store Location It is not surprising that brand sales are related to where people pass in a supermarket and that special displays are most effective when placed in heavy traffic locations. This is well illustrated in the sweater example shown in Figure 13-2. The sweater display located in a position where it was passed by 25 percent of store customers produced 4 unit sales—a poor showing relative to the unit sales from the special displays located in areas with high traffic density.

The other examples in the figure also show a positive relationship between people passing and the buying from a special display. Yet, exactly how well a display performs depends not only on its location but also on other selling efforts as well. The data on the new brand of shampoo, for example, show the number 3 checkout location to be superior to the health and beauty aids

[1]Unless otherwise indicated, the discussion on in-store merchandising effects is from *Progressive Grocer* (1971).

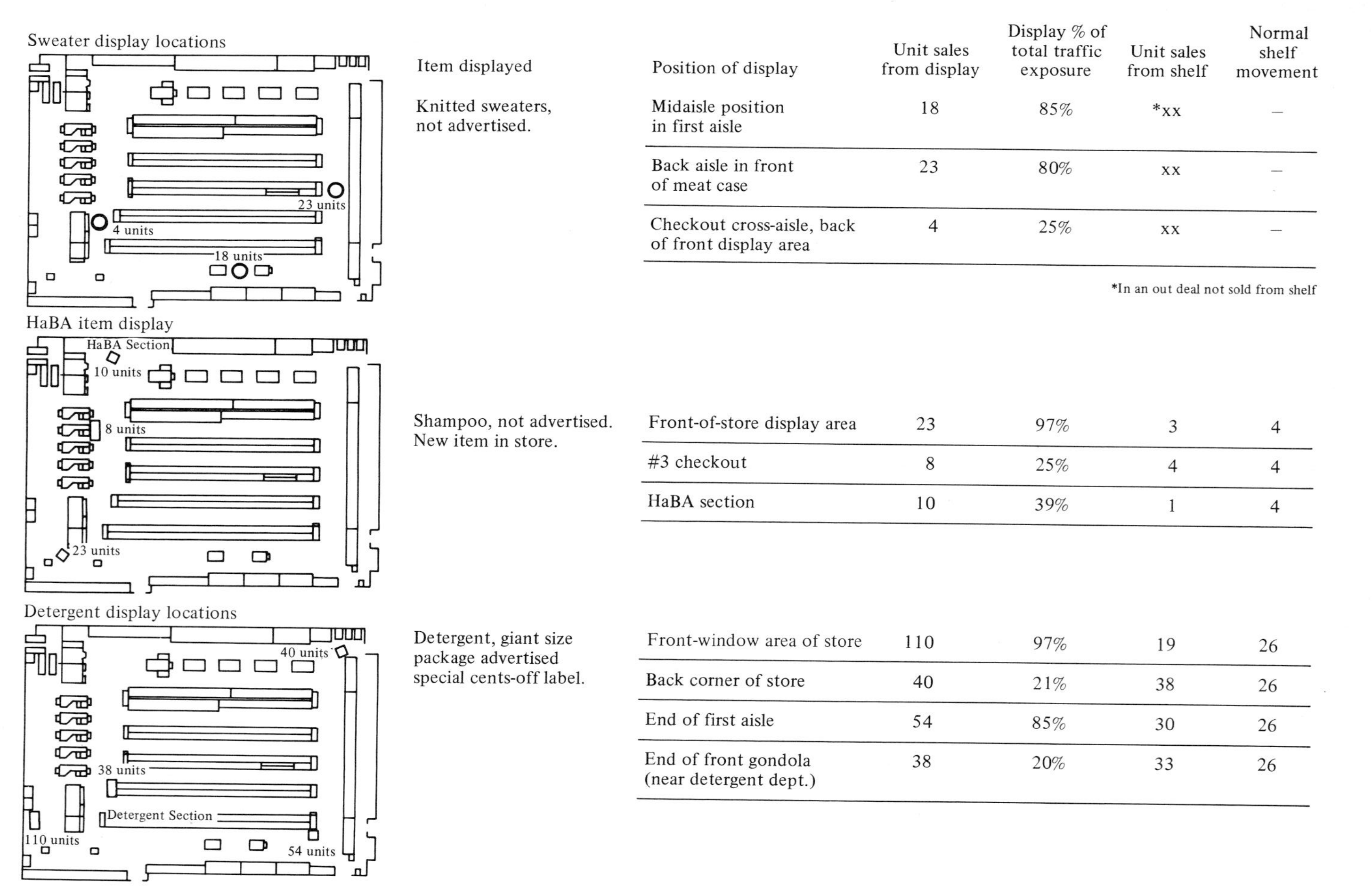

Item displayed	Position of display	Unit sales from display	Display % of total traffic exposure	Unit sales from shelf	Normal shelf movement
Knitted sweaters, not advertised.	Midaisle position in first aisle	18	85%	*xx	–
	Back aisle in front of meat case	23	80%	xx	–
	Checkout cross-aisle, back of front display area	4	25%	xx	–
Shampoo, not advertised. New item in store.	Front-of-store display area	23	97%	3	4
	#3 checkout	8	25%	4	4
	HaBA section	10	39%	1	4
Detergent, giant size package advertised special cents-off label.	Front-window area of store	110	97%	19	26
	Back corner of store	40	21%	38	26
	End of first aisle	54	85%	30	26
	End of front gondola (near detergent dept.)	38	20%	33	26

*In an out deal not sold from shelf

Figure 13-2 Effect of display location on sales. *Source: Progressive Grocer* (1971).

(HaBA) location when the impact of the special display on normal shelf sales is considered. When the checkout location was tested, it produced lower unit sales from the display, but it did not affect normal shelf sales as did the HaBA display. The front-of-store display area was the most effective location, but store managers cannot locate all their special displays at the same part of a store.

The third example in the figure illustrates customer reaction to a detergent brand, advertised and featuring a cents-off label, when displayed in different areas of the test stores. The coupling of special display with other promotional efforts indicated that the item will perform well on displays even in remote corners of the store and will not drastically affect shelf sales, which normally will increase as a result of effective advertising and price cuts.

The Effect of Time Even though displays are effective in increasing the sales of a brand, they have a temporal dimension: they can and do age quickly in terms of consumer interest. In general, the typical display tends to decrease in sales after the first week, but the degree of decline is relative to other promotional efforts and the seasonality of the item displayed.

Figure 13-3 shows the temporal effects of display effectiveness in four situations. Paper towels, which produced sales of 248 units during the first week, were also advertised in the local newspaper serving the test stores. No ads were used after the first week, and display sales dropped substantially. The special display tests on dog food showed an even more dramatic decline after the first week—the results of intentionally not restocking the display. In contrast, the canned soup displays were kept well stocked, and sales decline

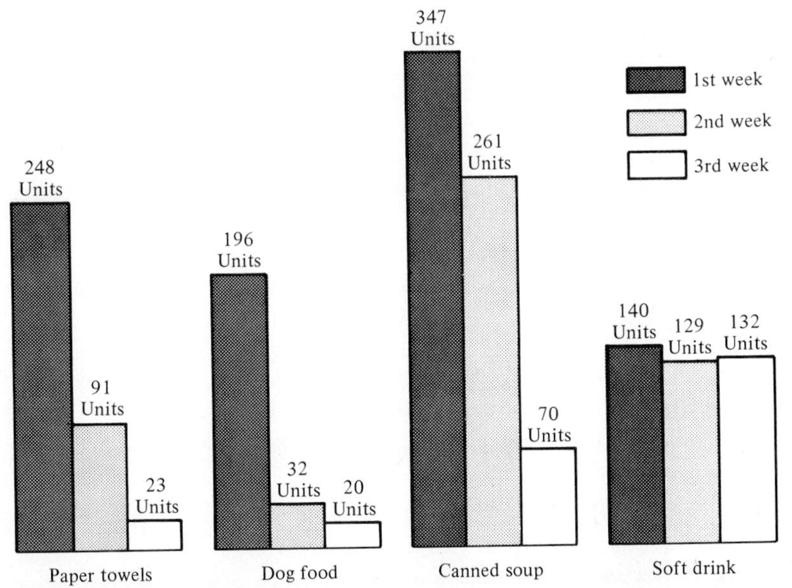

Figure 13-3 Length of display effectiveness. *Source: Progressive Grocer* (1971).

was substantially less each week. The general declining sales pattern is not shown for the soft drink experiment, indicating that rapidly consumed, seasonal-item displays can maintain sales level for longer periods of time.

Togetherness The *Progressive Grocer* experiments showed that "togetherness sells." When related or complementary items are jointly displayed, sales for each of the items are greater than when they are displayed separately. In one example, a display featured two seasonally related items—fresh lemons and instant tea—suggested as beverage go-togethers by point-of-purchase materials depicting a "Keep Cool" theme. In control stores, these items were also displayed, but in separate locations, with price signs but no tie-in suggestions. The results: sales were higher on lemons by 32 percent and on tea by 83 percent in stores using the combination display than in control stores using the separate-display approach. Table 13-4 illustrates the results of several related-item displays when compared with separate-item displays. In every case both individual and combined sales were higher when complementary products were jointly displayed.[2]

P-o-p, Signs, and Display Effectiveness Consumers tend to react favorably to special displays, as the previously described examples illustrate. Displays, however, tend to be more effective when used with colorful, eye-catching point-of-purchasing (p-o-p) materials to set the display theme and to make suggestions for the products' uses, or even when used with a simple, hand-lettered sign.

Consider, for example, the introduction of new brands in a supermarket, an occurrence which happens hundreds of times yearly. New items can become lost among the thousands of regularly stacked products if not properly identified. Point-of-purchase material, however, can properly identify new items; and once consumers are attraced to them, evaluations can be made and, if the product is acceptable, sales will generally be higher. To illustrate, *Progressive Grocer* tested three new items without and with point-of-purchase material. A new refrigerated item displayed in a dairy case reached weekly sales of 11 units without p-o-p and 38 units with p-o-p; a new salad dressing displayed on a shelf extender produced weekly sales of 5 units and 21 units, respectively, without and with p-o-p material; and the sales of a floor-displayed canned drink jumped from 19 to 41 units a week with the addition of point-of-purchase material.

Store-made signs typically are not acclaimed artistic successes. Nevertheless, consumers tend to react favorably to them. As the test results shown in Table 13-5 reveal, hand-lettered signs make an excellent showing even when contrasted to manufacturer-produced materials.

To summarize, special displays generally increase sales of a brand, at least

[2]A more complete discussion of the analysis of complementary products is presented in Chap. 15.

Table 13-4 Related-Item versus Separate Displays

Item	Separate display		Related-item display		Percent dollar sales difference
	Unit sales	Dollar sales	Unit sales	Dollar sales	
Picnic display					
Paper plates, white	21	13.80	43	29.67	+115
Paper plates, colored	8	6.32	28	12.12	+ 99
Stuffed olives	17	11.73	88	60.72	+418
Paper cups	24	11.76	38	18.62	+ 58
Potato chips	154	89.68	518	304.93	+240
Catsup	32	15.04	77	36.19	+141
Total	256	148.33	792	462.25	+212
Manufacturer banana-chocolate bits promotion					
Bananas	269	92.23	374	141.57	+ 54
Chocolate bits	10	4.90	47	23.03	+370
Total	279	97.13	421	164.60	+ 70
Dessert tie-in display					
Pound cake	12	5.84	44	19.83	+240
Strawberries	139	75.94	420	236.26	+211
Total	151	81.78	464	256.09	+213
Nonfood tie-in display					
Cleanser	10	4.90	27	13.23	+170
Cleaning brushes	3	.87	10	2.90	+233
Total	13	5.77	37	16.13	+180

Source: *Progressive Grocer* (1971).

for a short time, over normal shelf sales. More effectiveness is accomplished, however, when products are selected with consideration of their relationships to local consumer needs, seasonal demands, complementary usage, and promotional and advertising efforts by either manufacturers or the retailer.

Shelving

Special display may be the showpiece of in-store merchandising, but the shelf is the selling heart of the supermarket, for most supermarket sales come from consumers selecting products from the shelves of midstore gondolas. Thus, the way products are shelved affects consumer purchasing behavior, particularly with respect to shelf location and shelf facings.

Shelf Location Traditionally, the rule of thumb on shelf location sales effectiveness ranks eye level first, waist-level second, and knee or ankle level third. It is, of course, no more possible to locate all items at eye level than it is to locate all special displays in a 95 percent traffic location.

But beyond the physical impossibility of locating everything at eye level, store experiments have shown that there are other valid reasons for locating

Table 13-5 How Signs Affect Display Sales

Item	Type of display	Store-made sign (units sold)	Manufacturer sign (units sold)	No sign (units sold)
Facial tissue	Floor display	94	75	52
Bleach	Wire basket display	24	29	15
Refrigerated dough	In-case dairy display	22	38	6
Sponges	Extender display	15	—	9
Detergent	Floor display	29	34	10
Doughnuts	Table display	105	—	45

Source: *Progressive Grocer* (1971).

products on lower shelves. Generally, tests have demonstrated that consumer responses to shelf locations depend upon such factors as an item's package size, whether or not it is being advertised, its need for visibility, and its intended market segment. Some specific examples from the *Progressive Grocer* studies illustrate the generalization.

The importance of product size and weight as an influence on sales changes resulting from shelf shifts is illustrated by the effects of moving a 54-ounce juice item from a lower shelf to a top shelf. Instead of an increase in sales, which one might suspect, unit movement because of the difficulty of lifting such a heavy item from that height actually dropped off 15 percent.

Lower shelves also hold definite merchandising opportunities when the shelved product has special appeal to those customers who are only four feet tall or less—the children. In candy, sales increases in ranges of 14 percent to 39 percent have resulted from the placement of multipacks of penny candies, suckers, and TV-advertised products on the bottom shelf within reach of the juvenile crowd.

In the middle range of shelving heights, visibility variation becomes the major influence on product movement. Typical of the tested product shifts within this center range of shelving was the relocation of a grape jelly item from a waist-level position to eye level. Although the resulting change in visibility was not particularly dramatic, the shift did add 12 percent to the product's weekly sales. Data in Figure 13-4 (an average of a number of shelf relocations for products where visibility variation is the dominant factor), however, show how dramatically sales can change when an item is relocated. Is it any wonder that manufacturers continually vie for the more visible location?

Shelf Facings Manufacturers are as interested in obtaining adequate shelf facing for their brands as they are in getting a good shelf height. The underlying notion is that a "mass" display of a brand on a shelf will be more eye-catching and thereby generate a competitive advantage.

A number of experimental studies have been conducted by students of consumer behavior to determine how the number of facings influences sales (Cox, 1964; Kotzan and Evanson, 1969; Cox, 1970; and Hubbard, 1969–70).

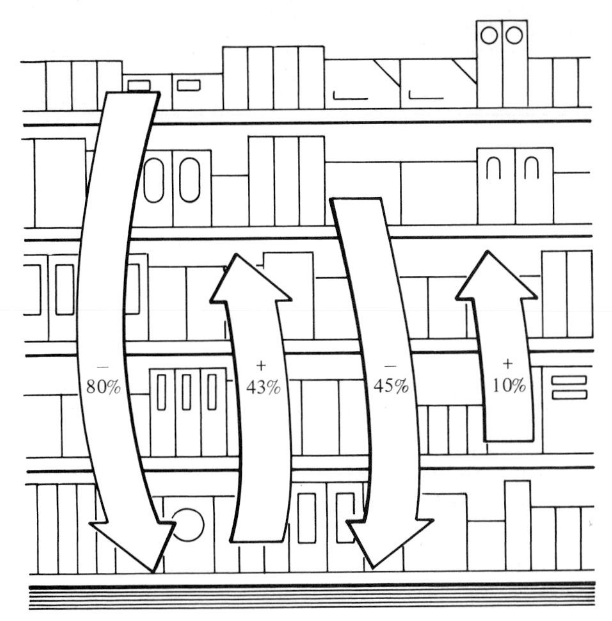

Figure 13-4 How shelf location shifts affect sales. *Source: Progressive Grocer* (1971).

These studies indicate that a brand can have too many as well as too few facings—that some products respond to increased facings while others do not. Table 13-6 illustrates how changing the number of facings can affect sales. The data in the table suggest that the typically fast-moving items react more dramatically to changes in shelf facings than typically slower-moving products like grapefruit juice.

PRICE

If asked the question, "How do consumers react to price changes?" a student from an introductory course on economics would typically answer, "If you lower prices, sales will increase." Generally the student's answer would be correct, reflecting his knowledge of a downward-sloping demand curve and his observations that whenever retailers wish to move older merchandise and/or attract customers, they employ such tactics as bargain-day sales, half-price sales, and loss leaders.

If asked another question, "If the price of a product is lowered 20 percent, how much will sales increase?" the same student might reply, somewhat pedantically, "It depends upon the price elasticity of the product, other things being equal." This answer, reflecting his knowledge of the economic concept of an elasticity index, would also be correct.

Elasticity is one of the most useful concepts in economics for analyzing consumer behavior. An *elasticity index* measures the reactions of consumers (sales) to changes in a variable such as price when both consumer reactions and

Table 13-6 How Shelf Facings Affect Sales

Item	Number of facings before	Number of facings after	Percent change in weekly unit sales
Grapefruit juice, 46 oz.	4	2	0%
Orange drink, 32 oz.	3	1	–29%
Household spray cleaner	2	4	+40
Household spray cleaner (same as above item)	3	1	–66
Liquid all-purpose cleaner	2	4	+25
No-stick pan spray	3	1	–60

Source: *Progressive Grocer* (1971).

prices are expressed in relative terms. For example, if the prices of both cigars and houses rise by 20 percent, the sales volume (in units) of cigars will remain about the same but housing sales will decline. Thus, there is little or no responsiveness to cigar price changes, indicating a near zero index of price elasticity, and some reaction to house price changes, indicating a significant figure (nonzero) for the price elasticity of housing.

Indexes of price elasticity are relatively easy to compute with standard statistical procedures, and at one time or another economists have computed the price elasticity of most products in the marketplace. The price elasticity for automobiles, for example, has been found in a number of studies to be around −1.0 (the negative sign indicating the relationship suggested by the student, that if prices decrease, sales will increase, and vice versa). In other words, a price change of 10 percent would produce a corresponding sales change of 10 percent—other things being equal.

If elasticity figures are so easily computed and so straightforward to use, why are prices and pricing considered so perplexing a problem to marketing managers, economists and other students of consumer behavior? The answer is found partially in the qualifier—other things being equal. Other things are not usually equal, and for many products these other things have been found to be of equal or greater importance than price changes for predicting behavior. Dyckman (1965), for example, developed an econometric model for predicting new car purchases for an extended period of time. He found four variables, when taken together, to be more important in explaining total new car purchases: income, price, existing stock of automobiles, and credit conditions. Not only did he need more than one variable to predict purchases, but he found that income changes were about twice as important as price changes in explaining car sales. In other words, while price was a determinant attribute, it was not as significant as people's incomes.

Another aspect contributing to the perplexity of pricing is the complexity of individual consumer reactions to prices and price changes. And whenever students of consumer behavior have examined the topic, they have found a number of different relationships.

One relationship deals with consumers' perceptions of price: How accurately do consumers perceive product prices? Generally, when consumers are given a price test, they display an amazing inability to recall accurately the prices of specific products (*Progressive Grocer,* 1964; and Brown, 1971). These findings probably should not come as any great shock, given the large number of products available to consumers. For instance, given that the typical supermarket carries over 7,000 items and the average time a homemaker spends shopping there on each trip to less than an hour, how could one expect this consumer to accurately perceive the prices of a large number of items? Besides,the customer can check the price on items of interest in the store. Nevertheless, prices to consumers are psychological as well as economic attributes of some products, and buyer perceptions of prices and price changes may affect their behavior toward products. Moreover, consumer perception of price may depend to a large degree on the place in which a product is sold, its advertising, and the importance the consumer ascribes to the price rather than its objective price tag.

Some of these interrelationships have been found whenever students of consumer behavior have observed consumers' reactions to product prices. Wells and LoSciuto (1966), for example, used the method of direct observation discussed in Chapter Two and found, among other things, that consumers reacted more strongly to prices of detergents than to prices of cereals. Findings such as this imply that marketers must have specific knowledge of which types of products consumers express a price concern for if pricing is to be used effectively as a sales-generating aspect of the marketing mix. Even when it is infeasible to calculate price elasticities for products, some generalizations about the degree of concern for prices is obvious. For example, when products are relatively expensive within the framework of a consumer's budget, the consumer will pay attention to price changes. If the price of a newspaper rises from 10 cents to 15 cents, hardly anyone stops buying his daily paper; but if there is a price jump of 50 percent on automobiles, many consumers pay attention and postpone plans to buy a new car. Also, when products are used somewhat habitually—such as cigarettes, cigars, alcoholic beverages, electricity, education, personal grooming articles, and gasoline—consumers typically are not concerned with price, unless, of course, prices change drastically as a result of shortages or other factors, causing the items to assume a larger position in the household budget.

But even when consumers are price conscious, the usual "lower price—greater sales" relationship is not always present. Within the range of prices consumers find acceptable (Gabor and Granger, 1964), they typically have a choice of various price lines. Invariably some consumers will choose brands from the higher price lines. Presumably in such cases consumers are using price as an indicator of product quality; that is, they are really selecting a higher-quality product but cannot distinguish quality except by price differences and/or brand- or store-image differences. A number of studies have supported the contention that price is used by consumers as an indicator of quality (Leavitt, 1954; Tull, Boring, and Gonsior, 1964; Smith and Broome, 1967;

McConnel, 1968; Stafford and Enis, 1969; Peterson, 1970; and Gardner, 1971). Shapiro (1968 and 1973) suggests that the importance of the "judging quality by price" phenomenon depends on these situations:

1 The more easily products can be evaluated, the less important the phenomenon will be.

2 The less expensive the product, compared with the psychological costs associated with seeking more information, the more the consumer will tend to judge quality by price.

3 The more prestigious the product, the more its quality will be judged by price.

To summarize, price changes can increase or decrease sales for many products, particularly if the price change is dramatic enough for consumers to feel the pinch on the family budget. Pricing is more effective, however, when consideration is given to the relationship of the product to people's concern for price, their perception of normal or acceptable prices, and other attributes by which they evaluate products.

SUMMARY

Although the future survival of a firm is determined largely by successful new products, the present well-being of a firm depends on the sales derived from established brands. As a result, repeat-purchasing behavior and the factors that affect it are important areas of market research. Marketers use store audits and consumer panels to keep track of the ongoings of their prospective markets.

Store audits track the movement of products through retail outlets and provide information on brand sales and brand shares. Data extracted from store audits can be used in making short-term decisions such as types of promotions to be used, and also in making long-term decisions such as changing product lines or distribution policies. Audit data are useful for spotting basic market trends, such as changes in consumer tastes, but they must be used with caution because the data can indicate contradictory conditions and often give only incomplete pictures of what is actually occurring in the marketplace.

To fill in the picture, marketers turn to consumer panels, which yield data on the actual purchasing behavior of individual homemakers. Panels indicate the percentage of a brand's customers who switch to other brands, how often they switch, and the brands they switch to. In addition to providing a more complete view of the market, the repeat-purchasing data obtained from consumer panels are used to predict the ultimate outcome of changes in marketing strategies for established brands. Outcome predictions can give marketers a chance to revise their strategies as needed. The information on repeat-purchasing patterns in response to special promotions, new merchandising techniques, and other efforts allows marketers to evaluate these programs in order to improve future efforts.

Store audits and consumer panels furnish enough data to derive usable predictions of consumer behavior, but they do not explain the reasons for that behavior. To understand the "why" of purchasing decisions, researchers examine consumer characteristics, product attributes, and the decision process itself. Although researchers have not found a strong relationship between brand loyalty and specific consumer characteristics such as age or education level, one researcher (Carman) has found a direct relationship between brand loyalty and store loyalty, and a direct relationship between store loyalty and personal consumer characteristics. Product attributes have been found to affect purchasing decisions, but often in opposite directions. Consumers of certain types of products tend on occasion to choose brands which they perceive as being substitutes for their preferred brand, while other consumers occasionally choose brands which are quite different from their usual choice. Until recently, students of consumer behavior have assumed that all decisions could be explained by definite, identifiable factors. Bass (1974) has proposed that some consumer decisions involve random, and therefore unpredictable, components.

Other facets of repeat-purchasing behavior include impulse buying and response to merchandising efforts. Studies show that consumers' buying behavior is becoming increasingly impulsive and, consequently, more easily influenced by in-store promotions and displays. Impulse buying is composed of four different types of behavior; pure impulse buying, reminder impulse buying, suggestion impulse buying, and planned impulse buying.

Research conducted in supermarkets and drugstores reveals that location within the store and shelf location and shelf facings of products all have significant effects on consumer purchasing rates. Special displays, signs, and p-o-p materials also affect consumers—often in a favorable manner—although effectiveness is limited by length of time and seasonality. Price, another merchandising variable, affects consumers in seemingly contradictory directions. For some products, increasing prices will have a negative effect on sales; but for other products, sales may actually increase as a result of higher prices. It seems that in certain situations consumers use price to judge quality.

REVIEW QUESTIONS

1 Why is the over-time observation of consumer behavior considered better than "snapshot" observation? How do marketers keep track of their markets over time?
2 Store audits provide information which is useful in making both short and long-term decisions. Identify the types of information which are obtainable from store audits, and indicate the prospective marketing decisions each type of information applies to.
3 The text states that consumer panel data put the C back in the S→C→R model. Using the concept of market dynamics, discuss why the C is important to marketers.
4 Does strong brand loyalty seem to be a function of individual consumer characteristics or product class? Discuss the research studies which suppport your answer. Are there contradictory findings? What are they?

5 Brand share can be predicted by multiplying ultimate penetration × repeat-purchasing rate × buying rate index. Define each of these variables and indicate why they are important in determining brand share.
6 Define the four types of impulse buying and discuss how in-store merchandising can affect each type of buying behavior.
7 Discuss the four brand-loyalty patterns identified by Brown. Brown found that the amount and type of loyalty vary greatly from one product category to another. How do specific product attributes, such as substitutable quality, affect brand loyalty?
8 Identify the factors that determine the effectiveness of in-store displays. Do you agree that most grocery displays should be changed at least once a month? Why or why not?
9 Why are manufacturers so concerned about having their products placed on the eye-level shelf? What types of products should not be placed on this shelf? Why?
10 In addition to elasticity, several other factors affect consumers' reactions to prices. Identify and discuss these factors.
11 In what situations will consumers tend to "judge quality by price"? When will this phenomenon be less important.

EXERCISE

Using the following schedule, record your gasoline purchases for one or two months.

Date of purchase	Location of dealer	Odometer reading	Brand purchased	Gallons purchased	Grade purchased			Payment	
					Reg.	Prem.	No lead	Cash	Credit card

At the end of the recording time period, construct an array for each category of purchase (brand, dealer, etc.) similar to the repeat-purchasing patterns described in the chapter. Do you exhibit brand loyalty? Dealer loyalty? Company loyalty? Grade loyalty? Explain your behavior for each category.

Compare your results with those of your classmates. Are there any differences in behaviors in the class? Why? Are the patterns of repeat buying explainable more by specific or by general characteristics?

REFERENCES

Bass, Frank M. "The Theory of Stochastic Preference and Brand Switching." *Journal of Marketing Research,* 11 (February 1974), 1–20.

———, Edgar A. Pessemier, and Donald R. Lehmann. "An Experimental Study of Relationships between Attitudes, Brand Preference, and Choice." *Behavioral Science,* 17 (November 1972), 532–541.

Brown, F. E. "Who Perceives Supermarket Prices Most Validly?" *Journal of Marketing Research,* 9 (February 1971), 110–113.

Brown, George H. "Brand Loyalty—Fact or Fiction?" *Advertising Age,* 23 (June 1952–January 1953) (a series).

Carman, James M. "Correlates of Brand Loyalty: Some Positive Results." *Journal of Marketing Research,* 7 (Feburary 1970), 67–76.

Cox, Keith R. "The Effect of Shelf Space upon Sales of Branded Products." *Journal of Marketing Research,* 7 (February 1970), 55–58.

———. "The Responsiveness of Food Sales to Shelf Space Changes in Supermarkets." *Journal of Marketing Research,* 1 (May 1964), 63–67.

Cunningham, Ross. "Brand Loyalty—What, Where, How Much." *Harvard Business Review,* 24 (January–February 1956), 116–128.

———. "Customer Loyalty to Store and Brand." *Harvard Business Review,* 39 (November–December, 1961), 127–137.

Dalquist, Eric. "As I See It." *Motor Trend* (April 1974), 6.

"Detroit Thinks Small." *Newsweek* (Apr. 1, 1974), 54–61.

Dyckman, Thomas R. "An Aggregate Demand Model for Automobiles." *Journal of Business,* 38 (July 1965).

Ehrenberg, A. S. C. *Repeat Buying: Theory and Applications.* Amsterdam: North-Holland Publishing Company, 1972.

Frank, Ronald E. "Brand Loyalty as a Basis for Market Segmentation." *Journal of Advertising Research,* 7 (June 1967), 27–33.

Gabor, A. and C. W. J. Granger. "Price Sensitivity of the Consumer." *Journal of Advertising Research,* 4 (December 1964), 40–44.

Gardner, David M. "Is There a Generalized Price-Quality Relationship?" *Journal of Marketing Research,* 8 (May 1971), 241–243.

Hubbard, Charles W. "The 'Shelving' of Increased Sales." *Journal of Retailing,* 45 (Winter 1969–1970), 75–84.

Kotzan, Jeffry A. and Robert V. Evanson. "Responsiveness of Drug Store Sales to Shelf Space Allocations." *Journal of Marketing Research,* 6 (November 1969), 465–469.

Kraft, Frederic B., Donald H. Granbois, and John O. Summers. "Brand Evaluation and Brand Choice: A Longitudinal Study." *Journal of Marketing Research,* 10 (August 1973), 235–241.

Kuehn, Alfred A. and Ralph L. Day. "Probablistic Models of Consumer Buying Behavior." *Journal of Marketing,* 28(October 1964), 27–31.

Leavitt, H. J. "A Note on Some Experimental Factors about the Meaning of Price." *Journal of Business,* 27 (1954), 205–210.

Lipstein, Benjamin. "The Dynamics of Brand Loyalty and Brand Switching." *Proceedings,* 5th Annual Conference of the Advertising Research Foundation, 1959.

McConnell, J. Douglas. "The Price-Quality Relationship in an Experimental Setting." *Journal of Marketing Research,* 5 (August 1968), 300–303.

"Merchandising Guide for the 70s." *Progressive Grocer* (January, February, March, June, September, and October 1971), a series.

Monroe, Kent B. "Buyers' Subjective Perceptions of Price." *Journal of Marketing Research* (February 1973), 70–80.

Parfitt, John. "Panel Research." In Robert M. Worcester (ed.), *Consumer Market Research Handbook.* Maidenhead, Berkshire, England: McGraw-Hill, 1972.

——— and B. J. K. Collins. "Use of Consumer Panels for Brand-Share Prediction." *Journal of Marketing Research,* 5 (May 1968), 131–145.

Peterson, Robert A. "The Price-Perceived Quality Relationship: Experimental Evidence."*Journal of Marketing Research,* 7 (November 1970), 525–528.

Progressive Grocer. "Colonial Study." *Progressive Grocer* (January 1964), C-81-96.

Shapiro, Benson P. "Price Reliance: Existence and Sources." *Journal of Marketing Research* (August 1973), 286–294.

———. "The Psychology of Pricing." *Harvard Business Review,* 46 (July–August 1968), 14–25, 160.

Sheth, Jagdish N. "Measurement of Multidimensional Brand Loyalty of a Consumer," *Journal of Marketing Research,* 7 (August 1970), 348–354.

Smith, Edward L. and Charles L. Broome. "A Laboratory Study of Consumers' Brand Preferences for Brands of Low Cost Consumer Goods." *Southern Journal of Business* (April 1967), 77–89.

Stafford, James E. and Ben M. Enis. "The Price-Quality Relationship: An Extension." *Journal of Marketing Research,* 6 (November 1969), 456–458.

Stern, Hawkins. "The Significance of Impulse Buying Today." *Journal of Marketing,* 26 (April 1962), 59–62.

Tull, D. S., R. A. Boring, and M. H. Gension. "A Note on the Relationship of Price and Imputed Quality," *Journal of Business,* 37 (1964), 186–191.

Wells, William D. and Leonard A. LoSciuto. "Direct Observation of Purchasing Behavior." *Journal of Marketing Research,* 3 (August 1966), 227–233.

Chapter 14

Consumer Spatial Behavior

To the casual observer the happenings in the marketplace may appear to be uncomplicated: "A store is a store is a store," and consumers shop stores of certain types fo buy certain products. To suggest this viewpoint, however, is roughly analogous to saying that an oak is a maple is a pine, since a tree is a tree is a tree from which wood is obtained, or to saying that first-degree murder is the same as manslaughter which is the same as suicide because "A death is a death is a death."

Consider the following "happenings," most of which take place hundreds of times daily:

- A woman drives to the supermarket, spends an hour pushing a cart, and buys, among other things, a pair of pantyhose, a new coffee percolator, and several magazines.
- A man walks to the corner drugstore and makes a savings account deposit in the branch bank located there.
- A teen bicycles to a hardware store buys stamps and mails a package at the post office branch located there.
- A homemaker thumbs through a catalog, picks up the phone, and orders

a pair of jeans for her son, a blouse for her daughter, a tricycle for another child, and a new hammer for her husband.

- A working wife driving home from work exits from the street long enough to pick up from a drive-in window a bucket of ready-to-eat, carry-out fried chicken for the family dinner.
- Ten nonworking homemakers get together in the home of an acquaintance for a morning "party." Several leave, having purchased a new kitchen gadget, floor polish, and window cleaner.
- A family of four drives across town to a freestanding discount store: the wife shops for food, the husband for automobile tires, one teen for backpacking equipment, and another for a new tape deck.
- Another family drives to a shopping center: they have lunch, take in a G-rated movie, and then sit on a bench in air-conditioned comfort and watch other people walk by.
- A husband and wife jet to a distant city: they spend the day shopping for Christmas gifts for the entire family in a single department store, dine at a restaurant-theater, watch the play, spend the night at a luxury hotel, and return home the next morning.

Incidents like these belie an uncomplicated view of the marketplace, both of the store and of the consumer. A store, or, more technically, a retail outlet, is only the framework through which goods, services, and other benefits are made available to the public. There are no magical product boundaries to this framework. As the incidents show, a supermarket is not just a place to buy food, a shopping center is not just a cluster of stores, and a "store" is not the only game in town.

Consumers, as suggested in Chapter Two, engage in many decisions and activities in many different settings and situations, such as those depicted in the incidents. One inescapable, pervasive activity revealed in the incidents, however, is spatail mobility—an acknowledgment to Detroit. In the 1930s and 1940s the auto liberated the shopper. And, free to roam, shoppers have traveled to the stores, shopping centers, and even cities that offered them what they wanted when they wanted it.

Spatial mobility, geographical population redistribution, and other consumer and competitive factors have caused the framework of the retail outlet to maintain an almost constant state of flux. To survive and prosper, retailers must attract shoppers and convert them to buyers. To do so requires an understanding of consumer spatial behavior or at least the ability to predict that behavior—the subject of this chapter.

Although complicated, often contradictory, and interrelated, consumer spatial behavior can be classified for purposes of analysis into three types of patronage decisions:

1 Interurban choice. Interurban decisions are those involving a geographical choice from the broadest types or retail aggregates available to consumers. The most common example is a consumer's choice to shop in city A as opposed to city B. Decisions of this type are made primarily by persons living in other than major metropolitan areas.

2 Intraurban choice. Intraurban decisions are those that involve a choice from among the retailing clusters within a broader urban area. An example is the choice of a regional shopping center over a downtown area.

3 Interoutlet choice. Interoutlet decisions take the form of choice from among competing retail outlets, such as deciding to shop in department store A instead of B or choosing a catalog outlet over a tire dealer.

While the decision types are presented in descending order of retail magnitude, and while each is not unrelated to the others, no hierarchy of decision is implied. Indeed, one person may follow a sequential order, selecting city, shopping cluster, and store, while another will simply select a store—a class decision that determines or precludes both the interurban and intraurban decisions. Nevertheless, each of the decision areas has developed as a topic for investigation in consumer research and the three types will serve as the organizational framework of this chapter.

INTERURBAN CHOICE

Traditionally the examination of interurban patronage has focused on developing empirically based models of consumer choice. The underlying thesis of such models is that if consumers' spatial behavior can be predicted by a straightforward formula, marketers can measure the retail trade influence of an area without resorting to expensive field surveys. Most of the work along these lines can be traced to the pioneering developments of William J. Reilly and Paul D. Converse which are called "laws of retail gravitation" because of their obvious similarity to Newton's law of gravitation.[1]

In the late 1920s, Reilly raised the central question, "Given two cities or trading centers located some distance apart, at what geographical point between them will consumers be indifferent as to where they travel for goods and what factors will determine this location?" This location or "breaking point" is the point up to which one city exercises the dominant drawing power and beyond which the other city dominates.

During the preasphalt days, the breaking point between cities could be found by driving along the main highways and locating the side road or roads where the depth and width of tire marks were about equal in both directions. Even today traffic counters can be used much in the same manner.

Reilly, however, sought a more straigthforward approach and conducted a series of studies in twenty states and the District of Columbia. Based on his field work, Reilly concluded:

> Two cities attract retail trade from any intermediate city or town in the vicinity of the breaking point approximately in direct proportion to the population of the two

[1]For a more comprehensive review of those early studies, see Schwartz (1963).

cities and in inverse proportion to the square of the distances from these two cities to the intermediate town (Reilly, 1931:9)[2]

Reilly did not believe that population and distance were the causes of consumer shopping choice—he recognized the drawing power of large retail stores, advertising, and other factors. Rather, he viewed population and distance as reliable indexes of all the other variables that could influence consumer choice. To demonstrate the accuracy of his formula, Reilly computed the breaking point between each of thirty pairs of trading centers, such as Atlanta and Birmingham, and then conducted field surveys in these areas to determine the actual breaking points between each of the thirty pairs of cities. The results are shown in Table 14-1. The predictions, while not perfect, are very close. In fact, 98 percent of the variation in the breaking-point distances of the consumer surveys is explained by Reilly's model (Schwartz, 1963).

Paul Converse extended the work of Reilly into the late 1940s and developed several refinements to the original model for certain situations and reformulated Reilly's formula to its most popular form:

$$\text{Breaking point, miles from B} = \frac{\text{miles between A and B}}{1 + \sqrt{\dfrac{\text{population of A}}{\text{population of B}}}} \qquad (14\text{-}2)$$

Based on his extensive tests of the model, Converse concluded:

1 The law of retail gravitation applies only to towns in the vicinity of the breaking points between two large towns.

2 Reilly's law applies only to the delineation of trading areas for shopping goods and particularly to fashion goods, sometimes referred to as "style" or "specialty" goods. This is so because a considerable part of convenience and bulk goods is purchased locally (Converse, 1946: 26).

Many consumer researchers have ignored the limitations established by Converse and, much to their surprise, have concluded the model no longer

[2]Mathematically, Reilly's statement is expressed as:

$$\frac{B_a}{B_b} = \left(\frac{P_a}{P_b}\right)\left(\frac{D_b}{D_a}\right)^2 \qquad (14\text{-}1)$$

Where B_a = the proportion of retail trade from the breaking point attracted by city A
B_b = the proportion attracted by city B
P_a = the population of city A
P_b = the population of city B
D_a = the distance from the intermediate city or town to city A
D_b = the distance from the intermediate vicinity to city B

Table 14-1 Location of Breaking-Point Towns for a National Sample of Retail Trading Centers

Breaking-point town	Reilly's Law prediction* (miles)	Field study results* (miles)
Collier, Georgia	66	64
Heflin, Alabama	89	87
Salada, Texas	55	55
Westfield, New York	60	58
Elkmont Springs, Tennessee	128	127
Springfield, Illinois	204	202
Middletown, Ohio	39	38
Northeast, Pennsylvania	109	113
East Springfield, Pennsylvania	76	80
Harmony, Ohio	37	38
Hillsbury, Texas	73	70
Midway between Tyler and Longview, Texas	139	133
Meriden, Connecticut	19	18
Midway between Giddings and Ledbetter, Texas	110	101
Devers, Texas	63	60
Schulenberg, Texas	114	109
Centerville, Indiana	61	62
Mt. Etna, Indiana	77	85
Uniontown, Indiana	62	74
Fender, Georgia	169	160
Chilhowie, Virginia	161	157
Kingsburg, California	223	215
Midway between Ocean Springs and Pascagoula, Mississippi	118	113
Palmer, Massachusetts	149	151
Meadville, Pennsylvania	111	110
Tipton, Missouri	169	171
Midway between Sinton and Skidmore, Texas	115	116
Midway between Kyle and San Marcos, Texas	58	55
Chehalis, Washington	102	101
Midway between Fredericksburg and Galansville, Virginia	71	69

*The distances presented in these columns are from the same city in each pair of trading centers studies.

Source: Reilly (1931), as reproduced in Schwartz (1963: 23).

works. No one in recent years, however, has duplicated the extensive tests originally conducted by Reilly, Converse, and others.

One reasonable criticism of the model relates to its assumption of the homogeneity of the population. By treating all consumers alike, the usefulness of the model is limited to the prediction of behavior on the average, and prediction must often be gained at the sacrifice of description. This limitation is related to the recent emphasis by students of consumer behavior on trying to identify consumers in smaller cities who tend to go out of town to shop for "shopping" goods even when those goods are available in their home towns—a supply factor typically not present in the original studies on the development of the gravity model.

Consumer Outshoppers

The search for the consumer outshopper is based on the assumption that consumers have a differential predisposition to forgo secondary costs such as time, money, and effort in their choice of one trade center rather than another, and on the findings of several studies that a substantial number of consumers do go out of town to shop (Hermann and Beik, 1968; Thompson, 1971; Reynolds and Darden, 1972; and Gillet and Scott, 1972).

The frequent outshoppers, when compared with the occasional outshoppers and those who do not shop out of town, tend to be better educated, have a higher income level, span a number of age groups (25–54), prefer to shop in the evening, and are more frequent buyers by mail. Also, they tend to be active, on-the-go, urban-oriented homemakers who are neither time-conscious nor loyal to any particular store. Furthermore, they express an overall dissatisfaction with local shopping conditions and a positive attitude toward larger urban shopping areas and exhibit their preferences by shopping out of town for a vast range of "shopping" goods (Reynolds and Darden, 1972; and Reynolds and Martin, 1974).

While the frequent outshoppers are readily identifiable, there is some doubt as to the feasibility of reaching them in an effective manner by marketers in small towns. Since they tend to hold a positive prejudice toward large urban areas and say they are not store-loyal, they seem to be saying, "I have a desire for a variety of shopping experiences"—a variety that probably would be economically infeasible for small-town merchants to provide.

Where economically feasible, however, the life style of the frequent outshoppers suggests several actions that might effectively reach them. One, small-town merchants could attempt to create a desirable townwide image based not only on attributes of their offerings, but also on the atmosphere of their community—an image of an enjoyable shopping experience. Two, the creation of an activity center featuring urban-oriented activities, such as travel and art exhibits, special lectures, and study groups, could be undertaken by merchants. Three, merchants should rethink their own role; they should view their facilities on an aggregate retail level and cooperate on a planned and coordinated basis, particularly with respect to store hours and townwide promotions (Reynolds and Darden, 1972).

INTRAURBAN CHOICE

The opening of Northgate, a regional shopping center in Seattle, in 1950 launched a retailing innovation that rapidly diffused to other metropolitan suburbs during the 1950s and 1960s. Planned shopping centers multiplied until they literally ringed the central cities of the metropolitan areas. These large, one-stop retailing clusters, surrounded by spacious parking areas, offered consumers an alternative to downtown shopping.

Given new shopping alternatives, consumers changed their spatial behavior and it became necessary for students of that behavior to explore new bases for predicting it. Several researchers tried Reilly's formula, substituting square footage of selling space and driving time for population and distance. Generally, however, the results were mixed and unsatisfactory. Other researchers have followed the lead of David Huff, who formulated a spatial model based on R. Duncan Luce's model of individual choice behavior (Huff, 1962; and Luce, 1959).

Huff's central thesis is that consumer spatial behavior is best described as a probabilistic phenomenon which can be modeled in terms of consumers' perceived utilities or benefits of alternative shopping centers. That is, the probability of a consumer choosing a given shopping center is equal to the ratio of the utility of that center to the combined utilities of all shopping centers under consideration.[3]

To illustrate, assume that a consumer has four shopping centers, j_1, j_2, j_3, and j_4 as his set of alternatives and plans to choose one at a given time. Assume further that the shopper perceives the relative utilities of each of the centers to be in the proportion 1:2:3:4. Over a repeated number of times, the consumer will choose j_4 about 40 percent of the time, as calculated from Eq. (14-3):

$$P_4 = \frac{4}{1 + 2 + 3 + 4} = 0.40$$

Utility, of course, is an abstract concept, and a countless number of attributes of centers and situations could determine a person's perceived utility of a center. In developing an operational model, Huff selected two variables which he believed would accurately reflect a center's utility: (1) square footage of selling space and (2) travel time. *Square footage of selling space* is used to approximate the impact of merchandise offerings of a center under the assumption that the larger the center, the more lines of merchandise available and the greater the utility of the center. *Travel time* is used to account for factors that tend to detract from the utility of a center. It is assumed that the farther the center from the consumer's home, the greater the cost and effort

[3]His theoretical formulation is:

$$P_j = \frac{u_j}{\sum_{j=1}^{n} u_j} \tag{14-3}$$

where P_j = the probability of a consumer choosing a shopping center
u_j = the utility of center j to the consumer
j = a set of shopping centers the consumer considers as alternatives (where $j = 1, \ldots, n$).

involved in traveling to that center and the less desirable the center will be to a consumer.[4]

After formulating the model, Huff conducted a pilot test in three California neighborhoods to see how well the model predictions would correspond with the actual shopping center choices of persons living in the neighborhoods. He found that he expected behavior of consumers as predicted by the model corresponded quite closely to the actual behavior reported by consumers in the survey.

Using the Model

The model has been used primarily to calculate the sales potential of an existing or proposed shopping center. This is accomplished by the following steps:

1 Divide the area surrounding the shopping center site into relatively homogeneous geographical segments. These segments could be census tracts or enumeration districts or they could be arbitrarily defined geographical divisions of the population, such as quadrants within a series of radii from the site of squares within a constructed grid. [These geographical segments represent the i's in the model (14-4).]

2 Determine the square footage of retail selling space of all shopping centers (the j's) included within the area of analysis.

3 Determine the travel time involved in getting from a particular geographical segment to each of the shopping centers.

4 Calculate the probability of consumers in each geographical segment going to the shopping center site under study for each type of product offered or planned for the shopping center; that is, apply Eq. (14-4) for each geographical segment.

5 Map the area surrounding the shopping center location by drawing lines connecting all the geographical segments having like probabilities.

6 Calculate from census or other sources the number of households within each of the geographical areas. Then multiply each of these figures by

[4]Formally, Huff states his empirical formula as:

$$P_{ij} = \frac{\dfrac{S_j}{T_{ij}{}^{\lambda}}}{\displaystyle\sum_{j=1}^{n} \frac{S_j}{T_{ij}{}^{\lambda}}} \qquad (14\text{-}4)$$

where P_{ij} = the probability of a consumer at a given point of origin i traveling to a given shopping center j

S_j = the size of a shopping center j

T_{ij} = the travel time involved in getting from a consumer's travel base i to shopping center j

λ = a parameter which is to be estimated empirically to reflect the effect of travel time on various kinds of shopping trips. This incorporation of the parameter reflected the conclusions of a number of previous studies that different types of merchandise supported different amounts of consumer shopping.

their respective probability values. This calculation gives the expected number of consumer households that will patronize the shopping center.

7 Determine the median household income of each of the geographical segments. Compare these figures with consumer expenditure data by income class (obtained from sources such as the BLS Survey of Consumer Expenditures) to determine the average annual expenditure on the various products offered by the shopping center.

8 Multiply each of the product expenditure figures by the expected number of consumer households from each geographical segment expected to patronize the shopping center under study. Add these individual estimates to arrive at a total annual sales potential by product category for the shopping center under study.

Some Problems

The consumer spatial model developed by Huff has several appealing features: (1) it is based on a theory of individual-choice behavior, (2) it incorporates variables that are readily obtainable, and (3) it can be applied in a straightforward manner to predict intraurban choice and to calculate sales potential for a shopping center location. Nevertheless, there are several problems related to the full utilization of the model.

One problem is inaccurate prediction in certain situations. Huff noted in his pilot test, for example, that the model consistently obtained poorer predictions in situations where more than one shopping center were in close proximity. This problem arises because the model assumes independence between centers. That is, the model does not allow the utility of one center to a consumer to be affected by its position relative to another center. This assumption is reasonable for single-purpose shopping trips. However, many shopping trips are multipurpose—consumers visit several retail outlets or combine shopping with nonshopping trips. The model is not intended to predict choice under the multipurpose trip assumption (Huff and Batsel, 1975).

Another problem of the utility model is whether or not the chosen variables, square footage and travel time, accurately reflect a consumer's perception of a center's utility. A study by Moore and Mason (1969) of the shopping patterns of 500 households north of Birmingham, Alabama, for example, revealed a strong pattern for residents of small incorporated communities to choose the central business district and for rural residents of similar socioeconomic characteristics to shop at a regional shopping center. Given the absence of socioeconomic, spatial, temporal, and physical barrier differences, the authors concluded that consumer perceptions of a given retail center lead to different shopping patterns.

Bucklin (1967) also questioned the role of square footage as the sole proxy for utility in models of intraurban choice. Based on the findings of his study, he concluded that "mass" variables such as population and square footage are adequate for models of interurban choice, image variables are necessary for interoutlet choice models, and the relative importance of mass and image measurements for intraurban choice depends on the type of shopping occasion: full search, directed search, or casual search. In the situation of "full search," where product selection is consequential and considerable comparison is desirable, mass variables are viewed as adequate indicators of a center's utility. As for "directed" or limited search for specific items, image is considered by Bucklin to play the dominant role as a measure of a center's utility. (This view, however, may be synonymous with the earlier statement that consumers may choose a store first and other spatial decisions follow.) Also, in the situation of "casual" search, where product selection is largely insignificant to the consumer and interstore comparisons are not viewed as rewarding, image is viewed as dominating mass as a measure of center utility.

INTEROUTLET CHOICE

The methods for studying consumer spatial behavior in interurban and intraurban situations were heavily oriented toward the use of directly observable variables and formal models of choice. By way of contrast, most of the history of research on interoutlet choice has been concerned with the nature of individual perceptions of outlets and consumer loyalty to stores shopped—an approach consistent with the notion that retailer success depends upon the ability to attract consumers and retain them as loyal customers.

The dollars and cents of this approach to retailers is apparent when the degree of shopping for items of merchandise is examined. Historically, marketers have acted on the premise that there were certain types of products for which consumers desired to shop—to search for from among the offerings of several retailers. Recent evidence from studies of female and male shoppers, however, reveals that the majority of consumers go to one store to buy so-called shopping goods (Udell, 1966; Dommermuth and Cundiff, 1967; Kleimenhagen 1966–1967; and Mason and Mayer, 1972). A corollary to these findings is that the store which attracts the shopper is likely to obtain the shopper's purchases.

These are, of course, exceptions to this generalization. For some goods, particularly socially visible and/or highly expensive products, there is a greater tendency for some consumers to shop around. For example, Dommermuth and Cundiff (1967) found that from 35 to 40 percent of the shoppers in their survey visited two or more stores before purchasing fashion items, and Mason and Mayer (1972) found that 61 percent of the men in their survey visited two or more outlets before purchasing a television set. But for most goods and for most consumers, the store first visited is likely to be the last one visited. Translated, "Shopper attraction means sales."

Store Image

Potential customers are attracted to a store or other form of retail outlet for several reasons, but perhaps the most important reason is the image of the store relative to image preferences of consumers. And whenever students of consumer behavior measure the images of retail stores in a community, they usually find that the stores have well-defined and widely shared images, both of the attributes of the stores and of the people who shop there.

Stores, like products, can be perceived along a large number of dimensions or attributes—a fact highlighted by a study of store perceptions of 744 Arizona department store customers conducted by Kunkel and Berry (1968). By answering three open-end questions, the respondents provided 3,737 statements describing their perceptions of three Phoenix department stores; statements of what they liked most and what they liked least, and statements of why they thought other people shopped in the stores. The authors were able to reduce the number of attributes by placing the statements into categories as shown in Figure 14-1. Even so, there remain twelve categories comprising almost fifty dimensions of department store image.

The findings of this study serve to emphasize a point made in Chapter 9: consumers frequently make choices based on only a few attributes of the total image—the large number of attributes uncovered in the department store study would simply be unmanageable as a basis for consumers to compare stores. Consequently, marketers cannot limit their studies of store choice to total image. In addition, they must find the "determinant" attributes of store image among target market segments and measure how well or how poorly consumers perceive their stores on the important aspects of image. This approach makes it possible to predict store choice and to plan marketing efforts when necessary to reposition a store in the minds of the consumers the store is trying to attract.

Often marketers will find that stores do fall short on certain features preferred by shoppers. A survey of a national sample of 500 homemakers illustrate this point. The homemakers were asked to rate each of 37 supermarket attributes on its "importance" to them. After rating the importance of the 37 factors, the housewives rated the "performance" of the store where they shopped most often on the same factors (arrayed in a different order on the questionnaire). When one compares the rankings (shown in Table 14-2) by importance and performance, phrases comparable to preference and perception, some immediate discrepancies show up among the most preferred attributes. Generally, the homemakers said they would like to see clearer supermarkets with prices clearly labeled, having better produce and meat departments, lower prices, and freshness dates marked on all products, and to have shorter waiting time for checkout—all features under the control of store management (Dietrich, 1973).

Given discrepancies such as those revealed in the supermarket study, a legitimate question is, "Will a concentrated effort to reposition a store along those dimensions increase the ability of the store to attract potential customers?" The answer is a qualified "yes"—qualified along the lines of the discussion in Chapter 9 of the fact that attitudes do not always predict behavior because of other influences at the time of decision, changing preferences, and available resources.

Figure 14-1 Dimensions of Store Image

01 Price of merchandise
- a Low prices
- b Fair or competitive prices
- c High or non-competitive prices
- d Values, except with specific regard to premiums, such as stamps, or quality of merchandise

02 Quality of merchandise
- a Good or poor quality of merchandise
- b Good or poor department(s), except with respect to assortment, fashion, etc.
- c Stock brand names

03 Assortment of merchandise
- a Breadth of merchandise
- b Depth of merchandise
- c Carries a brand I like

04 Fashion of merchandise

05 Sales personnel
- a Attitude of sales personnel
- b Knowledgeability of sales personnel
- c Number of sales personnel
- d Good or poor service

06 Locational convenience
- a Location from home
- b Location from work
- c Access
- d Good or poor location

07 Other convenience factors
- a Parking
- b Hours store is open
- c Convenience with regard to other stores
- d Store layout with respect to convenience
- e Convenience (in general)

08 Services
- a Credit
- b Delivery
- c Restaurant facilities
- d Other services (gift consultants, layaway plans, baby strollers, escalators, etc.)

09 Sales promotions
- a Special sales, including quality or assortment of sales merchandise
- b Stamps and other promotions
- c Fashion shows and other special events

10 Advertising
- a Style and quality of advertising
- b Media and vehicles used
- c Reliability of advertising

11 Store atmosphere
- a Layout of store without respect to convenience
- b External and internal decor of store
- c Merchandise display
- d Customer type
- e Congestion
- f Good for gifts, except with respect to quality, assortment or fashion of merchandise
- g "Prestige" store

12 Reputation on adjustments
- a Returns
- b Exchange
- c Reputation for fairness

Source: Kunkel and Berry (1968:26). Reprinted from *Journal of Marketing*, published by the American Marketing Association.

Another, related question is, "Can consumers' perceptions of these attributes actually be changed through marketing efforts?" The discussion of the influence of advertising and the effects of interpersonal communications in previous chapters suggests some of the possible answers to this complex question. In addition, there is evidence from a series of studies by Arnold and Tigert (1973–74) that substantially changing a marketing effort will affect consumers' perceptions of store attributes. Objective data on the price of a standard gorcery basket purchased in each of several supermarket chains over a two-year period (Figure 14-2) shows that on the first of November 1970,

Table 14-2 Consumer Rankings of Importance and Performance on 37 Supermarket Attributes

Importance to shoppers (rank)	Factor	Rating of store presently shopped (rank)
1	Cleanliness	7
2	All prices clearly labeled	15
3	Good produce department	9
4	Good meat department	13
5	Low prices	23
6	Accurate, pleasant checkout clerks	3
7	"Freshness" date marked on products	21
8	Shelves usually well-stocked	8
9	Good parking facilities	2
10	Good selection of nationally advertised brands	4
11	Good layout for fast, easy shopping	14
12	Good dairy department	5
13	Short wait for checkout	26
14	Aisles clear of boxes	27
15	Convenient store location	1
16	Frequent "sales" or "specials"	12
17	Helpful personnel in service departments	17
18	Don't run short of items on "special"	19
19	Good frozen foods department	11
20	Baggers on duty	20
21	New items that I see advertised are available	25
22	Manager is friendly and helpful	18
23	Pleasant atmosphere/decor	10
24	Good selection of low-priced "store" brand items	16
25	Not usually overcrowded	28
26	Unit pricing on shelves	32
27	Check cashing service	6
28	Carry purchases to car	29
29	Good drugs and toiletries section	24
30	Good assortment of non-foods merchandise	30
31	Open late hours	22
32	Eye-catching mass displays	31
33	Have in-store bakery	36
34	Trading stamps or other "extras"	33
35	Have deli department	34
36	People know my name	35
37	Sell hot foods to take out or eat in store	37

Source: Dietrich (1973:60).

Dominion instituted a dramatic price cut of about 12 percent and maintained a position of price leadership along with Miracle Food Mart, the previous price leader, thereafter. The monthly data collected by Arnold and Tigert on consumers' perceptions of chain prices, shown in Table 14-3, clearly correspond to the low-price strategy move by Dominion. The authors also found that

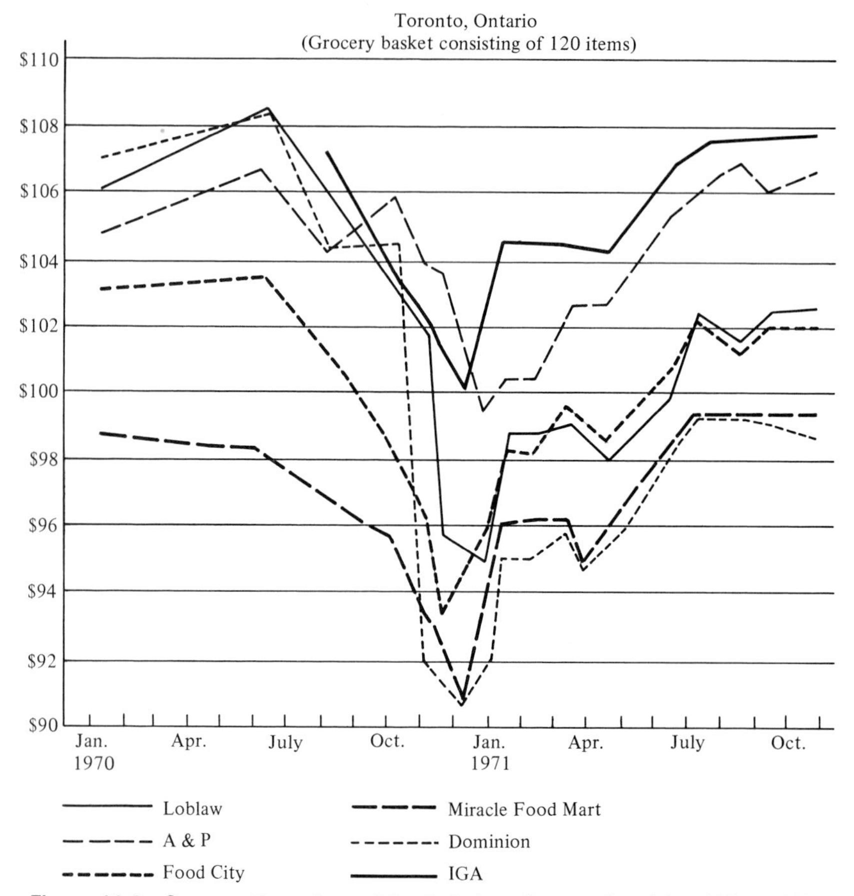

Figure 14-2 Comparative prices of food chains. *Source:* Arnold and Tigert (1973–1974: 7).

the change in price perception did not affect or "tarnish" the image of Dominion with respect to serice, a determinant attribute before and after the price change.

To summarize, shopper attraction can be influenced by how consumers perceive outlets, and marketing efforts can be initiated to change consumers' perceptions of important attributes of stores without damaging perception of other equally important aspects of image. From a marketing perspective, however, initial shopper attraction is but one aspect of the study of interoutlet choice. Ideally, once consumers have been attracted to a store, they will continue to shop there—to exhibit loyalty to the store.

Store Loyalty

Store loyalty, like brand loyalty, refers to a repetitive shopping pattern, and, as discussed in the preceding chapter, there is a degree of correspondence between consumers who are loyal to stores and those loyal to brands that implies a distribution strategy for brand manufacturers. Store loyalty also is

Table 14-3 Consumer Perceptions of Chains with Lowest Prices

	Percent of sample mentioning each chain											
	1970			1971								
Chain	October	November	December	January	February	March	April	May	July	August	September	October
1. A&P	16%*	10%	7%	6%	7%	8%	7%	6%	7%	8%	6%	7%
2. Dominion	7	29	34	32	31	32	30	27	26	29	27	33
3. Food City	18	18	16	18	15	13	9	10	12	14	12	10
4. Loblaws Group	15	11	7	9	8	9	15	14	13	13	14	10
5. MFM	32	29	32	29	35	33	34	36	34	30	34	34
6. Others	6	2	2	3	3	2	3	5	5	3	4	4
7. IGA	6	1	2	3	1	3	2	2	3	3	3	2
Totals	100%	100%	100%	100%	100%	100%	100%	100%	100%	100%	100%	100%
(N =	1900	1750	1457	1700	1520	1891	1032	1191	1294	1366	1451	1007)

*Read: Sixteen percent of the respondents in the October 1970 survey said that A&P has the lowest prices.
Source: Arnold and Tigert (1973–74: 10).

postulated to be a useful basis for market segmentation for retailers. To be useful to retailers the concept, like all bases for segmentation, must provide affirmative answers to these questions: (1) is the store-loyal consumer profitable? (2) If so, can the loyal consumer be identified? and (3) Can this consumer be reached?

Addressing the first question, Cunningham was quite explicit as to the dollars-and-cents importance of supermarket consumers' exhibiting high degrees of loyal behavior:

> For every one of these (high loyalty) families you can attract, you will get on the average 62.3% of its total food purchases (half again as much as the average family).
>
> In sum, your greatest opportunities lie in getting the best possible mix of consumer loyalties for the traffic that your store will carry. In a shopping area with many competitors, in fact, your best bet for holding and increasing sales volume is to improve the quality of your customer loyalty mix (Cunningham, 1961:136).

Enis and Paul (1970) have also explored the grocery expenditure patterns of store-loyal consumers. They found that (1) store-loyal behavior is independent of total amount of food expenditures; (2) more loyal consumers allocate much larger proportions of their expenditures to their first-choice stores than do less loyal consumers; (3) stores with the largest number of loyal consumers have the largest share of the market; and (4) loyal consumers are no more expensive to serve than nonloyal consumers.

In summary, the evidence on food shopping suggests that store-loyal behavior is an important basis for market segmentation.

The evidence for department store loyalty, however, is not as conclusive as for food outlet loyalty. Donnahoe (1956), using a store where twenty-four selected items were last purchased as a measure of loyalty, concluded that the loyal customer is so rare as to be a negligible factor in the total sales or sales potential of a given department store. He did find, however, that if a person buys one item in a store, the probability is increased that the person will make related purchases in the store. This finding suggests that if a department store can increase the number of loyal customers for certain items, it can also increase sales volume of complementary items. Thus, the evidence suggests that, for department stores, store loyalty is potentially a profitable basis for market segmentation.

Will personal characteristics of consumers distinguish loyal from nonloyal shoppers? Generally, in context of a type of store, the answer is "yes." But the specific answers to this question have been somewhat contradictory and sketchy because they have depended upon the particular mix of characteristics measured in each study, and students of consumer behavior have been prone to use consistently different mixes of characteristics in studies of store loyalty. Enis and Paul (1970), for instance, used a number of standardized personality measures and found that the more loyal consumers tended to express higher degrees of exhibition, achievement, and affiliation and lower degrees of deference. Their findings suggest that supermarket-loyal consumers are ones who shop where they feel noticed, wanted, and are known and treated respectfully—descriptions which suggest that retaining the loyal consumers requires a personalized approach to reach them. In another situation, Reynolds, Darden, and Martin (1974–75) used a number of life-style measures but not the standard personality measures. They concluded that the self-designated store-loyal consumer's life style suggests a portrait of a relatively conservative, inactive, time-conscious, radio and TV-user who is older and has less income and formal education than store-switching homemakers. While the appeals implied by this description may not be different from those drawn from the profile of the first study, the channel for reaching the loyal consumer—radio and TV—may be different.

In yet another instance, Lessig (1975) used even more store-specific measures. In an examination of panel data on food buying by ninety-one households, he found that images consumers have of alternative retail outlets provide useful information in the prediction of store loyalty. By establishing a connection between store image and store loyalty, the study by Lessig seems to say that what attracts consumers to begin what will keep attracting them over time, an indication that reinforces the importance of maintaining a proper image relative to consumer preferences.

At this stage in the knowledge of consumer behavior, the most viable conclusion is that store loyalty is an important aspect of store success, and store-loyal consumers can be identified and reached, but this must be accomplished through a store-by-store approach.

Consumer Differences

Another dimension that has proved important in the study of interoutlet patronage is the examination of the different types of consumers who tend to be frequent shoppers at various types of outlets. *Shopping frequency* refers to behavior toward a type of retail outlet, not loyalty to a particular firm within an outlet type. The two behaviors, of course, could overlap—an ideal situation for a given retailer—but studies have explored the two as different dimensions.

The rationale for identifying the frequent shopper is the same as that for all bases of market segmentation: to be able to reach effectively a potentially profitable group of consumers. To illustrate this approach, consumers of two widely differing types of retail outlets are examined: (1) heavy users of ready-to-eat carry-out fried chicken outlets (RECFC) and (2) in-home buyers.

RECFC In January 1969, Douglas Tigert (Tigert, Lathrope, and Bleeg, 1971), in connection with Market Facts, Inc., conducted a study of the heavy user of ready-to-eat, carry-out fried chicken drive-in restaurants. Based upon the responses of 857 female homemakers to a self-administered, 25-page questionnaire, the authors constructed the following profile of the heavy users—the women who purchased RECFC from a drive-in outlet once a month or more:

A Demographic profile of the heavy user:
  1. Works full time
  2. Above-average number of children
  3. Above-average income
  4. Not upscale in terms of education or occupation
  5. Lives in large cities in the South and Pacific regions of the United States
  6. Has own car

B Also heavy user of other products:
  1. Eye makeup
  2. Nail polish
  3. Cologne and toilet water
  4. Regular soft drinks
  5. Chewing gum and candy
  6. Gasoline
  7. New shoes
  8. Wide range of convenience foods:
     Frozen cakes
     Frozen fruit
     TV dinners
     Frozen side dishes
     Frozen main-course dinners
     Cake frosting mix
     Refrigerated biscuits
     Refrigerated dinner rolls
     Ready-to-serve frostings
     Refrigerated sweet rolls
     Canned spaghetti
     Toaster pastries
     Layer cake mix

C Life style profile of the heavy user:[5]
  1. Exhibits a zest for life
  2. Optimistic about personal and financial future
  3. Fashion and personal appearance conscious
  4. Pro-credit
  5. Active, on-the-go
  6. Influential with friends
  7. Venturesome
  8. Not afraid to borrow or invest money
  9. Swinging party-goer
  10. Shops in casual clothes at places like Sears and Wards

[5]Most of these are summary labels. For example, "not a homebody in a rut" is a summary for three statements: (1) I am a homebody, (2) Our days seem to follow a definite routine such as eating meals at a regular time, etc., and (3) I would like to have a maid to do the housework.

11 Liberal attitude toward discipline and sex
12 Likes science fiction
13 Doesn't think TV programs should be of a more serious type
14 Not a homebody in a rut
15 Enjoys bowling as a sport

Based on this rich description of the heavy user of carry-out fried chicken restaurants, Tigert and his associates presented the following implications for retailing strategy:

1 This product could be sold on credit through bank charge cards, American Express, gasoline cards, etc. In fact this type of franchise might well represent a good merger prospect for gasoline companies. Heavy users of RECFC are both borrowers and credit card users.

2 RECFC outlets might consider adding products to their line, should display space permit such a strategy. Examples are soft drinks, frozen foods, party snack chips, etc.

3 The concept of a friendly, informal atmosphere, already apparent, should be maintained. Formal or ultraconservative environments should be discouraged. Although they are concerned with personal appearance, heavy users also like to dress and shop in casual clothes.

4 Promotions for outlets could be tied in with bowling alleys, beauty parlors, dress shops, etc. For example, beauty parlors might offer coupons for chicken restaurants, and vice versa.

5 Promotions should not necessarily stress price-off coupons. Heavy users do not appear to be price conscious and, in fact, may be just the reverse, i.e., willing to pay more for quality and convenience.

6 In line with convenience theme, home delivery service should be seriously considered.

7 Promotions might be tied to the working-mother theme or to a party theme. For example, "Pick up a bucket on the way home from work," or "Order large quantities for your next party."

8 It is not at all clear that a move toward sit-in style restaurants and away from drive-ins would be appropriate for this product. Again, the convenience factor is important here.

9 Advertising might stress youth, families, parties, convenience, optimism, informality, and quality.

Some of the implications, of course, could be questioned. But this is a proverbial problem wherever one infers implications for action from survey results, and it is not the purpose of this discussion to argue pro or con concerning the implications.

Rather, it should be noted that each aspect of the overall heavy-user profile (demographic, other-product usage, and life style) contributes to the implications. Some of the implications can be inferred from one aspect, while others can be inferred from a combination of aspects. For example, Implication 1 can be inferred from the life style profile; Implication 7 can be inferred from a combination of the demographic and life style profiles.

In-Home Shoppers The first centennial of catalog marketing in 1972 largely went unheralded in the popular press. In retailing circles, however, a great deal of attention was being given to this form of marketing, for in 1971 catalog sales exceeded $10 billion and continued their decade trend of growing at a faster rate than total retail sales. Moreover, the demographic projections to 1984 implied an increasing growth potential. Students of consumer behavior also became increasingly interested in consumers' in-home buying behavior—an interoutlet choice away from the conventional retail store.

Traditionally, consumers had a limited choice of in-home shopping alternatives: mail order and door-to-door sales. Today they have a broad array of alternatives: mail order and mail-order catalogs, catalog desks in stores, catalog stores and sales agencies, telephone ordering, in-home party plans, and in-home selling. Watching the growth and continuing consumer acceptance of these alternatives, a student of consumer behavior asked the inevitable question, "Who tends to use them?" Are they the poor, elderly, and locked-in or unmobile consumers, or are they part and parcel of the more affluent and spatially mobile consumers? In other words, are in-home shoppers consumers who really have a choice in interoutlet decisions?

Generally, the answer is "yes." Studies of telephone buyers, mail order, and other forms of catalog buying indicate that it is the younger, more affluent risk-taking families with children that tend to be in-home buyers—at least, for those alternatives where the consumer takes the initiative in placing an order (Cox and Rich, 1964; Feldman and Starr, 1968; Gillett, 1970; and Reynolds, 1974). Moreover, these studies suggest that telephone and catalog shopping is motivated by desires to conveniently select from broad assortments of more fashionable styles and unusual items—after all, in most communities, the catalog is the "largest store in town."[6]

Marketers can also reach this segment of the market fairly effectively. To illustrate, consider catalog marketing. Even though consumers have numerous catalog buying alternatives, catalog circulation remains the primary operational tool for initially reaching the market. The very behavior of the frequent catalog buyer implies an interest in mail-order catalogs, and the distinguishing demographic characteristics of the frequent user provide the means for matching circulation with market location. Specifically, the frequent catalog buyer can be reached by direct mail through the use of zip codes corresponding to geographic areas with the greatest potential as defined by the demographic profile or through the use of commercially purchased mailing lists based on the configuration of discriminating demographic characteristics: age, income, and family size.

Also, special promotions and copy can be creatively developed to be consistent with the life style of the frequent buyers. Announcement and display messages emphasizing the assortment and unique items in the catalog can

[6]Preliminary evidence on in-home shopping where the salesperson takes the initiative instead of the consumer suggests a more locked-in consumer (Peters and Ford, 1972).

subtly capitalize on the consumers' positive attitudes toward assortment and negative attitudes toward local shopping conditions in smaller urban areas. Fashion and other illustrations can employ greater magazine-style photography to depict user images consistent with the venturesomeness of the frequent buyers. Since these buyers are self-confident risk-takers, a literal or "true" portrayal of items is unnecessary as long as stylish portrayals can be executed without being deceptive or misleading (Reynolds, 1974).

SUMMARY

The understanding of consumer spatial behavior is vital to marketers at various levels of the distribution chain. Retailers fail or prosper as a result of consumer spatial decisions, and a manufacturer's success depends largely on having the right product in the right outlets. As a result, researchers have attempted to identify the types of decisions and the determinant variables involved in this aspect of consumer behavior.

Spatial behavior is the result of three types of decisions: interurban choice, intraurban choice, and interoutlet choice. The study of interurban choice, pioneered by Reilly and Converse, examines the drawing power of large urban areas for consumers residing in smaller towns and rural areas. Using population and distance, Reilly developed a model which would indicate the breaking point at which consumers would no longer be drawn to a larger urban area. Converse reformulated Reilly's model and concluded that it applied only to shopping goods and to small towns located between two large urban areas. Another approach to interurban choice is to examine the personal characteristics of consumers who frequently shop outside their residential areas, and to develop a usable profile of this "outshopper." Retailers in both the home town and the large urban area can use this information to attract and hold customers.

Intraurban choice involves the decision by consumers to shop in one shopping center within their own area instead of another shopping center. Using square footage of selling space and travel time as determinant variables, Huff developed a model which will predict consumers' intraurban choices.

Consumers' interoutlet choices are influenced by such factors as the type of product being sought, store image, and store loyalty. Since research findings indicate that a majority of consumers go to one store to buy shopping goods, the outlet to which customers are first attracted usually gains their sales. A major factor that attracts consumers is store image, and most of the dimensions which determine store image are within management's control. Retailers need to determine which specific dimensions are the most important in attracting customers to their particular outlets and then develop these qualities to optimal levels in order to promote store loyalty. Research indicates that store-loyal consumers are especially important to grocery outlets, that they tend to spend a larger percentage of their food budget in their preferred store, and that they can be distinguished from other consumers by their personal characteristics.

Consumers who often patronize the same type of retail outlet are classified as *frequent shoppers.* We discuss two types of frequent shoppers: heavy users of ready-to-eat carry-out fried chicken and in-home buyers. The research in these areas illustrates the usefulness of developing consumer profiles for marketing strategy.

REVIEW QUESTIONS

1 Why has spatial mobility caused the framework of the retail outlet to maintain a constant state of flux? What other factors have contributed to this trend?
2 Define the three types of consumer spatial behavior decisions. Which type of decision does the work of Reilly and Converse pertain to? What are their conclusions?
3 Can frequent outshoppers be differentiated from other consumers? What are their distinguishing characteristics? Should local merchants consider these shoppers a lost cause? What can local merchants do to attract some of the frequent outshoppers?
4 Huff's spatial model is concerned with intraurban choice. What is his central thesis? What are the two variables Huff uses in designing his model of consumer choice? Discuss the findings of other researchers concerning these variables.
5 Why is store image so important to retailers? Can store image be successfully changed?
6 Store loyalty is important to manufacturers as well as to retailers. Why? What implications does this have for both groups?
7 Is store loyalty more important for one type of retail outlet than for any other type? If so, identify which type. Why is the store-loyal consumer so important?
8 Discuss the difference between shopping frequency and store loyalty. Can personal consumer characteristics be used to identify these behavior patterns? Give examples of the types of characteristics which seem to correlate with store loyalty and shopping frequency.

EXERCISE

In recent years, substantial interest and activity have been shown in the revitalization of shopping districts, especially with respect to environmental aspects such as streetscapes and landscapes. Such activities imply that environmental image influences consumers' choices of shopping districts and their enjoyment of the shopping experience.

Using Figure 14-1 as a guide, develop what you consider dimensions of a shopping-area image. Compare notes with classmates and develop a "final" set of dimensions. Discuss each of these dimensions in terms of how they affect the shopping experience of different types of consumers, such as young adults and the elderly.

REFERENCES

Arnold, Stephen J. and Douglas J. Tigert. "Market Monitoring through Attitude Research." *Journal of Retailing,* 49 (Winter 1973–1974), 3–22.

Bucklin, Louis P. "The Concept of Mass in Intra-urban Shopping." *Journal of Marketing,* 31 (October 1967), 37–42.

Converse, Paul D. "New Laws of Retail Gravitation." *Journal of Marketing,* 14 (October 1949).

———. *Retail Trade Areas in Illinois.* Urbana: University of Illinois Press, 1946.

Cox, Donald F. and Stuart U. Rich. "Perceived Risk and Consumer Decision Making: The Case of Telephone Shopping." *Journal of Marketing Research,* 1 (November 1964), 32–39.

Cunningham, Ross M. "Customer Loyalty to Store and Brand." *Harvard Business Review,* 39 (November–December 1961), 127–137.

Dietrich, Robert F. "37 Things You Can Do to Keep Your Customers—or Lose Them." *Progressive Grocer* (June 1973), 59–64.

Dommermuth, William P. and Edward W. Cundiff. "Shopping Goods, Shopping Centers, and Selling Strategies." *Journal of Marketing,* 31 (October 1967), 32–36.

Donnahoe, Alan S. "Research Study of Consumer Loyalty." *Journal of Retailing,* 1 (Spring 1956), 14–16.

Enis, Ben M. and Gordon W. Paul. " 'Store Loyalty' as a Basis for Market Segmentation." *Journal of Retailing,* 46 (Fall 1970), 42–56.

Feldman, Laurence P. and Alvin D. Starr. "Racial Factors in Shopping Behavior." In Keith Cox and Ben Enis (eds.), *A New Measure of Responsibility for Marketing.* Chicago: American Marketing Association, 1968.

Gillett, Peter L. "A Profile of Urban In-Home Shoppers." *Journal of Marketing,* 34 (July 1970), 40–45.

——— and Richard A. Scott. "Consumer Outshopping Patterns." Paper presented at the Annual Conference of the Southern Marketing Association, 1972.

Haines, George H., Jr., Leonard S. Simon, and Marcus Alexis. "Maximum Likelihood Estimation of Central-City Food Trading Areas." *Journal of Marketing Research,* 9 (May 1972), 154–159.

Herrmann, Robert O. and Leland L. Beik. "Shoppers' Movements outside Their Local Retail Area." *Journal of Marketing,* 32 (October 1968), 45–51.

Huff, David L. *Determination of Intra-Urban Retail Trade Areas.* Los Angeles: Division of Research, Graduate School of Business, University of California, Los Angeles, 1962.

——— and Larry Blue. *A Programmed Solution for Estimating Retail Sales Potentials.* Lawrence, Kans.: Center for Regional Studies, The University of Kansas, no date.

——— and Richard R. Batsell. "Conceptual and Operational Problems with Market Share Models of Consumer Spatial Behavior." in Mary Jane Schlinger (ed.), *Advances in Consumer Research.* Vol. 2. *Proceedings of the Annual Conference of the Association for Consumer Research,* 1975.

Kleimenhagen, Arnok. "Shopping, Specialty, or Convenience Goods." *Journal of Retailing* (Winter 1966–1967).

Kunkel, John H. and Leonard L. Berry. "A Behavioral Conception of Retail Image." *Journal of Marketing,* 32 (October 1968), 21–27.

Luce, R. Duncan. *Individual Choice Behavior.* New York: Wiley, 1959.

Mason, Joseph Barry and Morris L. Mayer. "Empirical Observations of Consumer Behavior." *Journal of Retailing,* 48 (Fall 1972), 17–31.

Monroe, Kent B. and Joseph B. Guiltinon. "A Path-Analytic Exploration of Retail Patronage Influences." *Journal of Consumer Research,* 2 (June 1975), 19–28.

Moore, Charles Thomas and Joseph Barry Mason. "A Research Note on Major Retail Center Patronage." *Journal of Marketing,* 33 (July 1969), 61–63.

Peters, William H. and Neil M. Ford. "A Profile of Urban In-Home Shoppers: The Other Half." *Journal of Marketing,* 36 (January 1972), 62–64.

Reilly, William J. *The Law of Retail Gravitation.* New York: William J. Reilly Company, 1931.

———. *Methods for the Study of Retail Relationships.* Austin, Tex.: University of Texas Press, 1929.

Reynolds, Fred D. "An Analysis of Catalog Buying Behavior." *Journal of Marketing,* 38 (July 1974), 47–51.

——— and William R. Darden. "Intermarket Patronage: A Psychographic Study of Consumer Outshoppers." *Journal of Marketing* (October 1972), 50–54.

——— and Warren S. Martin. "A Multivariate Analysis of Intermarket Patronage: Some Empirical Findings." *Journal of Business Research,* 2 (April 1974), 193–200.

———, William R. Darden, and Warren S. Martin. "Developing an Image of the Store Loyal Consumer." *Journal of Retailing* (Winter 1974–1975), 73–84.

Schwartz, George. *Development of Marketing Theory.* Cincinnati: South-Western Publishing Company, 1963.

Thompson, John R. "Characteristics and Behavior of Outshopping Consumers." *Journal of Retailing,* 47 (Spring 1971), 70–80.

Tigert, Douglas J., R. Lathrope, and M. J. Bleeg. "The Fast Food Franchise: Psychographic and Demographic Segmentation Analysis." *Journal of Retailing,* 47 (Spring 1971), 81–90.

Udell, Jon G. "Prepurchase Behavior of Buyers of Small Electrical Appliances." *Journal of Marketing,* 30 (October 1966), 50–52.

Chapter 15

The Analysis of Consumption

"Consumption," described unemotionally in Chapter 2 as a person's actual experience with a product, can take on value-laden connotations whenever a dictionary or thesaurus is consulted:

> **con-sump-tion** . . . *1.* act or process of consuming *2.* The utilization of economic goods, in the satisfaction of wants or in the process of production resulting chiefly in their destruction, deterioration, or transformation. . . .[1]
>
> WASTE.—*n.* *consumption,* expenditure, exhaustion; dispersion, leakage, loss, wear and tear, waste; prodigality.
>
> USE.—*n.* *use,* employ, exercise, application, appliance; disposal; consumption; agency, usefulness, etc.; benefit, recourse, resort, avail.
> *Conversion to use:* utilization, service, wear.
> *Way of using:* usage, employment, modus operandi [L.].
> *user,* consumer, market, demand.

[1]From Webster's New Collegiate Dictionary © 1976 by G. & C. Merriam Co., Publishers of the Merriam-Webster Dictionaries. Used by permission.

With such a large number of adjectives and synonyms to work with, it is possible to describe consumption from a variety of perspectives, some value-laden, others not. Consider this example:

> The average American in 1970 had a standard of living substantially more comfortable than that enjoyed by the kings of the Middle Ages. Not only was his home centrally heated, but it might well have had some form of air-conditioning (cooling) as well. His food supply was dependable and nutritionally balanced. His floors were carpeted and his walls were insulated. His wardrobe presented a clean change of clothes for every day in the week as well as the clothes required for special occasions, such as cocktail parties, hunting and fishing, the opera or theater, gardening and going to the dump, playing tennis, skiing, and snowmobiling (Webster, 1974:19).

The meaning of "consumption" as used in this chapter is most closely captured when it is viewed as a synonym of "use" or "way of using." *Consumption* is the way consumers use products, and the analysis of consumption is the same whether one considers the consequences of consumption as good, bad, or both.

As persons go about putting products to use, they experience in the most direct and personal manner the ability of a product or collection of products to meet their needs. This sensory experience takes place within the context of all other relevant influences and thereby becomes the primary basis for validating or invalidating purchasing decisions, communicating decisions, and forming attitudes toward products consumed.

Since consumption provides a direct influence on subsequent consumer behaviors, it is imperative for students of consumer behavior to explore it as fully as possible. Currently, there are three major types of analysis used to explore consumption: (1) analyzing expenditure patterns, (2) analyzing product usage rates, and (3) observing actual consumption. Each of these is discussed in detail in this chapter, which concludes with a section on current levels and trends in American consumption.

EXPENDITURE PATTERNS

Economists have long considered family budgetary or expenditure patterns to reflect consumption and savings. What a person or family spends is not, of course, actual consumption, but there is an analytical value to the idea that expenditures reflect consumption.

Probably no two persons, families, or households spend their money in exactly the same way. Yet numerous studies have shown that there is a predictable regularity in the way families of different income levels distribute their expenditures to major classes of goods and services.

A nineteenth-century statistician, Ernst Engel, is believed to have been the first person to isolate income-expenditure regularities. His statistical analysis led to the formulation of what are called "Engel's laws":

1 As income increases, the percentage spent for food declines.
2 As income increases, the percentage spent for clothing, rent, and home operation remains about the same.
3 As income increases, the percentage spent for all other goods and services increases.

Even today the expenditure patterns of families, on the average, change fairly regularly with income, just as they did over 100 years ago when Engel did his studies. Figure 15-1 shows the 1973 income-expenditure patterns of the urban United States population. Data in the figure, even though expressed in dollar amounts, show that percentage regularities found by Engel remain true today (the exception is the percentage spent on clothing).

The underlying explanation for these expenditure patterns is the "have–have not" income continuum of society. Poor families must, obviously, spend their incomes on the basic necessities of survival such as food. Poor families buy cheap, bulky carbohydrates, rent or own inexpensive houses with a minimum of "modern coveniences," and rarely spend any money on recreation, reading, and educational materials. In contrast, as incomes increase, life chances improve: people eat more and better—shifting their food expenditures to more expensive foods such as meats, fruits, vegetables, and a host of preprocessed foods. Yet, as the amount expended for food increases, the percentage spent for food declines, thereby leaving larger proportions to spend

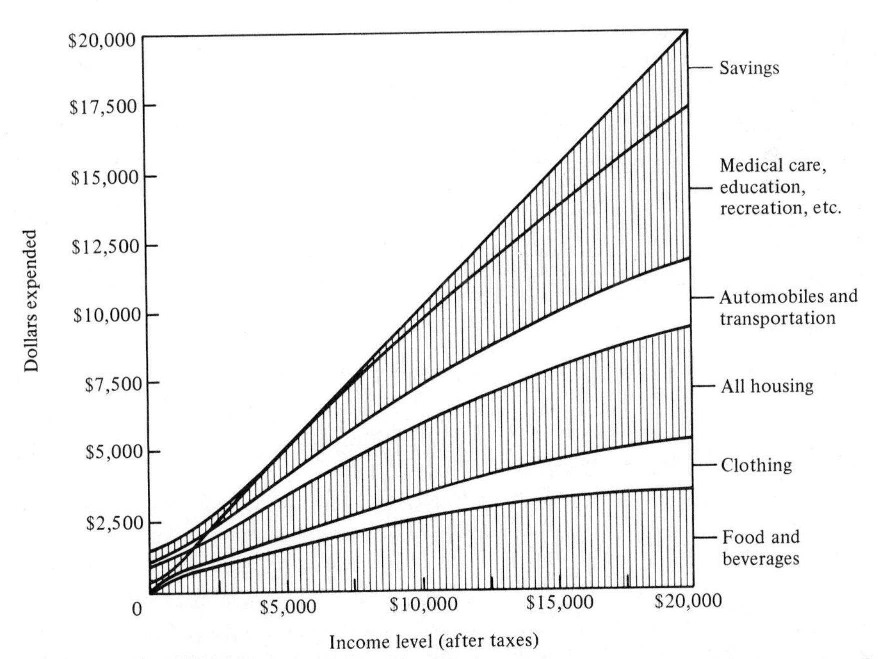

Figure 15-1 Expenditures for consumption at different income levels, 1973. *Source:* Samuelson (1973: 209).

on clothing, recreation, travel, and other "luxury" goods and services, even savings.

Income-expenditure patterns like Engel's can be helpful in a broad sort of way to anticipate changes in consumption patterns resulting from changes in incomes. More refined relationships, however, have been developed by statisticians of the U.S. Bureau of Labor Statistics. These are called "ratios of income sensitivity." These ratios are numerical values that relate percentage changes in consumer expenditures for products to percentage changes in income. Income sensitivity ratios are more useful than generalizations such as Engel's because they are more specific and cover a larger number of product categories. A selection of average population ratios are shown in Table 15-1. The coefficient 0.62 for food-at-home expenditures tells us that a 1 percent increase in income will produce a corresponding 0.62 percent increase in expenditures for food eaten at home.

Population averages such as those in Table 15-1 obscure the variations in expenditures by income classes. This is demonstrated in Table 15-2, which shows selected income sensitivity ratios for various income classes. The figure in the last column of the first row, for example, reveals that a 1 percent increase in income among families earning between $8,500 and $12,000 annually will produce a corresponding food-at-home expenditure increase of 0.35 percent instead of an average increase.

Marketers, armed with basic expenditure data for a product category by income class, an income sensitivity ratio for that product and income level, and knowledge of income changes, can calculate with reasonable accuracy changes in demand for the product category. The major problem in using such data is

Table 15-1 Income Sensitivity Ratios, 1955–1970

Item	Income elasticity[1]	Item	Income elasticity[1]
Total expenditures[2]	0.97	Semidurable housefurnishings	1.29
Food at home	0.62	Household supplies	0.96
Restaurant	0.51	Personal care services	0.76
Alcoholic beverages	0.77	Toilet articles, preparations	1.50
Tobacco	0.45	Medical care services	1.16
Women's, children's apparel	1.01	Drugs, supplies	1.49
Men's, boys' apparel	0.91	Automobile purchases	1.33
Footwear	0.59	Tires, tubes, accessories	1.72
Shelter	1.16	Gasoline and oil	1.05
Household operation services	1.06	Transportation services	0.56
Furniture	0.78	Sporting goods, toys	1.71
Household appliances	1.43	Foreign travel	1.61
Radio, TV, etc.	2.21	Higher education	1.55
China, glassware, utensils	1.22		

[1]Percentage change in personal consumption expenditures for each 1 percent rise in real disposable personal income.
[2]Personal consumption expenditures.
Source: The Conference Board (1972: 170).

their timeliness. Basic expenditure data are collected by the Department of Labor at roughly ten-year intervals, and the data change dramatically between collection dates. Moreover, the sensitivity ratios can change from time period to time period. The 0.62 for food at home in Table 15-1, for example, represents a ratio established for the period 1955–1970. The corresponding coefficient for the years 1948–1965 was 0.86. Also, the data are collected for product categories. There is no brand-specific information within the categories. Thus, the usefulness of expenditure patterns for the analysis of consumption is in determining demand for broad product categories.

PRODUCT USAGE RATES

As self-service retail stores have developed and spread throughout the country, manufacturers of consumer goods have found it increasingly difficult to get accurate information about the users of their products. While consumption expenditures are predictable for classes of products, not everyone buys everything, and some consumers buy large quantities of products that other consumers ignore. To help make decisions about what qualities to build into a product, how to package it, where to advertise it, and what to say in the advertising, a manufacturer must have more detailed consumption information concerning his customers and potential customers.

To fill this need, consumer research has often focused on the differences between those who use the product and those who do not, asking such questions as: How do buyers of sedans differ from buyers of station wagons? How do users of instant coffee differ from users of regular ground coffee? How do buyers of bubble gum differ from nonbuyers?

Table 15-2 Income Sensitivity Ratios by Income Level

	Income level (in dollars)						
Expenditure category	1,513 to 2,508	2,508 to 3,516	3,516 to 4,506	4,506 to 5,495	5,495 to 6,710	6,710 to 8,573	8,573 to 11,724
1 Food at home	1.20	0.62	0.70	0.82	0.55	0.51	0.35
2 Food away from home	1.60	0.90	0.32	*	1.50	1.32	1.11
3 Tobacco	1.25	1.00	0.59	0.55	0.55	0.32	*
4 Alcoholic beverages	1.08	1.82	1.05	1.40	1.23	0.90	0.86
5 Housing	0.53	0.67	0.56	0.54	0.47	0.51	0.70
6 Clothing	1.70	1.35	1.00	0.82	1.10	1.10	1.03
7 Personal care	1.15	0.82	0.44	0.50	0.55	0.76	0.60
8 Medical care	0.90	0.62	0.20	0.90	0.86	0.64	0.83
9 Recreation	1.60	0.78	1.15	0.55	1.64	1.05	1.19
10 Reading	0.73	2.08	0.70	0.55	1.08	0.64	0.83
11 Education	1.70	2.07	0.66	2.30	2.30	1.57	3.54
12 Transportation	1.90	2.75	1.50	0.80	0.82	0.95	0.86

*No change in expenditure level.
Source: U.S. Department of Labor (1965).

The Heavy Half

But for some product categories, merely being able to discriminate users from nonusers is not enough. If the product is so widely used that almost everyone uses some of it sometime, the population segment of greatest interest is a relatively small "heavy user" portion of the user group that accounts for the bulk of the sales volume. For instance, most people drink soft drinks at least occasionally, but less than a third of the consumer population drink soft drinks at the rate of one glass or more per day, and this heavy-user group accounts for more than three-quarters of the soft drinks sold. Less than 20 percent of homemakers use flour once a day or more, but they account for over half of total flour use. And less than 15 percent of the population make nearly 75 percent of the long distance telephone calls.

In a paper presented at a meeting of the Advertising Research Foundation, Dik Waren Twedt demonstrated the importance of the concept of the "heavy half" by showing that persons above the median of usage—the heavy half—account for 80 percent to 90 percent of total volume.

His data are shown in Table 15-3. The table is read cumulatively from left to right. It shows, reading across the top line, that the heaviest buyers—the top 10 percent—of concentrated fruit juice account for 39 percent of the sales volume, the top 20 percent account for 58 percent of the volume, and the top 50 per cent account for 89 percent of the volume. Reading down the 50 percent column, the data show that the heavy half account for 89 percent of the sales of concentrated fruit juice, 88 percent of the sales of beer, 83 percent of the sales of maragarine, and so on.

The fact that such large proportions of sales volume are accounted for by relatively small segments of the consumer population has tended to draw

Table 15-3 The Heavy Half

Products	% Buying	Purchase concentration deciles									
		10	20	30	40	50	60	70	80	90	100
Concentrated fruit juice	72	39	58	72	82	89	94	97	99	99	100
Beer	33	42	62	74	82	88	92	95	97	99	100
Margarine	89	31	50	64	75	83	90	94	97	99	100
Dog food	31	34	55	69	80	88	93	97	99	99	100
Cake mixes	75	32	52	67	77	85	90	94	97	99	100
Hair tonics	48	42	60	72	81	87	91	95	98	99	100
Cold cereal	96	36	57	76	80	87	92	96	98	99	100
Soaps and detergents	98	28	46	61	72	81	88	93	97	99	100
Toilet tissue	98	24	40	53	64	74	82	89	94	98	100
Canned hash	32	40	58	70	79	86	90	94	96	98	100
Cola beverages	78	44	65	77	84	90	93	96	98	99	100
Lemon-lime	58	56	72	81	86	91	94	96	98	99	100
Hair fixatives	46	52	68	76	83	88	92	95	98	99	100
Shampoo	82	32	50	63	73	81	87	92	96	98	100
Bourbon whiskey	41	48	66	76	84	89	91	92	95	98	100

Source: Twedt (1964).

attention away from the user group in general and focus it specifically on the "heavy user." For a great many products the prime question has become, "How do the heavy users differ from the light users and the nonusers?" rather than, "How do the users and the nonusers differ from each other?"

The task of identifying the heavy user of any product often is a difficult one, however, because of the complexity of consumption relationships among families. Consumer products fill an intricate mix of needs, and one usually cannot expect simple relationships between degree of product use and other consumer variables. It is not too surprising, then, that when Twedt (1964) presented his findings, he also made the following observations:

1 Demographic characteristics (age, education, income, race, etc.) are poor predictors of heavy usage.

2 Heavy usage of different products is relatively independent—the fact that a household uses a lot of aluminium foil tells us nothing about how much canned dog food that family will buy.

3 Among heavy users, there seems to be less, rather than more, brand loyalty. Not only do they buy more—they buy more often, and they buy more different brands.

4 The heavy users are not price buyers. They pay as much, or even a bit more, for a unit of purchase than do the light users.

Just as relatively small proportions of the consumer population account for major portions of the sales volume of most products, so also do limited segments of the population make up the audiences of magazines and television programs. Magazines are particularly selective. *Reader's Digest,* the second most widely disseminated magazine in the United States, reaches less than one-third of the American population, and the audiences of most magazines, especially magazines that appeal to special interest groups, are much smaller.

Marketers of nationally advertised consumer products must select specific magazines, television programs, and newspapers to carry their advertising messages. In the marketing manager's wildest dreams, he finds a way to make an exact match between the heavy users of his product and the audiences of a cleverly selected mix of advertising media. His advertising therefore goes to all heavy users of the product, and none of his advertising goes to light users or nonusers, so none of it is wasted.

A look at two housewives, "Mrs. Walker" and "Mrs. White," will show some of the difficulties of following this scheme. Both Mrs. Walker and Mrs. White are heavy users of detergent because both have large families containing many young children, but only one magazine, *Reader's Digest,* reaches them both, and the audience of *Reader's Digest* is so broad that most of it consists of light users or nonusers of detergents. (About half of the *Reader's Digest* readers are men, and a great many of the women in the *Reader's Digest* audience are beyond the life cycle stage of having young children.)

Mrs. Walker reads *Good Housekeeping* and Mrs. White reads *Family Circle.* Advertisements placed in both these magazines would reach both Mrs. Walker and Mrs. White, but they would also reach large numbers of people who do not buy much detergent. Television programs and newspapers, with audiences that are even broader and less homogeneous than the audiences of magazines, are even harder to select so as to take advantage of Twedt's concept of the heavy half.

But the product manager cannot go to the other extreme and place his advertising messages at random in any place that happens to be available. A detergent advertisement in *Playboy*, for instance, would not be seen by either Mrs. Walker or Mrs. White and would reach remarkably few of detergents' other heavy users. So advertisers do the best they can, selecting advertising media that give them the best possible audience of prospective customers, with full knowledge that the fit is bound to be far from perfect. With good information about their customers' media habits, they can at least avoid gross errors, and beyond that they can hope that the fit between the audience they would like to reach and the audience they actually do reach will not be too bad.

If, then, these atypical consumers are so difficult to identify beyond their usage rates, one might well ask, "How does the heavy half concept contribute to reaching target audiences other than in avoiding gross errors?" One important contribution evolving from the heavy half concept is the study of product use combinations.

Product Use Combinations

In the King and Summers study of opinion leadership described in a previous chapter, correlation coefficients were used to indicate the amount of opinion leadership overlap among various product categories. Each respondent was graded on an opinion leadership scale for each product category, correlations among these scale scores were computed, and the resulting pattern of relationships showed that there is more overlap in opinion leadership between some product categories than between some others.

The same method can be used to indicate the amount of overlap among products in terms of heavy versus light usage. Each respondent can be graded on a heavy user–light user scale for each product, correlations among these scale scores can be computed, and the resulting pattern of relationships will show whether there is more overlap in use between some products than between some others.

In his paper on the "heavy half" of product users, Twedt made a point of mentioning that the degree of overlap in product use is not great—that if a consumer is a heavy user of one product, there is no guarantee that this consumer will be a heavy user of any other product.

This is true, especially when products are perceived by consumers as substitute products—products which satisfy the same need and tend to be consumed separately, such as coffee and tea, automobiles and airplanes, and cigars and pipes.

But it would be strange indeed if such relationships were entirely absent. Not only are some products used separately because they are substitutes, but others are used together because they complement each other (beer and pretzels, coffee and cream, milk and cookies) and/or because they fill an intricate mix of needs for maintaining or extending a style of life.

In a paper presented at an annual conference of the American Marketing Association, William D. Wells (1967) demonstrated that there is indeed more overlap in use among some products than among others. The set of correlation coefficients is shown in Figure 15-2. These were computed from data obtained in a nationwide survey by the Brand Rating Research Corporation that asked homemakers about their degree of use of a variety of grocery products.

The coefficients on the upper left (numerals in darker print) show that there is more overlap in degree of use among laundry detergent, cold cereal, and canned soup than among any of these three products and the other products in the figure. These are products that are heavily used by large families with young children. The coefficients in the middle show higher than average overlap among shortening, sugar, and flour. These products are heavily used by homemakers who do an unusual amount of home baking. The coefficients in the lower right show overlap among plastic food wrap, plastic food bags, and aluminium foil. These products tend to be heavily used by affluent, older families.

Thus, even though the overalp is far from perfect, products can be seen to form use combinations that reflect need patterns. The need patterns in turn are the result of a complex set of relationships among the consumer's stage in life, education, income, and life style—among other variables. Nevertheless, product use combinations often suggest distinctive orientations toward sets or products in a manner analogous to the way a consistent set of behaviors indicates an underlying personality trait.

Consider, for example, the product category cosmetics. Three product use

Figure 15-2 Product Use Combinations

	Laundry detergent	Cold cereal	Canned soup	Shortening	Sugar	Flour	Plastic food wrap	Plastic food bags	Aluminum foil
Laundry detergent		**36**	**32**	14	26	21	12	07	06
Cold cereal	**36**		**27**	03	20	10	11	02	04
Canned soup	**32**	**27**		07	20	07	10	09	06
Shortening	14	03	07		**38**	**44**	09	07	07
Sugar	26	20	20	**38**		**41**	09	05	07
Flour	21	10	07	**44**	**41**		13	13	15
Plastic food wrap	12	11	10	09	09	13		**30**	**36**
Plastic food bags	07	02	09	07	05	13	**30**		**40**
Aluminum foil	06	04	06	07	07	15	**36**	**40**	

Source: Wells (1967).

combinations of cosmetic products have been isolated in a nationwide survey of 2,000 females: one group includes eye makeup, liquid face makeup base, lipstick, and hairspray; another group includes face cleansing cream, hand cream, perfume, and mouthwash; and a third includes hair shampoo, cream rinse, and home permanents.

Each of these combinations suggests somewhat different orientations toward personal grooming or the "embellisment of nature." The first group includes items that accentuate certain features the user sees when she looks in the mirror; this group might then be called a "decorative" orientation. The second set of products might reflect a "preservative" orientation, since all items in the cluster are those that protect against the undesirable rather than accentuate an attractive feature. The third group reflects an orientation toward special emphasis on care of the hair. It is interesting that hair spray belongs in the first group and not in the hair group. This suggests that use of hair spray has more to do with the picture the users see in the mirror (she wants to maintain that look) than with special interest in the hair itself (Wells, Banks, and Tigert, 1967).

Isolating product use combinations in this manner can yield a rich description of the user of a particular product. A copy writer scratching his head over how to reach the heavy user of cereal would find it useful to know that she is not just a lady with a lot of kids, but that she also is a peanut butter spreader, a clothes washer, a head shampooer, a Jello maker, a soup ladler, and a knee bandager.

Identifying market segments by product use combinations offers other marketing implications as well. Since the product set has a common set of heavy users, it makes sense to think in terms of marketing the products together. Just as special displays of complementary products yield greater sales than separate displays of the same products, cross-couponing, advertisement placement, product location in stores and mail-order catalogs, and joint promotions are candidates for effective "complementary" marketing.

Just as product use combinations appear when usage rates of products are correlated, so also do clusters of medium-use patterns emerge whenever viewing or readership measures are correlated (Banks, 1967; Swanson, 1967; Wells, Banks, and Tigert, 1967; Wells, 1969; Baumgarten and Ring, 1972; and Tigert, 1971). Tigert (1971), for example, explored the medium-use patterns of 1,800 female Canadians of 73 prime time television programs. His results are shown in Figure 15-3.

Findings such as those in the figure are not really surprising when we begin to think of the mass media as products in addition to channels of communication. In this context people "consume" television programs and magazine articles in terms of their particular set of interests and needs. Moreover, when students of consumer behavior have isolated media use patterns, they have been able to develop very descriptive life style profiles of the common core of users,—profiles which lead to marketing implications such as copy tone and product-medium matches.

Figure 15-3 Canadian Prime Time Television Factors for 1970

Movies
Academy Performance (CTV)
Friday Night Movies (CTV)
Wednesday Night Movies (CBC)

Sports
Hockey Night in Canada (Wednesday—CTV)
Wide World of Sport (CTV)
Hockey Night in Canada (Wednesday—CBC)
NFL Football (Cable)
Baseball Game of the Week (U.S. Channel)

Male Singers—I
Johnny Cash (CTV)
Dean Martin (CTV)
Andy Williams (CTV)
Glen Campbell (CTV)

Male Singers—II
This is Tom Jones (CTV)
Englebert Humperdinck (CTV)

Family Comedy
My 3 Sons (U.S. Channel)
Family Affair (CTV)

Variety Comedy
Jackie Gleason (CTV)
Carol Burnett Show (CTV)
Lucy (CTV)
Red Skelton (CBC)
Rowan & Martin Laugh-In (CBC)

Documentary
1st Tuesday (U.S. Channel)
60 Minutes (U.S. Channel)

Black Comedy
Bill Cosby (CBC)
Julia (CBC)

Impossible Adventures
Ironside (CTV)
It Takes a Thief (CTV)
Mannix (CTV)
Mod Squad (CTV)
The FBI (CTV)
Misson Impossible (CBC)

Fantasy Comedy
Bewitched (CTV)
Flying Nun (CTV)
Jeannie (CTV)

Female Star Comedy
Debbie Reynolds (CBC)
Doris Day Show (CBC)
Governor & J.J. (CBC)
Julia (CBC)

Westerns
Bonanza (CBC)
Gunsmoke (U.S. Channel)

Drama
McQueen (CBC)
The Bold Ones (CBC)
The Name of the Game (CBC)

U.S. News
CBS Evening News (Cronkite) (U.S. Channel)
Huntley-Brinkley Report (U.S. Channel)

Talk Shows
Johnny Carson (U.S. Channel)
Merv Griffin (U.S. Channel)

City-Country Comedy
Beverly Hillbillies (CBC)
Green Acres (CBC)

Honky Tonk (Canadian)
Pig & Whistle (CTV)
Diamond Lil's (CTV)

Canadian Documentary
Weekend (CBC)
Man Alive (CBC)
Man at the Centre (CBC)

Canadian Sing-Along
Tommy Hunter (CBC)
Sing-Along Jubilee (CBC)

Source: Tigert (1971: 241).

Thus far our discussion has centered on users versus nonusers and use combinations of products or media. Wells (1974) has demonstrated a useful refinement of those types of analyses of consumption: focus the analysis on those consumers who are both members of the audience of a particular vehicle *and* users of the product of interest. This refinement is useful to marketing managers because the overlap between audience membership and product consumption is never complete. Some members of a vehicle's audience will be nonusers of the product, and some users of the product will not be in the audience. In some cases the life style of those who are both members of an audience and users of a particular product or service will be unique.

The data in Table 15-4 illustrate this point. The *"Playboy"* column shows the responses of men who have taken an airline trip within the past year and are regular readers of *Playboy.* The *"National Geographic"* column gives the responses of men who have taken an airline trip within the past year and are regular readers of *National Geographic.* The figures in these two columns differ sharply from each other, and they differ sharply from the corresponding figures for *Playboy* and *National Geographic* readers who do not fly.

The air traveler who is reached through *Playboy* is not the same as the air traveler who is reached through *National Geographic,* even though both magazines would be selected by a computer routine that picks out vehicles with

Table 15-4 Airline Passengers and Magazine Readership

	Percent who "generally" or "definitely" agree	
	Playboy	National Geographic
I like skiing.	33	22
My greatest achievements are ahead of me.	78	55
We will probably move at least once in the next five years.	55	33
Men are smarter than women.	25	15
I like to golf.	44	30
I like to feel attractive to women.	72	55
I like gardening.	36	51
We often display the flag on national holidays.	46	59
I own many power tools.	34	47
Television commercials place too much emphasis on sex.	18	35
There is too much violence on television.	31	45
If Americans were more religious this would be a better country.	35	52
I will probably have more money to spend next year than I have now.	70	51
I like sports cars.	54	36
I like to play poker.	40	25
I would like to have my boss's job.	42	32
I would rather live in or near a big city than in or near a small town.	39	28
Most men would cheat on their wives if the right opportunity came along.	45	24
I enjoy going through an art gallery.	31	42
There are day people and night people; I am a day person.	42	58
I would rather spend a quiet evening at home than go out to a party.	31	45
Spiritual values are more important than material things.	40	60
If people would work harder and complain less this would be a better country.	58	71
Our home is furnished for comfort, not for style.	55	70

Source: Wells (1974:337). Reprinted from *Life Style and Psychographics*, published by the American Marketing Association.

unusually high concentrations of flyers. A simple comparison of flyers versus nonflyers or readers versus nonreaders would not have permitted these interesting differences to come to light.

OBSERVING CONSUMPTION

In the analysis of consumption by product usage rates, students of consumer behavior are looking beyond purchase behavior because of the logical belief that the reasons why people purchase or do not purchase a product are rooted in the use to which they put the product and the satisfaction derived in using it for a given purpose.

Typically, use behavior is studied by obtaining self-reports of use and/or frequency of use via a self-administered questionnaire. The following five questions about soap products illustrate how usage data are obtained from consumers:

1 How many bars of *heavy duty hand soap* (such as Lava) does your family use up in an average *month*?

None	1	2	3	4	5	6	More than 6
☐	☐	☐	☐	☐	☐	☐	☐

2 Approximately how many loads of wash do you yourself do in an average *week* in which you use a *laundry soap or detergent*?

None	1 or 2	3	4	5	6	7 or 8	9 or 10	More than 10
☐	☐	☐	☐	☐	☐	☐	☐	☐

3 Approximately how many washes do you do in an average *week* with a *soap for fine fabrics*?

	None	Less than one a week	1	2	3	4	5 or 6	More than 6
Washes by hand	☐	☐	☐	☐	☐	☐	☐	☐
Machine loads	☐	☐	☐	☐	☐	☐	☐	☐

4 About how many times a *week* do you use an *all purpose cleaner* like Mr. Clean, liquid Ajax or a similar product?

Don't use	Less than once a week	1	2	3	4	5 or 6	More than 6
☐	☐	☐	☐	☐	☐	☐	☐

5 How many different times a *day* do you use *scouring powder*?

Don't use	Less than once a day	1	2	3	4	5 or 6	More than 6
☐	☐	☐	☐	☐	☐	☐	☐

Notice how these usage questions are framed in terms of different time periods and situations for the various products. The frame of reference provides a good general orientation of the degree of use in context with normal usage periods and use situations such as machine versus hand washing. In the preceding section, we pointed out how this type of data is employed in understanding consumer behavior. For some products and some situations, however, the usage rate studies based on self-report fall short of yielding a comprehensive understanding of the role of a product or set of products in consumption. At times it is necessary to determine *how* people use products as well as *how often* they use them—information that can be obtained in part through direct observation.

Consider, for example, a situation where marketers have a desire to expand the market for a product such as baking soda. It is relatively easy to identify heavy, light, and nonusers of baking soda by self-report questions. It may be possible to describe these groups effectively and reach the heavy-user segment with brand-oriented appeals. But it is nearly impossible to convert light and nonusers to heavy use and heavy users to heavier use (thereby expanding the market) without also being able to communicate new ways to use baking soda. And it is difficult to suggest new uses without knowing how baking soda is being used. It makes little sense, for example, to tell homemakers to put baking soda in the refrigerator and in cat litter to remove unpleasant odors if they are already using it in these ways or if they do not own one or more cats or use cat litter.

Another situation where it is useful to know how consumers use a product is related to developing and/or testing new features of a product. If television or movie cameras placed in the kitchens or homemakers (with their full cooperation, of course) reveal that homemakers frequently must remove a number of items from the shelves in the refrigerator to get to other items at the rear of the shelves, it makes sense to think about developing shelves that slide or roll out of the refrigerator core for easy access to the rear of the shelves.

In essence, knowing how consumers use a product and the associations connected to its use helps establish dimensions of compatibility or incompatibility for new products or new features. Analoze, the pill that failed, is a classic example of the consequences of not knowing the associations people attach to how a product is consumed. Analoze was a cherry-flavored, combination pain killer and stomach sweetener with the relative advantage that it could be taken without water. Yet, despite favorable concept tests, the analogesic tablet was withdrawn after a poor showing during test marketing. A postmortem by the manufacturer revealed that headache sufferers had no confidence in a tablet not taken with water. Apparently consumers have taken headache remedies with water for so long that they associated water as an important part of pain relief (Schorr, 1961).

Thus far we have focused on how people use a particular product. It is also possible to take a broader focus and analyze how a collection of products are jointly and/or sequentially used to achieve a goal—in other words, "The way a purchaser of a product performs the total task of whatever it is that he or she is trying to accomplish when using the product—not baking a cake, but preparing a meal . . ." (Boyd and Levy, 1963). By examining "consumption systems" it is often helpful to wring the full meaning out of the way that products are used together to accomplish a broader goal. By understanding the total system, (desirably) the manufacturer will be able to "plug into" the system in a manner relevant to the consumer.

Consider, for example, the home laundry system which Harper Boyd and Sidney Levy (1963: 130–132) describe in their article on consumption systems as a dimension of consumer analysis. They provide a general description of the steps involved in laundering clothes, along with illustrations of marketing implications suggested by the description.

The week's accumulation of laundry is sorted into piles. The homemaker classifies the clothes to be processed, either by observation or by some predetermined set of "rules." Thus:

> Men's white shirts may be handled routinely, but an unusually soiled pair of trousers may require a decision to be made. The housewife may use such standards as appearance, soiling, wrinkling, odor, length of wearing, and type of cloth as bases for her decisions.
>
> Perhaps the men's shirts will be delivered to a Chinese laundry some distance away. (Here a special service is being used. Why is this service so unique? On the other hand, how much of a nuisance is it? Might the Chinese laundry begin pickup and delivery? Couldn't the large commercial laundries duplicate this type of laundering?)
>
> The sorting continues. (How distasteful is sorting to the housewife? Perhaps a powder to reduce odor and mildew in the laundry hamper would be useful. Or perhaps a method of precleaning clothes so that soaking is eliminated would be welcome. Could some kind of sorting rack attachment to an appliance facilitate the process?)
>
> White goods form one pile—sheets, pillowcases, towels, underwear, and so on. This requires hot water and bleach. Especially dirty spots may need individual attention with a brush. (Perhaps a tube of aerosol spray of a special cleaning substance could take care of these.)
>
> Another pile includes the colorful items—blouses, linen napkins, girls' frocks. These may or may not need hot water. They may possibly need a bit of mending. (Maybe a little laundry sewing kit would be handy for this.)
>
> Still another pile needs very special handling. Perhaps it includes socks, delicate undergarments, synthetics, woolens, to be subdivided into those needing cold water, warm water, hand washing, and so on. (Possibly the sink that has been designed out of laundry rooms still has its place after all.)
>
> Some things are to be dry cleaned—sent out or taken to a coin-operated machine. (When will home dry cleaning machines be available? And will there be a market for them?)

In doing the laundry, the products that will be used must be at hand—often a messy array of boxes, bottles (glass and plastic), spray cans, and jars. Like an alchemist, the homemaker will juggle an assortment that may include more than one brand of detergent, bluing, starch, bleach, water softener, spot remover, soap, and hand lotion! (Conceivably, there is room for an integrated line of laundry products with compatible ingredients and matched containers to help organize the array of cleaning staples.) Let us see how the system continues and note what other questions arise:

> Piles of clothes are put into the washing machine. Since the piles are of different volume and weight, there are problems in loading. Overloading is not uncommon; underloading is a wasteful irritation. (This problem has been solved by new models that adapt to smaller loads, but are there other refinements still possible?)
>
> There are different kinds of washing machines. The consumer has to judge which is best for her and then live with it. "I'd like one that does everything automatic, but my service man says those give more trouble, and that I'm better off with my simpler machine," is a statement commonly heard among housewives. (Clearly, reliability is still an area with marketing potential.)
>
> Nearby is the box of detergent. The giant box is a real chore to handle and to lug from the supermarket. (Volume delivery would seem a good solution; and perhaps home delivery of barrel-size containers would offer possibilities. Also, since laundries are such wet places, why don't they do something about the boxes that collapse? Plastic containers or plastic-bottom boxes would alleviate this problem.)
>
> Frequently the detergent is added to the wash by pouring from the box "about one cup." There is a general problem of imprecision; women are likely to overdo. (Perhaps the directions should be more explicit, or there should be warning lights or bells; and perhaps the detergent manufacturer could include measuring cups or one-cup automatic dispenser chutes.)
>
> What to do about bleach is a question that needs to be resolved. It is strong and threatening, but routinely useful; powder is safer, but possibly less effective. Bleach may be hard on clothes. It is disheartening to have clothes get frayed and threadbare. On the other hand, they will wear out and it is exciting to contemplate the possibility of a new garment. (The rapidity with which new types of bleaches enter the market indicates that there remains an unsatisfied need here).
>
> Washing chores vary with the kind of machines women have—whether a washer-dryer, or separate appliances. As the process goes on, the clothes are spread around in different states of handling—dirty, wet, dry, ironed, waiting ironing, from last time, poorly done pieces that need redoing, things that need touching up. (Laundries and utility rooms are not always well planned, even in new homes. There is still a market for intelligent architectural attention to working space and its organization. On the other hand, may there not also be a certain amount of pleasure in being ankle deep in clothes that are gradually working their way to cleanliness?)
>
> Dealing with lint is a problem. Lint removers (Scotch tape, sticky drums, and the like) for dry clothes, and lint removers in appliances are helpful, but still a bother. Washer and dryer lint traps are commonly neglected and may lead to mechanical problems. Many housewives end up washing dark things by hand to avoid lint. (Surely improvements are possible here.)

The homemaker continues with the laundry task, perhaps also attending to children and the preparation of meals, alert to clicks, buzzers, bells, agitator rhythm, and so on. Strangely enough, doing the home laundry is more complicated and more time-consuming than it used to be, owing to the proliferation of fabrics, machines, and washing ingredients. All the way through the system, many products are being used—softened water, implements, appliances, cleansers, aids—some casually, some with irritation, some with pleasure. Too much detergent may produce too many suds; too much softener makes the clothes feel smooth (even "slimy"); too much bleach is a hazard; the iron may scorch; a pipe leaks; buttons pop off; the dryer burns too hot—but the result may be, to the homemaker, a fragrant, warm, fluffy pile of gratifying accomplishment.

This analysis of the home laundry system is meant only to be suggestive; a properly done, more intensive, detailed analysis would be voluminous. But, even this overly general analysis does indicate how knowledge of the total system, more fully and carefully dissected, can alert the manufacturer to certain facts:

The homemaker is acting in an orderly or purposeful way, in the terms in which the problems and tasks are defined.

There are a series of interrelated steps which require consumer decision making based on knowledge, expectations, and standards (as well as on ignorance, surprise, and uncertainty).

Any laundry product is used with other products, with which it must be compatible.

Questions arise from this type of analysis that point the way to new products or to a clearer understanding of consumer motivations by which old products can be marketed more effectively.

Figure 15-4 illustrates this total home laundering system. The various circles also indicate how it is made up of several and sometimes overlapping subsystems.

TRENDS IN CONSUMPTION

Earlier we noted that consumer expenditure patterns are reflective of consumption and that, when combined with enabling characteristics such as income, they are particularly useful in gauging demand for broad product categories. They may also give some insight into what may happen in the future.

Some of the major trends in consumer expenditure patterns are shown in Table 15-5. Data in the table show total amounts of expenditures on major product categories for selected years beginning in 1929. Overall, total personal consumption expenditures increased from $77.2 billion in 1929 to $577.5 billion in 1969—a quantum leap of almost 750 percent. And while all produce expenditure categoires grew, some increased much more rapidly than others.

Figure 15-4 A home laundry system. *Source:* Boyd and Levy (1963: 133).

Personal care expenditures, for example, increased by 880 percent, compared with 530 percent for clothing and accessories.[2]

Changes in total expenditures patterns result from a variety of demographic and socioeconomic factors as discussed in previous chapters. Many of the shifts during the period 1929–1969 reflect the growth in income during this time

[2]To calculate the percent increase, divide the base year into the subsequent year of interest and multiply by 100 to remove the decimal.

Table 15-5 Personal Consumption Expenditures, U.S.,
(In billions of dollars)

Expenditure category	1929	1949	1959	1969
Total personal consumption expenditures	$77.2	$176.8	$311.2	$577.5
Food, beverages, and tobacco	21.2	56.6	85.2	131.9
Clothing and accessories	11.2	23.3	31.9	59.4
Personal care	1.1	2.3	5.0	9.7
Housing	11.5	19.3	43.7	84.0
Household operation	10.7	25.9	45.3	81.5
Medical care expenses	2.9	8.1	17.9	42.6
Personal business	4.2	6.2	13.9	31.9
Transportation	7.6	20.8	41.2	78.0
Recreation	4.3	10.0	17.4	36.3
Private education and research	0.7	1.5	3.4	9.7
Religious and welfare activities	1.2	2.2	4.4	8.1
Foreign travel and other	0.5	0.4	1.1	4.3
Total durables	9.2	24.6	44.3	90.0
Total nondurables	37.7	94.6	146.6	245.8
Total services	30.3	54.6	120.3	241.6

Source: U.S. Department of Commerce (1970).

period, as we would expect from Engel's laws. Other factors, however, also underlie many of the expenditure changes. Recreation expenditures, which increased over 800 percent during the period, are partly the result of higher incomes. These expenditures are also reflective of higher levels of education, increased leisure time, and more informal life styles.

The crucial question is, of course, "Are the past and present a prologue to the future?" In considering the future, which can never be predicted accurately, we must consider whether the same trends are likely or not, what shifts in tastes and desires are likely to occur, and so on. Clearly, it is difficult to appraise the future with any specific precision; but certain trends of the 1960s establish the base for projecting consumer demand to 1980, assuming, of course, that the past will be roughly duplicated in the future in terms of income-expenditure patterns modified by the demographics of the population.

Fabian Linden, of The Conference Board, making these assumptions, suggests that by 1980 consumer expenditures will exceed $1 trillion, measured in 1970 prices. This means that real, as opposed to inflated, personal consumption will increase by more than 50 percent during this decade, an interval in which the population will rise by 13 percent. Thus the population will grow and the average family will have about a third more to spend than it has today (Linden, 1972).

Growth of these dimensions will result in shifts in the pattern of consumer demand, just as there were shifts in the 1929–1969 data. The diversity within the overall growth during the 1970s, like that of the 1940s, 1950s, and 1960s, will be a reflection of increased income, the age composition of the population, educational and occupational changes, and changes in life styles. Here, briefly, are some major trends discussed in previous chapters which will affect the consumer's choice in the future:

1 Nineteen-eighty will be the era of the young affluent. The population of young families—those headed by persons in the age group 18–34—will grow twice as fast as the total number of families in the 1970s because of the postwar (1945–1960) baby boom. Also, the spending power of young families will almost double during the decade—a rate increase twice that for total spending.

2 Because the population of young families will rise sharply, there will be an increase in the number or births even with an anticipated low fertility level. The proportion of preschool children will increase, but the teen-age population will level off, reflecting the lower fertility level of the 1960s.

3 The younger "middle-age" families (ages 35–49) will also grow dramatically in the 1970s, but the older middle-age group will grow only slightly. Overall, this group will have the highest average income but will increasingly account for less of the total of family spending than in the past.

4 There will be a rapid rise in the number of older people—persons sixty-five and older. This means more people who have finished rearing their children and who will have extra income to spend for luxuries. Almost paradoxically, this also means more retired persons with less income relative to working income.

5 Overall, rising affluence. Perhaps the single most important trend of the 1970s is the continuous escalation of income. Growing opportunities for women, blacks, and other minorities will mean that these groups will share in the growth of incomes. In general, the spending power of upper-income groups (above $15,000) will more than double in the 1970s, and more and more families will be in the upper-income classes.

What do these trends portend for consumption in America? The overall forecast is shown in Figure 15-5. The trend lines suggest that durable goods—apartments and houses, appliances, automobiles, and boats—will constitute the fastest-growing sector of the consumer market. This is principally a reflection of the growth in the number of young adults with money. Nondurables, such as food, tobacco, alcohol, and clothing, will show the least rapid growth during the 1970s. This is because nondurables are not affected greatly by demographic changes in age composition but rather by total population growth, which will occur at a slower rate during the 1970s.

Service expenditures, the second fastest-growing sector, are expected to increase by about 60 percent during the 1970s. This projection is reflected in the derived demand for housing services, the impact of the elderly group on medical and personal care, and the desires of a better-educated population to broaden their horizons and experiences through travel.

Within the major expenditure categories there will continue to be diversity. Some product categories will grow more rapidly than others: Table 15-6 lists the average annual growth rates (projected) for specific product categories.

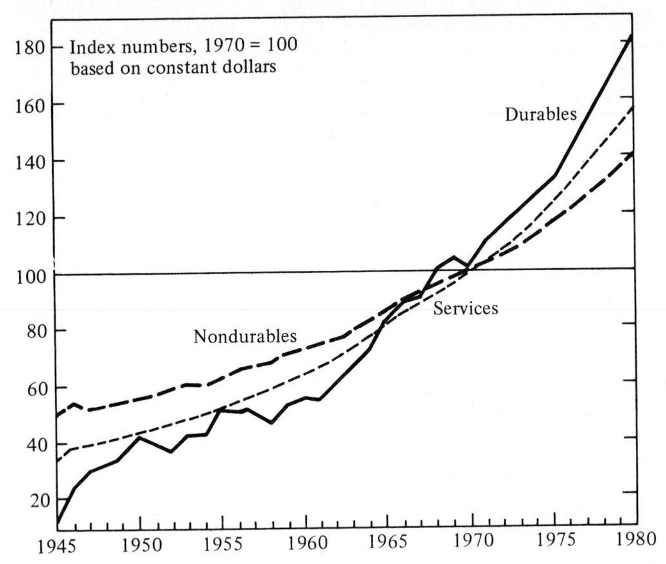

Figure 15-5 Consumer expenditures, 1945–1980. *Source:* Linden (1972).

It should be reiterated that these projections are the broad outlines of consumer expenditures in 1980. Nothing has been said about the diversity of brand choice as consumers continue to exercise their sovereign rights—within available offerings, of course, many of which may well undergo changes resulting from energy and energy-related shortages, inflation, governmental regulation, and technological accomplishments. Yet consumers do change their consumption patterns when faced with disrupting environmental influences and new concerns, as is illustrated by the following study designed to get the "drift" of the market in response to inflation in the mid-1970s.

Consumer Changes

In the previously mentioned 1975 Life Style study,[3] a special section of the questionnaire was devised to measure consumer changes. The section consisted of a set of activities listed after the following instruction to respondents:

> As times and circumstances change, people do less of some things and more of others. Below is a list of activities. For each activity, please indicate, *compared to this time last year,* whether you yourself are engaging in the activity a lot more, a little more, about the same amount, a little less or a lot less. Remember the comparison is with what you yourself were doing *this time last year.*

Consumers' responses are tabulated in Table 15-7. In the table, each activity is listed, along with the percent of females who said they were engaged

[3]Needham, Harper & Steers Advertising, Inc., 1975.

Table 15-6 The Discretionary Effect of Rising Income

Category	Income elasticity 1955–1970	Average annual growth rate 1955–1970	Average annual growth rate 1970–1980 (projected)
Disposable personal income	1.00	4.2	4.4
All expenditures	0.97	4.1	4.3
Durables	1.41	5.9	6.2
Cars[a]	1.33	5.6	5.8
Tires, tubes, and accessories	1.72	7.2	7.6
Furniture	0.78	3.3	3.4
Appliances	1.43	6.0	6.3
Television, radios, records, etc.	2.21	9.3	9.7
Other household durables[b]	1.22	5.1	5.4
Boats and sporting equipment	1.71	7.2	7.5
Nondurables	0.76	3.2	3.4
Food at home	0.62	2.6	2.7
Restaurant food	0.50	2.1	2.2
Alcoholic beverages	0.77	3.2	3.4
Tobacco	0.45	1.9	2.0
Women's apparel	1.01	4.3	4.5
Men's apparel	0.91	3.8	4.0
Footwear	0.59	2.5	2.6
Housefurnishings[c]	1.29	5.4	5.7
Household supplies	0.96	4.0	4.2
Drugs	1.49	6.3	6.6
Toilet goods	1.50	6.3	6.6
Gas and oil	1.05	4.4	4.6
Services	1.04	4.4	4.6
Shelter	1.16	4.9	5.1
Household operation	1.06	4.4	4.7
Gas and electricity	1.27	5.3	5.6
Telephone and telegraph	1.69	7.1	7.5
Domestic services	−0.34	−1.4	−1.5
Transportation	0.56	2.4	2.5
Automotive services	0.69	2.9	3.0
Local travel	−0.64	−2.7	−2.8
Intercity travel	1.30	5.4	5.7
Airline	2.68	11.3	11.8
Medical services	1.16	4.9	5.1
Physicians	0.97	4.1	4.3
Dentists	0.81	3.4	3.6
Personal care	0.76	3.2	3.4
Foreign travel	1.61	6.7	7.1
Higher education	1.55	6.5	6.8

[a]Expenditures for new cars plus the dealer's margin on the sale of used cars.
[b]China, tableware, utensils, garden tools, etc.
[c]Semidurable.
Source: Linden (1972).

Table 15-7 Consumer Changes (1974 to 1975)

Activity	Percent engaging in: More	Less	Difference
Staying home	35%	14%	+21%
Reading	40	11	+29
Watching television	24	18	+ 6
Eating dinner with the whole family	12	7	+ 5
Eating breakfast with the family	10	12	− 2
Going to the movies	9	43	−34
Going out to dinner	25	35	−10
Entertaining at home	23	28	− 5
Having fun	27	13	+14
Going to the grocery store	11	19	− 8
Shopping around for the lowest prices on food	65	3	+62
Looking at labels in the grocery store	62	2	+60
Saving and using "price off" coupons	52	4	+48
Buying nationally advertised brands	5	25	−20
Buying store brands	30	9	+21
Purchasing larger-size packages of food products	41	11	+30
Gardening	44	17	+27
Canning things at home	32	27	+ 5
Baking with a mix	11	27	−16
Baking from scratch	26	27	− 1
Buying sugar	3	67	−64
Buying candy	4	66	−62
Buying snack cakes	5	59	−54
Buying snack foods	9	58	−49
Buying cookies	8	51	−43
Buying soft drinks	10	48	−38
Buying jam or jelly	8	42	−34
Buying fruit	40	8	+32
Buying milk	28	10	+18
Buying bologna	9	32	−23
Buying hot dogs	11	30	−19
Buying frozen foods	18	23	− 5
Buying beef	16	20	− 4
Buying natural foods	16	23	− 7
Buying spaghetti, macaroni, or egg noodles	19	13	+ 6
Buying peanut butter	18	13	+ 5
Worrying about cholesterol	22	13	+ 9
Buying whipped margarine	9	40	−31
Buying regular margarine	15	19	− 4
Buying butter	22	27	− 5
Using salt	1	30	−29
Smoking	7	37	−30
Buying beer	7	40	−33
Worrying about money	42	15	+27
Saving money	27	30	− 3
Trying new products	18	20	− 2
Driving	28	28	0
Taking public transportation	9	31	−22
Thinking about buying a new car	22	56	−34
Thinking about buying a house	15	63	−48
Thinking about buying a new appliance	18	43	−25

Source: Needham, Harper & Steers Advertising, Inc., 1975.

in more (a lot more and a little more), the percent who reported less, and the difference—whether, overall, consumers were engaging more or less. (The percent of people reporting no change in their behavior on a given activity is implicit in the table, since "more" plus "less" plus "no change" equals 100 percent.)

The first group of activities reflect major changes in consumers' styles of living. Largely in response to higher prices and an uncertain economy, consumers shifted their orientations more toward home. They reported staying home and reading, watching television and eating dinner together as a family—all relatively inexpensive activities when compared with those engaged in less: movies, dinner out, and entertaining. The net result, however, was more fun.

The next four groups of activities in the table are with food. The activities focus mainly on food shopping and preparation; on concerns about nutrition; and on what is being consumed more and less in reaction to inflation and concern for nutrition. Obviously, consumers were not oblivious to rising prices. To partially counter, or at least adjust to, higher food prices, women told us they changed the way they shopped. They cut down somewhat on trips to the grocery store; they did more comparison shopping, examining labels, and using price coupons; many substituted store brands for nationally advertised brands and purchased larger-size packages; and they made an input at home through gardening and canning and baking less with mixes.

Coping with inflation, along with concerns for nutrition, produced a number of changes in what consumers bought as well as how they bought it. They reported cutting down the purchases of a large number of snack and snack-related foods—from candy and cookies to drinks and jelly—and increasing purchases of more wholesome foods for substitutions, such as fruit and milk. They also reduced their purchases of more expensive "luxury" foods such as beef and frozen foods and replaced these with less expensive but nutritious items. Their concern for nutrition and price also had an impact on the use of salt, butter, beer, and cigarettes.

Yes, consumers react to inflated food prices—they change where they shop, how they shop, and what they buy. But food is not a luxury. Food purchasing cannot be postponed indefinitely, as can the purchase of a new appliance, a house, a new car, or a vacation (reflected in the last four items in Table 15-7). Thus, instead of radically changing necessities such as food buying and driving, consumers attempt trade-offs and strategies designed for coping. The most important changes come in other areas of life—in the purchasing of luxury items and durables which can be postponed, and in their fundamental style of life itself.

SUMMARY

Product consumption is an integral part of the purhcase-repurchase cycle. Products that prove unsatisfactory to consumers when they are actually used will most likely not be repurchased. The analysis of consumption has focused on three main categories of consumer behavior: expenditure patterns, product usage rates, and actual consumption.

Aggregate expenditure patterns are influenced by income levels, and certain types of products are more sensitive to changes in income than others. Income sensitivity ratios, developed by the U. S. Bureau of Labor Statistics, measure the percentage change in expenditures for specific types of goods, such as furniture, as income levels rise or fall. A more general approach to expenditure patterns was devised by Engel, who recognized basic relationships between income and expenditures, such as the negative correlation between higher income levels and the percentage of income spent for food. Although Engel's laws were formulated in the nineteenth century, they still appear valid today.

Information about expenditure patterns is of little use to marketers unless it is supplemented with information about the consumers who purchase and use the products offered by those marketers. Consequently, a great deal of market research has been devoted to identifying and describing the consumers who are users of specific products. A result of this research is the "heavy half" concept formulated by Twedt, which postulates that for a given product, a small percentage of the overall consumer population represents the majority of sales. Practical application of this concept is difficult because of problems in identifying and reaching the heavy product user.

A method for making the "heavy half" concept more useful for marketers is to derive patterns of relationships between products. Basically, many products are part of a consumer system and therefore overlap in terms of use. Laundry products, for example, are used together to achieve certain consumer objectives. Consumers can be classified as heavy users of product groups, e.g., laundry products, which makes it easier to identify and reach them. Media usage patterns can be derived from research as well and, when combined with information on product usage, can be used effectively in developing market strategies.

In some cases the only way to develop effective market strategies is to actually observe product consumption. By this method of analysis marketers can discover exactly how their products are being used in the home—information which cannot be obtained from less direct methods of analysis. Such data are important when marketers are trying to promote new uses for established brands, improve their products, and develop new products to meet unsatisfied consumer needs.

Compilation of consumer expenditure patterns provides useful information on major shifts in spending habits over time, which reflect changes in demand for broad product categories. This class of data is crucial to marketers for their long-term planning of product lines and expected sales growth curves. It is important to note that historical data are useful but not infallible in predicting future expenditure patterns. Expenditure patterns shift in response to socioeconomic variables such as age, education level, amount of available leisure time, and changes in life style. Consumption patterns also shift in the short run as consumers seek to maintain a style of life in the face of such diversities as inflation, higher taxes, and uncertain economic conditions.

REVIEW QUESTIONS

1 Why should students of consumer behavior examine consumption? What are the three major types of analysis used to explore consumption?
2 Define Engel's laws. Are they still valid today? How do they differ from the "ratios of income sensitivity" developed by the U. S. Bureau of Labor Statistics?
3 What is the "heavy half" concept? In order to be useful to marketers, the heavy half concept is usually supplemented with study of product use combinations and media use patterns. Why? Give specific examples illustrating the importance of these additional factors to marketers.
4 Why is it useful to focus research on a combination of product users who are also users of a specific medium?
5 When is it necessary to use direct observation as well as self-report in obtaining product usage information?
6 What are "consumption systems," and how do they relate to product usage patterns?
7 Review the implications to marketing in the home laundry system. Which of the suggestions have found their way into the marketing economy of the 1970s?
8 In addition to income, several other factors influence consumption trends. Identify these factors and indicate what effects each factor will have on expenditure patterns in the near future.
9 Which sectors of the economy are expected to grow fastest during the next decade? Why?

EXERCISE

Select, as an observation point, a street intersection with a stop light and one that will allow you to observe motorists going from home to work in the morning and from work to home in the afternoon. Use a predetermined distance and a stopwatch to record times, and then calculate the speed with which motorists accelerate away from a stop light. Also record the type of vehicle, the number of persons in the vehicle, the sex of the driver, the relative age of the driver, and the direction (to indicate going toward or away from major points of employment) the vehicle is heading.

Is there any measurable variation in rate of acceleration away from the light? If so, do any of the variables observed help explain the variation? Discuss your findings with reference to a planned advertising campaign to make motorists aware of the need to conserve fuel by proper acceleration when leaving traffic lights.

REFERENCES

Banks, Seymour. "Patterns of Daytime Viewing Behavior." *Proceedings,* June Conference, American Marketing Association, 1967.

Baumgarten, Steven A. and L. Winston Ring. "An Evaluation of Media Readership Constructs and Audience Profiles by Use of Canonical Correlation Analysis." *Combined Proceedings,* American Marketing Association, 1971.

Boyd, Harper W., Jr. and Sidney J. Levy. "New Dimensionin Consumer Analysis." *Harvard Business Review,* 41 (November–December 1963), 129–140.

The Conference Board. *A Guide to Consumer Markets 1972/1973.* New York: The Conference Board, Inc., 1972.

Linden, Fabian. "The Consumer Market in 1980." *The Conference Board Record,* 9 (March, April, May, June 1972), a series.

Rienow, Robert and Leona Train Rienow. *Moment in the Sun.* New York: The Dial Press and Paul R. Reynolds, Inc., 1967.

Samuelson, Paul A. *Economics.* 9th ed. New York: McGraw-Hill, 1973.

Schorr, Burt. "The Mistakes: Many New Products Fail Despite Careful Planning Publicity." *Wall Street Journal* (1961). Quoted in E. M. Rogers, *Communication of Innovations.* New York: Free Press, 1971.

Swanson, Charles E. "Patterns of Nighttime Television Viewing." *Proceedings,* June Conference, American Marketing Association, 1967.

Tigert, Douglas J "Are Television Audiences Really Different?" *Combined Proceedings,* American Marketing Association, 1971.

Twedt, Dik W. "Some Practical Applications of 'Heavy-Half' Theory." *Proceedings,* 10th Annual Conference on the Advertising Research Foundation, 1964.

U. S. Department of Commerce, Office of Business Economics. *The National Income and Product Accounts of the United States, 1929–1965,* and *Survey of Current Business* (July 1970).

U. S. Department of Labor, Bureau of Labor Statistics. *Contrast in Spending by Urban Families,* Report No. 238-8, February 1965.

Webster, Jr., Frederick E. *Social Aspects of Marketing.* Englewood Cliffs, N. J.: Prentice-Hall, 1974.

Wells, William D. "Life Style and Psychographics: Definitions, Uses and Problems." In W. D. Wells (eds.), *Life Style and Psychographics.* Chicago: American Marketing Association, 1974.

———. "Patterns of Consumer Behavior." Paper delivered in Toronto at the 1967 Conference of the American Marketing Association.

———. "The Rise and Fall of Television Program Types." *Journal of Advertising Research,* 9 (September 1969), 21–27.

———, Seymour Banks and Douglas J. Tigert. "Order in the Data." In Reed Mayer (ed.), *Changing Marketing Systems: Consumer, Corporate and Government Interfaces.* Chicago: American Marketing Association, 1967.

Name Index

Subject Index